SAT*

ALL-IN-ONE

BY THE STAFF OF
KAPLAN EDUCATIONAL CENTERS

SIMON & SCHUSTER

*SAT is a registered trademark of the College Board, which is not affiliated with this book.

Kaplan Books
Published by Kaplan Educational Centers and Simon & Schuster
1230 Avenue of the Americas
New York, NY 10020

"On Seeing England for the First Time," by Jamaica Kincaid. Reprinted with permission of Wylie, Aitken & Stone, Inc.

From *Life Itself* by Francis Crick. Copyright © Francis Crick 1981. Reproduced with the Permission of Felicity Bryan Literary Agency.

FAR SIDE copyright 1986 & 1987 FARWORKS, INC. Reprinted with permission of UNIVERSAL PRESS SYNDICATE. All rights reserved.

"He cheated..." and "Reading skills..." ©1993 Frank Cotham and The Cartoon Bank, Inc.

Bizarro cartoons © 1987 & 1991, Chronicle Features. Reprinted with permission.

All other cartoons ©1993 Kaplan Educational Centers

"The Kaplan Advantage™ Stress Management System" by Dr. Ed Newman and Bob Verini,
© 1996, Kaplan Educational Centers

"College Admissions" section by R. Fred Zuker, © 1996, Kaplan Educational Centers

Cover Design: Gerard Capistrano, in collaboration with Frierson + Mee, Inc.
Design: Gerard Capistrano, Seth Godin, Charles Kreloff
Editors: Joyce Bermel, Tom Dyja
Executive Editor: Jay Johnson
Production: Chris Angelilli, Lisa DiMona, Martin Erb, Vic Lapuszynski, Frances Small
Layout: Julie Maner, Carol Markowitz
Project Management: Megan O'Connor
Copyediting: Doreen Beauregard, Jolanta Benal, Michelle Eldridge, Patricia Goff, Maude Spekes
Cartoons: Frank Cotham, Joe Dator, Holly Kowitt, Gary Larson, Rick Parker, Dan Piraro

Thanks to: Laura Barnes, Jeff Barton, Seppy Basili, Maureen Blair, Linda Calzaretta, Mike Cantwell,
Scott Dalla Valle, Fred Danzig, Craig Davis, Kenny Dinkin, Gordon Drummond,
Lee Fitzgerald, Kate Foster, Chris Hobson, Kate Holum, Eric Horowitz, Daniel Kane,
Chris Kent, Liza Kleinman, Gary Krist, Jon Krupp, Dianne Lake, Audrey Lee, Merideth Lee, Jason Levitis,
Rich Lowenthal, Joyce Lupack, Kate McCarthy, Ed Newman, Sam Nisson, James Pervin,
John Polstein, Donna Ratajczak, Robert Reiss, Joe Rosch, Amy Sgarro, Bob Stanton,
David Stuart, Bob Verini, Chris Woods, Susan Yanovich

ISBN 0–684–83378–6
ISSN 1088–0771

Manufactured in the United States of America
Published Simultaneously in Canada

August 1996

10 9 8 7 6 5 4 3 2 1

CONTENTS

TEN WAYS YOU CAN BOOST YOUR SCORE

GET FAMILIAR WITH THE TEST

The SAT is one of the most predictable experiences you'll have in your life. Before going into the test, you should know what to expect on every section, what the rules for each question type are, and what topics are covered. See pp. 7–9 for this information.

MAKE THE STRUCTURE OF THE TEST WORK FOR YOU

Most of the SAT is multiple choice. That means that the answer is right in front of you. No one cares how you got the answer—only whether you got it. You can make the test format work to your benefit. See pp. 1–6.

LEARN THE ANALOGIES THAT COME UP ALL THE TIME

Although baffling at first, SAT Analogies really test the same basic relationships over and over again. By becoming familiar with these "classic bridges," you can know what types of relationships to expect on the test. These bridges are explained on pp. 32–35.

KNOW WHAT TO LOOK FOR IN SENTENCE COMPLETIONS

Many Sentence Completions test your ability to understand the structure of sentences. By focusing on clue words, you can unwrap the meaning in seconds. See the list of clue words on p. 47.

READ ACTIVELY

Critical Reading on the SAT forces you to think about what you read. We show you how to unpack what the author says, pay attention to tone, and make inferences. See pp. 71–81.

BUILD YOUR VOCABULARY

Sooner or later, you're going to run into words you don't know. No one is expected to know all the words on the SAT. But don't worry—there are many techniques for finding the meanings of strange words, and for using what you do know about words to answer the question. See these strategies on pp. 22–24.

DO QCS QUICKLY AND EFFICIENTLY

Quantitative Comparisons questions appear on the math sections of the SAT. Difficult at first, they are a good source of quick points. You'll be repaid with interest for the time you spent practicing them. See the strategies on pp. 112–122.

UNDERSTAND THE TOP 10 MATH TRAPS

What makes some SAT math questions hard? It's not the numbers, and not always the concepts. Often, they're hard because of a trap—something the test maker hopes you'll fall for. We'll show you the most common traps and teach you how to avoid them on pp. 173–191.

LEARN TO USE YOUR CALCULATOR

You can use your calculator on the SAT. That means that thousands of students nationwide will be wasting their time using calculators on questions that are simple to solve with just a little thinking. We'll show you when to use your calculator and when not to on pp. 96–98.

DON'T PANIC

People panic because the test is unfamiliar to them. Throughout this book, we show you the classic problems and how to solve them, so that there's no need for you to panic on the day of the test.

FOREWORD

"**Y**ou can't prep for the SAT."

Some people wanted to believe that. For nearly 50 years the Educational Testing Service (ETS), the company that writes the SAT, and the College Board worked hard to make people believe it. Some myths die hard, and a few years ago, ETS and the College Board finally had to give it up.

More than 55 years ago, a young man named Stanley H. Kaplan knew that he could raise scores on the test. He perfected many special techniques and developed a course. Word spread, a business started, and eventually more than a quarter of a million high school students learned that you *could* increase your scores on the SAT. There were examples by the busload of students' scores increasing by 150, 200, 300 points or more. Finally, in the late 1980s, the College Board quietly inserted a change in the SAT information bulletin noting that it *was* possible to increase one's SAT score through formal and informal preparation.

There are other examples of Stanley Kaplan being ahead of his time. For decades he argued that the Scholastic *Aptitude* Test should be renamed the Scholastic *Assessment* Test, because the SAT was not an intelligence test. In 1994 ETS finally changed the official name of the SAT to the Scholastic Assessment Test.

Other myths surround the SAT. Some people believe that it measures high school achievement and is an absolute predictor of college performance. Again, not true. Despite the fact that female students score about 43 points lower than male students on the SAT (on the 400–1600 combined scale), females tend to earn higher grades than males in both high school and college.

So the SAT doesn't test intelligence, it may not be the best predictor of college success, and it doesn't necessarily reflect high school grades. But it is used in the college admission process, and preparation can improve your score!

ETS claims their test "measures the verbal and mathematical abilities you have developed over many years both in and out of school." In describing the 1994 changes in the SAT, the test makers stressed that the new test places more emphasis on critical reasoning and the ability to apply concepts in different contexts. These are admirable goals. But still the SAT is a test, and the thing the SAT measures best is how well you take the SAT.

Can you zero in on the hidden question behind the question? Can you work confidently, even when you've got five minutes and seven problems left? Can you relax and pace yourself while taking a test that feels like the three most important hours in your life? These are some of the skills the SAT rewards. Without them you can be intimidated, confused, maybe even panic-stricken. With them you control the test. You are equipped for your own peak performance.

Feeling in control and making the SAT your own are the most valuable things you can do for yourself as a test taker. And that's exactly what Kaplan has been doing for students over the last 55 years.

HOW TO USE THIS BOOK

Ideally, you should take a couple of months to work through this book, though it's certainly possible to read it in far less time. Here's how you should go about training with it:

1. Read the section entitled The Kaplan Advantage™ Stress Management System to set the stage for your training and testing success.

2. Read through each chapter completely, learning from the example problems and trying the practice problems. In Appendices A and B, you'll find word and root lists as well as the 100 most important math concepts to know.

4. When you've finished each chapter, review what you've learned in the Highlights box on the last page of the chapter.

5. Take the Practice Test *under strictly timed conditions*.

6. Score your Practice Test. Find out where you need help and then review the appropriate chapters.

7. Reread the Highlights boxes once more before taking your actual SAT.

8. Give yourself a day of rest right before the real exam.

If you have time, do just two or three chapters a week, and let it sink in slowly. Don't hesitate to take some time off from the SAT when you need to. Nobody can take this stuff day in and day out for weeks at a time without a break. You should also make a point of reading the College Admissions section (Appendix C), as well as the Kaplan Advantage™ Stress Management System, which can help you beat the test anxiety before—and during—the test.

The FastPrep and PanicPlans

Of course, many of you don't have a couple of months. Maybe you have only two or three weeks—or even less time than that. Don't freak! This book has been designed to work for students in your situation, too. If you go through a chapter or two every day, you can finish this book in a couple of weeks. If you have limited time to prepare for the SAT (six weeks or fewer), we suggest you do the following:

1. Take a slow, deep breath. Read The Kaplan Advantage™ Stress Management System to maximize your study and testing time.

2. Read the SAT Mastery chapter.

3. At the beginning of each chapter, read the FastPrep plan. This will tell you which areas of the chapter you should focus on. After you master each concept, check it off. If you are *really* short on time (less than a month), follow the Panic Plan suggestions (also found at the beginning of each chapter). The PanicPlan suggestions really streamline your study strategy.

4. Take the Practice Test *under timed conditions*.

5. Review your results, with special attention to the questions you missed.

6. Give yourself the day before the test off.

Scattered throughout the text you'll find "hints"—special points that we feel deserve emphasis and amplificaton. Pay special attention to these hints, which spotlight some very important test prep information. Sidebars also highlight key points, fun facts, and real-world stories.

A MESSAGE FROM ALL OF US AT KAPLAN

Welcome to Kaplan. You are preparing for the SAT with the nation's leader in test preparation. Each year, Kaplan raises students' scores through its courses, books, videos, online services, and digital products. We spend millions of dollars annually on research and development to ensure that our materials set the standards for the industry and reflect even the most minor test changes. With more than 160 centers and 1,000 satellite locations across the United States and abroad, Kaplan prepares more than 150,000 students each year for college and graduate admissions tests, professional licensing, and language exams. Kaplan is a wholly owned subsidiary of the Washington Post Company, which also owns *Newsweek* magazine.

Kaplan remains at the forefront of test preparation because of the outstanding team of professionals who create and deliver our products and services. Thanks to all of those who made this book—and your score improvement—possible.

Best of luck with the SAT!

Stanley Kaplan
Founder

Jonathan Grayer
President and CEO

THE KAPLAN ADVANTAGE™ STRESS MANAGEMENT SYSTEM

The countdown has begun. Your date with THE TEST is looming on the horizon. Anxiety is on the rise. The butterflies in your stomach have gone ballistic. Perhaps you feel as if the last thing you ate has turned into a lead ball. Your thinking is getting cloudy. Maybe you think you won't be ready. Maybe you already know your stuff, but you're going into panic mode anyway. Worst of all, you're not sure of what to do about it.

Don't freak! It is possible to tame that anxiety and stress—before *and* during the test. We'll show you how. You won't believe how quickly and easily you can deal with that killer anxiety.

MAKING THE MOST OF YOUR PREP TIME

Lack of control is one of the prime causes of stress. A ton of research shows that if you don't have a sense of control over what's happening in your life you can easily end up feeling helpless and hopeless. So, just having concrete things to do and to think about—taking control—will help reduce your stress. This section shows you how to take control during the days leading up to taking the test.

IDENTIFY THE SOURCES OF STRESS

In the space provided, jot down (in pencil) anything you identify as a source of your test-related stress. The idea is to pin down that free-floating anxiety so that you can take control of it. Here are some common examples to get you started:

- I always freeze up on tests.
- I'm nervous about the math (or the vocabulary or reading, etc.).

AVOID MUST-Y THINKING

Let go of "must-y" thoughts, those notions that you must do something in a certain way—for example, "I must get a great score, or else!" "I must meet Mom and Dad's expectations."

- I need a good/great score to go to Acme College.
- My older brother/sister/best friend/girl- or boyfriend did really well. I *must* match their scores or do better.
- My parents, who are paying for school, will be really disappointed if I don't test well.
- I'm afraid of losing my focus and concentration.
- I'm afraid I'm not spending enough time preparing.
- I study like crazy but nothing seems to stick in my mind.
- I always run out of time and get panicky.
- I feel as though thinking is becoming like wading through thick mud.

Sources of Stress

- I'm not spending enough time preparing
- Nothing seems to stick in my mind
- my parents who are paying for this school will be disappointed if I don't do well.
- getting the worst in class

Take a few minutes to think about the things you've just written down. Then rewrite them in some sort of order. List the statements you most associate with your stress and anxiety first, and put the least disturbing items last. Chances are, the top of the list is a fairly accurate description of exactly how you react to test anxiety, both physically and mentally. The later items usually describe your fears (disappointing Mom and Dad, looking bad, etc.). As you write the list, you're forming a hierarchy of items so you can deal first with the anxiety provokers that bug you most. Very often, taking care of the major items from the top of the list goes a long way toward relieving overall testing anxiety. You probably won't have to bother with the stuff you placed last.

TAKE STOCK OF YOUR STRENGTHS AND WEAKNESSES

Take one minute to list the areas of the test that you are good at. They can be general ("verbal") or specific ("analogies"). Put down as many as you can think of, and if possible, time yourself. Write for the entire time; don't stop writing until you've reached the one-minute stopping point.

Strong Test Subjects

* if I study a while I do good
* if it's something I am interested in I do good
* if I am Mentioned
* must need test
* not much thinking

Next, take one minute to list areas of the test you're not so good at, just plain bad at, have failed at, or keep failing at. Again, keep it to one minute, and continue writing until you reach the cutoff. Don't be afraid to identify and write down your weak spots! In all probability, as you do both lists you'll find you are strong in some areas and not so strong in others. Taking stock of your assets *and* liabilities lets you know the areas you don't have to worry about, and the ones that will demand extra attention and effort.

Weak Test Subjects

Now, go back to the "good" list, and expand it for two minutes. Take the general items on that first list and make them more specific; take the specific items and expand them into more general conclusions. Naturally, if anything new comes to mind, jot it down. Focus all of your attention and effort on your strengths. Don't underestimate yourself or your

VERY SUPERSTITIOUS

Stress expert Stephen Sideroff, Ph.D., tells of a client who always stressed out before, during, and even after taking tests. Yet, she always got outstanding scores. It became obvious that she was thinking superstitiously—subconsciously believing that the great scores were a result of her worrying. She also didn't trust herself, and believed that if she didn't worry she wouldn't study hard enough. Sideroff convinced her to take a risk and work on relaxing before her next test. She did, and her test results were still as good as ever— which broke her cycle of superstitious thinking.

abilities. Give yourself full credit. At the same time, don't list strengths you don't really have; you'll only be fooling yourself.

Expanding from general to specific might go as follows. If you listed "verbal" as a broad topic you feel strong in, you would then narrow your focus to include areas of this subject about which you are particularly knowledgeable. Your areas of strength might include analogies, ability to decipher unfamiliar words through knowledge of Latin, ability to recognize vocabulary bridges, etc.

Whatever you know comfortably (that is, almost as well as you know the back of your hand) goes on your "good" list. Okay. You've got the picture. Now, get ready, check your starting time, and start writing down items on your expanded "good" list.

Strong Test Subjects: An Expanded List

_____

_____

_____

_____

_____

_____

_____

_____

_____

_____

_____

_____

_____

_____

_____

_____

_____

_____

After you've stopped, check your time. Did you find yourself going beyond the two minutes allotted? Did you write down more things than you thought you knew? Is it possible you know more than you've given yourself credit for? Could that mean you've found a number of areas in which you feel strong?

You just took an active step toward helping yourself. Notice any increased feelings of confidence? Enjoy them.

Here's another way to think about your writing exercise. Every area of strength and confidence you can identify is much like having a reserve of solid gold at Fort Knox. You'll be able to draw on your reserves as you need them. You can use your reserves to solve difficult questions, maintain confidence, and keep test stress and anxiety at a distance. The encouraging thing is that every time you recognize another area of strength, succeed at coming up with a solution, or get a good score on a test, you increase your reserves. And, there is absolutely no limit to how much self-confidence you can have or how good you can feel about yourself.

IMAGINE YOURSELF SUCCEEDING

This next little group of exercises is both physical and mental. It's a natural followup to what you've just accomplished with your lists.

First, get yourself into a comfortable sitting position in a quiet setting. Wear loose clothes. If you wear glasses, take them off. Then, close your eyes and breathe in a deep, satisfying breath of air. Really fill your lungs until your rib cage is fully expanded and you can't take in any more. Then, exhale the air completely. Imagine you're blowing out a candle with your last little puff of air. Do this two or three more times, filling your lungs to their maximum and emptying them totally. Keep your eyes closed, comfortably but not tightly. Let your body sink deeper into the chair as you become even more comfortable.

With your eyes shut you can notice something very interesting. You're no longer dealing with the worrisome stuff going on in the world *outside* of you. Now you can concentrate on what happens *inside* you. The more you recognize your own physical reactions to stress and anxiety, the more you can do about them. You may not realize it, but you've begun to regain a sense of being in control.

Let images begin to form on the "viewing screens" on the back of your eyelids. You're experiencing visualizations from the place in your mind that makes pictures. Allow the images to come easily and naturally; don't force them. Imagine yourself in a relaxing situation. It might be in a special place you've visited before or one you've read about. It can be a fictional location that you create in your imagination, but a real-life memory of a place or situation you know is usually better. Make it as detailed as possible and notice as much as you can.

If you don't see this relaxing place sharply or in living color, it doesn't mean the exercise won't work for you. Some people can visualize in great detail, while others get only a sense of an image. What's important is not how sharp the details or colors, but how well you're able to manipulate the images. If you can conjure up finely detailed images, great. If you have only a faint sense of the images, that's okay—you'll still experience all the benefits of the exercise.

DON'T FORCE IT

Never try to force relaxation. You'll only get frustrated and find yourself even more uptight. Be passive.

OCEAN DUMPING

Visualize a beautiful beach, with white sand, blue skies, sparkling water, a warm sun, and seagulls. See yourself walking on the beach, carrying a small plastic pail. Stop at a good spot and put your worries and whatever may be bugging you into the pail. Drop it at the water's edge and watch it drift out to sea. When the pail is out of sight, walk on.

THE "NEW AGE" OF RELAXATION

Here are some more tips for beating stress:

• Massage, especially shiatsu—see if it's offered through your school's phys ed department, or at the local "Y."

• Check out a book on acupressure, and find those points on your body where you can press a "relax button."

• If you're especially sensitive to smells, you might want to try some aromatherapy. Lavender oil, for example, is said to have relaxing properties. Health food stores, drug stores, and New Age bookstores may carry aromatherapy oils.

• Many health food stores carry herbs and supplements that have relaxing properties, and they often have a specialist on staff who can tell you about them.

Think about the sights, the sounds, the smells, even the tastes and textures associated with your relaxing situation. *See* and *feel* yourself in this special place. Say your special place is the beach, for example. Feel how warm the sand is. Are you lying on a blanket, or sitting up and looking out at the water? Hear the waves hitting the shore, and the occasional seagull. Feel a comfortable breeze. If your special place is a garden or park, look up and see the way sunlight filters through the trees. Smell your favorite flowers. Hear some chimes gently playing and birds chirping.

Stay focused on the images as you sink farther back into your chair. Breathe easily and naturally. You might have the sensations of any stress or tension draining from your muscles and flowing downward, out your feet and away from you.

Take a moment to check how you're feeling. Notice how comfortable you've become. Imagine how much easier it would be if you could take the test feeling this relaxed and in this state of ease. You've coupled the images of your special place with sensations of comfort and relaxation. You've also found a way to become relaxed simply by visualizing your own safe, special place.

Now, close your eyes and start remembering a real-life situation in which you did well on a test. If you can't come up with one, remember a situation in which you did something (academic or otherwise) that you were really proud of—a genuine accomplishment. Make the memory as detailed as possible. Think about the sights, the sounds, the smells, even the tastes associated with this remembered experience. Remember how confident you felt as you accomplished your goal. Now start thinking about the upcoming test. Keep your thoughts and feelings in line with that successful experience. Don't make comparisons between them. Just imagine taking the upcoming test with the same feelings of confidence and relaxed control.

This exercise is a great way to bring the test down to earth. You should practice this exercise often, especially when the prospect of taking the exam starts to bum you out. The more you practice it, the more effective the exercise will be for you.

WHAT DO YOU WANT TO ACCOMPLISH IN THE TIME REMAINING?

The whole point to this next exercise is sort of like checking out a used car you might want to buy. You'd want to know up front what the car's weak points are, right? Knowing that influences your whole shopping-for-a-used-car campaign. So it is with your conquering-test-stress campaign: Knowing what your weak points are ahead of time helps you prepare.

So let's get back to the list of your weak points. Take two minutes to expand it just as you did with your "good" list. Be honest with yourself without going overboard. It's an accurate appraisal of the test areas that give you trouble. So, pick up your pencil, check the clock, and start writing.

Weak Test Subjects: An Expanded List

_____

_____

_____

_____

_____

_____

_____

_____

_____

_____

How did you do? Were you able to keep writing for the full two minutes? Has making this "weak" list helped you become more clear about the specific areas you need to address?

Facing your weak spots gives you some distinct advantages. It helps a lot to find out where you need to spend extra effort. Increased exposure to tough material makes it more familiar and less intimidating. (After all, we mostly fear what we don't know and are probably afraid to face.) You'll feel better about yourself because you're dealing directly with areas of the test that bring on your anxiety. You can't help feeling more confident when you know you're actively strengthening your chances of earning a higher overall test score.

EXERCISE YOUR FRUSTRATIONS AWAY

Whether it is jogging, walking, biking, mild aerobics, pushups, or a pick-up basketball game, physical exercise is a very effective way to stimulate both your mind and body and to improve your ability to think and concentrate. A surprising number of students get out of the habit of regular exercise, ironically because they're spending so much time prepping for exams. Also, sedentary people—this is a medical fact—get less oxygen to the blood and hence to the head than active people. You can live fine with a little less oxygen; you just can't think as well.

Any big test is a bit like a race. Thinking clearly at the end is just as important as having a quick mind early on. If you can't sustain your

STRESS TIP

Don't forget that your school probably has counseling available. If you can't conquer test stress on your own, make an appointment at the counseling center. That's what counselors are there for.

STRESS TIP

If you want to play music, keep it low and in the background. Music with a regular, mathematical rhythm—reggae, for example—aids the learning process. A recording of ocean waves is also soothing.

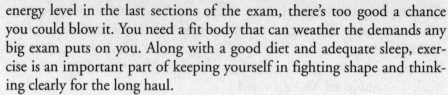

TAKE A HIKE, PAL

When you're in the middle of studying and hit a wall, take a short, brisk walk. Breathe deeply and swing your arms as you walk. Clear your mind. (And, don't forget to look for flowers that grow in the cracks of the sidewalk.)

CYBERSTRESS

If you spend a lot of time in cyberspace anyway, do a search for the phrase "stress management." There's a ton of stress advice on the 'Net, including material specifically for students.

energy level in the last sections of the exam, there's too good a chance you could blow it. You need a fit body that can weather the demands any big exam puts on you. Along with a good diet and adequate sleep, exercise is an important part of keeping yourself in fighting shape and thinking clearly for the long haul.

There's another thing that happens when students don't make exercise an integral part of their test preparation. Like any organism in nature, you operate best if all your "energy systems" are in balance. Studying uses a lot of energy, but it's all mental. When you take a study break, do something active instead of raiding the fridge or vegging out in front of the TV. Take a five- to 10-minute activity break for every 50 or 60 minutes that you study. The physical exertion gets your body into the act, which helps to keep your mind and body in sync. Then, when you finish studying for the night and hit the sack, you won't lie there, tense and unable to sleep because your head is overtired and your body wants to pump iron or run a marathon.

One warning about exercise, however: It's not a good idea to exercise vigorously right before you go to bed. This could easily cause sleep onset problems. For the same reason, it's also not a good idea to study right up to bedtime. Make time for a "buffer period" before you go to bed: For 30 to 60 minutes, just take a hot shower, meditate, simply veg out.

GET HIGH . . . NATURALLY

Exercise can give you a natural high, which is the only kind of high you should be aiming for. Using drugs (prescription or recreational) specifically to prepare for and take a big test is definitely self-defeating. (And if they're illegal drugs, you may end up with a bigger problem than the SAT on your hands.) Except for the drugs that occur naturally in your brain, *every* drug has major drawbacks—and a false sense of security is only one of them.

You may have heard that popping uppers helps you study by keeping you alert. If they're illegal, definitely forget about it. They wouldn't really work anyway, since amphetamines make it hard to retain information. Mild stimulants, such as coffee, cola, or over-the-counter caffeine pills can sometimes help as you study, since they keep you alert. On the down side, they can also lead to agitation, restlessness, and insomnia. Some people can drink a pot of high-octane coffee and sleep like a baby. Others have one cup and start to vibrate. It all depends on your tolerance for caffeine. Remember, a little anxiety is a good thing. The adrenaline that gets pumped into your bloodstream helps you stay alert and think more clearly. But, too much anxiety and you can't think straight at all.

Alcohol and other depressants are out, too. Again, if it's illegal, forget about it. Depressants wouldn't work anyway, since they lead to the inevitable hangover/crash, fuzzy thinking, and lousy sense of judgment. These would not help you ace the test.

Instead, go for endorphins—the "natural morphine." Endorphins have no side effects and they're free—you've already got them in your brain. It just takes some exercise to release them. Running around on the basketball court, bicycling, swimming, aerobics, power walking—these activities cause endorphins to occupy certain spots in your brain's neural synapses. In addition, exercise develops staying power and increases the oxygen transfer to your brain. Go into the test naturally.

TAKE A DEEP BREATH . . .

Here's another natural route to relaxation and invigoration. It's a classic isometric exercise that you can do whenever you get stressed out—just before the test begins, even *during* the test. It's very simple and takes just a few minutes.

Close your eyes. Starting with your eyes and—*without holding your breath*—gradually tighten every muscle in your body (but not to the point of pain) in the following sequence:

1. Close your eyes tightly.
2. Squeeze your nose and mouth together so that your whole face is scrunched up. (If it makes you self-conscious to do this in the test room, skip the face-scrunching part.)
3. Pull your chin into your chest, and pull your shoulders together.
4. Tighten your arms to your body, then clench your hands into tight fists.
5. Pull in your stomach.
6. Squeeze your thighs and buttocks together, and tighten your calves.
7. Stretch your feet, then curl your toes (watch out for cramping in this part).

At this point, every muscle should be tightened. Now, relax your body, one part at a time, *in reverse order*, starting with your toes. Let the tension drop out of each muscle. The entire process might take five minutes from start to finish (maybe a couple of minutes during the test). This clenching and unclenching exercise should help you to feel very relaxed.

AND KEEP BREATHING

Conscious attention to breathing is an excellent way of managing test stress (or any stress, for that matter). The majority of people who get into

NUTRITION AND STRESS: THE DOS AND DON'TS

Do eat:

- Fruits and vegetables (raw is best, or just lightly steamed or nuked)
- Low-fat protein such as fish, skinless poultry, beans, and legumes (like lentils)
- Whole grains such as brown rice, whole wheat bread, and pastas (no bleached flour)

Don't eat:

- Refined sugar; sweet, high-fat snacks (simple carbohydrates like sugar make stress worse and fatty foods lower your immunity)
- Salty foods (they can deplete potassium, which you need for nerve functions)

THE RELAXATION PARADOX

Forcing relaxation is like asking yourself to flap your arms and fly. You can't do it, and every push and prod only gets you more frustrated. Relaxation is something you don't work at. You simply let it happen. Think about it. When was the last time you tried to force yourself to go to sleep, and it worked?

STRESS TIP

A lamp with a 75-watt bulb is optimal for studying. But don't put it so close to your study material that you create a glare.

trouble during tests take shallow breaths. They breathe using only their upper chests and shoulder muscles, and may even hold their breath for long periods of time. Conversely, the test taker who by accident or design keeps breathing normally and rhythmically is likely to be more relaxed and in better control during the entire test experience.

So, now is the time to get into the habit of relaxed breathing. Do the next exercise to learn to breathe in a natural, easy rhythm. By the way, this is another technique you can use during the test to collect your thoughts and ward off excess stress. The entire exercise should take no more than three to five minutes.

With your eyes still closed, breathe in slowly and *deeply* through your nose. Hold the breath for a bit, and then release it through your mouth. The key is to breathe slowly and deeply by using your diaphragm (the big band of muscle that spans your body just above your waist) to draw air in and out naturally and effortlessly. Breathing with your diaphragm encourages relaxation and helps minimize tension.

As you breathe, imagine that colored air is flowing into your lungs. Choose any color you like, from a single color to a rainbow. With each breath, the air fills your body from the top of your head to the tips of your toes. Continue inhaling the colored air until it occupies every part of you, bones and muscles included. Once you have completely filled yourself with the colored air, picture an opening somewhere on your body, either natural or imagined. Now, with each breath you exhale, some of the colored air will pass out the opening and leave your body. The level of the air (much like the water in a glass as it is emptied) will begin to drop. It will descend progressively lower, from your head down to your feet. As you continue to exhale the colored air, watch the level go lower and lower, farther and farther down your body. As the last of the colored air passes out of the opening, the level will drop down to your toes and disappear. Stay quiet for just a moment. Then notice how relaxed and comfortable you feel.

QUICK TIPS FOR THE DAYS
JUST BEFORE THE EXAM

• The best test takers do less and less as the test approaches. Taper off your study schedule and take it easy on yourself. You want to be relaxed and ready on the day of the test. Give yourself time off, especially the evening before the exam. By that time, if you've studied well, everything you need to know is firmly stored in your memory banks.

• Positive self-talk can be extremely liberating and invigorating, especially as the test looms closer. Tell yourself things such as, "I choose to take this test" rather than "I have to"; "I will do well" rather than "I hope things go well"; "I can" rather than "I cannot." Be aware of negative, self-defeating thoughts and images and immediately counter any you become aware of. Replace them with affirming statements that encourage your self-esteem and confidence. Create and practice doing visualizations that build on your positive statements.

• Get your act together sooner rather than later. Have everything (including choice of clothing) laid out days in advance. Most important, know where the test will be held and the easiest, quickest way to get there. You will gain great peace of mind if you know that all the little details—gas in the car, directions, etcetera—are firmly in your control before the day of the test.

• Experience the test site a few days in advance. This is very helpful if you are especially anxious. If at all possible, find out what room your part of the alphabet is assigned to, and try to sit there (by yourself) for a while. Better yet, bring some practice material and do at least a section or two, if not an entire practice test, in that room. In this case, familiarity doesn't breed contempt, it generates comfort and confidence.

• Forego any practice on the day before the test. It's in your best interest to marshal your physical and psychological resources for 24 hours or so. Even race horses are kept in the paddock and treated like princes the day before a race. Keep the upcoming test out of your consciousness; go to a movie, take a pleasant hike, or just relax. Don't eat junk food or tons of sugar. And—of course—get plenty of rest the night before. Just don't go to bed too early. It's hard to fall asleep earlier than you're used to, and you don't want to lie there thinking about the test.

THUMBS UP FOR MEDITATION

Once relegated to the fringes of the medical world, meditation, biofeedback, and hypnosis are increasingly recommended by medical researchers to reduce pain from headaches, back problems—even cancer. Think of what these powerful techniques could do for your test-related stress and anxiety.

Effective meditation is based primarily on two relaxation methods you've already learned: body awareness and breathing. A couple of different meditation techniques follow. Experience them both, and choose the one that works best for you.

Breath Meditation

Make yourself comfortable, either sitting or lying down. For this meditation you can keep your eyes opened or closed. You're going to concentrate on your breathing. The goal of the meditation is to notice everything you can about your breath as it enters and leaves your body. Take three to five breaths each time you practice the meditation; this set of breaths should take about a minute to complete.

Take a deep breath and hold it for five to 10 seconds. When you exhale, let the breath out very slowly. Feel the tension flowing out of you along with the breath that leaves your body. Pay close attention to the air as it flows in and out of your nostrils. Observe how cool it is as you

STRESS TIP

Don't study on your bed, especially if you have problems with insomnia. Your mind may start to associate the bed with work, and make it even harder for you to fall asleep.

DRESS FOR SUCCESS

When you dress on the day of the test, put on loose layers. That way you'll be prepared no matter what the temperature of the room is. (An uncomfortable temperature will just distract you from the job at hand.)

And, if you have an item of clothing that you tend to feel "lucky" or confident in—a shirt, a pair of jeans, whatever—wear it. A little totem couldn't hurt.

BREATHE LIKE A BABY

A baby or young child is the best model for demonstrating how to breathe most efficiently and comfortably. Only its stomach moves as it inhales and exhales. The action is virtually effortless.

THINK GOOD THOUGHTS

Create a set of positive, but brief affirmations and mentally repeat them to yourself just before you fall asleep at night. (That's when your mind is very open to suggestion.) You'll find yourself feeling a lot more positive in the morning. Periodically repeating your affirmations during the day makes them even more effective.

inhale and how warm your breath is when you exhale. As you expel the air, say a cue word such as *calm* or *relax* to yourself. Once you've exhaled all the air from your lungs, start the next long, slow inhale. Notice how relaxed feelings increase as you slowly exhale and again hear your cue words.

Mantra Meditation

For this type of meditation experience you'll need a mental device (a mantra), a passive attitude (don't *try* to do anything), and a position in which you can be comfortable. You're going to focus your total attention on a mantra you create. It should be emotionally neutral, repetitive, and monotonous, and your aim is to fully occupy your mind with it. Furthermore, you want to do the meditation passively, with no goal in your head of how relaxed you're supposed to be. This is a great way to prepare for studying or taking the test. It clears your head of extraneous thoughts and gets you focused and at ease.

Sit comfortably and close your eyes. Begin to relax by letting your body go limp. Create a relaxed mental attitude and know there's no need for you to force anything. You're simply going to let something happen. Breathe through your nose. Take calm, easy breaths and as you exhale, say your mantra (*one, ohhm, aah, soup*—whatever is emotionally neutral for you) to yourself. Repeat the mantra each time you breathe out. Let feelings of relaxation grow as you focus on the mantra and your slow breathing. Don't worry if your mind wanders. Simply return to the mantra and continue letting go. Experience this meditation for 10 to 15 minutes.

HANDLING STRESS DURING THE TEST

The biggest stress monster will be the test itself. Fear not; there are methods of quelling your stress during the test.

•Keep moving forward instead of getting bogged down in a difficult question, game, or passage. You don't have to get everything right to achieve a fine score. So, don't linger out of desperation on a question that is going nowhere even after you've spent considerable time on it. The best test takers skip difficult material temporarily in search of the easier stuff. They mark the ones that require extra time and thought. This strategy buys time and builds confidence so you can handle the tough stuff later.

•Don't be thrown if other test takers seem to be working more busily and furiously than you are. Continue to spend your time patiently but doggedly thinking through your answers; it's going to lead to higher-quality test taking and better results. Don't mistake the other people's sheer activity as signs of progress and higher scores.

• *Keep breathing!* Weak test takers tend to share one major trait: They forget to breathe properly as the test proceeds. They start holding their breath without realizing it, or they breathe erratically or arrhythmically. Improper breathing hurts confidence and accuracy. Just as important, it interferes with clear thinking.

• Some quick isometrics during the test—especially if concentration is wandering or energy is waning—can help. Try this: Put your palms together and press intensely for a few seconds. Concentrate on the tension you feel through your palms, wrists, forearms, and up into your biceps and shoulders. Then, quickly release the pressure. Feel the difference as you let go. Focus on the warm relaxation that floods through the muscles. Now you're ready to return to the task.

• Here's another isometric that will relieve tension in both your neck and eye muscles. Slowly rotate your head from side to side, turning your head and eyes to look as far back over each shoulder as you can. Feel the muscles stretch on one side of your neck as they contract on the other. Repeat five times in each direction.

With what you've just learned here, you're armed and ready to do battle with the test. This book and your studies will give you the information you'll need to answer the questions. It's all firmly planted in your mind. You also know how to deal with any excess tension that might come along, both when you're studying for and taking the exam. You've experienced everything you need to tame your test anxiety and stress. You're going to get a great score.

STORIES FROM THE TRENCHES

Do you have any great stories, advice, or yuks related to tests or test stress? Well, share them (anonymously) with the rest of the class, please! Mail them to Kaplan, Book Group, 444 Madison Avenue, Suite 803, New York, NY 10022 (or fax us at 212–752–1845).

WHAT ARE "SIGNS OF A WINNER," ALEX?

Here's some advice from a Kaplan instructor who won big on *Jeopardy!*™ In the green room before the show, he noticed that the contestants who were quiet and "within themselves" were the ones who did great on the show. The contestants who did not perform as well were the ones who were fact-cramming, talking a lot, and generally being manic before the show. Lesson: Spend the final hours leading up to the test getting sleep, meditating, and generally relaxing.

From the day she was born, Emily's parents
knew she'd do well in school.

CHAPTER 1

SAT MASTERY

To perform well on the SAT, you need to draw on a set of skills that the College Board does not mention in any of their materials. You need to be a good SAT test taker.

Acquiring this ability, and the confidence it produces, is what this book is about.

THREE SIMPLE PRINCIPLES OF SAT MASTERY

There are three simple things you need to master the SAT:

- You need to have a basic understanding of SAT content.
- You need to hone the thinking and testing skills that underlie the SAT.
- You need to know the nature of the SAT.

Content and skills are obviously important. You can't do well without them. But understanding the nature of the SAT, its setup, its structure, and the tricks it often lays for you will allow you to gain points on the test that you might not otherwise have earned.

USING THE STRUCTURE OF THE SAT TO YOUR ADVANTAGE

The SAT is different from the tests that you're used to taking. On a school test, you probably go through the problems in order. You spend more time on the hard questions than on easy ones, since this is where you get more points. And you often show your work since the teacher tells you that how you approach a problem is as important as getting the answer right.

None of this works on the SAT. You can benefit from moving around within a section, the hard questions are worth the same as the easy ones, and it doesn't matter *how* you answer the question—only *what* your answer is.

To succeed in this peculiar context, you need to know some fundamentals about the overall structure of the SAT.

A DIFFERENT KIND OF TEST

The SAT's not like the tests you take in school. In school, you might need to get about 85 or 90 percent of the questions right to get a decent score. On the SAT, you sometimes need little more than 75 percent of the questions right to get a 1300—a very solid combined score.

1

THE SAT IS HIGHLY PREDICTABLE

Because the format and directions of the SAT remain unchanged from test to test, you can learn the setup in advance. On the day of the test, Analogies, QCs, Grid-ins—or the setup of any other question type or section—shouldn't be new to you.

One of the easiest things you can do to help your performance on the SAT is to understand the directions before taking the test. Since the instructions are always exactly the same, there's no reason to waste your time on the day of the test reading them. Learn them beforehand, as you go through this book, and skip them during the test.

MOST SAT QUESTIONS ARE ARRANGED BY ORDER OF DIFFICULTY

You've probably noticed that not all the questions on the SAT are equally difficult. Except for the Critical Reading problems, the questions are designed to get tougher as you work through a set.

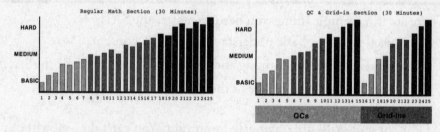

Questions get harder as you move through a section.

Here's how to use this pattern to your advantage. As you work, you should always be aware of where you are in the set. When working on the easy problems, you can generally trust your first impulse—the obvious answer is likely to be right.

As you get to the end of the set, you need to become more suspicious. Now the answers probably won't come easy. If they do, look at the problem again, because the obvious answer is likely to be wrong. Watch out for the answer that just "looks right." It may be a distractor—a wrong answer choice meant to entice you.

THERE'S NO MANDATORY ORDER TO THE QUESTIONS

You're allowed to skip around within each section of the SAT. High scorers know this. They move through the test efficiently. They don't dwell on any one question, even a hard one, until they've tried every question at least once.

When you run into questions that look tough, circle them in your test booklet and skip them for the time being. Go back and try again after you have answered the easier ones if you have time. On a second look, troublesome questions can turn out to be amazingly simple.

If you've started answering a question and get confused, quit and go on to the next question. Persistence may pay off in school, but it usually hurts your SAT score. Don't spend so much time answering one tough question that you use up three or four questions' worth of time. That costs you points, especially if you don't get the hard question right.

THERE'S A GUESSING PENALTY THAT CAN ACTUALLY WORK IN YOUR FAVOR

The test makers like to talk about the guessing penalty on the SAT. This is a misnomer. It's really a *wrong answer* penalty. If you guess wrong you get penalized. If you guess right, you're in great shape.

The fact is, if you can eliminate one or more answers as definitely wrong, you'll turn the odds in your favor and *actually come out ahead* by guessing. Here's how the penalty works:

- If you get an answer wrong on a Quantitative Comparison, which has four answer choices, you lose 1/3 point.

- If you get an answer wrong on other multiple-choice questions, which have five answer choices, you lose 1/4 point.

- If you get an answer wrong on a Grid-in math question, for which you write in your own answers, you lose nothing.

The fractional points you lose are meant to offset the points you might get "accidentally" by guessing the correct answer. With practice, however, you'll learn that it's often easy to eliminate *several* answer choices on some of the problems that you see. By learning the techniques for eliminating wrong answer choices you can actually turn the guessing "penalty" to your advantage.

THE ANSWER GRID HAS NO HEART

It sounds simple but it's extremely important: Don't make mistakes filling out your answer grid. When time is short, it's easy to get confused going back and forth between your test book and your grid. If you know the answer, but misgrid, you won't get the points.

To avoid mistakes on the answer grid:

Always Circle the Questions You Skip

Put a big circle in your test book around any question numbers you skip. When you go back, these questions will be easy to locate. Also, if you accidentally skip a box on the grid, you can check your grid against your book to see where you went wrong.

KAPLAN RULES

DON'T GUESS, unless you can eliminate at least one answer choice.
DON'T SKIP IT, unless you have absolutely no idea.

CIRCLE BEFORE YOU SKIP

A common cause of major SAT disasters is filling in all of the questions with the right answers—in the wrong spots.
Every time you skip a question, circle it in your test book and be double sure that you skip it on the answer grid as well.

Always Circle the Answers You Choose

Circling your answers in the test book makes it easier to check your grid against your book.

Grid Five or More Answers at Once

Don't transfer your answers to the grid after every question. Transfer your answers after every five questions, or at the end of each reading passage. That way, you won't keep breaking your concentration to mark the grid. You'll save time and you'll gain accuracy.

These fundamentals apply to every section of the test. But each question type also has its own structural peculiarities that make them easy to prep for. Some examples: On Grid-ins, the grid cannot accommodate five-digit answers, negatives, or variables. If you get such an answer, you know you've made a mistake and need to redo the problem.

Analogy answer choices are always ordered with the same parts of speech; this helps you determine if you're building an appropriate bridge.

Critical Reading questions with line references, "Little Picture" questions, can often be done quickly and don't require you to read the entire passage. You can do these first in a later reading passage if you're running out of time.

We'll show you lots of these structural elements, and the strategies you can use to take advantage of them, throughout this book.

APPROACHING SAT QUESTIONS

Apart from knowing the setup of the SAT, you've got to have a system for attacking the questions. You wouldn't travel around a foreign city without a map and you shouldn't approach the SAT without a plan. Now that you know some basics about how the test is set up, you can approach each section a little more strategically. What follows is the best method for approaching SAT questions systematically.

Think About the Question Before You Look at the Answer

The people who make the test love to put distractors among the answer choices. Distractors are answer choices that look like the right answer, but aren't. If you jump right into the answer choices without thinking first about what you're looking for, you're much more likely to fall for one of these traps.

Use Backdoor Strategies If the Answer Doesn't Come to You

There are usually a number of ways to get to the right answer on an SAT question. Most of the questions on the SAT are multiple choice. That means the answer is right in front of you—you just have to find it. This makes SAT questions open to a lot of ways of finding the answer. If you can't figure out the answer in a straightforward way, try other techniques. We'll talk about specific Kaplan methods such as backsolving, picking numbers, and eliminating weak Analogy bridges, in later chapters.

Guess Only When You Can Eliminate One Answer Choice

You already know that the wrong answer "penalty" can work in your favor. Don't simply skip questions that you can't answer. Spend some time with them to see if you can eliminate any of the answer choices. If you can, it pays for you to guess.

Pace Yourself

The SAT gives you a lot of questions in a short period of time. To get through a whole section, you can't spend too much time on any one question. Keep moving through the test at a good speed; if you run into a hard question, circle it in your test booklet, skip it, and come back to it later if you have time.

In the sidebar to the right are recommended average times per question. This doesn't mean that you should spend exactly 40 seconds on every Analogy. It's a guide. Remember, the questions get harder as you move through a problem set. Ideally, you can work through the easy problems at a brisk, steady clip, and use a little more of your time for the harder ones that come at the end of the set. One caution: Don't completely rush through the easy problems just to save time for the harder ones. These early problems are points in your pocket, and you're better off not getting to the last couple of problems than losing these easy points.

Locate Quick Points If You're Running out of Time

Some questions can be done quickly; for instance, some reading questions will ask you to identify the meaning of a particular word in the passage. These can be done at the last minute, even if you haven't read the passage. On most Quantitative Comparisons, even the hardest ones, you can quickly eliminate at least one answer, improving your chances of guessing correctly. When you start to run out of time, locate and answer any of the quick points that remain.

When you take the SAT, you have one clear objective in mind—to score as many points as you can. It's that simple. The rest of this book will help you do it.

RECOMMENDED TIMING	
Section	**On Average**
Analogies	40 seconds
Sentence Completions	40 seconds
Critical Reading*	75 seconds
Regular Math	70 seconds
QCs	45 seconds
Grid-ins	90 seconds

* Average time for Critical Reading includes time to read the passage. Spend about 30 seconds per question.

HIGHLIGHTS

• How to take advantage of the SAT's structure

• How to approach SAT questions systematically

CHAPTER 2

INSIDE THE SAT

Because it's a standardized test, you can feel safe in knowing that the structure, contents, and questions on the SAT will be pretty much what you should expect after working your way through this book. In this chapter, we will walk you through the structure of the SAT. When you sit down to take the test, you should already know what kind of questions you'll find, what the instructions say, how the test will be scored, and how you will be timed.

STRUCTURE OF THE TEST

There are six types of questions on the SAT, three verbal and three math. The likely number of questions you'll see of each type is listed below.

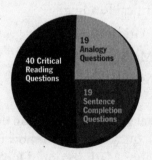 

Verbal

- 19 Analogies—Analogies test your ability to see relationships between words.

- 19 Sentence Completions—These test your ability to see how the parts of a sentence relate. About half will have one word missing from a sentence; the rest will have two words missing. Both types test vocabulary knowledge and reasoning ability.

KAPLAN RULES

Getting familiar with the SAT can get you a higher score on the SAT. Once you know the setup of the test and you've learned what to expect, you'll be more confident about your ability to master every section and question type. Familiarity gives you confidence and confidence gets you points.

• 40 Critical Reading questions, in four separate sets—Critical Reading tests your ability to read and understand a passage. The passages are long (400–850 words), and at least one passage contains two related readings. Some reading questions test your understanding of the content of the passage; others will require you to draw conclusions. Some will also explicitly test vocabulary in context.

Math

• 15 Quantitative Comparisons—QCs, as they're called, give you two quantities and ask you to compare them. You have to determine if one quantity is larger, if they're equal, or if you don't have enough information to decide. They test your knowledge of math, your ability to apply that knowledge, and your reasoning ability. They're also designed to be done quickly, making them a good source of quick points.

• 35 Regular Math—These are straightforward multiple-choice math questions, with five answer choices.

• 10 Grid-ins—These questions are open-ended, with no answer choices. Instead, you enter your response into a small grid. These questions test the same math concepts as the other types of questions.

SECTION BREAKDOWN

The SAT is divided into seven sections, which can appear in any order.

• Two 30-minute Verbal sections with Analogies, Sentence Completions, and Critical Reading.

• One 15-minute Verbal section with Critical Reading.

• One 30-minute section with QCs and Grid-ins.

• One 30-minute section with Regular Math.

• One 15-minute section with Regular Math.

There is also one 30-minute Experimental section. This section does not affect your score and is used to try out new questions. It can show up anyplace and it will look like any other Verbal or Math section. Don't try to figure out which section is experimental so you can nap during that period. First of all, you'll lose your momentum in the middle of the test. Second, and more important, you might be wrong.

DID YOU KNOW . . .

A little bit of improvement on the SAT can go a long way. Getting just one extra question right every 10 minutes on the SAT translates to 15 more questions right over the entire test. This improvement could boost your scaled score by close to 150 points.

SCORING

You get one point added to your score for each correct answer on the SAT, and lose a fraction of a point for each wrong answer (except for Grid-ins—but we'll go into that later). If you leave a question blank, you neither gain nor lose points. The totals are added up for all the Verbal and Math questions, and that produces two raw scores.

These numbers aren't your SAT scores. The raw scores are converted into scaled scores, each on a scale of 200 to 800, and these are the scores that are reported to you and the colleges you choose. (The reports include subscores as well, but most colleges focus on the two main scores.)

In April of 1995, the College Board adjusted or "recentered" the scoring of the SAT. The average scaled score (on a 200- to 800-point scale) for either Math or Verbal is now 500, for an average combined score of 1000 points. This is almost 100 points higher than the old combined averages. The test isn't any easier or harder; only the scoring has changed.

Bottom line: If you compared your SAT score with that of someone who took the test before 1995 (someone who got the exact number of questions right as you did), *your* score would probably be higher. Sounds great, right? Well, it's not so cut-and-dried.

Remember, everyone's score is adjusted, so you'll fall in the same percentile* range using this new scale as you would using the old. Plus, colleges are aware of these changes and are expecting higher scores in many cases. To get into a more exclusive school, you'll have to improve your score *relative* to your peers. That's the name of the game on the SAT.

SAT TIMING

The SAT:
- Is three hours long
- Includes two 10-minute breaks (after sections 2 and 4)

There are some rules about how you can and cannot allocate this time:
- You are not allowed to jump back and forth between sections.
- You are not allowed to return to earlier sections to change answers.
- You are not allowed to spend more than the allotted time on any section.
- You can move around within a section.
- You can flip through your section at the beginning to see what type of questions you have.

*Percent of SAT takers scoring at or below a given score

HIGHLIGHTS

• Structure of the test
• Scoring
• Timing

You'll get more familiar with the format and setup of the SAT as you work your way through this book. For now, just remember the basics we covered in Chapter 1: The SAT is predictable, there are elements built right into the test that allow you to prep for it, and you need to develop an approach to answering the questions.

Reading is important. It helps you find out what's on TV.

CHAPTER 3

INTRODUCING SAT VERBAL

Imagine yourself driving through Paris, France. As you approach an intersection, you see a red octagonal sign with the word *arrêtez* on it. Even if you don't speak a word of French, you come to a stop and look down the crossroads before driving on through the city.

If you didn't know the language, you probably took the information given to you—the shape, color, and location of the sign—and related it to what you already know. You may also have noticed, maybe subconsciously, that *arrêtez* sounds something like *arrest*, which means "stop."

The skills you displayed by making this deduction are skills of inference. To do well on SAT Verbal, you need to apply these same skills. The SAT does not test spelling or grammar. It does not test your knowledge of English literature or literary terms. It will never ask you to interpret a poem. SAT Verbal covers a fairly predictable, fairly limited body of skills and knowledge: vocabulary, verbal reasoning, and reading skills.

There are three scored Verbal sections on the SAT. The breakdown of the questions will go something like this:

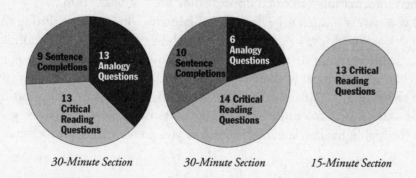

30-Minute Section　　*30-Minute Section*　　*15-Minute Section*

- One 30-minute section with nine Sentence Completions, 13 Analogies, and 13 Critical Reading questions
- One 30-minute section with 10 Sentence Completions, six Analogies, and 14 Critical Reading questions
- One 15-minute section with 13 Critical Reading questions

The Sentence Completions and Analogy sets are arranged by order of difficulty. The first few questions in a set are meant to be fairly straightforward and manageable. The middle few questions will be a little harder and the last few are the most difficult. Keep this in mind as you work and move through the early questions a little more quickly to leave yourself more time for the difficult ones.

Critical Reading is *not* arranged by difficulty. Any time you find yourself beginning to spend too much time on a question, you should skip it and return to it later.

HOW TO APPROACH SAT VERBAL

To do well on SAT Verbal, you need to be systematic in your approach to each question type and each of the three Verbal sections. Sentence Completions and Analogies are designed to be done relatively quickly. That means you can earn points fast, so you should do these first. Critical Reading takes a lot longer, so you can't just leave yourself five minutes to do a passage. Remember, you earn just as many points for an easy question as you do for a hard one.

TAPPING YOUR SAT VERBAL SKILLS

Although the test materials never explain this, a big key to doing well on the verbal part of the SAT is sharpening your verbal critical thinking skills —skills that you already use every day.

If you get to a movie 10 minutes late, do you give up and walk out, deciding you'll never understand what's going on? Probably not. Instead, you use your inference skills—the ability to draw valid conclusions from limited information—to catch up and enjoy the rest of the film.

If you have a sudden urge for a tub of popcorn, do you leave during the climactic scene? More likely, you use your ability to distinguish important concepts from minor details to pick a dull moment to make your move.

When your younger brother asks you what the movie was about, do you take two hours to explain it to him? You probably use your paraphrasing skills—the ability to condense complex ideas into a few words—to give him the highlights in a few minutes before you go back to ignoring him.

KNOW WHAT TO EXPECT

Doing your best on SAT Verbal comes from knowing what to expect, and knowing that you have the skills to handle it. You use words every day. You make your own ideas clear and you understand and respond to those of others. In all of these cases—talking with friends or talking with teachers, reading a textbook or reading a billboard, listening to lyrics or listening to your SAT proctor's instructions—you take limited information, process it through your own intellect and experience, and make sense of it. If you can learn to make the most of these skills on the test, you'll be well on the road to a much improved Verbal score.

HIGHLIGHTS

- The Verbal setup
- Tapping your Verbal skills
- Knowing what to expect

F·A·S·T P·R·E·P

✍ CHAPTER CHECKLIST

Once you've mastered a concept, check it off.

VOCABULARY

❏ A VOCABULARY BUILDING PLAN

❏ DECODING STRANGE WORDS

PANICPLAN

If you have a month or less to prep for the SAT, here's the best way to spend your time:

• Go straight to the section called "Decoding Strange Words on the Test" and try to master those skills.

CHAPTER 4

VOCABULARY

You know how to read. You can explain the relationship between *kitten* and *cat* to a three-year-old. You can finish a friend's sentence when she sneezes in the middle. So what makes the Verbal section such a challenge? Vocabulary. You may have a solid understanding of a Critical Reading passage but then get thrown by one tough vocabulary word. You may know the relationship between the original pair of words in an Analogy, but have a tough time finding the answer because all the choices have words you've never seen before. You may know precisely what kind of word to fill in on a Sentence Completion, and then find that all the answer choices look like they're in a foreign language.

All three Verbal question types—Analogies, Sentence Completions, and Critical Reading—depend upon your ability to work with unfamiliar words. You won't be asked to define words on the SAT. But you'll need to have a sense of their meaning in order to answer the questions.

TWO TYPES OF HARD WORDS

There are two types of hard SAT words:

- Unfamiliar words
- Familiar words with unfamiliar meanings

Some words are hard because you haven't seen them before. The words *scintilla* or *circumlocution,* for instance, are probably not part of your everyday vocabulary. But they might pop up on your SAT.

Easy words, such as *recognize* or *appreciation* may also trip you up on the test because they have secondary meanings that you aren't used to. Analogies and Critical Reading in particular will throw you familiar words with unfamiliar meanings.

To get a sense of your vocabulary strength, we've provided a representative list of words you might find on the SAT. Take a couple of minutes to look through it and see how many you know. Write your answer right in the book. Give yourself one point for each word you know. (Answers on p. 20.)

> ## WHO CARES?
>
> Somewhere in the process of studying for the Verbal section, you'll decide that knowing the difference between *taciturn* and *tenacious, obdurate* and *obloquy,* and even *plaudit* and *pusillanimous* is among the silliest things you've ever done. After all, no one on television talks that way.
>
> Your vocabulary says a lot about your ability to express yourself, as well as giving some valuable hints as to how well read you are. Colleges like students with big vocabularies, so humor them. Learn some new words.
>
> The single best way to do well on SAT verbal is to read as much as possible. Read newspapers and magazines to see words in use. Underline the ones you need to look up. If you recognize the words you see on the exam, you'll be on your way to acing the SAT.

irritate _____

truthful _____

conquer _____

passionate _____

inactive _____

eliminate _____

benevolent _____

elocution _____

irk _____

pragmatic _____

breadth _____

rectify _____

duplicity _____

impartial _____

abandon (n.) _____

vie _____

overt _____

august (adj.) _____

laud _____

voluble _____

flag (v.) _____

perspicacity _____

maladroit _____

sonorous _____

doleful _____

serpentine _____

rail (v.) _____

quiescence _____

idiosyncrasy _____

kudos _____

Turn the page for the definitions of the words in this list.

irritate	to annoy, bother
truthful	honest, straightforward, trustworthy
conquer	to defeat, overthrow
passionate	emotional, ardent, enthusiastic
inactive	not active, not moving
eliminate	to get rid of
benevolent	generous, kind
elocution	the study and practice of public speaking
irk	to irritate, anger, annoy
pragmatic	practical; moved by facts rather than abstract ideals
breadth	broadness, wideness
rectify	to correct
duplicity	deception, dishonesty, double-dealing
impartial	fair, just, unbiased, unprejudiced
abandon (n.)	total lack of inhibition
vie	to compete, contend
overt	apparent, unconcealed
august (adj.)	dignified, awe-inspiring, venerable
laud	to praise, applaud, honor
voluble	speaking much and easily, talkative; glib
flag (v.)	to droop, lose energy; to signal, to mark
perspicacity	shrewdness, astuteness, keenness of wit
maladroit	clumsy, tactless
sonorous	producing a full, rich sound
doleful	sad, mournful
serpentine	serpentlike; twisting, winding
rail (v.)	to scold with bitter or abusive language
quiescence	inactivity, stillness
idiosyncrasy	peculiarity of temperament, eccentricity
kudos	fame, glory, honor

If you scored 10 points or fewer, you should probably work on building your vocabulary. The techniques and tools in this chapter will help you improve your vocabulary and make the most out of what you do know about words.

If you scored between 10 and 20 points, your vocabulary is average. If you're willing to put in the time, using these techniques and tools can help you do better.

STRANGE WORD ORIGINS

Learning the derivation of words can often help you remember the meaning of words. Did you know...

Jovial (joyful) comes from the Roman deity Jove, who was known for his pleasant disposition.

Sardonic (characterized by bitter mockery) comes from sardinia, a mythical plant from the island of the same name. Ingestion of the plant caused convulsive laughter followed by death.

Maudlin (overly sentimental) comes from Mary Magdalene, a follower of Christ who is shown weeping in many paintings. Maudlin is an alternate pronunciation of Magdalene.

If you scored 20 points or more, your vocabulary is in great shape. You can polish it further, but you don't have to. If time is short, learn the strategies in Decoding Hard Words and concentrate on other aspects of the SAT that you find difficult.

A VOCABULARY BUILDING PLAN

A great vocabulary can't be built overnight, but you can develop a better SAT vocabulary with a minimum of pain.

Here's a plan:

Learn Words Strategically

The best words to learn are words that have appeared often on the SAT. The test makers are not very creative in their choice of words for each test; words that have appeared frequently are likely bets to show up again.

The word list in Appendix A (p. 211) gives you a jump on some common SAT words. Learn a few words a day from this list, spreading them over the time remaining before the SAT. Keep reviewing those you've already studied.

The word list groups words into common meaning families. For example, *loquacious, verbose,* and *garrulous* all mean "wordy, talkative." *Taciturn, laconic, terse, concise,* and *pithy* all mean "not talkative, not wordy." Instead of learning just one of these words, learn them all together—you get eight words for the price of one definition.

> *HINT: Be strategic. How well you use your time between now and the day of the test is just as important as how much time you spend prepping.*

Work with Word Roots

Most SAT words are made up of prefixes and roots that can get you at least partway to a definition. Often that's all you need to get a right answer.

Use the Root List in the back of this book to pick up the most valuable SAT roots. Target these words in your vocabulary prep. Learn a few new roots a day, familiarizing yourself with the meaning.

Personalize Your Vocabulary Study

Figure out a study method that works best for you, and stick to it.

- Use flashcards: Write down new words or word groups and run through them whenever you have a few spare minutes. Put one new word or word group on one side of a 3 x 5 index card and a short definition on the back.

- Make a vocabulary notebook: List words in one column and their meaning in another. Test yourself. Cover up the meanings, and see

PERSONALIZE YOUR HOME STUDY

- Use flashcards.
- Make a vocabulary notebook.
- Make a vocabulary tape.
- Look for hooks or phrases that will lodge a new word in your mind.

which words you can define from memory. Make a sample sentence using each word in context.

- Make a vocabulary tape: Record unknown words and their definitions. Pause for a moment before you read the definition. This will give you time to define the word in your head when you play the tape back. Quiz yourself. Listen to your tape in your portable cassette player. Play it in the car, on the bus, or whenever you have a few spare moments.

- Think of hooks that lodge a new word in your mind: Create visual images of words.

- Use rhymes and other devices that help you remember the words.

It doesn't matter which techniques you use, as long as you learn words steadily and methodically. Doing so over several months is ideal.

DECODING STRANGE WORDS ON THE TEST

Trying to learn every word that could possibly appear on the SAT is like trying to memorize the license plate number of every car on the freeway. It's not much fun, it'll give you a headache, and you probably won't pull it off.

No matter how much time you spend with flashcards, vocabulary tapes, or word lists, you're bound to face some mystery words on your SAT. No big deal. Just as you can use your basic multiplication skills to find the product of even the largest numbers, you can use what you know about words to focus on likely meanings of tough vocabulary words.

GO WITH YOUR HUNCHES

When you look at an unfamiliar word, your first reaction may be to say, "Don't know it. Gotta skip it." Not so fast. Vocabulary knowledge on the SAT is not an all-or-nothing proposition.

- Some words you know so well you can rattle off a dictionary definition of them.

- Some words you "sort of" know. You understand them when you see them in context, but don't feel confident using them yourself.

- Some words are vaguely familiar. You know you've heard them somewhere before.

HINT: If you think you recognize a word, go with your hunch.

Try to Recall Where You've Heard the Word Before

If you can recall a phrase in which the word appears, that may be enough to eliminate some answer choices, or even zero in on the right answer.

EXAMPLE

Between the two villages was a ---- through which passage was difficult and hazardous.
(A) precipice
(B) beachhead
(C) quagmire
(D) market
(E) prairie

To answer this question, it helps to know the word *quagmire*. You may remember *quagmire* from news reports referring to "a foreign policy *quagmire*" or "a *quagmire* of financial indebtedness." If you can remember how *quagmire* was used, you'll have a rough idea of what it means, and you'll see it fits. You may also be reminded of the word *mire*, as in "We got *mired* in the small details and never got to the larger issue." Sounds something like *stuck*, right? You don't need an exact definition. A *quagmire* is a situation that's difficult to get out of, so (C) is correct. Literally, a *quagmire* is a bog or swamp.

Decide If the Word Has a Positive or Negative "Charge"

Simply knowing that you're dealing with a positive or negative word can earn you points on the SAT.

Look at the word *cantankerous*. Say it to yourself. Can you guess whether it's positive or negative? Often words that sound harsh have a negative meaning while smooth sounding words tend to have positive meanings. If *cantankerous* sounded negative to you, you were right. It means "difficult to handle."

You can also use prefixes and roots to help determine a word's charge. *Mal, de, dis, un, in, im, a,* and *mis* often indicate a negative, while *pro, ben,* and *magn* are often positives.

Not all SAT words sound positive or negative; some sound neutral. But if you can define the charge, you can probably eliminate some answer choices on that basis alone.

EXAMPLE

He seemed at first to be honest and loyal, but before long it was necessary to ---- him for his ---- behavior.
(A) admonish . . steadfast
(B) extol . . conniving
(C) reprimand . . scrupulous
(D) exalt . . insidious
(E) castigate . . perfidious

You don't need an exact definition of the words that go in the blanks. You just need to know that negative words are needed in both blanks. (See Chapter 6 for more about Sentence Completions.) Then you can scan the answer choices for a choice that contains two clearly negative words. Choice (E) is right. *Castigate* means "punish or scold harshly," and *perfidious* means "treacherous."

Use Your Foreign Language Skills

Many of the roots you'll encounter in SAT words come from Latin. Spanish, French, and Italian also come from Latin, and have retained much of it in their modern forms. English is also a cousin to German and Greek. That means that if you don't recognize a word, try to remember if you know a similar word in another language.

Look at the word *carnal*. Unfamiliar? What about *carne*, as in *chili con carne*? *Carn* means "meat" or "flesh," which leads you straight to the meaning of *carnal*—pertaining to the flesh. You could decode *carnivorous* ("meat eating") in the same way.

You can almost always figure out something about strange words on the test because SAT words are never all that strange. Chances are that few words on the SAT will be totally new to you, even if your recollection is more subliminal than vivid.

When All Else Fails

Eliminate choices that are clearly wrong and make an educated guess from the remaining choices. A wrong answer won't hurt you much; a right answer will help you a lot.

HIGHLIGHTS

- How to expand your vocabulary
- How to decode strange words

F·A·S·T P·R·E·P

✍ CHAPTER CHECKLIST

Once you've mastered a concept, check it off.

ANALOGIES
- ❑ THE FORMAT
- ❑ BUILDING BRIDGES
- ❑ KAPLAN'S THREE-STEP METHOD
- ❑ TEST YOUR ANALOGY SMARTS
- ❑ NINE CLASSIC BRIDGES
- ❑ HOW TO FILL VOCABULARY GAPS
- ❑ ANALOGY PRACTICE SET

PANICPLAN

If you have a month or less to prep for the SAT, here's the best way to spend your time:

- Learn the Kaplan Three-Step Method for Analogies (pp. 28–29).
- Do the practice set on pp. 38–39.
- If you miss an answer, review pp. 34–38.

CHAPTER 5

ANALOGIES

nalogies may seem frightening at first because they don't look like anything you've ever done before. Once you get familiar with the format, however, you'll find there's a simple method for mastering this question type. In fact, prepping often gains you more points on Analogies than on any other Verbal question type. With practice, you can even learn to get the Analogy right when you don't know all of the vocabulary words involved.

THE FORMAT

There are 19 Analogies in all on the SAT. You'll probably see one set of 13 and one set of six. Each 30-minute Verbal section contains a set of Analogies. A question looks like this:

EXAMPLE

FLAKE : SNOW ::

(A) storm : hail

(B) drop : rain

(C) field : wheat

(D) stack : hay

(E) cloud : fog

The two words in capital letters are called the *stem words*. The instructions will tell you to choose the pair of words from the five answer choices that is related in the same way as this pair. In this example, the answer above is (B). A flake is a small unit of snow, just as a drop is a small unit of rain.

BUILDING BRIDGES

In every Analogy question, there exists a strong, definite connection between the two stem words. Your task is to identify this relationship, and then to look for a similar relationship among the answer pairs.

ANALOGIES ARE PART OF YOUR LIFE

Analogies can seem strange at first, until you realize that you speak and think in Analogies all the time.

Anytime you say "my sister is like a slug" you're drawing an Analogy between your sister and slugs—perhaps your sister is as gross as a slug, or perhaps she always falls asleep in bowls of beer. That may not be the kind of relationship that will appear on your SAT, but the way of thinking is the same.

What's a strong, definite relationship?

- The words *library* and *book* have a strong, definite connection. A library is defined as a place where books are kept. LIBRARY : BOOK could be a question stem.

- The words *library* and *child* do not have a strong, definite connection. A child may or may not have anything to do with a library. LIBRARY : CHILD would never be a question stem.

The best way to pinpoint the relationship between the stem words is to build a bridge. A bridge is a short sentence that relates the two words. Often, a bridge reads like a definition of one of the two words. For instance: "A LIBRARY is a place where BOOKS are kept."

The ability to find bridges is fundamental to Analogy success. Your bridge needs to capture the strong, definite connection between the words.

KAPLAN RULES

To solve an Analogy:

1. Build a bridge between the stem words.
2. Plug in the answer choices.
3. Adjust your bridge, if you need to.

KAPLAN'S THREE-STEP METHOD

The Kaplan Method for solving Analogies has three simple steps:

1. Build a bridge between the stem words.
2. Plug in the answer choices.
3. Adjust your bridge, if you need to.

Here's an Analogy stem. We've left out the answer choices because you need to focus first on the stem.

EXAMPLE

LILY : FLOWER ::

1. Build a Bridge
The best bridge here is, "A LILY is a type of FLOWER."

2. Plug in the Answer Choices
Here is the complete question.

EXAMPLE

LILY : FLOWER ::
(A) rose : thorn
(B) cocoon : butterfly
(C) brick : building
(D) maple : tree
(E) sky : airplane

Take the bridge you have built and plug in answer choices (A) through (E). If only one pair fits, it's the answer.

HINT: Be sure to try all five choices.

Here's how plugging in the answer choices works:

- (A) A rose is a type of thorn? No.
- (B) A cocoon is a type of butterfly? No.
- (C) A brick is a type of building? No.
- (D) A maple is a type of tree? Yes.
- (E) A sky is a type of airplane? No.

We've got four nos and only one yes, so the answer is (D).

3. Adjust Your Bridge If You Need To

If no answer choice seems to fit, your bridge is too specific and you should go back and adjust it. If more than one answer choice fits, your bridge is not specific enough. Look at this example.

WHAT MAKES A STRONG BRIDGE?

You might be lured into thinking the words *trumpet* and *jazz* have a strong bridge. They don't.

You can play lots of things on trumpets other than jazz—fanfares, taps, whatever. You can also play jazz on things other than trumpets.

Trumpet and *instrument* do have a strong bridge. A trumpet is a type of instrument. This is always true—it's a strong, definite relationship.

EXAMPLE

SNAKE : SLITHER ::
- (A) egg : hatch
- (B) wolf : howl
- (C) rabbit : hop
- (D) turtle : snap
- (E) tarantula : bite

With a simple bridge, such as "a snake slithers," you'd have a hard time finding the answer. All the answer choices make sense: an egg hatches, a wolf howls, a rabbit hops, a turtle snaps, a tarantula bites. Don't worry. Go back to step one and build another bridge, this time making it more specific. Think about what *slither* means.

New bridge: "Slithering is how a snake gets around."

(A) Hatching is how an egg gets around? No.

(B) Howling is how a wolf gets around? No.

(C) Hopping is how a rabbit gets around? Yes.

(D) Snapping is how a turtle gets around? No.

(E) Biting is how a tarantula gets around? No.

Four nos and one yes; the answer is (C).

HINT: If no answer fits, or too many answers fit, build a new bridge and plug in again.

WHAT PART OF SPEECH IS A STEM WORD?

Occasionally with an Analogy you might have to take a quick peek at the answer choices before you can build a bridge for the stem. The part of

NINE FAMOUS BRIDGES

Bridge on the River Kwai

Golden Gate Bridge

George Washington Bridge

Bridge Over Troubled Waters

Bridges of Madison County

Jeff Bridges

Lloyd Bridges

Tappan Zee Bridge

Bridget Fonda

speech of a stem word may be ambiguous. When you're not sure whether a stem word is a noun, verb, adjective, or adverb, look at the words directly beneath that stem word. As a rule, the words in a vertical row are all the same part of speech.

For example, you might see this:

VERB : NOUN ::
(A) verb : noun
(B) verb : noun
(C) verb : noun
(D) verb : noun
(E) verb : noun

or this:

ADJECTIVE : NOUN ::
(A) adjective : noun
(B) adjective : noun
(C) adjective : noun
(D) adjective : noun
(E) adjective : noun

but you'll *never* see this on an SAT Analogy:

NOUN : NOUN ::
(A) verb : noun
(B) noun : noun
(C) verb : verb
(D) verb : noun
(E) verb : noun

To establish the part of speech of a stem word, you don't usually have to look at more than choice (A).

How would you think through the following example?

EXAMPLE

PINE : DESIRE ::
(A) laugh : sorrow
(B) drink : thirst
(C) watch : interest
(D) listen : awe
(E) starve : hunger

The word *pine* can be a noun, but that's not likely here. You can't build a bridge between a tree with needlelike leaves and *desire*. Try another part of speech. A glance at the answer choices below *pine* (laugh, drink, watch, listen, and starve) tells you *pine* is being used as a verb.

What about *desire?* It could be a noun or a verb, but the answer choices beneath it (sorrow, thirst, interest, awe, and hunger) tell you it's used as a noun.

You've probably heard of someone pining away from unrequited love. As a verb, *pine* means "to yearn or suffer from longing." A good bridge would be: "To pine is to suffer from extreme desire." Plugging in the answer choices, you get:

(A) To laugh is to suffer from extreme sorrow? No.

(B) To drink is to suffer from extreme thirst? No.

(C) To watch is to suffer from extreme interest? No.

(D) To listen is to suffer from extreme awe? No.

(E) To starve is to suffer from extreme hunger? Yes.

Once again, four nos and one yes; the answer is (E).

TEST YOUR ANALOGY SMARTS

Try out what you've learned on these Analogies. (Answers on p. 33.)

1. SWEEP : BROOM ::
   (A) cut : scissors
   (B) soil : cloth
   (C) dry : bucket
   (D) thread : needle
   (E) wash : dish   Ⓐ Ⓑ Ⓒ Ⓓ Ⓔ

2. MAP : ATLAS ::
   (A) lock : key
   (B) road : highway
   (C) recipe : cookbook
   (D) concept : encyclopedia
   (E) theory : hypothesis   Ⓐ Ⓑ Ⓒ Ⓓ Ⓔ

3. HUNGRY : FAMINE ::
   (A) thirsty : rainfall
   (B) sick : plague
   (C) sated : dinner
   (D) dry : flood
   (E) sore : injury   Ⓐ Ⓑ Ⓒ Ⓓ Ⓔ

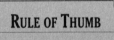

RULE OF THUMB

Try not to spend more than 40 seconds on each Analogy. Then you won't need to rush through Critical Reading, which comes next on the test.

NINE CLASSIC BRIDGES

It's easier to build bridges when you know the types of bridges that have appeared on the SAT in the past. While no one can give you a list of the words that will appear on SAT Analogies, you can learn what types of relationships to expect. The following classic bridges appear over and over again on the SAT. Don't memorize these bridges, or lists of words that fit these bridges. Instead, learn which types of bridges can lead you to the right answer on SAT Analogies and which cannot.

HINT: Become familiar with the types of bridges that connect stem words on the SAT. They can lead you to the right answer.

Classic bridges may take different forms, depending on what parts of speech are used. But the underlying concepts are what matter. Here are examples of nine classic types:

Bridge Type #1: DESCRIPTION

In many Analogies, one stem word is a person, place, or thing, and the other word is a characteristic of that person, place, or thing. Look at these examples:

PAUPER : POOR—A PAUPER is always POOR.

GENIUS : INTELLIGENT—A GENIUS is always INTELLIGENT.

TRAGEDY : SAD—A TRAGEDY is always SAD.

This classic bridge can also describe a person, place, or thing by what it is *not*.

PAUPER : WEALTHY—A PAUPER is never WEALTHY.

GENIUS : STUPID—A GENIUS is never STUPID.

TRAGEDY : HAPPY—A TRAGEDY is never HAPPY.

Try It Yourself

Here are more types of classic bridges. Fill in each blank with a stem word that will complete the bridge. There is more than one way to fill in each blank. The important thing is to get the right idea. See pp. 33–34 for suggested answers.

Bridge Type #2: CHARACTERISTIC ACTIONS

An INSOMNIAC can't ----.

A GLUTTON likes to ----.

A PROCRASTINATOR tends to ----.

Bridge Type #3: LACK

Something MURKY lacks ----.

A PESSIMIST lacks ----.

A PAUPER lacks ----.

DO IT YOURSELF

One way to see the inner workings of Analogies is to put some together yourself. Make sure you include five answer choices. This exercise will give you a good feel for the structure of SAT Analogies and may help you spot and avoid bad answer choices.

Bridge Type #4: CATEGORIES

MEASLES is a type of ----.

A MOTORCYCLE is a type of ----.

A POLKA is a type of ----.

Bridge Type #5: SIZE/DEGREE

To SPEAK very quietly is to ----.

To LIKE strongly is to ----.

To BRUSH is to ---- lightly.

Bridge Type #6: CAUSING/STOPPING

A REMEDY stops or cures an ----.

An OBSTACLE prevents ----.

Something INCENDIARY causes ----.

Bridge Type #7: PLACES

A JUDGE works in a ----.

A PLAY is performed on a ----.

BREAD is made in a ----.

Bridge Type #8: FUNCTION

GILLS are used for ----.

A PAINTBRUSH is used to ----.

A HELICOPTER is used for ----.

Bridge Type #9: PART/WHOLE

An ARMY is made up of ----.

A CROWD is made up of many ----.

An arrangement of FLOWERS is a ----.

Suggested Answers to Bridge Types

Your answers may vary from our suggested answers. As long as you've got the basic idea, that's okay.

CHARACTERISTIC ACTIONS

An INSOMNIAC can't SLEEP.

A GLUTTON likes to EAT.

A PROCRASTINATOR tends to DELAY.

ANSWERS TO ANALOGY QUESTIONS

1. (A) (A broom is used to sweep.)
2. (C) (An atlas is made up of many maps.)
3. (B) (Many are hungry during a famine.)

LACK

Something MURKY lacks CLARITY.

A PESSIMIST lacks OPTIMISM.

A PAUPER lacks MONEY.

CATEGORIES

MEASLES is a type of ILLNESS.

A MOTORCYCLE is a type of VEHICLE.

A POLKA is a type of DANCE.

SIZE/DEGREE

To SPEAK very quietly is to WHISPER.

To LIKE strongly is to LOVE (or ADORE).

To BRUSH is to TOUCH lightly.

CAUSING/STOPPING

A REMEDY stops or cures an ILLNESS.

An OBSTACLE prevents PROGRESS (or MOVEMENT).

Something INCENDIARY causes FIRE.

PLACES

A JUDGE works in a COURTROOM.

A PLAY is performed on a STAGE (or in a THEATER).

BREAD is made in a BAKERY.

FUNCTION

GILLS are used for BREATHING.

A PAINTBRUSH is used to PAINT.

A HELICOPTER is used for FLYING.

PART/WHOLE

An ARMY is made up of SOLDIERS.

A CROWD is made up of many PEOPLE.

An arrangement of FLOWERS is a BOUQUET.

HOW TO FILL VOCABULARY GAPS

Sometimes on an SAT Analogy, you simply don't know one of the stem words. When this happens, the basic three-step process won't do much good. You can't even do step one; you can't build a bridge using a word you don't know. You need another plan.

The best backup strategy is not to focus on the stem pair. Instead, try looking at the answer pairs and eliminate those that simply can't be right. If you can knock out even one, guessing from the remaining choices is to your advantage. You may be surprised at how far this strategy can take you.

Before you guess, take these three steps to eliminate some answer choices. (And remember, even if you can eliminate only one answer choice, guessing comes out in your favor.)

1. Eliminate answer choices with weak bridges.

2. Eliminate any two answer choices with identical bridges.

3. Eliminate answer choices with bridges that couldn't work with the stem pair no matter what that unknown word means.

Here's how you do it.

Eliminate Answer Choices with Weak Bridges

You learned earlier that a strong, definite relationship always exists between the pair of stem words. The answer pairs, however, don't always have a good bridge—and any choice without a good bridge can't be right. In other words, you can eliminate certain answer choices without looking at the stem at all.

Try this exercise. Here is a list of six answer pairs without any stem pairs—answers without questions. Try to make a bridge for each pair. If no strong bridge is possible, mark the pair with an X. (Answers on page 37.)

dog : house

aquatic : water

nocturnal : animal

infantile : toy

steak : potatoes

raisin : grape

In many cases, this method alone will allow you to eliminate one, two, or even three answer choices.

Eliminate Answer Choices with Identical Bridges

There's another way of eliminating some wrong choices that's so obvious you might not think of it. If two choices have the same bridge, it follows that neither one can be more right than the other. And since they can't

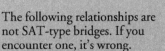

KAPLAN RULES

The following relationships are not SAT-type bridges. If you encounter one, it's wrong.

• Synonyms (Example: predict : foretell)

• Antonyms (Example: wealthy : impoverished)

• Members of the same category (Example: dog : cat)

both be right, they must both be wrong. For example, look at the following question:

> **EXAMPLE**
>
> LEGERDEMAIN : MAGICIAN ::
> (A) baggage : immigrant
> (B) justice : pragmatist
> (C) sluggishness : racer
> (D) diplomacy : diplomat
> (E) indifference : fanatic

What if you don't know what *legerdemain* means? (C) seems like a possible answer because this pair of words has a strong bridge: "Sluggishness is the opposite of what you'd expect from a racer." But choice (E) has a very similar bridge: "Indifference is the opposite of what you'd expect from a fanatic."

Since a question can't have two right answers, and both (C) and (E) have the same bridge, both must be wrong. The correct answer is (D).

Eliminate Answer Choices with Bridges That Can't Fit the Stem
What do you do with answer pairs that can't be eliminated by either of the first two methods? The next step is to find bridges for the remaining answers, and then to plug in the stem word pair. It's true that you don't even know what one of the stem words means. But in some cases you'll see that the stem word pair can't fit the answer bridge no matter what that unknown word means. Here's an example.

> **EXAMPLE**
>
> GENUFLECT : KNEE ::
> (A) pierce : ear
> (B) hold : hand
> (C) nod : neck
> (D) stub : toe
> (E) pick : tooth

You may not know what *genuflect* means. Since you can't work directly with this stem, take a look at the answer choices instead.

Answer pair (A) has a strong bridge: To pierce an ear is to put a hole in it. Now try plugging *genuflect* and *knee* into this same bridge: To genuflect a knee is to put a hole in it. Hmmm. Can you really imagine that there exists a verb in the English language that means "to put a hole in a knee?" No way. The concept doesn't even make sense. So GENUFLECT : KNEE and pierce : ear can't possibly have the same bridge. (A) can't be the right answer.

The same technique can be used to eliminate choice (E). Picking your teeth is a way of cleaning between them. Is there a comparable way of cleaning between your knees? Not likely.

So you've been able to eliminate two of the answer choices—without knowing what *genuflect* means. Sometimes, of course, this technique demands a bit more intuition. Without knowing for sure, you might just have a feeling that there wouldn't be a word for a very large telephone or for a group of hammers. If you're guessing anyway, go with these hunches. The correct answer is (C).

Putting It Together

Now apply all three answer-eliminating techniques to one question. (Pretend that you don't know the word *scimitar* even if you do.)

EXAMPLE

SCIMITAR : SWORD ::
(A) diamond : ring
(B) greyhound : dog
(C) saddle : horse
(D) lance : shield
(E) forest : tree

Choice (A): A diamond may adorn a ring, but plenty of rings don't have diamonds, and plenty of diamonds don't have rings. Choice (A) has a weak bridge. Eliminate.

Choice (B): A greyhound is a kind of dog. Could a scimitar be a kind of sword? It sounds possible.

Choice (C): A saddle is used for riding a horse. A scimitar is used for riding a sword? That can't make sense. Eliminate.

Choice (D): A lance and a shield are both part of the traditional gear of a knight, but that's all we can say to connect them. Again, a weak bridge. Eliminate.

Choice (E): A forest is a group of trees. Could a scimitar be a group of swords? Maybe.

Without knowing a stem word, you've gotten down to two answer choices—(B) and (E). Is there more likely to be a word for a kind of sword or for a group of swords? Take your best guess.

(B) is, in fact, the answer.

ANSWERS AND EXPLANATIONS FOR WEAK BRIDGES

A dog may or may not live in a house.—*Weak bridge*
Aquatic means "having to do with water."—*Strong bridge*
Not all animals are nocturnal, or active at night.—*Weak bridge*
You don't have to be infantile, or immature, to play with a toy.—*Weak bridge*
You can eat steak and potatoes, but you don't have to.—*Weak bridge*
A raisin is, by definition, a dried-up grape.—*Strong bridge*

DON'T FALL FOR SAME SUBJECT TRAPS

Same Subject Traps are wrong answer choices that lure you in by giving you words that remind you of stem words. *The same subject doesn't make it right.*

Remember, you're looking for an answer choice that has the same relationship as the stem, not an answer choice that reminds you of the stem.

A DOUBLE VOCABULARY GAP

What if you don't know either of the stem words? You can still eliminate weak bridges and identical bridges. For example:

> **EXAMPLE**
>
> MANUMISSION : THRALL ::
> (A) submission : employee
> (B) prediction : artist
> (C) promotion : rank
> (D) tip : waiter
> (E) parole : prisoner

Promotion is the act of raising a soldier in rank. A tip is a type of gratuity or reward given to a waiter. Parole is the act of freeing a prisoner. These are all good bridges, and none of them repeat, so (C), (D), and (E) are all possible answers. But submission is not a characteristic of every employee, and there's no particular connection between prediction and artist. So eliminate (A) and (B).

To make your final decision, of course, you still have to guess. But now that you've eliminated answer choices, guessing works in your favor. The answer here happens to be (E), since manumission is the act of freeing a thrall, or slave.

HINT: When all else fails, make an educated guess.

ANALOGY PRACTICE SET

1. COPPER : METAL ::
   (A) grain : sand
   (B) helium : gas
   (C) stem : flower
   (D) tree : trunk
   (E) stone : clay   Ⓐ Ⓑ Ⓒ Ⓓ Ⓔ

2. BROOM : DIRT ::
   (A) brush : bristles
   (B) fork : plate
   (C) rake : leaves
   (D) mirror : face
   (E) scissors : blades   Ⓐ Ⓑ Ⓒ Ⓓ Ⓔ

3. COWARD : BRAVERY ::
   (A) eccentric : conformity
   (B) hero : fortitude
   (C) prophet : vision
   (D) sage : wisdom
   (E) comedian : humor   Ⓐ Ⓑ Ⓒ Ⓓ Ⓔ

4. REVERE : ADMIRE ::
   (A) cherish : conceive
   (B) release : reject
   (C) guess : solve
   (D) propose : change
   (E) despise : disdain Ⓐ Ⓑ Ⓒ Ⓓ Ⓔ

5. PERPLEXING : CONFUSION ::
   (A) appalling : dismay
   (B) static : change
   (C) unpleasant : chaos
   (D) dignified : pride
   (E) grave : regret Ⓐ Ⓑ Ⓒ Ⓓ Ⓔ

6. AMUSING : MIRTH ::
   (A) ailing : health
   (B) painful : sympathy
   (C) optimistic : objectivity
   (D) protective : insecurity
   (E) terrifying : fear Ⓐ Ⓑ Ⓒ Ⓓ Ⓔ

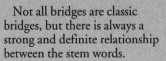

RULE OF THUMB

Not all bridges are classic bridges, but there is always a strong and definite relationship between the stem words.

7. FOOD : MENU ::
   (A) accounting : inventory
   (B) index : foreword
   (C) silverware : spoon
   (D) merchandise : catalog
   (E) films : credits Ⓐ Ⓑ Ⓒ Ⓓ Ⓔ

8. IMPERCEPTIBLE : DETECT ::
   (A) fundamental : begin
   (B) inconceivable : imagine
   (C) rugged : seize
   (D) costly : overcharge
   (E) immense : notice Ⓐ Ⓑ Ⓒ Ⓓ Ⓔ

9. PERSEVERE : DOGGED ::
   (A) comply : obedient
   (B) inspire : pompous
   (C) hesitate : reckless
   (D) speak : laconic
   (E) retard : expeditious Ⓐ Ⓑ Ⓒ Ⓓ Ⓔ

10. ENTHRALLING : TEDIUM ::
    (A) witty : frivolity
    (B) insipid : appetite
    (C) glaring : illumination
    (D) wearisome : redundancy
    (E) trite : originality Ⓐ Ⓑ Ⓒ Ⓓ Ⓔ

HIGHLIGHTS

- The Kaplan Three-Step Method
- How to build a bridge
- Nine classic bridges
- How to eliminate a weak bridge
- What to do if you don't know a stem word

Explanations for Analogy Practice Set

1. (B) (Copper is a kind of metal.)
2. (C) (A broom is used to clear away dirt.)
3. (A) (A coward does not display bravery.)
4. (E) (To revere is to admire very much.)
5. (A) (Something that is perplexing causes confusion.)
6. (E) (Something that is amusing causes mirth.)
7. (D) (A menu is a list of available food.)
8. (B) (If something is imperceptible, you cannot detect it.)
9. (A) (A dogged person is one who perseveres.)
10. (E) (Something that is enthralling lacks tedium.)

F·A·S·T P·R·E·P

CHAPTER CHECKLIST

✍ *Once you've mastered a section, check it off.*

SENTENCE COMPLETIONS
- ❑ THE FORMAT
- ❑ KAPLAN'S FOUR-STEP METHOD
- ❑ PICKING UP ON CLUES
- ❑ TACKLING HARD QUESTIONS
- ❑ PRACTICE SET

PANICPLAN

If you have a month or less to prep for the SAT, here's the best way to spend your time:

- Learn the Kaplan Four-Step Method for Sentence Completions (pp. 44–47).
- Do the practice set on pp. 53–54. If you miss an answer, read example questions on pp. 47–53.

CHAPTER 6

SENTENCE COMPLETIONS

Of all the verbal question types, Sentence Completions are probably the most student-friendly. Unlike Analogies, they give you some context in which to think about vocabulary words, and unlike Critical Reading, they only require you to pay attention to a single sentence at a time.

> **STATISTIC:** *The 19 Sentence Completions count for about one-fourth of your verbal score.*

THE FORMAT

There are 19 Sentence Completions in all on the SAT. You'll probably see one set of nine and one set of ten. They appear in both 30-minute Verbal Sections. The instructions for Sentence Completions look something like this:

> Select the lettered word or set of words that best completes the sentence.

> **EXAMPLE**
> Today's small, portable computers contrast markedly with the earliest electronic computers, which were ----.
> (A) effective
> (B) invented
> (C) useful
> (D) destructive
> (E) enormous

In the example, the new computers, which are small and portable, are contrasted with old computers. You can infer that the old computers must be the opposite of small and portable, so (E), *enormous,* is right.

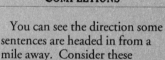

MASTERING COMPLETIONS

You can see the direction some sentences are headed in from a mile away. Consider these examples:

"I still want to be your friend. . . ."

"Despite your impressive qualifications. . . ."

"If I ever get my hands on you, you little. . . ."

You could probably finish off these sentences on your own with pretty much the same language that the speaker would use. That's because the tone and structure of a sentence often clue you in to the meaning of the sentence.

On SAT Sentence Completions, you need to fill in missing pieces. Do this by using the sentence's clue words (e.g., *despite, although*) and structural clues (construction and punctuation) to determine where the sentence is headed.

KAPLAN'S FOUR-STEP METHOD

Here's the basic method for Sentence Completions:

1. Read the Sentence Carefully

Think about the sentence before looking at the answer choices. Figure out what the sentence means, taking special note of clue words.

> **HINT:** *Clue words such as* and, but, such as, *and* although *tell you where a sentence is heading.*

2. Anticipate the Answer

Predict the word that goes in the blanks. Do this before looking at the answer choices.

> **HINT:** *You don't have to make an exact prediction. A rough idea of the kind of word you'll need will do. It's often enough simple to predict whether the missing word is positive or negative.*

3. Compare Your Prediction with Each Answer Choice, and Pick the Best Match

> **HINT:** *Scan every answer choice before deciding.*

4. Read the Sentence with Your Answer Choice in the Blank or Blanks

> **HINT:** *Only one choice will make sense.*

If you've gone through the four steps and more than one choice seems possible, don't get stuck on the sentence. If you can eliminate at least one answer as wrong, guess and move on. If a question really stumps you, skip it and come back when you're done with the section.

Here's how the four-step method works on some examples.

EXAMPLE

Alligators, who bask in the sun for hours, appear to be ---- creatures, yet they are quite capable of sudden movement.

(A) active
(B) violent
(C) stern
(D) content
(E) sluggish

KAPLAN RULES

To solve a Sentence Completion question:

1. Read the sentence carefully.

2. Anticipate the answer.

3. Compare your prediction with each answer choice, and pick the best match.

4. Read the sentence with your answer choice in the blank or blanks.

Read the sentence carefully, looking for clue words. *Yet* is a major clue. It tells you that the sentence switches direction midstream. The word in the blank must be the opposite of *sudden*.

Predict the word that goes in the blank. You can guess that alligators seem like lazy or idle creatures.

Compare your prediction with each answer choice, and pick the best match. (A), *active,* has nothing to do with being lazy or idle. Neither does (B), *violent.* Neither does (C), *stern.* Neither does (D), *content.* But (E), *sluggish,* means inactive or slow-moving, so pick (E).

Check your answer by plugging it into the sentence. Let's check: "Alligators, who bask in the sun for hours, appear to be sluggish creatures, yet they are quite capable of sudden movement." Sounds okay. Finally, scan the other choices to make sure this is the best choice. None of the other choices works in the sentence, so (E) is correct.

> **HINT:** *Don't read the sentence five times, plugging in every answer choice. That method takes too much time and makes you vulnerable to traps. Think about the question before you look for the answer.*

EXAMPLE

The king's ---- decisions as a diplomat and administrator led to his legendary reputation as a just and ---- ruler.

(A) quick . . capricious

(B) equitable . . wise

(C) immoral . . perceptive

(D) generous . . witty

(E) clever . . uneducated

Read the sentence carefully, looking for clue words. A big clue here is the phrase *led to.* You know that the kind of decisions the king made led to his reputation as a just and ---- ruler. So whatever goes in both blanks must be consistent with *just.*

Predict the word that goes in the blank. Notice that both blanks must be similar in meaning. Because of his ---- decisions, the king is viewed a certain way, as a just and ---- ruler. So if the king's decisions were good, he'd be remembered as a good ruler, and if his decisions were bad, he'd be remembered as a bad ruler. *Just,* which means "fair," is a positive-sounding word; you can predict that both blanks will be similar in meaning, and that both will be positive words. Write a "+" in the blanks or over the columns of answer choices to remind you.

Compare your prediction with each answer choice, and pick the best match. One way to do this is to determine which answers are positive and which are negative.

In (A), *quick* and *capricious* aren't similar. (*Capricious* means "erratic or fickle.")

In (B), *equitable* means "fair." *Equitable* and *wise* are similar and they're both positive. When you plug them in, they make sense, so (B)'s right.

In (C), *immoral* and *perceptive* aren't similar at all. *Perceptive* is positive but *immoral* isn't.

In (D), *generous* and *witty* are both positive qualities, but they aren't really similar and they don't make sense in the sentence.

In (E), *clever* and *uneducated* aren't similar. *Clever* is positive but *uneducated* isn't.

Check your answer by plugging it into the sentence. "The king's equitable decisions as a diplomat and administrator led to his legendary reputation as a just and wise ruler." (B) makes sense in the sentence. Finally, a scan of the other choices reveals that none works as well. So (B) is our answer.

EXAMPLE

Charlie Parker was ---- artist, inspiring a generation of modern jazz musicians with his brilliant improvisations and experiments in bebop style.

(A) an arbitrary
(B) a benign
(C) a seminal
(D) an emphatic
(E) a candid

Read the sentence carefully, looking for clue words. The big clue is: Whatever goes in the blank must fit with the phrase *inspiring a generation.*

DON'T BE AN IMPULSE ANSWER BUYER

It's hard to know what to buy when you don't know what you're shopping for. Same thing with Sentence Completions.

You should make a prediction of the answer you're looking for before you go to the answer choices. This way, you won't fall for a distractor. You'll find the answer you want rather than the answer the test maker wants you to find.

Predict the word that goes in the blank. The sentence tells you Parker inspired a generation of musicians, so you can predict that he was an influential artist.

Compare your prediction with each answer choice, and pick the best match.

(A) arbitrary: Too negative—you need a positive word.

(B) benign: *Benign* means "mild or gentle"—again, not what you want.

(C) seminal: Most closely matches your prediction—it means "containing the seeds of later development."

(D) emphatic: Might sound reasonable at first, but it means "expressive or forceful," which is not the same as "major or important."

(E) candid: *Candid* means "frank or open," which doesn't adequately describe how Parker influenced a generation.

(C), *seminal* is the answer. Notice that you could have found this answer by elimination, without actually knowing what the word means. Check your answer by plugging it into the sentence. Charlie Parker was a seminal, or influential, artist inspiring a generation with his brilliant improvisations. Sounds fine.

PICKING UP ON CLUES

To do well on Sentence Completions, you need to see how a sentence fits together. Clue words help you do that. The more clues you get, the clearer the sentence becomes, and the better you can predict what goes in the blanks.

What do we mean by clue words? Take a look at this example:

> **EXAMPLE**
>
> Though some have derided it as ----, the search for extraterrestrial intelligence has actually become a respectable scientific endeavor.

Here, *though* is an important clue. *Though* contrasts the way some have derided, belittled, or ridiculed the search for extraterrestrial intelligence with the fact that that search has become respectable. Another clue is *actually*. *Actually* completes the contrast—though some see the search one way, it has actually become respectable.

You know that whatever goes in the blank must complete the contrast implied by the word *though*. So for the blank, you need something that describes the opposite of *a respectable scientific endeavor*. A word such as *useless* or *trivial* would be a good prediction for the blank.

GET A CLUE

Clue words help you get to the right answer. Look for the following types of words:

Contrasts:
- but
- however
- although

Continuations:
- ; (a semicolon)
- also
- and
- because
- due to
- notably

Try using clue words to predict the answers to the questions below. First, look at the sentences without the answer choices and:

- Circle clue words.
- Think of a word or phrase that might go in each blank.
- Write your prediction below each sentence.

1. One striking aspect of Caribbean music is its ---- of many African musical ----, such as call-and-response singing and polyrhythms.

   _____   _____

2. Although Cézanne was inspired by the Impressionists, he ---- their emphasis on the effects of light and ---- an independent approach to painting that emphasized form.

   _____   _____

3. They ---- until there was no recourse but to ---- a desperate, last-minute solution to the problem.

   _____   _____

4. Her normally ---- complexion lost its usual glow when she heard the news of her brother's accident.

   _____

Here are the same questions with their answer choices. Now find the right answer to each question, referring to the predictions you just made. See the next page for the answers.

1. One striking aspect of Caribbean music is its ---- of many African musical ----, such as call-and-response singing and polyrhythms.
   (A) recruitment . . groups
   (B) proficiency . . events
   (C) expectation . . ideas
   (D) absorption . . forms
   (E) condescension . . priorities

2. Although Cézanne was inspired by the Impressionists, he ---- their emphasis on the effects of light and ---- an independent approach to painting that emphasized form.
   (A) accepted . . developed
   (B) rejected . . evolved
   (C) encouraged . . submerged
   (D dismissed . . aborted
   (E) nurtured . . founded   Ⓐ Ⓑ Ⓒ Ⓓ Ⓔ

3. They ---- until there was no recourse but to ---- a desperate, last-minute solution to the problem.
   (A) compromised . . try
   (B) delayed . . envision
   (C) procrastinated . . implement
   (D debated . . maintain
   (E) filibustered . . reject   Ⓐ Ⓑ Ⓒ Ⓓ Ⓔ

4. Her normally ---- complexion lost its usual glow when she heard the news of her brother's accident.
   (A) wan
   (B) pallid
   (C) sallow
   (D) ashen
   (E) sanguine   Ⓐ Ⓑ Ⓒ Ⓓ Ⓔ

TACKLING HARD QUESTIONS

The last few Sentence Completions in a set are usually difficult. If you're getting stuck, here are a few special techniques to pull you through.

- Avoid tricky wrong answers.
- Take apart tough sentences.
- Work around tough vocabulary.

Avoiding Tricky Wrong Answers

Towards the end of a set, watch out for tricky answer choices. Avoid:

- Opposites of the correct answer
- Words that sound right because they're hard
- Two-blankers in which one word fits but the other doesn't

HINT: *Questions go from easiest to hardest—the higher the question number, the harder the question.*

ANSWERS TO PICKING UP ON CLUES

1. (D)—Clue: *aspect*
   The only choice that could logically complete a description of Caribbean music is (D): Caribbean music is characterized by its absorption of many African musical forms.

2. (B)—Clue: *Although*
   Although indicates that Cézanne must have somehow differed from the Impressionists. So he must have (B) rejected or (D) dismissed their emphasis on the effects of light. For the second blank, there's no reason to say that Cézanne aborted an independent approach to painting. Only (B) works for both blanks.

3. (C)—Clues: *until, desperate*
   For the first blank, you can predict that they must have waited until only a "desperate solution" was possible. (C) and (D) fit this prediction. (C) implement, or carry out, makes more sense in the second blank.

4. (E)—Clue: *usual glow*
   If her complexion had a "usual glow" it must have been normally rosy. The only choice that means rosy is (E) sanguine.

Two-Blankers

Two-blank sentences can be easier than one-blankers.

• Try the easier blank first.

• Eliminate all choices that won't work for that blank.

The following example would be the seventh question out of a 10-problem set.

> **EXAMPLE**
>
> Granted that Joyce is extremely ----, it is still difficult to imagine her as a professional comedian.
>
> (A) dull
>
> (B) garrulous
>
> (C) effusive
>
> (D) conservative
>
> (E) witty

A Sentence Like This May Show up Towards the End of a Set

Read this sentence carefully or you may get tricked. If you read too quickly, you might think, "If Joyce is hard to imagine as a comedian, she's probably extremely dull or conservative. So I'll pick either (A) or (D)." But the sentence is saying something else.

Pick up the Clues

The key is the clue word *granted*. It's another way of saying *although*. So the sentence means, "Sure Joyce is funny, but she's no professional comedian." Therefore, the word in the blank must resemble *funny*. That means (E), *witty*, is correct.

Don't Pick an Answer Just Because It Sounds Hard

Garrulous means "talkative" and *effusive* means "overly expressive." You might be tempted to pick one of these simply because they sound impressive. But they're put there to trick you. Don't choose them without good reason.

Now let's look at a two-blank sentence. The following example is another seventh question out of a 10-problem set.

> **EXAMPLE**
>
> When the state government discovered that thermal pollution was killing valuable fish, legislation was passed to ---- the dumping of hot liquid wastes into rivers and to ---- the fish population.
>
> (A) discourage . . decimate
>
> (B) regulate . . quantify
>
> (C) facilitate . . appease
>
> (D) discontinue . . devastate
>
> (E) prohibit . . protect

Look at All the Choices

Check out the first blank first. Legislation was not passed to facilitate dumping, so that eliminates choice (C). The other four are all possible.

Now check the second blanks. The legislature wouldn't pass a law to decimate, or quantify, or devastate the fish population, so (A), (B), and (D) are wrong. Only choice (E), *prohibit . . protect,* fits for both blanks. The legislature might well pass a law to prohibit dumping hot liquids and to protect fish.

> **HINT:** *Don't jump at an answer choice because one blank fits.*
> *Check both blanks.*

Taking Apart Tough Sentences

Look at the following example, the seventh question of a nine-problem set.

> **EXAMPLE**
>
> Although this small and selective publishing house is famous for its ---- standards, several of its recent novels have a mainly popular appeal.
> (A) proletarian
> (B) naturalistic
> (C) discriminating
> (D) imitative
> (E) precarious

What if you were stumped, and had no idea which word to pick? Try this strategy.

> **HINT:** *Listen to the part of the sentence around the blank.*
> *Rule out funny-sounding answer choices.*

The process might go like this:

Proletarian standards? Hmmm . . . sounds funny.

Naturalistic standards? Not great.

Discriminating standards? That's got a familiar ring.

Imitative standards? Weird-sounding.

Precarious standards? Nope.

(C) sounds best and, as it turns out, is correct. Although the small publishing house has discriminating, or picky, standards, several of its recent novels appeal to a general audience.

Now try a complex sentence with two blanks. Remember our rules:

• Try the easier blank first.

• Save time by eliminating all choices that won't work for one blank.

The following example is the fifth question out of a nine-problem set.

EXAMPLE

These latest employment statistics from the present administration are so loosely documented, carelessly explained, and potentially misleading that even the most loyal Senators will ---- the ---- of the Presidential appointees who produced them.

(A) perceive . . intelligence

(B) understand . . tenacity

(C) recognize . . incompetence

(D) praise . . rigor

(E) denounce . . loyalty

It's not so easy to see what goes in the first blank, so try the second blank. You need a word to describe Presidential appointees who produced the "loosely documented," "carelessly explained," and "misleading" statistics. So it's got to be negative. The only second-word answer choice that's definitely negative is (C), *incompetence,* or inability to perform a task. Now try *recognize* in the first blank. It fits, too. (C) must be correct.

Working Around Tough Vocabulary

The following example is the second question out of a nine-problem set.

EXAMPLE

Despite her ---- of public speaking experience, the student council member was surprisingly cogent, and expressed the concerns of her classmates persuasively.

(A) hope

(B) depth

(C) method

(D) lack

(E) union

If you don't know what *cogent* means, work around it.

> **HINT**: *Look in the sentence for the definition of a hard word.*

From the sentence, especially the clue word *and,* you know that *cogent* goes with *expressed the concerns of her classmates persuasively.* So you don't have to worry about what *cogent* means. All you need to know is that the

KAPLAN RULES

If you find a word you don't understand, look in the sentence for its definition.

student council member was persuasive despite a ---- of speaking experience. Only (D), lack, fits. "Despite her lack of public speaking experience, the student council member expressed the concerns of her classmates persuasively." (By the way, *cogent* means "convincing, believable," roughly the same as "expressing concern persuasively.")

Let's look at this Sentence Completion problem. This time the tough vocabulary is in the answer choices. This example is the sixth question out of nine questions.

Advances in technology occur at such a fast pace that dictionaries have difficulty incorporating the ---- that emerge as names for new inventions.

(A) colloquialisms

(B) euphemisms

(C) compensations

(D) neologisms

(E) clichés

Again, look at the sentence. Whatever goes in the blank has to describe "names for new inventions." If you don't know what the word *colloquialisms* or *euphemisms* means, don't give up. Rule out as many choices as you can, and guess among the remaining ones.

You can eliminate (C) and (E) right off the bat. They don't describe names for new inventions. Now you can make an educated guess. Again, educated guessing will help your score more than guessing blindly or skipping the question.

Or, if you studied your word roots, you might know that *neo-* means "new," so the word *neologisms* might be the best choice for names of new inventions. In fact, it's the right answer. Neologisms are newly coined words.

HINT: *To help yourself earn extra points, study the Root List in Appendix A.*

If All Else Fails
If you're really stumped, don't be afraid to guess. Eliminate all answer choices that seem wrong and guess from the remaining choices.

SENTENCE COMPLETIONS PRACTICE SET

1. In the years following World War II, almost all Canadian Inuits ---- their previously nomadic lifestyle; they now live in fixed settlements.
   (A) abandoned
   (B) continued
   (C) fashioned
   (D) preserved
   (E) rebuilt

   Ⓐ Ⓑ Ⓒ Ⓓ Ⓔ

2. A newborn infant's ---- skills are not fully ----, for it cannot discern images more than ten inches from its face.
(A) perceptual . . stimulated
(B) visual . . developed
(C) descriptive . . ripened
(D) olfactory . . shared
(E) average . . familiar

Ⓐ Ⓑ Ⓒ Ⓓ Ⓔ

3. Some geysers erupt regularly while others do so ----.
(A) consistently
(B) copiously
(C) perennially
(D) sporadically
(E) violently

Ⓐ Ⓑ Ⓒ Ⓓ Ⓔ

4. Because of the lead actor's ---- performance, the play received poor reviews from influential theater critics, and was canceled only one week after it opened.
(A) erudite
(B) corporeal
(C) overwrought
(D) fractious
(E) resplendent

Ⓐ Ⓑ Ⓒ Ⓓ Ⓔ

5. Sociologists have found that, paradoxically, many children of unorthodox, creative parents grow up to be rather tame ----.
(A) idealists
(B) conformists
(C) individualists
(D) alarmists
(E) elitists

Ⓐ Ⓑ Ⓒ Ⓓ Ⓔ

6. In Han mortuary art, the ---- and the ---- are combined; one tomb may contain eerie supernatural figures placed next to ordinary like-nesses of government administrators at work.
(A) fantastic . . mundane
(B) inventive . . remorseful
(C) illusory . . derivative
(D) enlightened . . conservative
(E) unique . . historical

Ⓐ Ⓑ Ⓒ Ⓓ Ⓔ

EXPLANATIONS

Sentence Completions Practice Set

1. (A)—*Nomadic* means "wandering, transient." If Inuit people now live in fixed settlements, we can predict that they rejected, or abandoned, "their previously nomadic lifestyle."

2. (B)—If a newborn infant "cannot discern (or perceive) images more than 10 inches from its face," then the infant's ability to see things has not fully evolved. In other words, its visual skills are not fully developed. The word *olfactory,* choice (D), means "relating to sense of smell."

3. (D)—The clue words *while others* indicate contrast. If some geysers "erupt regularly," we can predict that others do so irregularly. The best choice is (D), since *sporadically* means "infrequently or irregularly."

4. (C)—If the play "received poor reviews" and was canceled because of something about the lead actor's performance, that performance must have been quite bad. The word *overwrought,* choice (C), means "overdone" or "excessively agitated." It is one of two negative words in the answer choices, and the only one that could logically describe a performance.

5. (B)—Paradoxically (or contrary to what one would expect), children of creative and unorthodox parents grow up to be something other than creative and unorthodox. We need a word that contrasts with *creative and unorthodox* and goes along with *tame.* (B) is the best choice; conformists are people who follow established norms and customs without challenging anything or anyone.

6. (A)—If "one tomb contains eerie supernatural figures" and "ordinary likenesses of government administrators," it's likely that Han mortuary art combines the unearthly or bizarre with the ordinary or mundane. The best answer is (A). In Han art, the fantastic (eerie supernatural figures) and the mundane (administrators) are combined.

HIGHLIGHTS

- The Kaplan four-step method
- Use clue words
- How to avoid tricky wrong answers
- How to take apart tough sentences
- How to work around tough vocabulary

F·A·S·T P·R·E·P

CHAPTER CHECKLIST

 Once you've mastered a section, check it off.

DOING YOUR BEST ON CRITICAL READING
- ❏ HOW TO READ A PASSAGE
- ❏ KAPLAN'S FIVE-STEP METHOD FOR CRITICAL READING QUESTIONS
- ❏ PAIRED PASSAGES—A (NOT-SO) SPECIAL CASE
- ❏ WHAT TO DO WHEN TIME IS RUNNING OUT

HOW TO DO SPECIFIC QUESTION TYPES
- ❏ BIG PICTURE QUESTIONS
- ❏ LITTLE PICTURE QUESTIONS
- ❏ VOCABULARY-IN-CONTEXT QUESTIONS

PANICPLAN

If you have a month or less to prep for the SAT, here's the best way to spend your time:

- Since Critical Reading makes up half of the Verbal section of the SAT, it's important that you read the whole chapter.

- Pay special attention to the practice test on pp. 61–63.

CHAPTER 7

CRITICAL READING: THE BASICS

Improving your Critical Reading score means building the skills you have and applying them to the SAT. You don't need outside knowledge to answer the Critical Reading questions. And you don't need an amazing vocabulary, since unfamiliar words will be defined for you.

Critical Reading passages and questions are very predictable, since the test makers use a formula to write them. You'll be given four reading passages, 400 to 850 words each, drawn from the arts, humanities, social sciences, sciences, and fiction. One of these is a "paired passage" consisting of two related excerpts. You'll be asked about the overall tone and content of a passage, the details, and what the passage suggests. You'll also be asked to compare and contrast the related passages.

THE FORMAT

Critical Reading instructions tell you to answer questions based on what is stated or implied in the accompanying passage or passages. As with other question types, you should get familiar enough with the Critical Reading format that you don't waste time reading the directions again on the day of the test.

Each reading passage begins with a brief introduction. Related questions follow the passage.

> **HINT**: *Don't skip the brief introductions. They'll help you focus your reading.*

Critical Reading questions have a specific order: The first few questions ask about the beginning of the passage, the last few about the end.

Questions following "paired passages" are generally ordered. The first few questions relate to the first passage, the next few to the second passage, and the final questions ask about the passages as a pair. Generally, but not always. You'll learn more about this on p. 69.

IF YOU CAN READ THIS, YOU CAN DO WELL ON SAT VERBAL

If you bought a new VCR, as soon as you unpacked it you'd read the instruction manual to figure out how to hook it up and get it working.

You probably wouldn't sit down and read the whole book, though. You'd skip the pages that contain step-by-step instructions on how to record programs from the TV until you'd gotten the VCR connected and plugged in.

If the manual said, "connect the xygupts to terminal c," you'd probably figure out how to do that, even though you don't know the word *xygupts*.

In setting up your VCR, you'd have demonstrated that you know how to read with a purpose; know how and when to deal with details; and can figure out the meaning of unfamiliar words from context.

How NOT to Read

DON'T wait for important information to jump out and hit you in the face. Search for important points. As you read, ask yourself, "What's this all about? What's the point of this?"

DON'T read the passage thoroughly. It's a waste of your time. Skim the passage to get the drift.

DON'T skim so quickly that you miss the passage's main point. Read quickly but don't race.

DON'T get caught up in details.

Ask Yourself

• What's this passage about?

• What's the point of this?

• Why did someone write this?

• What's the author trying to say?

• What are the two or three most important things in this passage?

Critical Reading questions are not ordered by difficulty. Unlike the other kinds of questions on the SAT, the location of a Critical Reading question tells you nothing about its potential difficulty. So don't get bogged down on a hard Critical Reading question. The next one might be a lot easier.

HOW TO READ A PASSAGE

Some students find Critical Reading passages dull or intimidating. Remember that each passage is written for a purpose—the author wants to make a point, describe a situation, or convince you of his or her ideas. As you're reading, ask yourself, "What's the point of this? What's this all about?" This is active reading, and it's the key to staying focused on the page.

Active reading doesn't mean reading the passage word-for-word. It means reading lightly, but with a focus. This is what we mean by skimming.

> **HINT:** *The questions will help you fill in the details by directing you back to important information in the passage.*

Getting hung up on details is a major Critical Reading pitfall. You need to grasp the outline, but you don't need to get all the fine features.

> **HINT:** *The less time you spend on reading the passages, the more time you'll have to answer the questions—and that's where you score points. To increase your reading speed and skimming skills, turn to the skimming exercises in Chapter 8, pp. 73–75.*

TEST YOUR CRITICAL READING SMARTS

Test your reading skills on the following sample passage, keeping our tips in mind. Remember that active reading will make this difficult passage—and every passage—more doable.

EXAMPLE

In this essay, the author writes about her childhood on a Caribbean island that was an English colony for many years.

When I saw England for the first time, I was a child in school sitting at a desk. The England I was looking at was laid out on a map gently, beautifully, delicately, a very special jewel; it lay on a bed of sky blue, its yellow form mysterious, because though it looked like a leg of mutton*, it could not really look like anything so familiar as a leg of mutton because it was England. England was a special jewel all right, and only special people got to wear it. The people who got to wear England were English people. They wore it well and they wore it everywhere: in jungles, in deserts, on plains, in places where they were not welcome, in places they should not have been. When my teacher had pinned this map up on the blackboard, she said, "This is England"—and she said it with authority, seriousness, and adoration, and we all sat up. We understood then—we were meant to understand then—that England was to be our source of myth and the source from which we got our sense of reality, our sense of what was meaningful, our sense of what was meaningless—and much about our own lives and much about the very idea of us headed that last list.

At the time I was a child sitting at my desk seeing England for the first time, I was already very familiar with the greatness of it. Each morning before I left for school, I ate a breakfast of half a grapefruit, a bowl of oat porridge, bread and butter and a slice of cheese, and a cup of cocoa. The can of cocoa was often left on the table in front of me. It had written on it the name of the company, the year the company was established, and the words "Made in England." Those words, "Made in England," were written on the box the oats came in too. The shoes I wore were made in England; so were my socks and cotton undergarments and the satin ribbons I wore tied at the end of two plaits of my hair. My father, who might have sat next to me at breakfast, was a carpenter and cabinet maker. The shoes he wore to work would have been made in England, as were his khaki shirt and trousers, his underpants and undershirt, his socks and brown felt hat. Felt was not the proper material from which a hat that was expected to provide shade from the hot sun should be made, but my father must have seen and admired a picture of an Englishman wearing such a hat in England. As we sat at breakfast a car might go by. The car, a Hillman or a Zephyr, was made in England. The very conception of the meal itself, breakfast, and its substantial quality and quantity was an idea from England; we somehow knew that in England they began the day with this meal called breakfast and a proper breakfast was a big breakfast.

At the time I saw this map—seeing England for the first time—I did not say to myself, "Ah, so that's what it looks like," because there was no longing in me to put a shape to those three words that ran through every part of my life, no matter how small; for me to have had such a

Line (5)

(10)

(15)

(20)

(25)

(30)

(35)

(40)

(45) longing would have meant that I lived in a certain atmosphere, an atmosphere in which those three words were felt as a burden. But I did not
live in such an atmosphere. My father's brown felt hat would develop a
hole in its crown, the lining would separate from the hat itself, and six
weeks before he thought that he could not be seen wearing it—he was
a very vain man—he would order another hat from England. And my
(50) mother taught me to eat my food in the English way: the knife in the
right hand, the fork in the left, my elbows held still close to my side.
When I had finally mastered it, I overheard her saying to a friend, "Did
you see how nicely she can eat?" But I knew then that I enjoyed my food
more when I ate it with my bare hands, and I continued to do so when
(55) she wasn't looking. And when my teacher showed us the map, she
asked us to study it carefully, because no test we would ever take would
be complete without this statement: "Draw a map of England."

I did not know then that the statement "Draw a map of England"
was something far worse than a declaration of war. I did not know then
(60) that this statement was part of a process that would result in my erasure,
not my physical erasure, but my erasure all the same. I did not know
then that this statement was meant to make me feel in awe and small
whenever I heard the word "England": awe at its existence, small
because I was not from it. I did not know very much of anything then—
(65) certainly not what a blessing it was that I was unable to draw a map of
England correctly.

*the flesh of a sheep

It's important to learn how to read the passage quickly and efficiently.
Remember, though, that reading the passage won't earn you points—it's
the questions that count.

KAPLAN'S FIVE-STEP METHOD FOR CRITICAL READING QUESTIONS

Here's Kaplan's proven approach to Critical Reading questions:

1. Read the question stem.
2. Locate the material you need.
3. Come up with an idea of the right answer.
4. Scan the answer choices.
5. Select your answer.

1. Read the Question Stem
This is the place to really read carefully. Take a second to make sure you
understand what the question is asking.

> **KAPLAN RULES**
>
> To approach Critical Reading:
> • Read the question stem.
> • Locate the material you need.
> • Come up with an idea of the right answer.
> • Scan the answer choices.
> • Select your answer.

2. Locate the Material You Need

If you are given a line reference, read the material surrounding the line mentioned. It will clarify exactly what the question is asking.

If you're not given a line reference, scan the text to find the place where the question applies, and quickly reread those few sentences. Keep the main point of the passage in mind.

3. Come up with an Idea of the Right Answer

Don't spend time making up a precise answer. You need only a general sense of what you're after, so you can recognize the correct answer quickly when you read the choices.

4. Scan the Answer Choices

Scan the choices, looking for one that fits your idea of the right answer. If you don't find an ideal answer, quickly eliminate wrong choices by checking back to the passage. Rule out choices that are too extreme or go against common sense. And get rid of answers that sound reasonable, but don't make sense in the context of the passage.

5. Select Your Answer

You've eliminated the obvious wrong answers. One of the few remaining should fit your ideal. If you're left with more than one contender, consider the passage's main idea, and make an educated guess.

Now Try the Questions
(Answers on p. 63.)

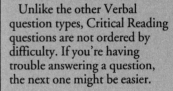

HAVING TROUBLE?

Unlike the other Verbal question types, Critical Reading questions are not ordered by difficulty. If you're having trouble answering a question, the next one might be easier.

1. According to the author, England could not really look like a leg of mutton (line 5) because
   - (A) maps generally don't give an accurate impression of what a place looks like
   - (B) England was too grand and exotic a place for such a mundane image
   - (C) England was an island not very different in appearance from her own island
   - (D) the usual metaphor used to describe England was a precious jewel
   - (E) mutton was one of the few foods familiar to her that did not come from England

2. The author's reference to felt as "not the proper material" (line 31) for her father's hat chiefly serves to emphasize her point about the
   - (A) extremity of the local weather
   - (B) arrogance of island laborers
   - (C) informality of dress on the island
   - (D) weakness of local industries
   - (E) predominance of English culture   Ⓐ Ⓑ Ⓒ Ⓓ Ⓔ

61

3. The word *conception* as used in line 36 means
   (A) beginning
   (B) image
   (C) origination
   (D) notion
   (E) plan

   Ⓐ Ⓑ Ⓒ Ⓓ Ⓔ

4. The word *substantial* in line 36 means
   (A) important
   (B) abundant
   (C) firm
   (D) down-to-earth
   (E) materialistic

   Ⓐ Ⓑ Ⓒ Ⓓ Ⓔ

5. In the third paragraph, the author implies that any longing to put a shape to the words "made in England" would have indicated
   (A) a resentment of England's predominance
   (B) an unhealthy desire to become English
   (C) an inability to understand England's authority
   (D) an excessive curiosity about England
   (E) an unfamiliarity with English customs

   Ⓐ Ⓑ Ⓒ Ⓓ Ⓔ

6. The author cites the anecdotes about her father and mother in lines 46–55 primarily to convey their
   (A) love for their children
   (B) belief in strict discipline
   (C) distaste for anything foreign
   (D) reverence for England
   (E) overemphasis on formal manners

   Ⓐ Ⓑ Ⓒ Ⓓ Ⓔ

7. The word *erasure* (line 60) as used by the author most nearly means
   (A) total annihilation
   (B) physical disappearance
   (C) sense of insignificance
   (D) enforced censorship
   (E) loss of freedom

   Ⓐ Ⓑ Ⓒ Ⓓ Ⓔ

8. The main purpose of the passage is to
   (A) advocate a change in the way a subject is taught in school
   (B) convey the personality of certain figures from the author's childhood
   (C) describe an overwhelming influence on the author's early life
   (D) analyze the importance of a sense of place to early education
   (E) relate a single formative episode in the author's life

   Ⓐ Ⓑ Ⓒ Ⓓ Ⓔ

9. For the author, the requirement to "Draw a map of England" (lines 58–66) represented an attempt to
   (A) force students to put their studies to practical use
   (B) glorify one culture at the expense of another
   (C) promote an understanding of world affairs
   (D) encourage students to value their own heritage
   (E) impart outmoded and inappropriate knowledge

   Ⓐ Ⓑ Ⓒ Ⓓ Ⓔ

10. At the end of the passage, the author suggests that her inability "to draw a map of England correctly" indicated a
   (A) heartfelt desire to see the country in person rather than through maps
   (B) serious failure of the education she received
   (C) conscious rejection of the prestige of a foreign power
   (D) harmful preoccupation with local affairs and customs
   (E) beneficial ignorance of her own supposed inferiority

   Ⓐ Ⓑ Ⓒ Ⓓ Ⓔ

Applying the Five-Step Method
Try Kaplan's five-step method on question one from the sample reading passage on pp. 59–60.

1. Read the Question Stem
In this case, the question is straightforward: Why couldn't England really look like a leg of mutton? (Notice that *mutton* is defined for you at the end of the passage—you aren't expected to know the meaning of unfamiliar terms.)

2. Locate the Material You Need
You're given a clue: The answer lies somewhere near the fifth line. But don't read just that line—read the line or two before and after as well. By doing so, you learn that England was mysterious and special, so it couldn't look like something as familiar (to the author) as a leg of mutton.

3. Come up with an Idea of the Right Answer
After reading those couple of lines, you'd expect the answer to be something like, "England was too special to look like a familiar leg of mutton."

4. Scan the Answer Choices
Choice (B) comes close to the ideal—it should have popped out. But if you weren't sure, you could have quickly eliminated the other choices. Thinking of the main idea would have helped you eliminate (A) and (C). England was precious—like a jewel—but the author doesn't imply that England was usually compared to a jewel (D). And you never learn where mutton comes from (E).

WHAT'S MUTTON?
When a word is too obscure for the SAT, they'll define it at the bottom of the reading passage.

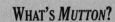

ANSWERS TO CRITICAL READING QUESTIONS

1. (B)
2. (E)
3. (D)
4. (B)
5. (B)
6. (D)
7. (C)
8. (C)
9. (B)
10. (E)

5. Select Your Answer

Choice (B) is the only one that works here. By reading the material surrounding the line reference and putting an answer into your own words, you should have been able to choose (B) with confidence.

> **PRACTICE:** *Now try the five-step method on the remaining questions for the passage on pp. 59–60.*

> **HINT:** *From the questions, you can "fill in" the information you don't get in a quick reading. It's a way of working backwards, to reconstruct the passage.*

BIG PICTURE, LITTLE PICTURE, AND VOCABULARY-IN-CONTEXT

Most SAT Critical Reading questions fall into three basic types. "Big Picture" questions test your overall understanding of the passage's biggest points. "Little Picture" questions ask about localized bits of information. Vocabulary-in-Context questions ask for the meaning of a single word.

In the passage on pp. 59–60, question eight is an example of a Big Picture question. Question two is an example of a Little Picture question. Question three is a Vocabulary-in-Context question.

> **HINT:** *Remember to skip around if you need to. You can tackle whichever passages you like in any order you like within the same section. But once you've read through the passage, try all the questions that go with it.*

The Big Picture

Big Picture questions test your overall understanding of a passage. They might ask about:

- The main point or purpose of a passage
- The author's attitude or tone
- The logic underlying the author's argument
- How ideas relate to each other

PRACTICE

If you're having a problem finding the main point of a passage and answering Big Picture questions, work on the paraphrasing exercises in Chapter 8.

One way to see the Big Picture is to read actively. As you read, ask yourself, "What's this all about? What's the point of this?"

> **HINT:** *Still stumped after reading the passage? Do the Little Picture questions first. They can help you fill in the Big Picture.*

Turn back to the passage you tried on pp. 59–60. What did you get out of the first reading? Something like, "England was a profound influence on the author's early life, but not a completely positive influence"? That would have been enough.

Now look at question eight. It's a Big Picture question, asking for the main point of the passage. Use the five-step method to find your answer.

1. Read the Question Stem
Simple enough: What's the main point of the passage?

2. Locate the Material You Need
In this case, you're asked about the overall point. You should have grasped a sense of that from reading the passage.

3. Get an Idea of the Right Answer
Again, you need just a rough statement. Here, something like this would do: "The purpose is to describe how England was a huge influence, but maybe not a completely positive one, in the author's young life."

4. Scan the Answer Choices
(C) should have popped out. But (D) might have looked good, too, if you focused on the words "sense of place." So put those two aside as contenders. How a subject was taught in school (A), figures in the author's childhood (B), and a single formative episode (E) are too narrow.

5. Select Your Answer
You've crossed off the poor choices, and you're down to two possibilities. Which matches your ideal? (C) comes closer. Look closely at (D) and you'll see that it's too general. Go with the best choice.

Little Picture Questions
More than two-thirds of Critical Reading questions ask about the Little Picture. Little Picture questions usually give you a line reference or refer you to a particular paragraph—a strong clue to where in the passage you'll find your answer.

Little Picture questions might:

• Test whether you understand significant information that's stated in the passage

• Ask you to make inferences or draw conclusions based on a part of the passage

• Ask you to relate parts of the passage to one another

Question two is a Little Picture question. You're asked about the felt hat of the author's father—what does this point emphasize? Applying Kaplan's

Step Two, locate the material you'll need. You're given a clue—a line reference—to help you here. Reread that, and the lines before and after it as well.

> **HINT:** *Don't pick farfetched inferences. SAT inferences tend to be strongly implied in the passage.*

So why did the father wear a felt hat, which was probably quite hot in the tropical sun? Because it was English. That's what correct choice (E) says. Rereading that bit of the passage should have led you right to that answer. (A) comes close, but doesn't fit the main point of the passage. Even with Little Picture questions, grasping the main point of the passage can help you find the correct answer.

> **HINT:** *Beware of answer choices that provide a reasonable answer to the stem, but don't make sense in the context of the passage.*

Vocabulary-in-Context Questions

Vocabulary-in-Context questions ask about an even smaller part of the passage than other Little Picture questions do. They ask about the usage of a single word. These questions do not test your ability to define hard words such as *archipelago* and *garrulous*. They do test your ability to infer the meaning of a word from context.

In fact, the words tested in these questions will probably be familiar to you—they are usually fairly common words with more than one definition. Many of the answer choices will be definitions of the tested word, but only one will work in context. Vocabulary-in-Context questions always have a line reference, and you should always use it!

> **HINT:** *CONTEXT is the most important part of Vocabulary-in-CONTEXT questions.*

Sometimes one of the answer choices will jump out at you. It'll be the most common meaning of the word in question—but it's rarely right! We call this the "obvious" choice. For example, say *curious* is the word being tested. The obvious choice is *inquisitive*. But *curious* also means "odd," and that's more likely to be the answer. Using context to find the answer will help prevent you from falling for this trap. You can use these choices to your advantage, though. If you get stuck on a Vocabulary-in-Context question, you can eliminate the "obvious" choice and guess.

> **HINT:** *If a question has an "obvious" choice, steer clear of it.*

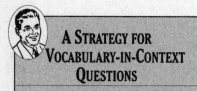

A STRATEGY FOR VOCABULARY-IN-CONTEXT QUESTIONS

Once you find the tested word in the passage, you can treat a Vocabulary-in-Context question like a Sentence Completion.

Pretend the word is a blank in the sentence. Read a line or two around the "blank," if you need to.

Then predict a word for the "blank." Check the answer choices for a word that comes close to your prediction.

Vocabulary-in-Context Practice
(Answers on p. 69.)

1. Embodied and given life in the social realities of her own period, Jane Austen's satire still has currency in ours.

   In the lines above, *currency* most nearly means
   (A) usualness
   (B) stylishness
   (C) prevalence
   (D) funds
   (E) relevance   Ⓐ Ⓑ Ⓒ Ⓓ Ⓔ

2. A perpetual doubting and a perpetual questioning of the truth of what we have learned is not the temper of science.

   In the lines above, *temper* most nearly means
   (A) disposition
   (B) nature
   (C) anger
   (D) mood
   (E) mixture   Ⓐ Ⓑ Ⓒ Ⓓ Ⓔ

3. Captain Wentworth had no fortune. He had been lucky in his profession, but, spending freely what had come freely, had realized nothing.

   Which most nearly captures the meaning of the word *realized* in the sentence above?
   (A) understood
   (B) accomplished
   (C) learned
   (D) accumulated
   (E) fulfilled   Ⓐ Ⓑ Ⓒ Ⓓ Ⓔ

4. Anyone with more than a superficial knowledge of Shakespeare's plays must necessarily entertain some doubt concerning their true authorship.

   In the lines above, *entertain* most nearly means
   (A) amuse
   (B) harbor
   (C) occupy
   (D) cherish
   (E) engage   Ⓐ Ⓑ Ⓒ Ⓓ Ⓔ

5. Many people who invested in the booming art market of the 1980s were disappointed; few of the works appreciated in value.

In the lines above, *appreciated* most nearly means
(A) admired
(B) applauded
(C) spiraled
(D) increased
(E) acknowledged

Ⓐ Ⓑ Ⓒ Ⓓ Ⓔ

6. Charles de Gaulle's independence of mind can be seen by the fact that he negotiated with Algerian nationalists, although he was pressed by his advisors, French colonists, and the army itself to continue the war.

Which most nearly captures the meaning of the word *pressed* in the sentence above?
(A) squeezed
(B) urged
(C) troubled
(D) required
(E) compelled

Ⓐ Ⓑ Ⓒ Ⓓ Ⓔ

7. Today some would say that those struggles are all over——that all the horizons have been explored——that all the battles have been won—— that there is no longer an American frontier. But I trust that no one in this vast assemblage will agree with those sentiments.

In the lines above, *sentiments* most nearly means
(A) beliefs
(B) results
(C) loyalties
(D) challenges
(E) emotions

Ⓐ Ⓑ Ⓒ Ⓓ Ⓔ

8. The convicts made their escape by scaling the prison walls and stealing away under the cover of darkness.

Which most nearly captures the meaning of the word *stealing* in the line above?
(A) seizing
(B) taking
(C) slipping
(D) grabbing
(E) abducting

Ⓐ Ⓑ Ⓒ Ⓓ Ⓔ

PAIRED PASSAGES—A (NOT-SO) SPECIAL CASE

Don't let the paired passages worry you—they're not twice as hard as the single reading selections. In fact, students often find the paired passages the most interesting on the test. With paired passages, focus as you read on the relationship between the two passages. Just as with single passages, the questions following paired passages can help fill in the picture.

Questions following paired passages tend to be ordered, with the first few questions relating to the first passage, the next few to the second passage, and the final questions asking about the passages as a pair. This is the best way to tackle the questions in any case, even if the test makers mix in a question about both passages amidst questions on the first passage (it's been known to happen).

How to Do Paired Passages

- Skim the first passage, looking for the drift (as you would with a single passage).
- Do the questions that relate to the first passage.
- Skim the second passage, looking for the drift and thinking about how the second passage relates to the first.
- Do the questions that relate to the second passage.
- Now you're ready to do the questions that ask about the relationship between the two passages.

Alternately skimming passages and answering questions is especially important if you're short of time. You'll be able to answer at least some of the questions before time runs out. By the time you've looked at both passages and answered the questions about each passage, you'll have a firm sense of the relationship between the pair. That will help you to answer the last group of questions.

Active reading can help you answer these questions, too. Remember to ask yourself, "What are these passages about? What is each author's point? What is similar about the two passages? What is different?"

WHAT TO DO WHEN TIME IS RUNNING OUT

It's always best to skim the passage before you hit the questions. But if you only have a few minutes left, here's how to score points even while time is running out.

You can answer Vocabulary-in-Context questions and many Little Picture questions without reading the passage. If the question has a line reference, locate the material you need to find your answer and follow the five-step method as usual. You won't have the overall picture to guide you, but you might be able to reach the correct answer just by understanding the "Little Picture."

ANSWERS TO VOCABULARY-IN-CONTEXT

1. (E)
2. (B)
3. (D)
4. (B)
5. (D)
6. (B)
7. (A)
8. (C)

HIGHLIGHTS

- How to read the passage
- How to use Kaplan's five-step method for answering questions
- Big Picture and Little Picture questions
- Vocabulary-in-Context
- Paired passages

F·A·S·T P·R·E·P

CHAPTER CHECKLIST

 Once you've mastered a section, check it off.

BUILDING READING SKILLS
- ❑ SKIMMING
- ❑ PARAPHRASING
- ❑ MAKING INFERENCES

PANICPLAN

If you have a month or less to prep for the SAT, here's the best way to spend your time:

- Read the section on skimming, pp. 71–75.
- Hold off on the rest of the chapter until you've covered all the basics in this book.
- If you have time to come back, work on the paraphrasing and inference sections.

CHAPTER 8

CRITICAL READING SKILLS

SKIMMING, PARAPHRASING, MAKING INFERENCES

In Chapter 7 you learned the basics of Critical Reading—what it looks like, what to expect, how to read the passages, how to tackle the questions. This chapter will help you improve the Critical Reading skills tested on the SAT—skimming, paraphrasing, and drawing inferences. You already have these skills.

- Skimming means reading quickly and lightly. You do this when you look information up in a phone book, or glance at a newspaper article only long enough to get the gist of the story.

- When you restate something in your own words, that's paraphrasing. You do it all the time in daily life—when you give a phone message, or retell a story.

- When you deduce information from a statement or situation, you're making inferences. You do it every day. If your best friend stopped talking to you, you'd probably infer that your friend was mad at you, even if your friend didn't actually say so.

SKIMMING

> **HINT:** *Don't read each word separately. Move your eyes lightly over the page, grouping words.*

Skimming is a specific reading style where you read quickly and in less detail than usual. These two characteristics are what make skimming the best way to read SAT passages. You want to read quickly because time is

READ THIS QUICKLY

Joe stood at the edge of town, a cigarette in his left hand, a bottle of bourbon in his right. He'd had tough ones before, but this was gonna be the end of him. He looked back towards the light of the city below him. "If only I could get Martinez to talk," he thought to himself. In a flash, Joe was back in the Mustang racing towards town. . . .

What was this little story about? Chances are, even with a quick read, you took away some information that helped you piece it together. That's because you've already developed your reading skills (you're reading this, aren't you?).

Your challenge on the SAT is to apply these skills in a peculiar context and not to be intimidated by the passages they throw at you.

limited, and you want to read lightly because the questions direct you to the details you need. Spending a lot of time with the passage before you see the questions just doesn't make sense. So skimming works well—as long as you read with three things in mind:

- The content of the passage
- The organization of the passage
- The author's purpose or point of view

If you have a general idea of these three things when you're done skimming, then you're ready for the questions.

In order to be an effective skimmer, you need to practice. Treat your practice sessions as an opportunity to learn. In time, you'll notice improvement.

- Practice frequently, in short sessions.
- Use these methods every time you read.

How to Skim

To improve your reading speed, get your eyes to move quickly and lightly along each line of type. Think about the way you usually read. Do you dwell on each word, as if you were plodding through a field of mud? Or do your eyes move quickly over the page, as if you were walking on hard, dry ground?

The way your eyes habitually move across each line of type and return to the beginning of the next line is your tracking style. That's what you'll work on here. The object is to make it light and swift, rather than heavy and deliberate.

Improving your tracking style will help you perform your best when under pressure.

Skimming Tips

Don't Subvocalize

Subvocalizing is "sounding out" words as you read. Even if you don't move your lips, you're probably subvocalizing if you read one word at a time. Subvocalizing costs you time—because you can't read faster than you speak. If you group words, you won't subvocalize.

WHAT DO WE MEAN BY SKIMMING?

Skimming is still reading. It means reading quickly, looking only for the main ideas and the organization of the passage.

Keep Asking Yourself Where the Author's Going
Stay alert for the author's signals. Each SAT passage takes you on a journey, and every passage contains phrases or paragraph breaks that signal the next phase of this journey. As you skim, notice where each passage changes course.

Keep Your "Footsteps" Light
Don't read a passage slowly and deliberately. On the other hand, don't race as fast as you can. The idea is to increase your reading rate slightly while remaining comfortable.

Skimming Exercises
Now try a few exercises to see how skimming works. Read the following paragraph word by word.

> The prohibitive prices of some exhibits, as well as the continued depression of the local economy, prevented the 1939 World's Fair from being a great financial success. In a cultural sense, however, the Fair was enormously successful, and a landmark event of the era. As one historian noted, the Fair became "a cultural document of American values and aspirations at a crucial crossroads." After a decade of hardship, many Americans were ready to embrace a vision of social harmony, prosperity, and a bright future.

Now read the same paragraph, concentrating phrase by phrase.

> The prohibitive prices/ of some exhibits, /as well as/ the continued depression/ of the local economy, /prevented/ the 1939 World's Fair/ from being/ a great financial success. /In a /cultural sense,/ however,/ the Fair/ was enormously successful,/ and a landmark event/ of the era./ As one historian noted,/ the Fair became / "a cultural document/ of American values and aspirations/ at a crucial crossroads." /After a decade /of hardship,/ many Americans/ were ready to embrace/ a vision of social harmony,/ prosperity,/ and a bright future.

OKAY TO SLASH?

Don't put slash marks in your test booklet on the real SAT. You're allowed to, but it's a waste of time.

The point is to make "mental" slash marks so that you get in the habit of moving briskly through the passage.

Here's another paragraph. Put in the slash marks yourself, phrase by phrase.

> The theme of the 1939 World's Fair was "Building the World of Tomorrow." Indeed, the modern and the futuristic were everywhere apparent. The main symbols of the Fair were the Trylon and the Perisphere, a huge pyramid and orb which were lit up at night in a dazzling display. The most popular exhibit, sponsored by General Motors, was the Futurama, which claimed to provide visitors with a glimpse of automotive America in 1960. Patrons were carried by individual moving chairs on a simulated cross-country voyage, along a superhighway which would allow drivers to reach speeds up to 100 miles an hour.

No two readers will mark up this paragraph the same way, because each person sees phrases differently. That's okay. What's important is to begin working phrase-by-phrase, instead of word-by-word.

Now try another method. Read the following paragraphs, letting your eyes move down the page, and coming to rest at only two places per line:

> The *Catcher in the Rye*, published in 1951, is the only novel written by J.D. Salinger in a career that lasted less than twenty years. It is the story of Holden Caulfield, a sensitive, rebellious New York City teen-ager taking his first hesitant steps into adulthood. Holden flees the confines of his snobbish Eastern prep school, searching for innocence and truth, but finds only "phoniness." Filled with humor and pathos, The *Catcher in the Rye* won wide critical acclaim at the time of its publication. In the four decades since then, however, it has become a true phenomenon, selling hundreds of thousands of copies each year, and Holden Caulfield has gained the status of a cultural icon. What accounts for this book's remarkable hold on generation after generation of American youth?
>
> Holden Caulfield is the narrator of The *Catcher in the Rye,* and his narration is a stylistic tour de force, revealing Salinger's masterful ear for the linguistic idioms and rhythms of adolescent speech. Slang evolves continuously, of course, and yesterday's "in" expressions are usually passé by tomorrow. But Holden's characteristic means of expression—the vernacular of a teen-age social misfit, desperately trying to find his niche—transcends the particulars of time and place. Like another 1950s icon, James Dean in "Rebel Without a Cause," Holden Caulfield has "outlived" his era and become an enduring symbol of sensitive youth, threatened by an indifferent society.

See how your eye takes in whole phrases, though you haven't read every word? That's another skimming method.

Remember, skim the passage before you turn to the questions. When you tackle the questions, you'll focus more tightly on parts of the passage.

Many questions will direct you back to specific lines or paragraphs, so you won't be desperately searching for relevant information.

PARAPHRASING

> **HINT:** *A good paraphrase accurately restates the meaning of the original, without adding or losing important points.*

WHY SKIM?

You gain points by answering the questions, not by reading the passages. Read quickly for the main idea and the structure, so you'll know where to look for the answers to the questions. The place to really concentrate is on the questions.

What happens when your best friend misses a day of school? You probably tell her or him what went on that night on the phone, or the next day before class. You'd be paraphrasing—condensing a day's worth of events into a few minutes, highlighting the most important things. Critical Reading questions often ask you to do a similar thing. They ask what a passage, or part of it, says. The right answer accurately paraphrases the meaning of the passage or excerpt, that is, it restates the meaning without losing any important points. Let's see how this works. Here are a few sentences from a Critical Reading passage:

EXAMPLE

No doubt because it painted a less than flattering picture of American life in America for Asian immigrants, *East Goes West* was not well received by contemporary literary critics. According to them, Kang's book displayed a curious lack of insight regarding the American effort to accommodate those who had come over from Korea. The facet of the novel reviewers did find praiseworthy was Han's perseverance and sustained optimism in the face of adversity.

The passage indicates that the response of critics to *East Goes West* was one of
(A) irony regarding the difference between Han's expectations and reality
(B) admiration of the courage and creativity Kang showed in breaking from literary tradition
(C) confusion about the motivation of the protagonist
(D) qualified disapproval of Kang's perception of his adopted homeland
(E) anger that Kang had so viciously attacked American society

There's a lot going on in the passage, but don't let it confuse you. Follow our advice:

Kaplan's Four-Step Paraphrasing Method

1. Read the question stem. That's the partial sentence leading into the answer choices.
2. Read the lines you're referred to, searching for the relevant phrases. (If a question gives you a line reference, be sure to read a line or two before and after the keyed line.)

3. Predict a good paraphrase for what's being asked.

4. Find a similar answer choice.

Now Apply Kaplan's Method to the Reading Question Above

1–2. After reading the stem and relevant lines of the passage (in this case, we found them for you), the key phrases should have popped out: "not well received," "a curious lack of insight," and "the facet reviewers did find praiseworthy."

3. Predicted paraphrase: The critics were displeased with Kang's view of the immigrant's experience, but approved of the hero's persistence.

4. Look for the answer choice that means the same as your paraphrase.

Choice (D) comes closest. Qualified means "modified" or "limited," so qualified disapproval captures both the negative and the positive reaction the reviewers had.

Notice that Choice (E) is too negative, and choice (B) is too positive. Choices (A) and (C) don't reflect what the extract says. So (D) is the answer.

Practice Paraphrasing

The excerpts on the following page will help you recognize a good paraphrase quickly. Follow the method you've just learned. Notice as you go if your paraphrase includes too much or too little information, or if it has the wrong focus. If so, adjust it.

Each excerpt is followed by a space in which you can write your own paraphrase. Compare your paraphrase with the answer choices and pick the best approximation. Answers on p. 81.

1. He was not in love with Margaret, and he believed, though one could never be sure, that she was not in love with him—that her preference was for the handsome young clergyman who read Browning with her every Tuesday afternoon. But he was aware also that she would marry him if he asked her; he knew that the hearts of four formidable parents were set on the match; and in his past experience his mother's heart had invariably triumphed over his less intrepid resolves.

The protagonist believes that Margaret will marry him because (give the reason in your own words):

_____

_____

Now find the best paraphrase:

(A) she wouldn't have the resolve to refuse him

(B) they are in love with each other

(C) they both feel parental pressure

(D) she knows the clergyman won't marry her

(E) his mother will talk her into accepting him

2. Only with effort can the camera be forced to lie: basically it is an honest medium: so the photographer is much more likely to approach nature in a spirit of inquiry, of communion, instead of with the saucy swagger of self-dubbed "artists."

The distinction made in the passage between a photographer and an "artist" can best be summarized as which of the following (summarize the distinction in your own words):

_____

_____

Now find the best paraphrase:

(A) The photographer's job is to record the world, and the artist's is to embellish it.

(B) The photographer's work is realistic, while the artist's is impressionistic.

(C) The artist finds his inspiration in the urban environment, the photographer in nature.

(D) The photographer has a more open and unassuming attitude toward the natural world than the artist does.

(E) Photographers are more pretentious than artists are.

3. The following excerpt is from a speech given by Frederick Douglass.

"What to the American slave is your Fourth of July? I answer, a day that reveals more to him than all other days of the year, the gross injustice and cruelty to which he is the constant victim. To him your celebration is a sham; your boasted liberty an unholy license; your national greatness, swelling vanity. . . ."

According to Douglass, for slaves, the Fourth of July (complete the sentence in your own words):

_____

_____

Now find the best paraphrase:
(A) highlights the hypocrisy of stated American ideals
(B) reveals the injustice of not being invited to participate
(C) is a reminder of the greatness of their homeland
(D) shows the depravity of the celebrants
(E) is a completely meaningless day

MAKING INFERENCES

Inferences are conclusions you reach that are hinted at, but not directly stated, in the reading passage. When you infer, you're "reading between the lines." In Critical Reading:

• If you're given a line reference, be sure to read a line or two around it.

• Always look for evidence in the passage to support an inference.

Many SAT questions test your power to make accurate inferences.

EXAMPLE

My father was a justice of the peace, and I supposed that he possessed the power of life and death over all men and could hang anybody that offended him. This distinction was enough for me as a general thing; but the desire to become a steamboat man kept intruding, nevertheless. I first wanted to be a cabin boy, so that I could come out with a white apron on and shake a tablecloth over the side, where all my old comrades could see me. Later I thought I would rather be the deck hand who stood on the end of the stage plank with a coil of rope in his hand, because he was particularly conspicuous.

The author makes the statement that "I supposed he possessed the power of life and death over all men and could hang anybody that offended him" primarily to suggest the
(A) power held by a justice of the peace in a frontier town
(B) naive view that he held of his father's importance
(C) respect that the townspeople had for his father
(D) possibility of miscarriages of justice on the American frontier
(E) harsh environment in which he was brought up

The answer is implied here. The author doesn't say "my view of my father's importance at the time was naive." But the idea is implicit in the excerpt.

As the author explains it, he supposed at the time that his father was all powerful and that he could kill almost anyone. On a first reading, that probably struck you as odd. You also probably wondered why the son was proud of it. But read the passage carefully and you'll realize the tone is ironic. The author is making fun of his youthful ideas. So the correct answer has to be (B).

Don't Go Too Far with Inferences

SAT inferences tend to be straightforward and consistent with the overall idea of the passage. They are not extreme, complex, or subtle. In fact, they're incredibly predictable. (You can use this to your advantage.) That's why Choices (A) and (E) go too far.

- Is it realistic that the author's father could hang anyone he wanted? Even if he could, would the author be proud of it? Very unlikely.

- Do the boy's early assumptions about his father's power indicate anything about the environment he grew up in? Not a thing.

Look at another question about the same excerpt:

EXAMPLE

The author decides that he would rather become a deck hand than a cabin boy because
(A) the job offers higher wages
(B) he believes that the work is easier
(C) he wants to avoid seeing his older friends
(D) deck hands often go on to become pilots
(E) the job is more visible to passersby

The author never says, "I decided to become a deck hand because the job was more visible to passersby." He *does* say he wanted to become a cabin boy so his old comrades could see him. And he adds the deck hand job would make him conspicuous. Between the lines, the correct answer, (E), is strongly implied.

Inference Practice

To sharpen your ability to deal with all kinds of inferences, do the following exercise. (Answers on p. 81.)

1. The graduating classes were the nobility of the school. Like travelers with exotic destinations on their minds, the graduates were remarkably forgetful. They came to school without their books, or tablets, or even pencils. Volunteers fell over themselves to secure replacements for the missing equipment. Even the teachers were respectful of the now quiet and aging seniors, and tended to speak to them, if not as equals, as beings only slightly lower than themselves.

    In the lines above, the author most likely mentions the eagerness of the "volunteers" in order to
    (A) indicate the ambition of younger school members
    (B) explain a double standard in teachers' attitudes
    (C) underline the respect with which seniors were treated
    (D) emphasize how careless seniors were with their equipment
    (E) point out a shortage in school supplies

2. Without knowing exactly what he'd done, Marc realized that he'd really done it now, and he felt the silence incriminating him. "Now wait just a minute. Hold on there," he said, producing a laugh from somewhere. Marc was the statesman of the class. People joked about how much money he was going to make coming out of law school. But he was groping for his words now, his eyes flickering over the countertop as if the words he was looking for were visible there.

    In the lines above, Marc's reputation as "the statesman of the class" is most likely mentioned in order to indicate that
    (A) he is noted for his diplomacy
    (B) many people resent his success
    (C) he is generally an articulate speaker
    (D) he is a popular student on campus
    (E) his ambitions are not realistic

    Ⓐ Ⓑ Ⓒ Ⓓ Ⓔ

3. Everyone seems to agree that there is something wrong with the way science is being taught these days. But no one is at all clear about what went wrong or what is to be done about it. The term "scientific illiteracy" has become almost a cliché in educational circles. Graduate schools blame the colleges, colleges blame the high schools, the high schools blame the elementary schools, which, in turn, blame the family. I suggest that the scientific community is partly, perhaps largely, to blame.

In the lines above, the phrase "almost a cliché in educational circles" is used to indicate
(A) the lack of unity between different sectors of education
(B) the widespread concern about the way science is being taught
(C) the inability of many scientists to communicate effectively
(D) the ignorance displayed by the scientific community about literature
(E) the extent of agreement over specific educational reforms

ANSWERS TO PARAPHRASING AND INFERENCE QUESTIONS

Paraphrasing

1. (C) Their parents want them to get married.

2. (D) A photographer is more open to nature and less pretentious than an "artist" is.

3. (A) The Fourth of July is a sham because the holiday celebrates freedom and they are not free.

Inferences

1. (C)

2. (C)

3. (B)

HIGHLIGHTS

• How to skim
• How to paraphrase
• How to make inferences

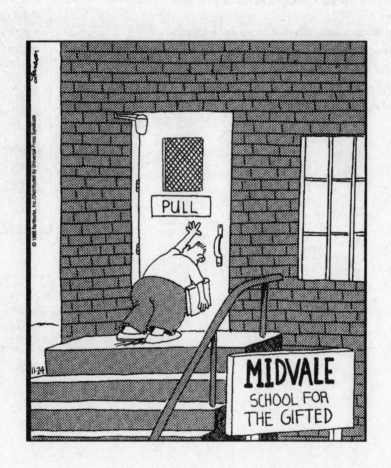

CHAPTER 9

INTRODUCING SAT MATH

Mathematics is many things. It is linear algebra and complex analysis. It is topology and trigonometry. It is number theory and multivariable calculus. Mathematics is a huge and daunting field, which requires years of study to master. But SAT Math is different. To ace the SAT, you need only a small body of mathematical knowledge covering basic concepts in arithmetic, algebra, and geometry. These concepts have been distilled into 100 principles that appear as an appendix to this book.

A solid grasp of these principles will get you a good SAT score. Understanding the ways in which these principles are tested—the twists and turns that the test makers throw into many SAT problems—can get you a great score.

This chapter explains:

- The SAT Math sections
- The SAT Math question types
- How to approach SAT Math problems
- Picking numbers
- Backsolving

Then, in chapters 10 through 15 you'll learn:

- When to use your calculator
- Specific strategies for solving Regular Math questions, Quantitative Comparisons (QCs), and Grid-ins
- How to avoid math traps the test makers have set
- How to make educated guesses on difficult math problems

SAT MATH: THE WARNING SIGNS

- When smoke starts coming out of your calculator, you're overusing it.
- If you are counting on your fingers and starting to remove your socks, you're off the track.
- If your answer depends on calculating the weight of the moon, in kilograms, you've read something wrong.
- "One potato, two potato" is not a useful guessing technique.

HOW SAT MATH IS SET UP

There are three scored Math sections on the SAT:
- One 30-minute section with 25 Regular Math questions
- One 30-minute section with a set of 15 QCs and a set of 10 Grid-ins
- One 15-minute section with 10 Regular Math questions

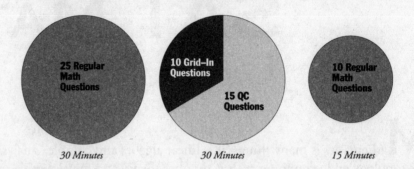

Difficulty Level

All sets of SAT Math questions are designed to start off basic and gradually increase in difficulty.

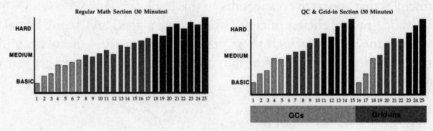

The 10 Regular Math questions also get more difficult.

Always be aware of the difficulty level as you go through a question set. Easy problems call for different strategies. The harder the questions, the more traps you will encounter. If you know you're dealing with a hard question (even though it may look easy), you'll be prepared.

DON'T READ THE DIRECTIONS ON TEST DAY— KNOW WHAT TO EXPECT

You'll save a lot of time on the SAT Math by knowing the directions. They take a fair amount of time to plow through and they are the same for every test. With just a little prior experience, you'll know what to do with each question type and you'll skip the directions and go straight to the first question.

At the start of each Math section you will find the following information:

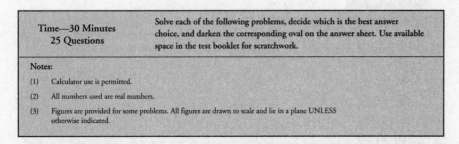

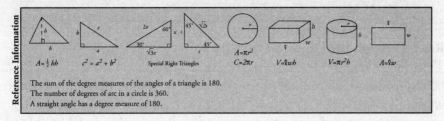

Note (2) means you won't have to deal with imaginary numbers, such as i (the square root of -1).

Note (3) tells you diagrams are drawn to scale, which means you can use these diagrams to estimate measurements. However, if the diagrams are labeled "Figure not drawn to scale," you can't do this.

Saying the figures "lie in a plane" simply means you are dealing with flat figures, like rectangles or circles, unless the question says otherwise.

The math information you're given includes many basic geometry formulas. By the day of the test you should know all these formulas by heart. But if you forget one at the last minute, you'll find them in the directions.

The Grid-ins and QCs have slightly different instructions, which we'll discuss in detail in Chapter 11 and Chapter 12.

HOW TO APPROACH SAT MATH

To maximize your Math score, you need to learn to use your time efficiently. Then you won't get bogged down on a single hard question and miss other problems you could have solved if you'd had more time.

The key to working systematically is: Think about the question before you look for the answer. A few seconds spent up front looking for traps, thinking about your approach, and deciding whether to tackle the problem now or come back to it later will pay off in SAT points. On basic problems, you may know what to do right away. But on hard problems, the few extra seconds are time well spent.

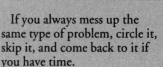

RULE OF THUMB

If you always mess up the same type of problem, circle it, skip it, and come back to it if you have time.

Now apply it to the problem below:

EXAMPLE

12. At a certain diner, Joe orders three doughnuts and a cup of coffee and is charged $2.25. Stella ordered two doughnuts and a cup of coffee and is charged $1.70. What is the price of two doughnuts?

   (A) $0.55
   (B) $0.60
   (C) $1.10
   (D) $1.30
   (E) $1.80

Read Through the Question

This means the *whole* question. If you try to start solving the problem before reading it all the way through, you may end up doing unnecessary work.

Decide whether the question is basic, medium, or hard. All SAT Math questions are arranged in order of difficulty. Within a set, the first questions are basic, the middle ones moderately difficult, and the last ones are hard. Question 12 above is a moderately difficult word problem.

> **HINT:** *On difficult questions, watch out for Math Traps. Hard questions are often misleadingly worded to trip up careless readers. (For more on Math Traps, see Chapter 14, p. 173.)*

Make sure you know what's being asked. Question 12 looks straightforward but read through it carefully and you'll see a slight twist. You're asked to find the cost of *two* doughnuts, not one. Many people will find the price of a single doughnut and forget to double it.

Decide Whether to Do the Problem or Skip It for Now

- If you have no idea what to do, skip the problem and circle it in your test booklet. Spend your time on the problems you can solve.

- If you think you can solve it, but it will take a lot of time, circle the question number in your test booklet and make a note to come back to it later if you have time.

- If you can eliminate one or more answer choices, do so and make an educated guess. Mark that you guessed in your test booklet, and try solving later if time permits. (For details on educated guessing, see Chapter 15, p. 199.)

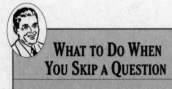

WHAT TO DO WHEN YOU SKIP A QUESTION

Circle it in your test booklet and make sure you skip it on your answer grid.

If You Do Tackle the Problem, Look for the Fastest Approach
Look for hidden information. On an easy question all the information you need to solve the problem may be given up front, in the stem, or in a diagram. But in a harder question, you may need to look for hidden information that will help you solve the problem. Since questions are arranged in order of difficulty, you should be a little wary of question 12. If you get the answer too easily, you may have missed something. In this case, you're asked to find the price of two doughnuts, not one. For more on Hidden Instructions see Chapter 14.

Look for shortcuts. Sometimes the obvious way of doing a problem is the long way. If the method you choose involves lots of calculating, look for another route. There's usually a shortcut you can use that won't involve tons of arithmetic.

In question 12, for example, the cost of doughnuts and coffee could be translated into two distinct equations using the variables d and c. You could find c in terms of d, then plug this into the other equation. But if you think carefully, you'll see there's a quicker way: The difference in price between three doughnuts and a cup of coffee and two doughnuts and a cup of coffee is the price of one doughnut. So one doughnut costs $2.25 - $1.70 = $0.55. (Remember, you have to find the price of *two* doughnuts. Twice $0.55 is $1.10.)

Use a variety of strategies. Chapter 13, Classic Problem-Solving Techniques, reviews many strategies for specific problem types that will help you get to the answer faster. You can also use special Kaplan methods, such as Picking Numbers and Backsolving. (For more on these methods, see pp. 88–92 in this chapter.)

If You Get Stuck, Make an Educated Guess
If you're not sure what to do, or if you've tried solving a problem but got stuck, cut your losses. Eliminate any answer choices you can, and make an educated guess.

HINT: When you skip a question, make a note in your test booklet to come back to it later, if you have time.

Let's say it's taking too long to solve the doughnut problem. Can you eliminate any answer choices? The price of two doughnuts and a cup of coffee is $1.70. That means the cost of two doughnuts alone can't be $1.80, which eliminates choice (E). Now you can choose between the remaining choices, and your odds of guessing correctly have improved. (See Chapter 15, Math Guessing.)

If you practice using this approach to the Math problems on the SAT, you will save time and avoid mistakes on the day of the test.

WHEN YOU'RE STUCK

The great thing about Math, even if you hate it, is that there are usually a lot of different ways to get to the right answer. On the SAT, there are two methods in particular that are really useful when you don't see the straightforward way to solve the problem—picking numbers and backsolving. These strategies can take longer than traditional methods, but they're worth trying if you have enough time.

PICKING NUMBERS

Sometimes you can get stuck on a math question just because it's too general or abstract. A good way to get a handle on such a question is to bring it down to earth and make it more explicit by temporarily substituting particular numbers. This "picking numbers" strategy works especially well with even/odd questions.

> **EXAMPLE**
>
> If a is an odd integer and b is an even integer, which of the following must be odd?
>
> (A) $2a + b$
> (B) $a + 2b$
> (C) ab
> (D) a^2b
> (E) ab^2

Rather than try to think this one through abstractly, it's easier for most people simply to pick numbers for a and b. There are rules that predict the evenness or oddness of sums, differences, and products, but there's no need to memorize these rules. When it comes to adding, subtracting, and multiplying evens and odds, what happens with one pair of numbers generally happens with all similar pairs.

Just say, for the time being, that $a = 3$ and $b = 2$. Plug those values into the answer choices and there's a good chance that only one choice will be odd:

> (A) $2a + b = 2(3) + 2 = 8$
> (B) $a + 2b = 3 + 2(2) = 7$
> (C) $ab = (3)(2) = 6$
> (D) $a^2b = (3^2)(2) = 18$
> (E) $ab^2 = (3)(2^2) = 12$

Choice (B) is the only odd one for $a = 3$ and $b = 2$, so it must be the one that's odd no matter what odd number a and even number b actually stand for. The answer is (B).

Another good situation for using the "picking numbers" strategy is when the answer choices to a percent problem are all percents.

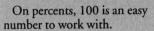

EXAMPLE

From 1985 to 1990, the population of City X increased by 20 percent. From 1990 to 1995, the population increased by 30 percent. What was the percent increase in the population over the entire 10-year period 1985–1995?

(A) 10%
(B) 25%
(C) 50%
(D) 56%
(E) 60%

Instead of trying to solve this problem in the abstract, pick a number for the original 1985 population and see what happens. There's no need to pick a realistic number. You're better off picking a number that's easy to work with. And in percent problems the number that's easiest to work with is almost always 100. Say the 1985 population was 100, then what would the 1990 population be? Twenty percent more than 100 is 120. Now, if the 1990 population was 120, what would the 1995 population be? What's 30 percent more than 120? Be careful. Don't just add 30 to 120. You need to find 30 percent of 120 and add that on. Thirty percent of 120 is (.30)(120) = 36. Add 36 to 120 and you get a 1995 population of 156. What percent greater is 156 than 100? That's easy—that's why we picked 100 to start with. It's a 56 percent increase. The answer is (D).

A third good situation for using the "picking numbers" strategy is when the answer choices to a word problem are not numbers, but algebraic expressions.

EXAMPLE

If n apples cost p dollars, then how may dollars would q apples cost?

(A) $\frac{np}{q}$

(B) $\frac{nq}{p}$

(C) $\frac{pq}{n}$

(D) $\frac{n}{pq}$

(E) $\frac{p}{nq}$

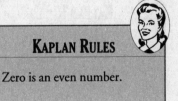

The only thing that's hard about this question is that it uses variables instead of numbers. So, make it real. Pick numbers for the variables. Pick numbers that are easy to work with. Say $n = 2$, $p = 4$, and $q = 3$. Then the question becomes: "If two apples cost $4.00, how many dollars would three apples cost?" That's easy—$6.00. When $n = 2$, $p = 4$, and $q = 3$, the correct answer should equal 6. Plug those values into the answer choices and see which ones yield 6:

RULE OF THUMB

Avoid picking weird numbers like 0 and 1, as these often give several "possibly correct" answers.

(A) $\dfrac{np}{q} = \dfrac{(2)(4)}{3} = \dfrac{8}{3}$

(B) $\dfrac{nq}{q} = \dfrac{(2)(3)}{3} = \dfrac{6}{3} = 2$

(C) $\dfrac{pq}{n} = \dfrac{(4)(3)}{2} = \dfrac{12}{2} = 6$

(D) $\dfrac{n}{pq} = \dfrac{2}{(4)(3)} = \dfrac{2}{12} = \dfrac{1}{6}$

(E) $\dfrac{p}{nq} = \dfrac{4}{(2)(3)} = \dfrac{4}{6} = \dfrac{2}{3}$

Choice (C) is the only one that yields 6, so it must be the correct answer.

When picking numbers for an abstract word problem like this one, it's important to try all five answer choices. Sometimes more than one choice will yield the correct result, in which case one or more choices work coincidentally with the numbers you picked. When that happens, pick another set of numbers to weed out the coincidences. Avoid picking weird numbers such as 0 and 1, as these often give several "possibly correct" answers.

BACKSOLVING

On some Math questions, when you can't figure out the question, you can try working backwards from the answer choices. Plug the choices back into the question until you find the one that works.

Backsolving works best:

- When the question is a complex word problem and the answer choices are numbers

- When the alternative is setting up multiple algebraic equations

Don't backsolve:

- If the answer choices include variables

- On algebra questions or word problems that have ugly answer choices such as radicals and fractions (plugging them in takes too much time)

KAPLAN RULES

Remember the answer is always in front of you on multiple choice questions. Your job is to find it.

How Backsolving Works

When the Question Is Complex and the Answer Choices Are Simple

SPEED TIP

To speed things up, start with the middle-range number. Since answer choices are always listed in increasing or decreasing order, that means starting with choice (C). If (C) is too large, move to the smaller choices. If it's too small, move to the bigger ones.

> **EXAMPLE**
>
> An office has 27 employees. If there are seven more women than men in the office, how many employees are women?
>
> (A) 8
> (B) 10
> (C) 14
> (D) 17
> (E) 20

> **HINT:** *Sometimes backsolving is faster than setting up an equation.*

The five answer choices represent the possible number of women in the office, so try them in the question stem. The choice that gives a total of 27 employees, with seven more women than men, will be the correct answer.

Plugging in choice (C) gives you 14 women in the office. Since there are seven more women than men, there are seven men in the office. But 14 + 7 < 27. The sum is too small, so there must be more than 14 women. Eliminate answer choices (A), (B), and (C).

Either (D) or (E) will be correct. Plugging in (D) gives you 17 women in the office and 17 − 7, or 10 men. 17 + 10 = 27 employees total. Answer choice (D) is correct.

Algebra Problems for Which You Need to Solve Multiple Equations

> **EXAMPLE**
>
> If $a + b + c = 110$, $a = 4b$, and $3a = 2c$, then $b =$
> (A) 6
> (B) 8
> (C) 9
> (D) 10
> (E) 14

You're looking for b, so plug in the answer choices for b in the question and see what happens. The choice that gives us 110 for the sum $a + b + c$ must be correct.

Start with the midrange number, 9, choice (C).

- If $b = 9$, then $a = 4 \times 9 = 36$.
- $2c = 3a = 3 \times 36 = 108$.
- $c = 54$.
- $a + b + c = 36 + 9 + 54 = 99$.

Since this is a smaller sum than 110, the correct value for b must be greater. Therefore, eliminate answer choices (A), (B), and (C).

Now plug in either (D) or (E) and see if it works. If it doesn't, the remaining choice must be correct.

Short of time? Try guessing between (D) and (E). But guess intelligently. Since (C) wasn't far wrong, you want a number just slightly bigger. That's choice (D).

HIGHLIGHTS

- Approaching SAT Math
- Picking Numbers
- Backsolving

F·A·S·T P·R·E·P

CHAPTER CHECKLIST

 Once you've mastered a section, check it off.

CALCULATORS AND THE SAT
- ❑ WHAT KIND OF CALCULATOR SHOULD I BRING?
- ❑ WHEN SHOULD I USE A CALCULATOR?
- ❑ WHEN *SHOULDN'T* I USE A CALCULATOR?

PanicPlan

If you have a month or less to prep for the SAT, here's the best way to spend your time:
- Skim pp. 98–100 (on common calculator mistakes).

CHAPTER 10

CALCULATORS AND THE SAT

Y ou are allowed to use a calculator on the SAT. That's a mixed blessing. The good news is you can do computation faster. The bad news is you may be tempted to waste time using a calculator on questions that shouldn't involve lengthy computation.

Remember, you never *need* a calculator to solve an SAT problem. If you ever find yourself doing extensive calculation on the SAT—elaborate long division or long, drawn-out multiplication—stop and look again because you probably missed a shortcut.

SHOULD I BRING A CALCULATOR?

You definitely want to bring your calculator on the day of the test. The fact is, there are some problems for which using the calculator will really come in handy. By using your calculator on particular problem types and by zeroing in on the parts of problems that need calculation, you can increase your score and save yourself time on the SAT.

WHAT KIND OF CALCULATOR SHOULD I BRING?

The best calculator to bring is one you're comfortable with. The most important thing is not how fancy your calculator is, but how good you are at using it. Remember, you won't be doing logs, trig functions, or pre-programmed formulas on the SAT. Most of the time you'll be multiplying and dividing.

> **THE MORE YOU KNOW ABOUT THE SAT . . .**
>
> . . . the less you'll use your calculator.
>
> Studies have shown that students who regularly use calculators score better on the SAT than those who don't.
>
> But using a calculator too much could actually hurt your score. In fact, the better you are at the SAT, the less you'll need your calculator.

You can use the following calculators on the SAT:

- A four-function calculator (that adds, subtracts, multiplies, divides)
- A scientific calculator (that also does radicals, exponents, etcetera)
- A graphing calculator (that displays the graph of an equation in a coordinate plane)

But the following are not allowed:

- A calculator that prints out your calculations
- A hand-held minicomputer or a laptop computer
- Any calculator with a typewriter keypad
- A calculator that "speaks," makes strange noises, or requires an electrical outlet for use

WHEN SHOULD I USE A CALCULATOR?

Calculators help the most on Grid-ins and the least on QCs.

The reason for this is that QCs are designed to be done very quickly, and never involve much computation—if you think you need a calculator on them, then you're missing something. Both Grid-ins and Regular Math will sometimes involve computation—never as the most important part of the question, but often as a final step.

Since Grid-ins don't give you answer choices to choose from, it's especially important to be sure of your work. Calculators can help you avoid careless errors.

Remember, a calculator can be useful when used selectively. Not all parts of a problem are necessarily easier on a calculator. Consider this problem:

KAPLAN RULES

The best calculator in the world won't help if the batteries are dead or if you forget to put them in. Make sure you have fresh batteries in your machine on the day of the test.

> **EXAMPLE**
>
> If four grams of cadmium yellow pigment can make 3 kilograms of cadmium yellow oil paint, how many kilograms of paint could be produced from 86 grams of pigment?

This word problem has two steps. Step one is to set up the following proportion:

$$\frac{4 \text{ gms}}{3 \text{ kgs}} = \frac{86 \text{ gms}}{x \text{ kgs}}$$

A little algebraic engineering tells you that:

$$x \text{ kgs} = \frac{3 \text{ kgs} \times 86 \text{ gms}}{4 \text{ gms}}$$

Here's where you whip out that calculator. This problem has now been reduced down to pure calculation: $(3 \times 86) \div 4 = 64.5$.

Your calculator will also be especially useful for picking numbers and backsolving.

When You Pick Numbers
When you plug in real numbers to replace variables in complex equations, your calculator can speed things up. (See Picking Numbers, Chapter 9, pp. 88–90.)

When You Backsolve
When you plug multiple-choice answers into a problem to see which answer is right, your calculator can speed up the process. (See Backsolving, Chapter 9, pp. 90–92.)

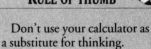

RULE OF THUMB

Don't use your calculator as a substitute for thinking.

WHEN SHOULDN'T I USE A CALCULATOR?

Don't be fooled. On most SAT problems you may be tempted to use your calculator, but many questions will be easier without a calculator. That's particularly true on QCs.

Consider this problem:

EXAMPLE

Column A	Column B
$\dfrac{5}{8} + \dfrac{9}{14}$	$\dfrac{4}{9} + \dfrac{10}{21}$

Sure, you could grab your calculator and divide out those fractions. Relatively quickly you could calculate the new values and compare the columns.

But why bother?

If you just compare these terms to $\frac{1}{2}$ you'll be out of this problem much faster. After all, $\frac{5}{8}$ and $\frac{9}{14}$ from Column A are both greater than $\frac{1}{2}$, and $\frac{4}{9}$ and $\frac{10}{21}$ (from Column B) are both less than $\frac{1}{2}$. Column A must be greater. Using your calculator on this one would only slow you down.

Be careful on non-QC questions, too. Consider this:

EXAMPLE

If $x^2 \times 8^2 = 49 \times 64 \times 81$, $x^2 =$

(A) 49^2
(B) 56^2
(C) 63^2
(D) 72^2
(E) 81^2

Now if you punch in $49 \times 64 \times 81$ you'll get 254,016. But that won't be too helpful. Look at the answer choices! Instead realize that:

$$(x^2) \times 8^2 = (49 \times 81) \times 64$$

8^2 is the same as 64, so get rid of the 64s on both sides. You get:

$$x^2 = 49 \times 81$$

So that's $x^2 = 7^2 \times 9^2$ or $x^2 = 7 \times 7 \times 9 \times 9$, which is 63×63 or 63^2. No calculator required.

COMMON MISTAKE #1: CALCULATING BEFORE YOU THINK

On the Grid-in problem below, how should you use your calculator?

EXAMPLE

The sum of all the integers from 1 to 44, inclusive, is subtracted from the sum of all the integers from 7 to 50, inclusive. What is the result?

The Wrong Approach
• Grab calculator.
• Punch in all the numbers.
• Put down answer and hope you didn't hit any wrong buttons.

CALCULATOR ABUSE: THE WARNING SIGNS

• Punching in numbers before you've read the question.
• Hand cramps from punching in too many numbers.
• Repeatedly spelling *hello* or *Shell Oil* on your calculator rather than answering the question.

The wrong approach is to punch in all the numbers from 1 to 44, find their sum, then do the same for numbers 7 through 50, and subtract the first sum from the second. Doing that means punching 252 keys. The odds are you'll slip up somewhere, hit the wrong key, and get the wrong answer. Even if you don't, punching in all those numbers takes too much time.

The Kaplan Method
- Think first.
- Decide on the best way to solve it.
- Only then, use your calculator.

The right approach is to *think first*. The amount of computation involved in solving this directly tells you that there *must* be an easier way. You'll see this if you realize that both sums are of the same number of consecutive integers. Each integer in the first sum has a corresponding integer six units greater than it in the second sum, like so:

$$
\begin{array}{ll}
1 & 7 \\
+2 & +8 \\
+3 & +9 \\
\cdot & \cdot \\
\cdot & \cdot \\
\cdot & \cdot \\
+42 & +48 \\
+43 & +49 \\
+44 & +50 \\
= & =
\end{array}
$$

There are 44 pairs of integers that are six units apart. So the total difference between the two sums will be the difference between each pair of integers times the number of pairs.

Now take out your calculator, punch "6 x 44 =," and get the correct answer of 264, with little or no time wasted.

> **WARNING:** *If you're punching buttons for long stretches at a time, you're approaching the problem the wrong way.*

RULE OF THUMB

Different calculators do chain calculations different ways. Make sure you know how your calculator does chains so you don't miscalculate.

HIGHLIGHTS

• Bring your calculator to the SAT

• Practice using it before the day of the test

• Think before you calculate

COMMON MISTAKE #2: FORGETTING THE ORDER OF OPERATIONS

Watch out. Even when you use your calculator, you can't just enter numbers in the order they appear on the page—you've got to follow the order of operations. This is a very simple error but it can cost you lots of points.

The order of operations, or PEMDAS, means you do whatever is in:

Parentheses first, then deal with
Exponents, then
Multiplication and
Division, and finally
Addition and
Subtraction

For example, say you want to find the value of the expression

$$\frac{x^2+1}{x+3} \quad \text{when } x = 7$$

If you just punched in "7 × 7 + 1 ÷ 7 + 3 =" you would get the wrong answer. The correct way to work it out is:

$$(7^2 + 1) \div (7 + 3) = (7 \times 7 + 1) \div (7 + 3) = (49 + 1) \div 10 = 50 \div 10 = 5$$

Combining a calculator with an understanding of when and how to use it can help you boost your score.

Midway through the exam,
Allen pulls out a bigger brain.

F·A·S·T P·R·E·P

CHAPTER CHECKLIST

Once you've mastered a section, check it off.

GRID-INS
- ❑ THE FORMAT
- ❑ FILLING IN THE GRID
- ❑ PRACTICE GRIDDING

PANICPLAN

If you have a month or less to prep for the SAT, here's the best way to spend your time:

- Read this entire chapter. It's pretty short and the gridding tips that we discuss can help prevent you from making careless mistakes that cost you points.

- Do the gridding drills at the end of the chapter.

CHAPTER 11

GRID-INS

In high school math class, you usually don't get five answer choices to choose from on a test. And you don't lose a quarter of a point for a wrong answer. Instead, you are given a problem and you're asked to find the answer.

The Grid-in section on the SAT is a lot like the math tests you're already used to taking. Unlike other questions on the SAT, Grid-ins have no multiple-choice answers and there's no penalty for wrong answers. You have to figure out your own answer and fill it in on a special grid. Note that some Grid-ins have only one correct answer, while others have several, or even a range of correct answers.

THE FORMAT

You'll get 10 Grid-ins, following the QCs, in one of the Math Sections. To get an idea of what the instructions will look like on the day of the test day, turn the page.

For each question, you'll see a grid with four boxes and a column of ovals beneath each. First write your numerical answer in the boxes, one digit, decimal point, or fraction bar per box. Then fill in the corresponding ovals below.

WARNING:

- *The computer cannot scan the numerical answer in the boxes; you must fill in the corresponding ovals.*

- *Fill in no more than one oval per column.*

- *Make the oval you grid match your number above that oval.*

> ### GRID-INS HAVE NO HEART
>
> The fact that there's an entire chapter devoted to showing you how to do Grid-ins should tell you something: It's really easy to mess them up.
>
> The SAT is scored by computer. If you write the correct answer in the boxes at the top of the grid but forget to grid in the bubbles, you don't get the points.
>
> If you forget to convert a mixed number to a fraction or decimal equivalent, you won't get credit for your answer. The golden rule: Be careful.

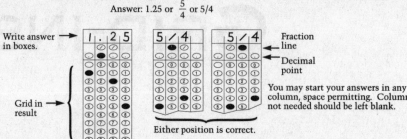

For each of the questions below (16-25), solve the problem and indicate your answer by darkening the ovals in the special grid. For example:

Answer: 1.25 or $\frac{5}{4}$ or 5/4

Write answer in boxes.

Grid in result

Fraction line

Decimal point

You may start your answers in any column, space permitting. Columns not needed should be left blank.

Either position is correct.

- It is recommended, though not required, that you write your answer in the boxes at the top of the columns. However, you will receive credit only for darkening the ovals correctly.

- Grid only one answer to a question, even though some problems have more than one correct answer.

- Darken no more than one oval in a column.

- No answers are negative.

- Mixed numbers cannot be gridded. For example: the number $1\frac{1}{4}$ must be gridded as 1.25 or 5/4.

(If [1 1/4] is gridded, it will be interpreted as $\frac{11}{4}$ not $1\frac{1}{4}$.)

- Decimal Accuracy: Decimal answers must be entered as accurately as possible. For example, if you obtain an answer such as 0.1666..., you should record the result as .166 or .167. **Less accurate values such as .16 or .17 are not acceptable.**

Acceptable ways to grid $\frac{1}{6}$ =.1666...

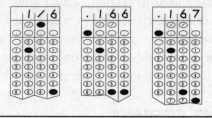

Grid-in Instructions

FILLING IN THE GRID

The grid cannot accommodate

- Negative answers
- Answers with variables
- Answers greater than 9999
- Answers with commas
- Mixed numbers

Recommendation: Start your answer in the first column box. Do that even if your answer has only one or two figures. If you always start with the first column, your answers will always fit. Since there is no oval for 0 in the first column, grid an answer of 0 in any other column. (Technically, you can start in any column, but follow this rule to avoid mistakes.)

In a fractional answer, grid (/) in the correct column. The sign (/) separates the numerator from the denominator. It appears only in columns two and three.

TWO GRID-IN TIPS

1. Always start from the left.

2. Guess when you can. Skip it when you haven't a clue. Be sure to circle the question number in your test booklet if you skip it.

There's no wrong-answer penalty for Grid-ins. So if you have time, take an educated guess. It can't hurt.

Example: If you get an answer of 5/8. Grid (/) in column two.

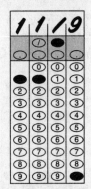

Example: If you get an answer of 11/9. Grid (/) in column three.

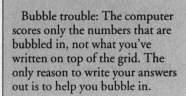
WARNING: *A fractional answer with four digits won't fit.*

Change mixed numbers to decimals or fractions before you grid. If you try to grid a mixed number, it will be read as a fraction, and be counted wrong. For example, $4\frac{1}{2}$ will be read as the fraction $\frac{41}{2}$, which is $20\frac{1}{2}$.

So first change mixed numbers to fractions or decimals, then grid in. In this case:

- Change $4\frac{1}{2}$ to $\frac{9}{2}$ and grid in as shown below.

- Or change $4\frac{1}{2}$ to 4.5 and grid in the decimal.

Watch where you put your decimal points.

- For a decimal less than 1, such as .127, enter the decimal point in the first box as shown in the figure above.

- Put a zero before the decimal point only if it's part of the answer—don't just put one there to make your answer *look* more accurate.

- Never grid a decimal point in the last column.

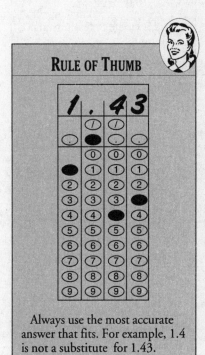

With long or repeating decimals, grid the first three digits only and plug in the decimal point where it belongs. Say three answers are .45454545, 82.452312, and 1.428743. Grid .454, 82.4, and 1.42, respectively.

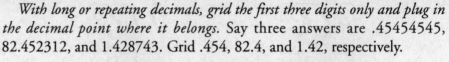

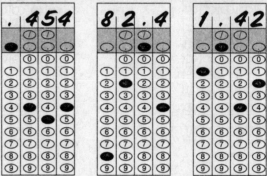

You could round 1.428743 up to the nearest hundredth (1.43), but it's not required. So don't bother, since you could make a mistake. Shorter, less accurate answers—such as 1.4—are wrong.

On Grid-ins with more than one right answer, choose one, and enter it. Say you're asked for a two-digit integer that is a multiple of 2, 3, and 5. You might answer 30, 60, or 90. Whichever you grid would be right.

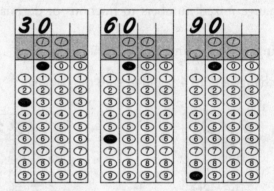

Some Grid-ins have a range of possible answers. Suppose you're asked to grid a value of m, given that $1 - 2m < m$ and $5m - 2 < m$. Solving for m in the first inequality, you find that $\frac{1}{3} < m$. Solving for m in the second inequality, you find that $m < \frac{1}{2}$. So $\frac{1}{3} < m < \frac{1}{2}$. Grid in any value between $\frac{1}{3}$ and $\frac{1}{2}$. (Gridding in $\frac{1}{3}$ or $\frac{1}{2}$ would be wrong.) When the answer is a range of values, it's often easier to work with decimals: $.333 < m < .5$. Then you can quickly grid .4 (or .35 or .45, etcetera) as your answer.

Write your answers in the number boxes. You will make fewer mistakes if you write your answers in the number boxes. You may think that gridding directly will save time, but writing first and then gridding ensures accuracy, which means more points.

PRACTICE GRIDDING

With just a little practice, you can master the gridding-in process. Complete the Grid-ins below, following our instructions. After you finish, check your work against the grids on the next page.

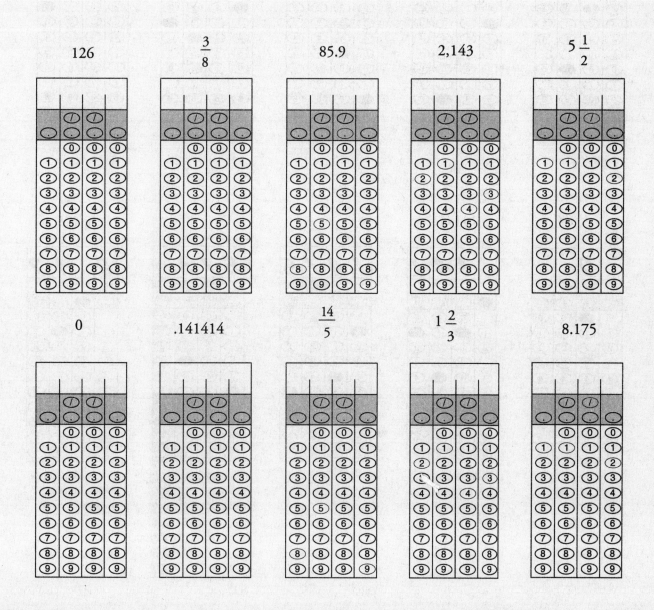

GRIDDING ANSWERS

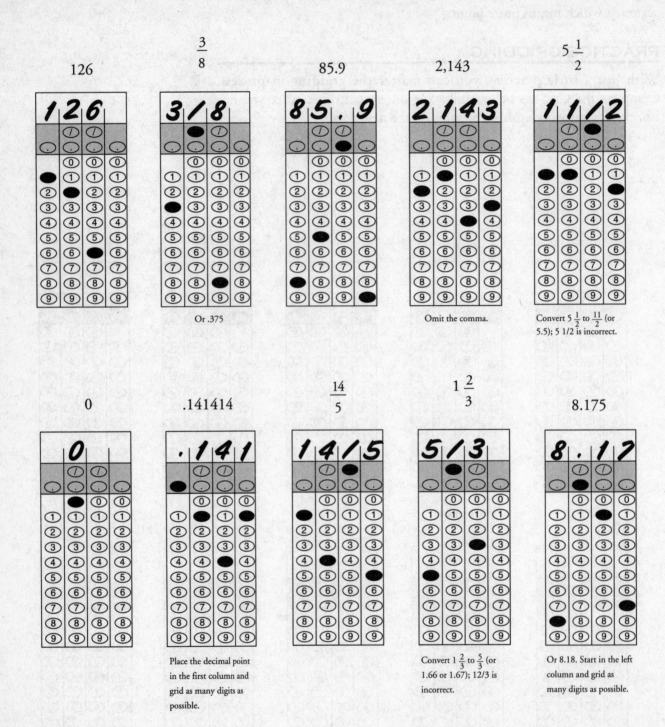

126

$\frac{3}{8}$

Or .375

85.9

2,143

Omit the comma.

$5\frac{1}{2}$

Convert $5\frac{1}{2}$ to $\frac{11}{2}$ (or 5.5); 5 1/2 is incorrect.

0

.141414

Place the decimal point in the first column and grid as many digits as possible.

$\frac{14}{5}$

$1\frac{2}{3}$

Convert $1\frac{2}{3}$ to $\frac{5}{3}$ (or 1.66 or 1.67); 12/3 is incorrect.

8.175

Or 8.18. Start in the left column and grid as many digits as possible.

F·A·S·T P·R·E·P

CHAPTER CHECKLIST

 Once you've mastered a section, check it off.

QUANTITATIVE COMPARISONS
- ❑ COMPARE PIECE BY PIECE
- ❑ MAKE ONE COLUMN LOOK LIKE THE OTHER
- ❑ DO THE SAME THING TO BOTH COLUMNS
- ❑ PICK NUMBERS
- ❑ REDRAW THE DIAGRAM
- ❑ AVOID QC TRAPS

PANICPLAN

If you have a month or less to prep for the SAT, here's the best way to spend your time:

- Skim pp. 111–113.
- Learn the two rules for choice (D) on page 112.
- Do the practice problems on pp. 123–124. If you miss an answer, review the strategy before continuing.

CHAPTER 12

QUANTITATIVE COMPARISONS

In Quantitative Comparisons, instead of solving for a particular value, you need to compare two quantities. At first, QCs may appear really difficult because of their unfamiliar format. However, once you become used to them, they can be quicker and easier than the other types of math questions.

THE FORMAT

Where They Appear
The 15 QCs appear in the Math section that also contains the 10 Grid-in questions. They are arranged in order of increasing difficulty.

The Questions
In each question, you'll see two mathematical expressions. They are boxed, one in Column A, the other in Column B. Your job is to compare them.

Some questions include additional information about one or both quantities. This information is centered, unboxed, and essential to making the comparison.

> **HINT:** To score high on QCs, learn what the answer choices stand for.

The Directions
The directions you'll see will look something like those on the next page. Familiarize yourself with them now.

THE ANSWER CHOICES

If you remember anything from this chapter, it should be a thorough understanding of the four answer choices.

You won't have time to keep referring to the directions. You've got to know them cold.

(A) if Column A is greater

(B) if Column B is greater

(C) if the columns are equal

(D) if more information is needed to determine the relationship

(E) will not be scored

D-Day

As soon as you find that more than one relationship is possible, you know the answer is (D). Don't waste your time looking for other possibilities.

Directions for Quantitative Comparison Questions

Compare the boxed quantity in Column A with the boxed quantity in Column B. Select answer choice

- A if Column A is greater;
- B if Column B is greater;
- C if the columns are equal; or
- D if more information is needed to determine the relationship.

An E response will be treated as an omission.

Notes:
1. Some questions include information about one or both quantities. That information is centered and unboxed.
2. A symbol that appears in both Column A and Column B stands for the same thing in both columns.
3. All numbers used are real numbers.

EXAMPLES

	Column A	Column B	Answers
E1	3×4	$3 + 4$	● Ⓑ Ⓒ Ⓓ Ⓔ
E2	x	160	Ⓐ Ⓑ ● Ⓓ Ⓔ
E3	$x + 1$	$y - 1$	Ⓐ Ⓑ Ⓒ ● Ⓔ

(E2: $x°$ $20°$)

(E3: x and y are positive)

WARNING: *Never pick choice (E) as the answer to a QC.*

TWO RULES FOR ANSWER CHOICE (D)

Choices (A), (B), and (C) all represent definite relationships between the quantities in Column A and Column B. But choice (D) represents a relationship that cannot be determined. Here are two things to remember about choice (D) that will help you decide when to pick it:

1. Choice (D) is never correct if both columns contain only numbers. The relationship between numbers is unchanging, but choice (D) means more than one relationship is possible.

2. Choice (D) is correct if you can demonstrate two different relationships between the columns. Suppose you ran across the following QC:

Column A	Column B
$2x$	$3x$

If x is a positive number, Column B is greater than Column A. If $x = 0$, the columns are equal. If x equals any negative number, Column B is less than Column A. Since more than one relationship is possible, the answer is (D). In fact, as soon as you find a second possibility, stop work and pick choice (D).

RULE OF THUMB

Usually there's a simpler way to solve a QC than using your calculator.

COMPARE, DON'T CALCULATE: KAPLAN'S SIX STRATEGIES

Here are six Kaplan strategies that will enable you to make quick comparisons. In the rest of this chapter you'll learn how they work and you'll try them on practice problems.

Strategy 1: Compare piece by piece.
This works on QCs that compare two sums or two products.

Strategy 2: Make one column look like the other.
This is a great approach when the columns look so different that you can't compare them directly.

Strategy 3: Do the same thing to both columns.
Change both columns by adding, subtracting, multiplying, or dividing by the same amount on both sides in order to make the comparison more apparent.

Strategy 4: Pick numbers.
Use this to get a handle on abstract algebra QCs.

Strategy 5: Redraw the diagram.
Redrawing a diagram can clarify the relationships between measurements.

Strategy 6: Avoid QC traps.
Stay alert for questions designed to fool you by leading you to the obvious, wrong answer.

Now learn how these strategies work.

STRATEGY 1: COMPARE PIECE BY PIECE

EXAMPLE

Column A	Column B

$$w > x > 0 > y > z$$

$w + y$ | $x + z$

In the problem above, there are four variables—w, x, y, and z. Compare the value of each "piece" in each column. If every "piece" in one column is greater than a corresponding "piece" in the other column and the only operation involved is addition, the column with the greater individual values will have the greater total value.

From the given information we know that $w > x$ and $y > z$. Therefore, the first term in Column A, w, is greater than the first term in Column B, x. Similarly, the second term in Column A, y, is greater than the second term in Column B, z. Since each piece in Column A is greater than the corresponding piece in Column B, Column A must be greater; the answer is (A).

STRATEGY 2: MAKE ONE COLUMN LOOK LIKE THE OTHER

When the quantities in Columns A and B are expressed differently, you can often make the comparison easier by changing one column to look like the other. For example, if one column is a percent and the other a fraction, try converting the percent to a fraction.

EXAMPLE

Column A	Column B
$x(x-1)$	$x^2 - x$

Here Column A has parentheses, and Column B doesn't. So make Column A look more like Column B: Get rid of those parentheses. You end up with $x^2 - x$ in both columns, which means they are equal and the answer is (C).

Try another example, this time involving geometry.

EXAMPLE

Column A	Column B

The diameter of circle O is d and the area is a.

$\dfrac{\pi d^2}{2}$	a

Make Column B look more like Column A by rewriting a, the area of the circle, in terms of the diameter, d. The area of any circle equals πr^2, with r as the radius.

Since the radius is half the diameter, we can plug in $\frac{d}{2}$ for r in the area formula to get $\pi(\frac{d}{2})^2$ in Column B. Simplifying we get $\frac{\pi d^2}{4}$. Since both columns contain π, we can simply compare $\frac{d^2}{2}$ with $\frac{d^2}{4}$. Since $\frac{d^2}{4}$ is half as much as $\frac{d^2}{2}$, and d^2 must be positive, Column A is greater.

Choice (A) is correct.

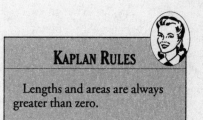

KAPLAN RULES

Lengths and areas are always greater than zero.

STRATEGY 3: DO THE SAME THING TO BOTH COLUMNS

Some QC questions become much clearer if you change not just the appearances, but the values of both columns. Treat them like two sides of an inequality, with the sign temporarily hidden.

You can add or subtract the same amount from both columns and multiply or divide by the same positive amount without altering the relationship. You can also square both columns if you're sure they're both positive. But watch out. Multiplying or dividing an inequality by a negative number reverses the direction of the inequality sign. Since it alters the relationship between the columns, avoid multiplying or dividing by a negative number.

> **HINT:** *Don't multiply or divide both QC columns by a negative number.*

In the QC below, what could you do to both columns?

EXAMPLE

Column A	Column B
	$4a + 3 = 7b$
$20a + 10$	$35b - 5$

All the terms in the two columns are multiples of 5, so divide both columns by 5 to simplify. You're left with $4a + 2$ in Column A and $7b - 1$ in Column B. This resembles the equation given in the centered information. In fact, if you add 1 to both columns, you have $4a + 3$ in Column A and $7b$ in Column B. The centered equation tells us they are equal. Thus choice (C) is correct.

In the next QC, what could you do to both columns?

EXAMPLE

Column A	Column B

$$y > 0$$

$1 + \dfrac{y}{(y+1)}$	$1 + \dfrac{1}{(1+y)}$

Solution: First subtract 1 from both sides. That gives you $\dfrac{y}{(1+y)}$ in Column A, and $\dfrac{1}{(1+y)}$ in Column B. Then multiply both sides by $(1 + y)$, which must be positive since y is positive. You're left comparing y with 1.

You know y is greater than 0, but it could be a fraction less than 1, so it could be greater or less than 1. Since you can't say for sure which column is greater, the answer is (D).

KAPLAN RULES

Some surprising things can happen when you play around with negative numbers and fractions. Keep things like this in mind:

- When you square a positive fraction less than 1, the result is smaller than the original fraction.

- When you square a negative number, the result is a positive number.

- When you square 0 and 1, they stay the same.

STRATEGY 4: PICK NUMBERS

If a QC involves variables, try picking numbers to make the relationship clearer. Here's what you do:

- Pick numbers that are easy to work with.
- Plug in the numbers and calculate the values. Note the relationship between the columns.
- Pick another number for each variable and calculate the values again.

EXAMPLE

Column A	Column B

$$r > s > t > w > 0$$

$\frac{r}{t}$	$\frac{s}{w}$

Try $r = 4$, $s = 3$, $t = 2$, and $w = 1$. Then Column A $= \frac{r}{t} = \frac{4}{2} = 2$. And Column B $= \frac{s}{w} = \frac{3}{1} = 3$. So in this case Column B is greater than Column A.

Always Pick Another Number and Calculate Again

In the example above, we first found Column B was bigger. But that doesn't mean Column B is always bigger and that the answer is (B). It *does* mean the answer is not (A) or (C). But the answer could still be (D)—not enough information to decide.

If time is short, guess between (B) and (D). But whenever you can, pick another set of numbers and calculate again.

As best you can, make a special effort to find a second set of numbers that will alter the relationship. Here for example, try making r a lot larger. Pick $r = 30$ and keep the other variables as they were. Now Column A $= \frac{30}{2}$ = 15. This time, Column A is greater than Column B, so answer choice (D) is correct.

> **HINT:** *If the relationship between Columns A and B changes when you pick other numbers, (D) must be the answer.*

Pick Different Kinds of Numbers

Don't assume all variables represent positive integers. Unless you're told otherwise, variables can represent zero, negative numbers, or fractions. Since different kinds of numbers behave differently, always pick a different kind of number the second time around. In the example above, we plugged in a small positive number the first time and a larger number the second.

In the next three examples, we pick different numbers and get different results. Since we can't find constant relationships between Columns A and B, in all these cases the answer is (D).

DON'T OVER (D) IT

Choice (D) doesn't mean *you* can't determine which is greater—it means no one can.

If you frequently find (D) is your answer, double-check your work.

EXAMPLE

Column A	Column B
w	$-w$

If $w = 5$, Column A = 5 and Column B = −5, so Column A is greater.
If $w = -5$, Column A = −5 and Column B = 5, so Column B is greater.

Column A	Column B
	$x \neq 0$
x	$\frac{1}{x}$

If $x = 3$, Column A = 3 and Column B = $\frac{1}{3}$, so Column A is greater.

If $x = \frac{1}{3}$, Column A = $\frac{1}{3}$ and Column B = $\frac{1}{\frac{1}{3}}$ = 3, so Column B is greater.

Column A	Column B
x	x^2

If $x = \frac{1}{2}$, Column A = $\frac{1}{2}$ and Column B = $\frac{1}{4}$, so Column A is greater.

If $x = 2$, Column A = 2 and Column B = 4, so Column B is greater.

KAPLAN RULES

Remember:

Not all numbers are positive.

Not all numbers are integers.

STRATEGY 5: REDRAW THE DIAGRAM

- Redraw a diagram if the one that's given misleads you.
- Redraw scale diagrams to exaggerate crucial differences.

Some geometry diagrams may be misleading. Two angles or lengths may look equal as drawn in the diagram, but the given information tells you that there is a slight difference in their measures. The best strategy is to redraw the diagram so that their relationship can be clearly seen.

EXAMPLE

Column A   Column B

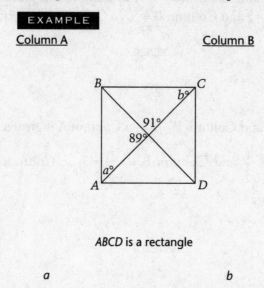

ABCD is a rectangle

a   b

Redraw this diagram to exaggerate the difference between the 89-degree angle and the 91-degree angle. In other words, make the larger angle much larger, and the smaller angle much smaller. The new rectangle that results is much wider than it is tall.

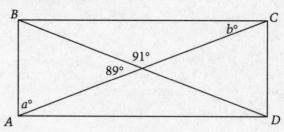

In the new diagram, where the crucial difference jumps out, *a* is clearly greater than *b*.

STRATEGY 6. AVOID QC TRAPS

To avoid QC traps, always be alert. Don't assume anything. Be especially cautious near the end of the question set.

Don't Be Tricked by Misleading Information

EXAMPLE

Column A   Column B

John is taller than Bob.

John's weight in pounds   Bob's weight in pounds

The test makers hope you think, "If John is taller, he must weigh more." But there's no guaranteed relationship between height and weight, so you don't have enough information. The answer is (D). Fortunately, problems like this are easy to spot if you stay alert.

Don't Assume

A common QC mistake is to assume that variables represent positive integers. As we saw in using the Picking Numbers strategy, fractions or negative numbers often show another relationship between the columns.

EXAMPLE

Column A   Column B

When 1 is added to the square of x the result is 37.

x 6

It is easy to assume that x must be 6, since the square of x is 36. That would make choice (C) correct. However, it is possible that $x = -6$. Since x could be either 6 or -6, the answer is (D).

HINT: *Be aware of negative numbers!*

Don't Forget to Consider Other Possibilities
The following question appears at the end of the QC section.

> **EXAMPLE**
>
> Column A   Column B
>
> $$\begin{array}{r} R \\ S \\ T \\ \hline 1\,W \end{array}$$
>
> In the addition problem above, R, S, and T are different digits that
> are multiples of 3, and W is a digit.
>
> W   8

Since you're told that R, S, and T are digits and different multiples of 3,
most people will think of 3, 6, and 9, which add up to 18. That makes W
equal to 8, and Columns A and B equal. But that's too obvious for a QC at
the end of the section.

There's another possibility. Zero is also a multiple of 3. So the three digits could be 0, 3, and 9, or 0, 6, and 9, which give totals of 12 and 15,
respectively. That means W could be 8, 2, or 5. Since the columns could be
equal, or Column B could be greater, answer choice (D) must be correct.

Don't Fall for Look-Alikes

> **EXAMPLE**
>
> Column A   Column B
>
> $\sqrt{5} + \sqrt{5}$ $\sqrt{10}$

At first glance, forgetting the rules of radicals, you might think these
quantities are equal and that the answer is (C). But use some common
sense to see this isn't the case. Each $\sqrt{5}$ in Column A is bigger than $\sqrt{4}$, so
Column A is more than 4. The $\sqrt{10}$ in Column B is less than another
familiar number, $\sqrt{16}$, so Column B is less than 4. The answer is (A).

Now use Kaplan's six strategies to solve nine typical QC questions. Then
check your work against our solutions.

TEST YOUR QC SMARTS

<u>Column A</u>   <u>Column B</u>

1. $x^2 + 2x - 2$ $x^2 + 2x - 1$

Ⓐ Ⓑ Ⓒ Ⓓ Ⓔ

$x = 2y$
$y > 0$

2. 4^{2y} 2^x

Ⓐ Ⓑ Ⓒ Ⓓ Ⓔ

$\dfrac{x}{y} = \dfrac{z}{4}$

x, y, and z are positive

3. $6x$ $2yz$

Ⓐ Ⓑ Ⓒ Ⓓ Ⓔ

---

q, r, and s are positive integers
$qrs > 12$

4. $\dfrac{qr}{5}$ $\dfrac{3}{s}$

Ⓐ Ⓑ Ⓒ Ⓓ Ⓔ

$x > 1$
$y > 0$

5. y^x $y^{(x+1)}$

Ⓐ Ⓑ Ⓒ Ⓓ Ⓔ

$7p + 3 = r$
$3p + 7 = s$

6. r s

Ⓐ Ⓑ Ⓒ Ⓓ Ⓔ

In triangle XYZ, the measure of angle X equals the measure of angle Y.

7. The degree measure   The degree measure
of angle Z of angle X plus the
                      degree measure of
                      angle Y

Ⓐ Ⓑ Ⓒ Ⓓ Ⓔ

$h > 1$

8. The number of $\dfrac{60}{h}$
minutes in h
hours

Ⓐ Ⓑ Ⓒ Ⓓ Ⓔ

Column A	Column B

Square A   Square B

Note: Figures not drawn to scale.

9. $\dfrac{\text{Perimeter of square } A}{\text{Perimeter of square } B}$ $\dfrac{\text{Length of } WY}{\text{Length of } PR}$

Ⓐ Ⓑ Ⓒ Ⓓ Ⓔ

ANSWERS TO QC TEST

1. (B)

Comparing the respective pieces of the two columns, the only difference is the third piece: -2 in Column A and -1 in Column B. We don't know the value of x, but whatever it is, x^2 in Column A must have the same value as x^2 in Column B, and $2x$ in Column A must have the same value as $2x$ in Column B. Since any quantity minus 2 must be less than that quantity minus 1, Column B is greater than Column A.

2. (A)

Replacing the x exponent in Column B with the equivalent value given in the problem, we're comparing 4^{2y} to 2^{2y}. Since y is greater than 0, raising 4 to the $2y$ power will result in a greater value than raising 2 to the $2y$ power.

3. (B)

Do the same thing to both columns until they resemble the centered information. When we divide both columns by $6y$ we get $\frac{6x}{6y}$, or $\frac{x}{y}$ in Column A, and $\frac{2yz}{6y}$, or $\frac{z}{3}$ in Column B. Since $\frac{x}{y} = \frac{z}{4}$, and $\frac{z}{3} > \frac{z}{4}$ (because z is positive), $\frac{z}{3} > \frac{x}{y}$.

4. (D)

Do the same thing to both columns to make them look like the centered information. When we multiply both columns by $5s$ we get qrs in Column A and 15 in Column B. Since qrs could be any integer greater than 12, it could be greater than, equal to, or less than 15.

5. (D)

Try $x = y = 2$. Then Column A $= y^x = 2^2 = 4$. Column B $= y^{x+1} = 2^3 = 8$, making Column B greater. But if $x = 2$ and $y = \frac{1}{2}$, Column A $= (\frac{1}{2})^2 = \frac{1}{4}$ and Column B $= (\frac{1}{2})^3 = \frac{1}{8}$. In this case, Column A is greater than Column B, so the answer is (D).

6. (D)

Pick a value for p, and see what effect this has on r and s. If $p = 1$, $r = (7 \times 1) + 3 = 10$, and $s = (3 \times 1) + 7 = 10$, and the two columns are equal. But if $p = 0$, $r = (7 \times 0) + 3 = 3$, and $s = (3 \times 0) + 7 = 7$, and Column A is smaller than Column B. Since there are at least two different possible relationships, the answer is choice (D).

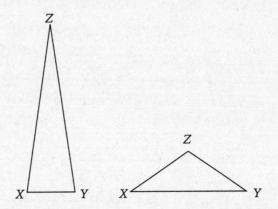

7. (D)

Since angle X = angle Y, this is an isosceles triangle. We can draw two diagrams with X and Y as the base angles of an isosceles triangle. In one diagram, make the triangle tall and narrow, so that angle X and angle Y are very large, and angle Z is very small. In this case, column B is greater. In the second diagram, make the triangle short and wide, so that angle Z is much larger than angle X and angle Y. In this case, Column A is greater. Since more than one relationship between the columns is possible, the correct answer is choice (D).

8. (A)

The "obvious" answer here is choice (C), because there are 60 minutes in an hour, and 60 appears in Column B. But the number of minutes in h hours would equal 60 times h, not 60 divided by h. Since h is greater than 1, the number in Column B will be less than the actual number of minutes in h hours, so Column A is greater. (A) is correct.

HIGHLIGHTS

- The four QC answer choices
- Never fill in answer choice (E) on your grid
- Know the two rules for answer choice (D)
- Compare, don't calculate
- Compare piece by piece
- Make one column look like the other
- Do the same thing to both columns
- Pick numbers
- Redraw the diagram
- Avoid QC traps

9. (C)

We don't know the exact relationship between Square *A* and Square *B*, but it doesn't matter. The problem is actually just comparing the ratios of corresponding parts of two squares. Whatever the relationship between them is for one specific length in both squares, the same relationship will exist between them for any other corresponding length. If a side of one square is twice the length of a side of the second square, the diagonal will also be twice as long. The ratio of the perimeters of the two squares is the same as the ratio of the sides. Therefore, the columns are equal. (C) is correct.

F·A·S·T P·R·E·P

👉 *Once you've mastered a section, check it off.*

Classic Problem-Solving Techniques
- ❏ Remainders
- ❏ Averages
- ❏ Ratios
- ❏ Rates
- ❏ Percents
- ❏ Combinations
- ❏ Simultaneous equations
- ❏ Symbolism
- ❏ Special triangles
- ❏ Multiple and oddball figures

PanicPlan

If you have a month or less to prep for the SAT, here's the best way to spend your time:

- In each of the 10 sections, try the sample problems.
- Review any section where you have trouble.

CHAPTER 13

CLASSIC PROBLEM-SOLVING TECHNIQUES

The test makers are not paid to be creative. In fact, there are certain types of problems that they like to use again and again on the SAT. This chapter gives you 10 of their favorite problem types, along with Kaplan's classic techniques for solving them.

REMAINDERS

Remainder questions can be easier than they look. You might think you have to solve for a certain value, but often you don't.

EXAMPLE

When n is divided by 7, the remainder is 4. What is the remainder when $2n$ is divided by 7?

(A) 0
(B) 1
(C) 2
(D) 3
(E) 4

The question above doesn't depend on knowing the value of n. In fact, n has an infinite number of possible values.

HINT: *Pick a number for n.*

Which number should you pick? Since the remainder when n is divided by 7 is 4, pick any multiple of 7 and add 4. The easiest multiple to work with is 7. So, $7 + 4 = 11$. Use 11 for n.

Plug 11 into the question and see what happens.

SIX THINGS MORE DIFFICULT THAN SAT MATH

1. Open-heart surgery
2. Dunking on Michael Jordan
3. Getting Dead tickets
4. Beating curfew without getting caught
5. Reading *Moby Dick* without falling asleep
6. Getting a date for the prom

What is the remainder when $2n$ is divided by 7?

$$2(11) \div 7 =$$

$$22 \div 7 =$$

$$\frac{22}{7} = 3 \text{ remainder } 1$$

The remainder is 1 when $n = 11$. So the answer is (B). The remainder will also be 1 when $n = 18, 25,$ or 46.

QC Remainders

Column A	Column B

When p is divided by 5 the remainder is 3.
When q is divided by 5 the remainder is 4.

p $\qquad\qquad\qquad\qquad\qquad$ q

The centered information tells you that p can be any of the integers 3, 8, 13, 18, 23,...; and that q can be any of the integers 4, 9, 14, 19, 24,....

So how do p and q compare? You can't tell; p could be small and q big, or the other way around. The answer is (D), not enough information to decide.

> **SPEED TIP**
>
> When picking a number for a remainder problem, add the remainder to the number you're dividing by.

Practice Problems: Remainders

1. When z is divided by 8, the remainder is 5. What is the remainder when $4z$ is divided by 8?

   (A) 1
   (B) 3
   (C) 4
   (D) 5
   (E) 7

   Ⓐ Ⓑ Ⓒ Ⓓ Ⓔ

Column A   Column B

   When x is divided by 6 the remainder is 3.
   When y is divided by 6 the remainder is 4.

2. x y Ⓐ Ⓑ Ⓒ Ⓓ Ⓔ

   When m is divided by 5 the remainder is 2.
   When n is divided by 5 the remainder is 1.

3. The remainder   The remainder when
    when $m + n$ is mn is divided by 5
    divided by 5   Ⓐ Ⓑ Ⓒ Ⓓ Ⓔ

Answers to Remainder Problems

1. (C)

Let $z = 13$ and plug in $4z = 4(13) = 52$, which leaves a remainder of 4 when divided by 8.

2. (D)

We determine that x can be any of the integers 3, 9, 15, 21,..., and y can be any of the integers 4, 10, 16, 22,.... Since x could be greater than or less than y, the correct answer must be choice (D).

3. (A)

The variable m can be any integer that ends in either a 2 or a 7; n can be any integer that ends in either a 1 or a 6. Plugging in will show that in any case, $m + n$ will leave a remainder of 3 when divided by 5, and mn will leave a remainder of 2 when divided by 5, so Column A is greater.

AVERAGES

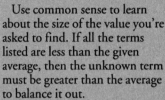

EXAMPLE

The average weight of five dogs in a certain kennel is 32 pounds. If four of the dogs weigh 25, 27, 19, and 35 pounds, what is the weight of the fifth dog?

(A) 28
(B) 32
(C) 49
(D) 54
(E) 69

> ### USE YOUR HEAD
>
> Use common sense to learn about the size of the value you're asked to find. If all the terms listed are less than the given average, then the unknown term must be greater than the average to balance it out.
> Likewise, if adding a new value, x, to a group of numbers raises the average value of the group, then x must be greater than the average of the original numbers.

Instead of giving you a list of values to plug into the average formula, SAT average questions often put a slight spin on the problem. They tell you the average of a group of terms and ask you to find the value of the missing term.

HINT: Work with the sum.

Let x = the weight of the fifth dog. Plug this into the average formula:

$$32 = \frac{25 + 27 + 19 + 35 + x}{5}$$

$$32 \times 5 = 25 + 27 + 19 + 35 + x$$

So the average weight of the dogs, times the number of dogs, equals the total weight of the dogs, or, mathematically:

$$\text{Average} \times \text{Number of Terms} = \text{Sum of Terms}$$

Remember this manipulation of the average formula so that whenever you know the average of a group of terms and the number of terms, you can find the total sum.

Now you can solve for the weight of the fifth dog:

$$32 \times 5 = 25 + 27 + 19 + 35 + x$$
$$160 = 106 + x$$
$$54 = x$$

So the weight of the fifth dog is 54 pounds, choice (D).

> ### CALCULATOR FUN
>
> This is a good time to use your calculator. Enjoy yourself.

Practice Problems: Averages

REGULAR MATH

1. The average (arithmetic mean) of six numbers is 16. If five of the numbers are 15, 37, 16, 9, and 23, what is the sixth number?
   (A) −20
   (B) − 4
   (C)   0
   (D)   6
   (E) 16

   (A) (B) (C) (D) (E)

2. Bart needs to buy five gifts with $80. If two of the gifts cost a total of $35, what is the average (arithmetic mean) amount Bart can spend on each of the remaining three gifts?
   (A) $45
   (B) $17
   (C) $16
   (D) $15
   (E) $10

   (A) (B) (C) (D) (E)

3. The average (arithmetic mean) of five numbers is 8. If the average of two of these numbers is −6, what is the sum of the other three numbers?
   (A) 28
   (B) 34
   (C) 46
   (D) 52
   (E) 60

   (A) (B) (C) (D) (E)

Answers to Averages Practice Problems

1. (B)

Average $\times$ Number of Terms = Sum of Terms

$16 \times 6 = 15 + 37 + 16 + 9 + 23 + x$

$96 = 100 + x$

$-4 = x$

2. (D)

Bart has $80 and spent $35 on two gifts; therefore he has $45 left to spend on the remaining three. So,

$x = \dfrac{\$45}{3}$

$x = \$15$

3. (D)

Average $\times$ Number of Terms = Sum of Terms

The sum of all five numbers is

$$8 \times 5 = 40$$

The sum of two of these numbers is

$$(-6) \times 2 = -12$$

So, the difference of these two sums, $40 - (-12) = 52$, is the sum of the other numbers.

RATIOS

EXAMPLE

Out of every 50 chips produced in a certain factory, 20 are defective. What is the ratio of nondefective chips produced to defective chips produced?

(A) 2:5

(B) 3:5

(C) 2:3

(D) 3:2

(E) 5:2

HINT: Identify the parts and the whole in the problem.

Find the parts and the whole in the problem. In this case the total number of chips is the whole, and the number of nondefective chips and the number of defective chips are the parts that make up this whole.

You're given a part-to-whole ratio—the ratio of defective chips to all chips, and asked to find a part-to-part ratio—the ratio of nondefective chips to defective chips.

If 20 chips out of every 50 are defective, the remaining 30 chips must be nondefective. So the part-to-part ratio of nondefective to defective chips is 30/20, or 3/2, which is equivalent to 3:2—answer choice (D).

If you hadn't identified the part and the whole first it would be easy to get confused and compare a part to the whole, like the ratios in answer choices (A) and (B).

This approach also works for ratio questions that ask you to find actual quantities. For example:

Out of every five chips produced in a certain factory, two are defective. If 2,200 chips were produced, how many were defective?

Here you need to find a quantity—the number of defective chips.

HINT: If you're looking for the actual quantities in a ratio, set up and solve a proportion.

You're given a part-to-whole ratio (the ratio of defective chips to all chips), and the total number of chips produced. You can find the answer by setting up and solving a proportion.

TRAIN YOUR BRAIN

Use common sense to check your math on this example to the right. Most of the chips are nondefective, so the ratio must be greater than 1. If you reversed the terms and thought (C) was the answer, that would tell you that you did something wrong.

$$\frac{\text{Number of defective chips}}{\text{Total number of chips}} = \frac{2}{5} = \frac{x}{2,200}$$

x = Number of defective chips

$5x = 4,400$

$x = 880$

HINT: *Remember that ratios compare only relative size—they don't tell you the actual quantities involved.*

KAPLAN RULES

When you look at a ratio, make sure you know if you're dealing with *parts* to *parts* or *parts* to *whole*.

You also need to see if the parts that you're given add up to the whole. For example, the number of male and female students in a classroom must add up to the whole. The number of students with blond hair and the number of students with brown hair are parts, but do not necessarily add up to the whole.

Practice Problems: Ratios

1. The ratio of right-handed pitchers to left-handed pitchers in a certain baseball league is 11:7. What fractional part of the pitchers in the league are left-handed?

(A) $\frac{6}{7}$

(B) $\frac{6}{11}$

(C) $\frac{7}{11}$

(D) $\frac{7}{18}$

(E) $\frac{11}{18}$

Ⓐ Ⓑ Ⓒ Ⓓ Ⓔ

2. In a group of 24 people who are either homeowners or renters, the ratio of homeowners to renters is 5:3. How many homeowners are in the group?

(A) 15
(B) 14
(C) 12
(D) 9
(E) 8

Ⓐ Ⓑ Ⓒ Ⓓ Ⓔ

3. Magazine A has a total of 28 pages, 16 of which are advertisements and 12 of which are articles. Magazine B has a total of 35 pages, all of them either advertisements or articles. If the ratio of the number of pages of advertisements to the number of pages of articles is the same for both magazines, then Magazine B has how many more pages of advertisements than Magazine A?

(A) 2
(B) 3
(C) 4
(D) 5
(E) 6

Ⓐ Ⓑ Ⓒ Ⓓ Ⓔ

Answers to Ratios Problems

1. (D)

The parts are the number of right-handed (11) and the number of left-handed pitchers (7). The whole is the total number of pitchers (right-handed + left-handed), which is 11 + 7, or 18. So:

$$\frac{\text{part}}{\text{whole}} = \frac{\text{left-handed}}{\text{total}} = \frac{7}{11 + 7} = \frac{7}{18}.$$

2. (A)

The parts are the number of homeowners (5) and the number of renters (3). The whole is the total (homeowners + renters). So:

$$\frac{\text{part}}{\text{whole}} = \frac{\text{homeowners}}{\text{homeowners + renters}} = \frac{5}{5 + 3} = \frac{5}{8}.$$

TIME TROUBLE?

Use logic to narrow your choices. Most are homeowners, so the answer must be more than half of 24, or 12. Either (A) or (B) is the right answer.

Since we are trying to find an actual quantity, set up a proportion.

$$\frac{\text{Homeowners}}{\text{Total people}} = \frac{5}{8} = \frac{x}{24}$$
$$8x = 120$$
$$x = 15$$

3. (C)

The $\frac{\text{part}}{\text{whole}}$ ratio of advertisements (16) to total pages (28) in Magazine A is $\frac{16}{28}$, or $\frac{4}{7}$. Magazine B has the same ratio, so if there are 35 pages in Magazine B, $\frac{4}{7} \times 35$—or 20 pages—are advertisements. Therefore, there are four more pages of advertisements in Magazine B than in Magazine A.

RATES

EXAMPLE

If eight oranges cost a dollars, b oranges would cost how many dollars?

(A) $8ab$

(B) $\frac{8a}{b}$

(C) $\frac{8}{ab}$

(D) $\frac{a}{8b}$

(E) $\frac{ab}{8}$

A rate is a ratio that compares quantities that are measured in different units. In the problem above the units are oranges and dollars.

What makes the rate problem above difficult is the presence of variables. It's hard to get a clear picture of the relationship between the units.

> **HINT:** *Pick numbers for the variables to make the relationship between the units clearer.*

Pick numbers for a and b that are easy to work with in the problem.

Let $a = 16$. Then eight oranges cost \$16.00. So the cost per orange at this rate is $\frac{16 \text{ dollars}}{8 \text{ oranges}} = \$2$ per orange. Let $b = 5$. So the cost of five oranges at this rate is five oranges $\times$ \$2.00 per orange = \$10.00.

Now plug in $a = 16$ and $b = 5$ into the answer choices to see which one gives you a value of 10.

Choice (A): $8 \times 16 \times 5 = 640$. Eliminate.

Choice (B): $\frac{8 \times 16}{5} = \frac{128}{5}$. Eliminate.

Choice (C): $\frac{8}{16 \times 5} = \frac{1}{10}$. Eliminate.

Choice (D): $\frac{16}{8 \times 5} = \frac{2}{5}$. Eliminate.

Choice (E): $\frac{16 \times 5}{8} = 10$.

Since (E) is the only one that gives the correct value, it is correct.

Practice Problems: Rates

REGULAR MATH

1. If David paints at the rate of h houses per day, how many houses does he paint in d days, in terms of h and d?

   (A) $\dfrac{h}{d}$

   (B) hd

   (C) $h + \dfrac{d}{2}$

   (D) $h - d$

   (E) $\dfrac{d}{h}$

2. Bill has to type a paper that is p pages long, with each page containing w words. If Bill types an average of x words per minute, how many hours will it take him to finish the paper?

   (A) $60wpx$

   (B) $\dfrac{wx}{60p}$

   (C) $\dfrac{60wp}{x}$

   (D) $\dfrac{wpx}{60}$

   (E) $\dfrac{wp}{60x}$

   Ⓐ Ⓑ Ⓒ Ⓓ Ⓔ

3. If Seymour drove 120 miles in x hours at constant speed, how many miles did he travel in the first 20 minutes of his trip?

   (A) $60x$

   (B) $3x$

   (C) $\dfrac{120}{x}$

   (D) $\dfrac{40}{x}$

   (E) $\dfrac{6}{x}$

   Ⓐ Ⓑ Ⓒ Ⓓ Ⓔ

Answers to Rates Problems

1. (B)

Pick numbers for h and d. Let $h = 2$ and $d = 3$; that is, suppose he paints two houses per day and he paints for three days, so in three days he can paint six houses. You multiply the rate (h) by the number of days (d). The only answer choice that equals 6 when $h = 2$ and $d = 3$ is choice (B).

2. (E)

Pick numbers for p, w, and x that work well in the problem. Let $p = 3$ and let $w = 100$. So there are three pages with 100 words per page, or 300 words total. Say he types five words a minute, so $x = 5$. So he types 5×60, or 300 words an hour. Therefore, it takes him one hour to type the paper. The only answer choice that equals 1 when $p = 3$, $w = 100$, and $x = 5$ is choice (E).

3. (D)

Let $x = 4$. That means that he drove 120 miles in four hours, so his speed was $\frac{120 \text{ miles}}{4 \text{ hours}}$, or 30 miles per hour. Since 20 minutes $= \frac{1}{3}$ of an hour, the distance he traveled in the first 20 minutes is $\frac{1}{3}$ hours $\times$ 30 miles per hour $= 10$ miles. The only answer choice that equals 10 when $x = 4$ is choice (D).

PERCENTS

Last year Julie's annual salary was $20,000. This year's raise brings her to an annual salary of $25,000. If she gets the same percent raise every year, what will her salary be next year?

(A) $27,500

(B) $30,000

(C) $31,250

(D) $32,500

(E) $35,000

KNOW YOUR PERCENTS

When you need to, you can figure out a percent equivalent on your calculator by dividing the numerator by the denominator. You'll save time by knowing some common percent equivalents.

$$\frac{1}{5} = 20\%$$

$$\frac{1}{4} = 25\%$$

$$\frac{1}{3} = 33\frac{1}{3}\%$$

$$\frac{1}{2} = 50\%$$

$$\frac{2}{3} = 66\frac{2}{3}\%$$

$$\frac{3}{4} = 75\%$$

In percent problems, you're usually given two pieces of information and asked to find the third. When you see a percent problem, remember:

• If you are solving for a percent:

$$\text{Percent} = \frac{\text{Part}}{\text{Whole}}$$

• If you need to solve for a part:

$$\text{Percent} \times \text{Whole} = \text{Part}$$

This problem asks for Julie's projected salary for next year—that is, her current salary plus her next raise.

You know last year's salary ($20,000) and you know this year's salary ($25,000), so you can find the difference between the two salaries:

$$\$25,000 - \$20,000 = \$5,000 = \text{her raise}$$

Now find the percent of her raise, by using the formula

$$\text{Percent} = \frac{\text{Part}}{\text{Whole}}$$

Since Julie's raise was calculated on last year's salary, divide by $20,000.

HINT: *Be sure you know which Whole to plug in. Here you're looking for a percent of $20,000, not $25,000.*

$$\text{Percent raise} = \frac{\$5,000}{\$20,000} = \frac{1}{4} = 25\%$$

You know she will get the same percent raise next year, so solve for the part. Use the formula Percent × Whole = Part. Her raise next year will be

$$25\% \times \$25,000 = \frac{1}{4} \times 25,000 = \$6,250$$

MIRROR IMAGE

x percent of y = y percent of x

20% of 50 = 50% of 20

$$\frac{1}{5} \times 50 = \frac{1}{2} \times 20$$

$$10 = 10$$

Add that sum to this year's salary and you have her projected salary: $25,000 + $6,250 = $31,250, or answer choice (C).

Make sure that you change the percent to either a fraction or a decimal before beginning calculations.

Practice Problems: Percents

QC

Column A	Column B
1. 5% of 3% of 45	6.75

Ⓐ Ⓑ Ⓒ Ⓓ Ⓔ

GRID-IN

2. Eighty-five percent of the members of a student organization registered to attend a certain field trip. If 16 of the members who registered were unable to attend, resulting in only 65 percent of the members making the trip, how many members are in the organization?

REGULAR MATH

3. If a sweater sells for $48 after a 25 percent markdown, what was its original price?
   (A) $56
   (B) $60
   (C) $64
   (D) $68
   (E) $72

Ⓐ Ⓑ Ⓒ Ⓓ Ⓔ

Answers to Percent Problems

1. (B)

Percent $\times$ Whole = Part. Five percent of (3 percent of 45) = .05 $\times$ (.03 $\times$ 45) = .05 $\times$ 1.35 = .0675, which is less than 6.75 in Column B.

2. (80)

You need to solve for the Whole, so identify the Part and the Percent. If 85 percent planned to attend and only 65 percent did, 20 percent failed to attend, and you know that 16 students failed to attend.

$$\text{Percent} \times \text{Whole} = \text{Part}$$
$$\frac{20}{100} \times \text{Whole} = 16$$
$$\text{Whole} = 16 \times \frac{100}{20}$$
$$\text{Whole} = 80$$

3. (C)

We want to solve for the original price, the Whole. The percent markdown is 25 percent, so $48 is 75 percent of the whole.

$$\text{Percent} \times \text{Whole} = \text{Part}$$
$$75 \text{ percent} \times \text{Original Price} = \$48$$
$$\text{Original Price} = \frac{\$48}{0.75} = \$64$$

COMBINATIONS

EXAMPLE

If Alice, Betty, and Carlos sit in three adjacent empty seats in a movie house, how many different seating arrangements are possible?

(A) 3
(B) 4
(C) 5
(D) 6
(E) 8

Combination problems ask you to find the different possibilities that can occur in a given situation.

HINT: Simply count the number of possibilities by listing them in a quick but systematic way.

To solve this problem, let the first letter of each name stand for that person. First, find all the combinations with Alice in the first seat:

ABC
ACB

Using the same system, try Betty in the first seat, and then Carlos:

BAC
BCA
CAB
CBA

At this point we've exhausted every possibility. So there are six possible arrangements, and that's answer choice (D).

Some problems set up conditions that limit the possibilities somewhat. Some may ask for the number of distinct possibilities, meaning that if the same combination shows up twice in different forms, you should count it only once. Consider the following problem.

WARNING

Don't use complex formulas to solve combinations problems. SAT combinations questions are simple enough that you can write down the possibilities and count them.

EXAMPLE

Set I: {2, 3, 4, 5}
Set II: {1, 2, 3}

If x is a number generated by multiplying a number from Set I by a number from Set II, how many possible values of x are greater than 5?
(A) 3
(B) 4
(C) 5
(D) 6
(E) 7

Again, list the possibilities in a systematic way, pairing off each number in the first set with each number in the second set, so every combination is included:

$2 \times 1 = 2$ $4 \times 1 = 4$
$2 \times 2 = 4$ $4 \times 2 = 8$
$2 \times 3 = 6$ $4 \times 3 = 12$
$3 \times 1 = 3$ $5 \times 1 = 5$
$3 \times 2 = 6$ $5 \times 2 = 10$
$3 \times 3 = 9$ $5 \times 3 = 15$

How many of these values are greater than 5? Going down the list: 6, 6, 9, 8, 12, 10, and 15. Although there are seven answers for x that are greater than 5, two of them are the same. So there are six different values of x greater than 5, not seven. The answer is (D).

HINT: *Always write down the possibilities as you organize them, so you can count them accurately, and so you don't count the same combination twice.*

Practice Problems: Combinations

REGULAR MATH

1. A three-digit code is made up of three different digits from the set {2,4,6,8}. If 2 is always the first digit in the code, how many three-digit codes can be formed?

    (A) 16
    (B) 12
    (C) 10
    (D) 8
    (E) 6

    Ⓐ Ⓑ Ⓒ Ⓓ Ⓔ

QC

Column A   Column B

Five people attend a meeting. Each person shakes hands once with every other person at the meeting.

2. The total number   15
   of handshakes that
   take place

    Ⓐ Ⓑ Ⓒ Ⓓ Ⓔ

REGULAR MATH

3. Three people stop for lunch at a hot dog stand. If each person orders one item and there are three items to choose from, how many different combinations of food could be purchased? (Assume that order doesn't matter; e.g., a hot dog and two sodas are considered the same as two sodas and a hot dog.)

    (A) 6
    (B) 9
    (C) 10
    (D) 18
    (E) 27

    Ⓐ Ⓑ Ⓒ Ⓓ Ⓔ

Answers to Combinations Problems

1. (E)

Every code starts with 2, so the last two digits determine the number of possibilities. The last two digits could be: 46, 48, 64, 68, 84, and 86. That makes six combinations that fit the conditions.

2. (B)

Be careful not to count each handshake twice. Call the five people *A, B, C, D,* and *E*. We can pair them off like this:

A with *B, C, D,* and *E* (four handshakes)

B with *C, D,* and *E* (three more—note that we leave out *A*, since the handshake between *A* and *B* is already counted)

C with *D* and *E* (two more)

D with *E* (one more)

The total is 4 + 3 + 2 + 1, or 10 handshakes.

3. (C)

To find the number, let's call the three items they can purchase *A, B,* and *C*. The possibilities:

All three order the same thing: *AAA, BBB, CCC*

Two order the same thing: *AAB, AAC, BBA, BBC, CCA, CCB*

All three order something different: *ABC*

So there are 10 different ways the three items could be ordered.

SIMULTANEOUS EQUATIONS

EXAMPLE

If $p + 2q = 14$ and $3p + q = 12$, then $p =$

(A) -2

(B) -1

(C) 1

(D) 2

(E) 3

In order to get a numerical value for each variable, you need as many different equations as there are variables to solve for. So, if you have two variables, you need two independent equations.

You could tackle this problem by solving for one variable in terms of the other, and then plugging this expression into the other equation. But the simultaneous equations that appear on the SAT can usually be handled in an easier way.

> **HINT:** *Combine the equations—by adding or subtracting them—to cancel out all but one of the variables.*

You can't eliminate p or q by adding or subtracting the equations in their present form. But if you multiply the second equation by 2:

$$2(3p + q) = 2(12)$$
$$6p + 2q = 24$$

Now when you subtract the first equation from the second, the qs will cancel out so you can solve for p:

$$6p + 2q = 24$$
$$-[p + 2q = 14]$$
$$\overline{}$$
$$5p + 0 = 10$$

If $5p = 10$, $p = 2$.

REMEMBER

When subtracting one equation from another, be sure to distribute the minus sign to each term. In the example to the left,

$$-p - 2q = -14$$

RULE OF THUMB

Simultaneous equations on the SAT are almost always easy to combine.

Practice Problems: Simultaneous Equations

REGULAR MATH

1. If $x + y = 8$ and $y - x = -2$, then $y =$
   (A)   −2
   (B)   3
   (C)   5
   (D)   8
   (E)   10

Ⓐ Ⓑ Ⓒ Ⓓ Ⓔ

GRID-IN

2. If $4a + 3b = 19$ and $a + 2b = 6$, then $a + b =$

REGULAR MATH

3. If $m - n = 5$ and $2m + 3n = 15$, then $m + n =$
   (A)   1
   (B)   6
   (C)   7
   (D)   10
   (E)   15

Ⓐ Ⓑ Ⓒ Ⓓ Ⓔ

Answers to Simultaneous Equations Problems

1. (B)
When you add the two equations, the xs cancel out and you find that $2y = 6$, so $y = 3$.

2. (5)
Adding the two equations, you find that $5a + 5b = 25$. Dividing by 5 shows that $a + b = 5$.

3. (C)
Multiply the first equation by 2, then subtract the first equation from the second to eliminate the ms and find that $5n = 5$, or $n = 1$:

$$2m + 3n = 15$$
$$\underline{-2m + 2n = -10}$$
$$5n = 5$$
$$n = 1$$

Plugging this value for n into the first equation shows that $m = 6$:

$$m - n = 5$$
$$m - 1 = 5$$
$$m = 6$$

So $m + n = 7$:

$$m + n = 6 + 1 = 7$$

Choice (C) is correct.

KAPLAN RULES

Intimidated by symbols? The test makers put symbolism on the SAT to test your ability to think. Once you get over your fear of seeing something completely unknown, you'll realize the math is usually quite easy.

SYMBOLISM

You should be quite familiar with the arithmetic symbols $+$, $-$, $\times$, $\div$, and %. Finding the value of $10 + 2$, $18 - 4$, 4×9, or $96 \div 16$ is easy.

However, on the SAT, you may come across bizarre symbols. You may even be asked to find the value of $10 \star 2$, $5 \circledast 7$, $10 \circledast 6$, or $65 \heartsuit 2$.

The SAT test makers put strange symbols in questions to confuse or unnerve you. Don't let them. The question stem always tells you what the strange symbol means. Although this type of question may look difficult, it is really an exercise in plugging in. Look at the following example:

> **EXAMPLE**
>
> If $a \star b = \sqrt{a+b}$ for all nonnegative numbers, what is the value of $10 \star 6$?
> (A) 0
> (B) 2
> (C) 4
> (D) 8
> (E) 16

To solve, just plug in 10 for a and 6 for b into the expression $\sqrt{a+b}$. That equals $\sqrt{10+6}$ or $\sqrt{16}$ or 4, choice (C).

How about a more involved symbolism question?

> **EXAMPLE**
>
> If $a \blacktriangle$ means to multiply a by 3 and $a \circledast$ means to divide a by -2, what is the value of $((8 \circledast)\blacktriangle) \circledast$?
> (A) −6
> (B) 0
> (C) 2
> (D) 3
> (E) 6

HINT: When a symbolism problem includes parentheses, do the operations inside the parentheses first.

First find $8 \circledast$. This means to divide 8 by -2, which is -4. Working out to the next set of parentheses, we have $(-4)\blacktriangle$, which means to multiply -4 by 3, which is -12. Lastly, we find $(-12) \circledast$, which means to divide -12 by -2, which is 6, choice E.

HINT: When two or three questions include the same symbol, expect the last question to be the most difficult, and be extra careful.

Practice Problems: Symbolism

Column A   Column B

If $x \neq 0$, let $\spadesuit\, x$ be defined by $\spadesuit\, x = x - \dfrac{1}{x}$

1.   −3 $\spadesuit -3$

ⒶⒷⒸⒹⒺ

REGULAR MATH

2. If $r \heartsuit s = r(r - s)$ for all integers r and s, then $4 \heartsuit (3 \heartsuit 5)$ equals

(A)   −8

(B)   −2

(C)   2

(D)   20

(E)   40

ⒶⒷⒸⒹⒺ

Questions 3 – 4 refer to the following definition:
$$c \star d = \frac{(c - d)}{c}, \text{ where } c \neq 0.$$

3. $12 \star 3 =$

(A) −3

(B) $\dfrac{1}{4}$

(C) $\dfrac{2}{3}$

(D) $\dfrac{3}{4}$

(E) 3

ⒶⒷⒸⒹⒺ

---

4. If $9 \star 4 = 15 \star k$, then $k =$

(A) 3

(B) 6

(C) $\dfrac{20}{3}$

(D) $\dfrac{25}{3}$

(E) 9

ⒶⒷⒸⒹⒺ

Answers to Symbolism Problems

1. (B)

Plug in −3 for x: ♠ $x = -3 - \dfrac{1}{-3} = -3 + \dfrac{1}{3} = -2\dfrac{2}{3}$, which is greater than −3 in Column A.

2. (E)

Start in the parentheses and work out: $(3 ♥ 5) = 3(3 - 5) = 3(-2) = -6$; $4 ♥ (-6) = 4[4 - (-6)] = 4(10) = 40$.

3. (D)

Plug in 12 for c and 3 for d: $\dfrac{12 - 3}{12} = \dfrac{9}{12} = \dfrac{3}{4}$.

4. (C)

Plug in on both sides of the equation:

$$\frac{9 - 4}{9} = \frac{15 - k}{15}$$
$$\frac{5}{9} = \frac{15 - k}{15}$$

Cross-multiply and solve for k:

$$75 = 135 - 9k$$
$$-60 = -9k$$
$$\frac{-60}{-9} = k$$
$$\frac{20}{3} = k$$

SPECIAL TRIANGLES

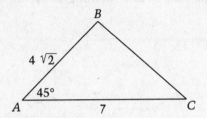

Note: Figure not drawn to scale.

EXAMPLE

In the triangle above, what is the length of side *BC?*
(A) 4
(B) 5
(C) $4\sqrt{2}$
(D) 6
(E) $5\sqrt{2}$

HINT: *Look for the special triangles in geometry problems.*

Special triangles contain a lot of information. For instance, if you know the length of one side of a 30–60–90 triangle, you can easily work out the lengths of the others. Special triangles allow you to transfer one piece of information around the whole figure.

The following are the special triangles you should look for on the SAT.

Equilateral Triangles
All interior angles are 60° and all sides are of the same length.

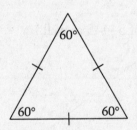

Isosceles Triangles

Two sides are of the same length and the angles facing these sides are equal.

Right Triangles

Contain a 90° angle. The sides are related by the Pythagorean theorem. $a^2 + b^2 = c^2$ where a and b are the legs and c is the hypotenuse.

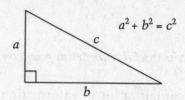

The "Special" Right Triangles

Many triangle problems contain "special" right triangles, whose side lengths always come in predictable ratios. If you recognize them, you won't have to use the Pythagorean theorem to find the value of a missing side length.

The 3–4–5 Right Triangle

(Be on the lookout for multiples of 3–4–5 as well.)

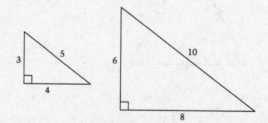

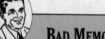

BAD MEMORY?

If you forget the triangle ratios, you can find a description of the isosceles right triangle and 30–60–90 triangle in the information box at the start of every Math section on the SAT.

The Isosceles Right Triangle
(Note the side ratio—$1:1:\sqrt{2}$.)

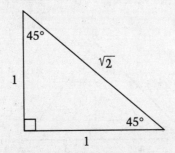

The 30–60–90 Right Triangle
(Note the side ratio—$1:\sqrt{3}:2$, and which side is opposite which angle.)

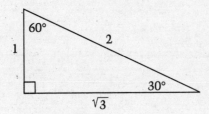

Getting back to our example, you can drop a vertical line from B to line AC. This divides the triangle into two right triangles.

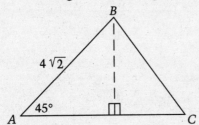

That means you know two of the angles in the triangle on the left: 90° and 45°. So this is an isosceles right triangle, with sides in the ratio of $1:1:\sqrt{2}$. The hypotenuse here is $4\sqrt{2}$, so both legs have length 4. Filling this in, you have:

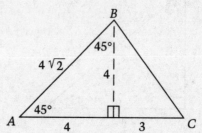

Now you can see that the legs of the smaller triangle on the right must be 4 and 3, making this a 3–4–5 right triangle, and the length of hypotenuse *BC* is 5.

Practice Problems: Special Triangles

REGULAR MATH

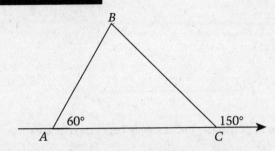

Note: Figure not drawn to scale.

1. In triangle ABC above, if $AB = 4$, then $AC =$

 (A) 10
 (B) 9
 (C) 8
 (D) 7
 (E) 6

 Ⓐ Ⓑ Ⓒ Ⓓ Ⓔ

QC

Column A  Column B

In the coordinate plane, point R has coordinates (0,0) and point S has coordinates (9,12).

2. The distance from   16
 R to S

 Ⓐ Ⓑ Ⓒ Ⓓ Ⓔ

REGULAR MATH

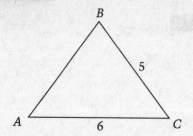

3. If the perimeter of triangle *ABC* above is 16, what is its area?

(A)   8
(B)   9
(C)   10
(D)   12
(E)   15

Answers to Special Triangles Problems

1. (C)

Angle *BCA* is supplementary to the angle marked 150°, so angle *BCA* = 180° − 150° = 30°. Since the sum of interior angles of a triangle is 180°, angle *A* + angle *B* + angle *BCA* = 180°, so angle *B* = 180° − 60° − 30° = 90°. So triangle *ABC* is a 30–60–90 right triangle, and its sides are in the ratio 1: $\sqrt{3}$: 2. The side opposite the 30°, *AB*, which we know has length 4, must be half the length of the hypotenuse, *AC*. Therefore *AC* = 8, and that's answer choice (C).

2. (B)

Draw a diagram. Since *RS* isn't parallel to either axis, the way to compute its length is to create a right triangle with legs that are parallel to the axes, so their lengths are easy to find. If the triangle formed is not a special triangle, we can then use the Pythagorean theorem to find the length of *RS*.

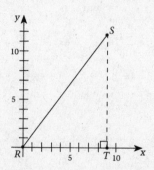

Since *S* has a *y*-coordinate of 12, it's 12 units above the *x*-axis, so the length of *ST* must be 12. And since *T* is the same number of units to the right of the *y*-axis as *S*, given by the *x*-coordinate of 9, the distance from the origin to *T* must be 9. So we have a right triangle with legs of 9 and 12. You should recognize this as a multiple of the 3–4–5 triangle. $9 = 3 \times 3$; $12 = 3 \times 4$; so the hypotenuse *RS* must be 3×5, or 15. That's the value of Column A, so Column B is greater.

3. (D)
To find the area you need to know the base and height. If the perimeter is 16, then $AB + BC + AC = 16$; that is, $AB = 16 - 5 - 6 = 5$. Since $AB = BC$, this is an isosceles triangle. If you drop a line from vertex *B* to *AC*, it will divide the base in half. This divides the triangle up into two smaller right triangles:

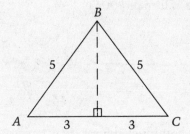

These right triangles each have one leg of 3 and a hypotenuse of 5; therefore they are 3–4–5 right triangles. So the missing leg (which is also the height of triangle *ABC*) must have length 4. We now know that the base of *ABC* is 6 and the height is 4, so the area is $\frac{1}{2} \times 6 \times 4$, or 12, answer choice (D).

MULTIPLE AND ODDBALL FIGURES

**BREAKING UP
IS EASY**

When you see a shape that isn't a triangle, rectangle, or circle try breaking it into familiar figures.

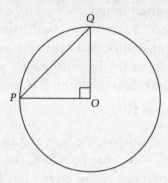

EXAMPLE

In the figure above, if the area of the circle with center O is 9π, what is the area of triangle POQ?

(A) 4.5

(B) 6

(C) 9

(D) 3.5π

(E) 4.5π

In a problem that combines figures, you have to look for the relationship between the figures.

HINT: _Look for pieces the figures have in common._

For instance, if two figures share a side, information about that side will probably be the key.

In this case the figures don't share a side, but the triangle's legs are important features of the circle—they are radii. You can see that $PO = OQ =$ the radius of circle O.

The area of the circle is 9π. The area of a circle is πr^2, where $r =$ the radius. So $9\pi = \pi r^2$, $9 = r^2$, and the radius $= 3$. The area of a triangle is $\frac{1}{2}$ base times height. Therefore, the area of ΔPOQ is $\frac{1}{2}$ (leg$_1$ $\times$ leg$_2$) $= \frac{1}{2}$ $(3 \times 3) = \frac{9}{2} = 4.5$, answer choice (A).

But what if, instead of a number of familiar shapes, you are given something like this?

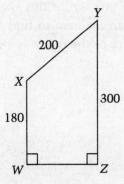

What is the perimeter of quadrilateral *WXYZ*?

(A)   680
(B)   760
(C)   840
(D)   920
(E) 1,000

Try breaking the unfamiliar shape into familiar ones. Once this is done, you can use the same techniques that you would for multiple figures. Perimeter is the sum of the lengths of the sides of a figure, so you need to find the length of *WZ*. Drawing a perpendicular line from point *X* to side *YZ* will divide the figure into a right triangle and a rectangle. Call the point of intersection *A*.

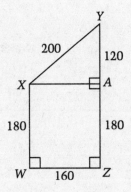

RULE OF THUMB

Multiple figures are almost always made up of either several familiar shapes put together, or one familiar shape with a recognizable piece shaded or cut out of it.

Opposite sides of a rectangle have equal length, so *WZ* = *XA* and *WX* = *ZA*. *WX* is labeled as 180, so *ZA* = 180. Since *YZ* measures 300, *AY* is 300 − 180 = 120. In right triangle *XYA*, hypotenuse *XY* = 200 and

YOU CAN LOOK IT UP

A list of the 100 Math Principles you need to know can be found in Appendix B, SAT Math in a Nutshell. Review it to see what areas you might need to brush up on.

leg AY = 120; you should recognize this as a multiple of a 3-4-5 right triangle. The hypotenuse is 5 × 40, one leg is 3 × 40, so XA must be 4 × 40 or 160. (If you didn't recognize this special right triangle you could have used the Pythagorean theorem to find the length of XA.) Since WZ = XA = 160, the perimeter of the figure is 180 + 200 + 300 + 160 = 840, answer choice (C).

Practice Problems: Multiple and Oddball Figures

REGULAR MATH

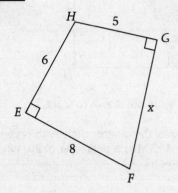

1. What is the value of *x* in the figure above?

    (A)   4
    (B) $3\sqrt{3}$
    (C) $3\sqrt{5}$
    (D) $5\sqrt{3}$
    (E)   9

    Ⓐ Ⓑ Ⓒ Ⓓ Ⓔ

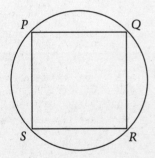

2. In the figure above, square *PQRS* is inscribed in a circle. If the area of square *PQRS* is 4, what is the radius of the circle?

    (A)   1
    (B) $\sqrt{2}$
    (C)   2
    (D) $2\sqrt{2}$
    (E) $4\sqrt{2}$

    Ⓐ Ⓑ Ⓒ Ⓓ Ⓔ

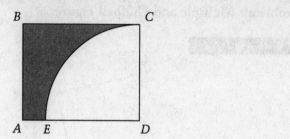

Note: Figure not drawn to scale.

3. In the figure above, the quarter circle with center *D* has a radius of 4 and rectangle *ABCD* has a perimeter of 20. What is the perimeter of the shaded region?

(A) $20 - 8\pi$
(B) $10 + 2\pi$
(C) $12 + 2\pi$
(D) $12 + 4\pi$
(E) $4 + 8\pi$

Ⓐ Ⓑ Ⓒ Ⓓ Ⓔ

Answers to Multiple and Oddball Figure Problems

1. (D)

Draw a straight line from point H to point F, to divide the figure into two right triangles.

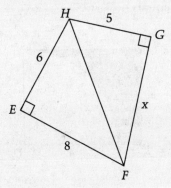

$\triangle EFH$ is a 3–4–5 right triangle with a hypotenuse of length 10. Use the Pythagorean theorem in $\triangle FGH$ to find x:

$$x^2 + 5^2 = 10^2$$
$$x^2 + 5^2 = 100$$
$$x^2 = 75$$
$$x = \sqrt{75}$$
$$x = \sqrt{25}\,\sqrt{3}$$
$$x = 5\,\sqrt{3}$$

2. (B)

Draw in diagonal QS and you will notice that it is also a diameter of the circle.

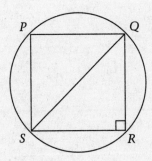

Since the area of the square is 4 its sides must each be 2. Think of the diagonal as dividing the square into two isosceles right triangles. Therefore, the diagonal $= 2\sqrt{2} =$ the diameter; the radius is half this amount or $\sqrt{2}$.

3. (C)

The perimeter of the shaded region is $BC + AB + AE +$ arc EC. The quarter circle has its center at D, and point C lies on the circle, so side DC is a radius of the circle and equals 4.

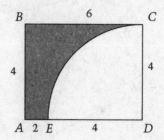

Opposite sides of a rectangle are equal so AB is also 4. The perimeter of the rectangle is 20, and since the two short sides account for 8, the two longer sides must account for 12, making BC and AD each 6. To find AE, subtract the length of ED, another radius of length 4, from the length of AD, which is 6; $AE = 2$. Since arc EC is a quarter circle, the length of the arc EC is $\frac{1}{4}$ of the circumference of a whole circle with radius 4: $\frac{1}{4} \times 2\pi r = \frac{1}{4} \times 8\pi = 2\pi$. So the perimeter of the shaded region is $6 + 4 + 2 + 2\pi = 12 + 2\pi$.

F·A·S·T P·R·E·P

CHAPTER CHECKLIST

 Once you've mastered a section, check it off.

HOW TRAPS WORK AND HOW TO AVOID THEM

- ❏ THE WRONG WAY TO ANSWER THE QUESTIONS
- ❏ AVOIDING THE TRAPS
- ❏ FINDING THE RIGHT ANSWERS

KAPLAN'S TOP 10 SAT MATH TRAPS

- ❏ PERCENT INCREASE/DECREASE
- ❏ WEIGHTED AVERAGES
- ❏ RATIO:RATIO:RATIO
- ❏ EXPRESSIONS THAT LOOK EQUAL— BUT AREN'T
- ❏ UNSPECIFIED ORDER
- ❏ LENGTH:AREA RATIOS
- ❏ NOT ALL NUMBERS ARE POSITIVE INTEGERS
- ❏ HIDDEN INSTRUCTIONS
- ❏ AVERAGE RATES
- ❏ COUNTING NUMBERS

PANICPLAN

If you have a month or less to prep for the SAT, here's the best way to spend your time:

- Skim pp. 176–191.
- Do the first practice set, pp. 173–175. If you miss an answer, identify the trap that caught you and study that section.
- Do the second practice set, pp. 192–195. If you get any answer wrong, identify the trap and study that section. If you get all the answers right, you're strong at avoiding traps.

CHAPTER 14

TOP TEN SAT MATH TRAPS

It's time for us to let you in on a little secret that will allow you to breeze through the entire SAT, get into any college you want, succeed in life, and find eternal happiness.

If you believed a word of the preceding paragraph, you need to pay special attention to this chapter. This chapter presents 10 common SAT traps. Traps lure you into one answer, usually one that's easy to get to. But they conceal the correct answer, which requires some thought. If you're not wary of traps on the SAT, they may trip you up. Learn to recognize common traps and you'll gain more points.

HINT: If you see what appears to be a basic problem late in a question set, there is probably a trap.

WATCH OUT FOR TRAPS

The following 10 questions have one thing in common—they all have traps. Take 12 minutes to try to work through all of them. Then check your answers on p. 176.

1. Jackie purchased a new car in 1990. Three years later she sold it to a dealer for 40 percent less than she paid for it in 1990. The dealer then added 20 percent onto the price he paid and resold it to another customer. The price the final customer paid for the car was what percent of the original price Jackie paid in 1990?

    (A) 40 percent
    (B) 60 percent
    (C) 72 percent
    (D) 80 percent
    (E) 88 percent

KAPLAN'S FAVORITE TRAP

When the hands of your watch show 12:30, how many degrees separate the hour hand from the minute hand?

The obvious answer is 180 degrees. That's a trap. (At 12:30 the hour hand doesn't point directly at the 12; it's halfway between the 12 and the 1.) The test makers hoped that you would jump to the obvious answer, without taking the time to think it through.

Over the years, the SAT has had plenty of problems like this one. Traps catch unwary students who forget to think through the problem before they answer it. How do you prevent yourself from falling for other SAT Math traps? Read this chapter.

2. In a class of 27 students, the average (arithmetic mean) score of the boys on the final exam was 83. If the average score of the 15 girls in the class was 92, what was the average of the whole class?

(A) 86.2
(B) 87.0
(C) 87.5
(D) 88.0
(E) 88.2

Ⓐ Ⓑ Ⓒ Ⓓ Ⓔ

3. Mike's coin collection consists of quarters, dimes, and nickels. If the ratio of the number of quarters to the number of dimes is 5:2, and the ratio of the number of dimes to the number of nickels is 3:4, what is the ratio of the number of quarters to the number of nickels?

(A) 5 to 4
(B) 7 to 5
(C) 10 to 6
(D) 12 to 7
(E) 15 to 8

Ⓐ Ⓑ Ⓒ Ⓓ Ⓔ

Column A	Column B
$p > q > 1$	

4. $p^2 - q^2$ $(p - q)^2$ Ⓐ Ⓑ Ⓒ Ⓓ Ⓔ

A, *B*, and *C* are points on a line such that point *A* is 12 units away from point *B* and point *B* is four units away from point *C*.

5. The distance from   16
point *A* to point *C*   Ⓐ Ⓑ Ⓒ Ⓓ Ⓔ

6. The area of a   Twice the area of a
square with a   square with a
perimeter of 14   perimeter of 7   Ⓐ Ⓑ Ⓒ Ⓓ Ⓔ

7. If $n \neq 0$, then which of the following must be true?

    I. $n^2 > n$
   II. $2n > n$
  III. $n + 1 > n$

(A) I only
(B) II only
(C) III only
(D) I and III only
(E) I, II, and III

Ⓐ Ⓑ Ⓒ Ⓓ Ⓔ

8. At a certain restaurant, the hourly wage for a waiter is 20 percent greater than the hourly wage for a dishwasher, and the hourly wage for a dishwasher is half as much as the hourly wage for a cook's assistant. If a cook's assistant earns $8.50 an hour, how much less than a cook's assistant does a waiter earn each hour?

   (A) $2.55
   (B) $3.40
   (C) $4.25
   (D) $5.10
   (E) $5.95   Ⓐ Ⓑ Ⓒ Ⓓ Ⓔ

9. A car traveled from *A* to *B* at an average speed of 40 miles per hour and then immediately traveled back from *B* to *A* at an average speed of 60 miles per hour. What was the car's average speed for the round-trip, in miles per hour?

   (A) 45
   (B) 48
   (C) 50
   (D) 52
   (E) 54   Ⓐ Ⓑ Ⓒ Ⓓ Ⓔ

10. The tickets for a certain raffle are consecutively numbered. If Louis sold the tickets numbered from 75 to 148 inclusive, how many raffle tickets did he sell?

   (A) 71
   (B) 72
   (C) 73
   (D) 74
   (E) 75   Ⓐ Ⓑ Ⓒ Ⓓ Ⓔ

HOW MATH TRAPS WORK AND HOW TO AVOID THEM

How did you do? If you got any wrong answers, unless you calculated incorrectly, chances are you got caught in a trap. The same traps occur again and again on the SAT. Learn how they work and how to avoid them. Once you can deal with traps, you'll do much better on the harder math questions.

To see how they work, look again at the 10 sample questions. Each contains one of the Top 10 Math Traps.

ANSWERS

1. (C)
2. (D)
3. (E)
4. (A)
5. (D)
6. (A)
7. (C)
8. (B)
9. (B)
10. (D)

TRAP 1: PERCENT INCREASE/DECREASE

EXAMPLE

Jackie purchased a new car in 1990. Three years later she sold it to a dealer for 40 percent less than she paid for it in 1990. The dealer then added 20 percent onto the price he paid and resold it to another customer. The price the final customer paid for the car was what percent of the original price Jackie paid in 1990?

(A) 40 percent
(B) 60 percent
(C) 72 percent
(D) 80 percent
(E) 88 percent

The Wrong Answer

The increase/decrease percentage problem usually appears at the end of a section and invariably contains a trap. Most students will figure that taking away 40 percent, and then adding 20 percent gives you an overall loss of 20 percent, and pick choice (D), 80 percent, as the correct answer.

The Trap

When a quantity is increased or decreased by a percent more than once, you cannot simply add and subtract the percents to get the answer.

In this kind of percent problem:

- The first percent change is a percent of the starting amount.

- The second change is a percent of the new amount.

Avoiding the Trap

Percents can be added and subtracted only when they are percents of the same amount.

Finding the Right Answer

We know:

- The 40 percent less that Jackie got for the car is 40 percent of her original price.

- The 20 percent the dealer adds on is 20 percent of what the dealer paid, a much smaller amount.

- Adding on 20 percent of that smaller amount is not the same thing as adding back 20 percent of the original price.

So We Can Solve the Problem

- Use 100 for a starting quantity, whether or not it makes sense in the real situation. The problem asks for the relative amount of change. So you can take any starting number, and compare it with the final

TOP 10 TRAP #1

To get a combined percent increase or decrease, don't just add the percents.

result. Because you're dealing with percents, 100 is the easiest number to work with.

> **HINT:** *Pick 100 as the starting quantity and see what happens.*

- If Jackie paid $100.00 for the car, what is 40 percent less?

- In the case of $100.00, each percent equals $1.00 dollar, so she sold it for $60.00.

- If the dealer charges 20 percent more than his purchase price, he's raising the price by 20 percent of $60.00, which is $12.00 (not 20 percent of $100.00, which is $20.00).

- Therefore the dealer sold the car again for $60.00 + $12.00, or $72.00.

- Finally, what percent of the starting price ($100.00) is $72.00? It's 72 percent. So the correct answer here is choice (C).

TOP TEN TRAP #2

Don't just average the averages.

TRAP 2: WEIGHTED AVERAGES

EXAMPLE

In a class of 27 students, the average (arithmetic mean) score of the boys on the final exam was 83. If the average score of the 15 girls in the class was 92, what was the average of the whole class?

(A) 86.2
(B) 87.0
(C) 87.5
(D) 88.0
(E) 88.2

The Wrong Answer

If you simply average 83 and 92 to come up with 87.5 as the class average, you fell for the trap.

The Trap

You cannot combine averages of different quantities by taking the average of those averages.

In an average problem, if one value occurs more frequently than others it is "weighted" more. Remember that the average formula calls for the sum of all the terms, divided by the total number of terms.

Avoiding the Trap

Work with the sums, not the averages.

Finding the Right Answer

If 15 of the 27 students are girls, the remaining 12 must be boys.

We can't just add 83 to 92 and divide by two. In this class there are more girls than boys, and therefore the girls' test scores are "weighted" more—they contribute more to the class average. So the answer must be either (D) or (E). To find each sum, multiply each average by the number of terms it represents. After you have found the sums of the different terms, find the combined average by plugging the sums into the average formula.

$$\text{Total class average} = \frac{\text{Sum of girls' scores} + \text{Sum of boys' scores}}{\text{Total number of students}}$$

$$= \frac{(\text{\# of girls} \times \text{girls' average score}) + (\text{\# of boys} \times \text{boys' average score})}{\text{Total number of students}}$$

$$= \frac{15(92) + 12(83)}{27} = \frac{1{,}380 + 996}{27} = 88$$

So the class average is 88, answer choice (D).

STUMPED?

Use logic. There are more girls than boys, so the average would be closer to the girls' average—92. The only choices that are closer to 92 than 83 are (D) and (E).

TRAP 3: RATIO:RATIO:RATIO

> **EXAMPLE**
>
> Mike's coin collection consists of quarters, dimes, and nickels. If the ratio of the number of quarters to the number of dimes is 5:2, and the ratio of the number of dimes to the number of nickels is 3:4, what is the ratio of the number of quarters to the number of nickels?
>
> (A) 5:4
> (B) 7:5
> (C) 10:6
> (D 12:7
> (E) 15:8

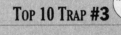

MONEY

Don't be distracted by money. In the example to the left, we care only about the *number* of coins, not their value.

The Wrong Answer
If you chose 5:4 as the correct answer, you fell for the classic ratio trap.

The Trap
Parts of different ratios don't always refer to the same whole.

In the classic ratio trap, two different ratios each share a common part that is represented by two different numbers. The two ratios do not refer to the same whole, however, so they are not in proportion to each other. To solve this type of problem, restate both ratios so that the numbers representing the common part (in this case "dimes") are the same. Then all the parts will be in proportion and can be compared to each other.

Avoiding the Trap
Make sure parts of ratios refer to the same whole.

Finding the Right Answer
To find the ratio of quarters to nickels, restate both ratios so that the number of dimes is the same in both. We are given two ratios:

Quarters:dimes = 5:2   Dimes:nickels = 3:4

The number corresponding to dimes in the first ratio is 2.

The number corresponding to dimes in the second ratio is 3.

To restate the ratios, find the least common multiple of 2 and 3.

The least common multiple of 2 and 3 is 6.

TOP 10 TRAP #3

Don't take one number from one ratio and compare it to another number from another ratio.

Restate the ratios with the number of dimes as 6:

Quarters:dimes = 15:6   Dimes:nickels = 6:8

The ratios are still in their original proportions, but now they're in proportion to each other and they refer to the same whole.

The ratio of quarters to dimes to nickels is 15:6:8, so the ratio of quarters to nickels is 15:8, which is answer choice (E).

TRAP 4: EXPRESSIONS THAT LOOK EQUAL—BUT AREN'T

EXAMPLE

Column A	Column B
	$p > q > 1$
$p^2 - q^2$	$(p - q)^2$

The Wrong Answer
If you said the expressions were equal, you'd be wrong.

The Trap
At first glance the expressions look like they're equal—but they're not.

This common SAT trap happens most often in QCs. Problems like this trap students who are too hasty, who answer on the basis of appearance, without considering the mathematical rules involved.

Avoiding the Trap
If two quantities seem obviously equal, double-check your answer, using your math knowledge and the techniques discussed in Chapter 12, Quantitative Comparisons (p. 111).

This is an example of the general rule that whenever an answer to a question late in a section looks obviously correct, it probably isn't.

Finding the Right Answer
In this case you can use the make-one-column-look-more-like-the-other technique discussed in Chapter 12.

Factor Column A and rewrite Column B:

Column A	Column B
$(p - q)(p + q)$	$(p - q)(p - q)$

Now use the do-the-same-thing-to-both-columns technique. Both columns contain $(p - q)$. You know than $p > q$, so $p - q$ is a positive number. Therefore, you can divide both columns by $p - q$:

Column A	Column B
$p + q$	$p - q$

Since q is positive, adding q in Column A will get you more than subtracting q in Column B. Column A is greater, so the answer is (A).

This trap does not apply only to quadratics. Below are some other quantities that the hasty student might mistake as equal. Go through this list and make sure you can tell why these expressions are not equal except for special cases.

- $(x + y)^2$ does NOT equal $x^2 + y^2$
- $(2x)^2$ does NOT equal $2x^2$
- $x^{20} - x^{18}$ does NOT equal x^2
- $x^3 + x^3$ does NOT equal x^6
- $\sqrt{x} + \sqrt{x}$ does NOT equal $\sqrt{2x}$
- $\sqrt{x} - \sqrt{y}$ does NOT equal $\sqrt{x-y}$
- $\dfrac{1}{x} + \dfrac{1}{y}$ does NOT equal $\dfrac{1}{x+y}$

You could prove that any of these quantities need not be equal using the Picking Numbers technique.

TRAP 5: UNSPECIFIED ORDER

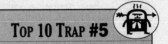

EXAMPLE

<u>Column A</u>   <u>Column B</u>

A, B, and *C* are points on a line such that point *A* is 12 units away from point *B* and point *B* is 4 units away from point *C*.

The distance from   16
point *A* to point *C*

The Wrong Answer

First you should always draw a diagram to help you visualize the relationship between the points.

In this diagram, the distance from *A* to *C* is 16, which is the same as Column B. But choice (C) is not the right answer.

The Trap

Don't assume that there is only one arrangement of the points—in this case, alphabetical order. We are not told what the relationship between *A* and *C* is. In fact *C* could lie to the left of *B*, like so:

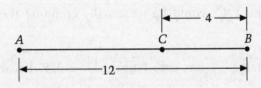

Avoiding the Trap

Don't assume points lie in the order they are given or in alphabetical order. Look for alternatives.

Finding the Right Answer

In this case, the distance from *A* to *C* is 8, which is less than Column B. Since we have two possible relationships between the columns, the answer must be (D)—you can't be certain from the data given.

TOP 10 TRAP #6

The ratio of areas is not the same as the ratio of lengths.

TRAP 6: LENGTH:AREA RATIOS

EXAMPLE

<u>Column A</u>

The area of a square with a perimeter of 14

<u>Column B</u>

Twice the area of a square with a perimeter of 7

The Wrong Answer
Twice the perimeter doesn't mean twice the area. Choice (C) is wrong.

The Trap
In proportional figures, the ratio of the areas is not the same as the ratio of the lengths.

Avoiding the Trap
Understand that the ratio of the areas of proportional figures is the square of the ratio of corresponding linear measures.

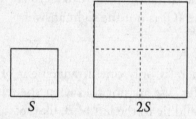

Finding the Right Answer
One way to solve this QC would be to actually compute the respective areas.

A square of perimeter 14 has side length $\frac{14}{4}$ = 3.5. Its area then is $(3.5)^2$ = 12.25. On the other hand, the area of the square in Column B is $(\frac{7}{4})^2 = (1.75)^2$ = 3.0625. Even twice that area is still less than the 12.25 in Column A. The answer is (A).

A quicker and more clever way to dodge this trap is to understand the relationship between the linear ratio and the area ratio of proportional figures. In proportional figures, the area ratio is the *square* of the linear ratio.

In the example above, we are given two squares with sides in a ratio of 14:7 or 2:1.

Using the rule above, we square the linear 4:1 ratio. The areas of the two figures will be in a four-to-one ratio.

The same goes for circles:

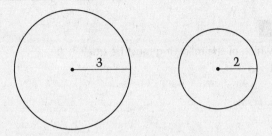

In the figure above, we are given two circles with radii in a 3:2 ratio. Using the rule above, we square the linear 3:2 ratio. The areas of the two circles will be in a 9:4 ratio.

TRAP 7: NOT ALL NUMBERS ARE POSITIVE INTEGERS

EXAMPLE

If $n \neq 0$, then which of the following must be true?

I. $n^2 > n$

II. $2n > n$

III. $n + 1 > n$

(A) I only

(B) II only

(C) III only

(D) I and III only

(E) I, II, and III

The Wrong Answer

In the example above, if you considered only positive integers greater than 1 for the value of n, you would assume that all three statements are true. However, that is not the case.

The Trap

Not all numbers are positive integers.

Don't forget there are negative numbers and fractions as well. This is important because negative numbers and fractions between 0 and 1 behave very differently from positive integers.

Avoiding the Trap

When picking numbers for variables, consider fractions and negative numbers.

Finding the Right Answer

Looking at statement I, you may assume that when you square a number, you end up with a larger number as a result. For example, $4^2 = 16$, or $10^2 = 100$. However, when you square a fraction between 0 and 1, the result is quite different: $(\frac{1}{2})^2 = \frac{1}{4}$. $(\frac{1}{10})^2 = \frac{1}{100}$. You get a smaller number.

In statement II, what happens when you multiply a number by 2? $7 \times 2 = 14$; $25 \times 2 = 50$. Multiplying any positive number by 2 doubles that number, so you get a larger result. However, if you multiply a negative number by 2, your result is smaller than the original number. For example, $-3 \times 2 = -6$.

Finally, look at statement III. What happens when you add 1 to any number? Adding 1 to any number gives you a larger number as a result. For example, $5 + 1 = 6$; $\frac{1}{2} + 1 = 1\frac{1}{2}$; and $-7 + 1 = -6$. That should be pretty obvious.

Therefore, only statement III must be true. That makes choice (C) correct. If you didn't consider fractions or negative numbers, you would have fallen into the trap and answered the question incorrectly.

HINT: *This trap appears most often in QC problems, so watch out.*

TRAP 8: HIDDEN INSTRUCTIONS

TOP 10 TRAP #8

Make sure you're answering the question that's asked. Hint: underline the last phrase in the question.

> **EXAMPLE**
>
> At a certain restaurant, the hourly wage for a waiter is 20 percent greater than the hourly wage for a dishwasher, and the hourly wage for a dishwasher is half as much as the hourly wage for a cook's assistant. If a cook's assistant earns $8.50 an hour, how much less than a cook's assistant does a waiter earn each hour?
>
> (A) $2.55
> (B) $3.40
> (C) $4.25
> (D) $5.10
> (E) $5.95

The Wrong Answer

To solve this problem, you must find the hourly wage of the waiter.

The cook's assistant earns $8.50 an hour. The dishwasher earns half of this—$4.25 an hour. The waiter earns 20 percent more than the dishwasher—$4.25 × 1.2 = $5.10.

So the waiter earns $5.10 an hour, and you might reach automatically to fill in answer choice (D). But (D) is the wrong answer.

The Trap

A small step, easily overlooked, can mean the difference between a right and wrong answer.

In this case the word is "less." After spending all this time finding the waiter's hourly wage, in their moment of triumph many students skip right over the vital last step. They overlook that the question asks not what the waiter earns, but how much less than the cook's assistant the waiter earns.

Avoiding the Trap

Make sure you answer the question that's being asked. Watch out for hidden instructions.

Finding the Right Answer

You have figured out that the waiter earns $5.10 an hour. And the cook's assistant earns $8.50 an hour. To find out how much less than the cook's assistant the waiter earns, subtract the waiter's hourly wage from the cook's assistant's hourly wage.

The correct answer is (B).

PEEK-A-BOO

Hidden instructions come in many forms. Watch out for questions that give all the information in one unit (say minutes) and ask you for the answer in another unit (say seconds or hours). Read carefully and solve for the correct quantity.

TRAP 9: AVERAGE RATES

TOP 10 TRAP #9

> **Any time it says "average rate"** in the question, be alert: You usually can't just average the rates to get the right answer.

EXAMPLE

A car traveled from A to B at an average speed of 40 miles per hour and then immediately traveled back from B to A at an average speed of 60 miles per hour. What was the car's average speed for the round-trip, in miles per hour?

(A) 45

(B) 48

(C) 50

(D) 52

(E) 54

The Wrong Answer

Do you see which answer choice is too "obvious" to be correct? The temptation is simply to average 40 and 60. The answer is "obviously" 50 (C). But 50 is wrong.

The Trap

To get an average speed, you can't just average the rates.

Why is the average speed not 50 mph? Because the car spent more time traveling at 40 mph than at 60 mph. Each leg of the round trip was the same distance, but the first leg, at the slower speed, took more time.

Avoiding the Trap

You can solve almost any Average Rate problem with this general formula:

$$\text{Average Rate} = \frac{\text{Total Distance}}{\text{Total Time}}$$

Use the given information to figure out the total distance and the total time. But how can you do that when many problems don't specify the distances?

Finding the Right Answer

In our sample above, we are told that a car went from A to B at 40 miles per hour and back from B to A at 60 miles per hour. In other words, it went half the total distance at 40 mph and half the total distance at 60 mph.

How do you use the formula:

$$\text{Average Rate} = \frac{\text{Total Distance}}{\text{Total Time}}$$

if you don't know the total distance?

STUMPED?

Use common sense. The car spent more time at 40 mph so the answer will be less than 50— i.e., weighted more heavily towards 40 (remember weighted averages, trap #2).

If you saw this much but couldn't get the answer, you could guess between (A) and (B). (More on guessing in Chapter 15.)

HINT: Pick a number! Pick any number you want for the total distance.

Divide that total distance into half distances. Calculate the time needed to travel each half distance at the different rates.

HINT: Pick a number that's easy to work with.

A good number to pick here would be 240 miles for the total distance, because you can figure in your head the times for two 120-mile legs at 40 mph and 60 mph:

$$A \text{ to } B: \frac{120 \text{ miles}}{40 \text{ miles per hour}} = 3 \text{ hours}$$

$$B \text{ to } A: \frac{120 \text{ miles}}{60 \text{ miles per hour}} = 2 \text{ hours}$$

$$\text{Total time} = 5 \text{ hours}$$

Now plug "total distance = 240 miles" and "total time = 5 hours" into the general formula:

$$\text{Average Rate} = \frac{\text{Total Distance}}{\text{Total Time}} = \frac{240 \text{ miles}}{5 \text{ hours}} = 48 \text{ miles per hour}$$

Correct answer choice: (B).

TRAP 10: COUNTING NUMBERS

EXAMPLE

The tickets for a certain raffle are consecutively numbered. If Louis sold the tickets numbered from 75 to 148 inclusive, how many raffle tickets did he sell?

(A) 71
(B) 72
(C) 73
(D) 74
(E) 75

The Wrong Answer

If you subtract 75 from 148 and get 73 as the answer, you are wrong.

The Trap

Subtracting the first and last integers in a range will give you the difference of the two numbers. It won't give you the number of integers in that range.

Avoiding the Trap

To count the number of integers in a range, subtract and then add 1.

If you forget the rule, pick two small numbers that are close together, such as 1 and 4. Obviously, there are four integers from 1 to 4, inclusive. But if you had subtracted 1 from 4, you would have gotten 3. In the diagram below, you can see that 3 is actually the distance between the integers, if the integers were on a number line or a ruler.

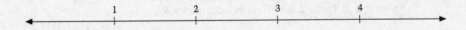

Finding the Right Answer

In the problem above, subtract 75 from 148. The result is 73. Add 1 to this difference to get the number of integers. That gives you 74. The correct answer choice is (D).

The word "inclusive" tells you to include the first and last numbers given. So, for example, "the integers from 5 to 15 inclusive" would include 5 and 15. Questions always make it clear whether you should include the outer numbers or not, since the correct answer hinges on this point.

MORE PRACTICE

Now that you can recognize the Top 10 Traps, try the following test. This time, try to identify the trap in each problem. Check your answers on pp. 195–196.

Column A	Column B

A car traveled the first half of a 100-kilometer distance at an average speed of 120 kilometers per hour, and it traveled the remaining distance at an average speed of 80 kilometers per hour.

1. The car's average speed, in kilometers per hour, for the 100 kilometers   100

Ⓐ Ⓑ Ⓒ Ⓓ Ⓔ

The ratio of $\frac{1}{4}$ to $\frac{2}{5}$ is equal to the ratio of $\frac{2}{5}$ to x.

2. x $\frac{3}{5}$

Ⓐ Ⓑ Ⓒ Ⓓ Ⓔ

3. $14 - 6$ $\sqrt{14^2 - 6^2}$

Ⓐ Ⓑ Ⓒ Ⓓ Ⓔ

4. $\dfrac{a+b}{3}$ $a + b$

Ⓐ Ⓑ Ⓒ Ⓓ Ⓔ

John buys 34 books at $6.00 each, and 17 at $12.00 each.

5. The average price John pays per book $9.00

Ⓐ Ⓑ Ⓒ Ⓓ Ⓔ

On a certain highway Town X lies 50 miles away from Town Y, and Town Z lies 80 miles from Town X.

6. The number of minutes a car traveling at an average speed of 60 miles per hour takes to travel from Town Y to Town Z 30

Ⓐ Ⓑ Ⓒ Ⓓ Ⓔ

a, b, and c are positive numbers.
$b < c$

7. $(a + b)^2$ $a^2 + c^2$

Ⓐ Ⓑ Ⓒ Ⓓ Ⓔ

8. The area of a circle with a diameter of 3   The sum of the areas of three circles each with a diameter of 1

Ⓐ Ⓑ Ⓒ Ⓓ Ⓔ

Column A   Column B

Jane invests her savings in a fund that adds 10 percent interest
to her savings at the end of every year.

9. The percent by which   31 percent
    her money has increased
    after three years   Ⓐ Ⓑ Ⓒ Ⓓ Ⓔ

$x > 1$

10. $7^{2x} - 7^x$ 7^x Ⓐ Ⓑ Ⓒ Ⓓ Ⓔ

---

11. Pump 1 can drain a 400-gallon water tank in 1.2 hours. Pump 2
    can drain the same tank in 1.8 hours. How many minutes longer
    than pump 1 would it take pump 2 to drain a 100-gallon tank?

    (A) 0.15
    (B) 1.2
    (C) 6
    (D) 9
    (E) 18   Ⓐ Ⓑ Ⓒ Ⓓ Ⓔ

---

12. Volumes 12 through 30 of a certain encyclopedia are located on
    the bottom shelf of a bookcase. If the volumes of the encyclopedia
    are numbered consecutively, how many volumes of the encyclope-
    dia are on the bottom shelf?

    (A) 17
    (B) 18
    (C) 19
    (D) 29
    (E) 30   Ⓐ Ⓑ Ⓒ Ⓓ Ⓔ

---

13. A reservoir is at full capacity at the beginning of summer. By the
    first day of fall, the level in the reservoir is 30 percent below full
    capacity. Then during the fall a period of heavy rains raises the
    level by 30 percent. After the rains, the reservoir is at what percent
    of its full capacity?

    (A) 100 percent
    (B)   95 percent
    (C)   91 percent
    (D)   85 percent
    (E)   60 percent   Ⓐ Ⓑ Ⓒ Ⓓ Ⓔ

14. Two classes, one with 50 students, the other with 30, take the same exam. The combined average of both classes is 84.5. If the larger class averages 80, what is the average of the smaller class?

(A) 87.2
(B) 89.0
(C) 92.0
(D) 93.3
(E) 94.5   Ⓐ Ⓑ Ⓒ Ⓓ Ⓔ

15. In a pet shop, the ratio of puppies to kittens is 7:6 and the ratio of kittens to guinea pigs is 5:3. What is the ratio of puppies to guinea pigs?

(A)   7:3
(B)   6:5
(C)   13:8
(D)   21:11
(E)   35:18   Ⓐ Ⓑ Ⓒ Ⓓ Ⓔ

16. A typist typed the first n pages of a book, where $n > 0$, at an average rate of 12 pages per hour and typed the remaining n pages at an average rate of 20 pages per hour. What was the typist's average rate, in pages per hour, for the entire book?

(A) $14\frac{2}{3}$

(B) 15

(C) 16

(D) 17

(E) 18   Ⓐ Ⓑ Ⓒ Ⓓ Ⓔ

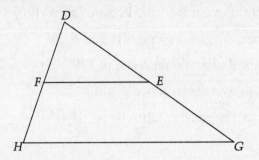

17. In triangle *DGH* above, *DE* = *EG*, *EF* ∥ *GH*, and the area of triangle *DGH* is 30. What is the area of triangle *DEF*?

(A)   7.5
(B)   15
(C)   22.5
(D)   60
(E)   It cannot be determined from the information given.

Ⓐ Ⓑ Ⓒ Ⓓ Ⓔ

DID YOU FALL FOR THE TRAPS?

How did you do? Did you spot the trap in each problem? Use the answers below to see what your weaknesses are. Each wrong answer represents one trap you need to work on. Go back and reread the section on that trap. Then try the problems again, until you answer correctly.

1.   (B) Trap: Average rates (see p. 189)

2.   (A) Trap: Ratio:ratio:ratio (see p. 179)

3.   (B) Trap: Expressions that look equal—but aren't (see p. 181)

4.   (D) Trap: Not all numbers are positive integers (see p. 186)

5.   (B) Trap: Weighted averages (see p. 178)

6.   (D) Trap: Unspecified order (see p. 183)

7.   (D) Trap: Expressions that look equal—but aren't (see p. 181)

8.   (A) Trap: Length:area ratio (see p. 184)

9.   (A) Trap: Percent increase/decrease (see p. 176)

10. (A) Trap: Expressions that look equal—but aren't (see p. 181)

11. (D) Trap: Hidden instructions (see p. 188)

12. (C) Trap: Counting numbers (see p. 191)

HIGHLIGHTS

- To get a combined percent increase, don't just add the percents.
- Don't just average the averages.
- Don't take one number from one ratio and compare it to another number from another ratio.
- Don't be fooled by appearances.
- Don't assume that there's just one way to draw the diagram.
- The ratio of areas is not the same as the ratio of lengths.
- Not all numbers are positive integers. Don't forget to consider zero, fractions, and negative numbers.
- Make sure you're answering the question that's asked. Hint: Underline the last phrase in the question.
- Any time it says "average rate" in the question, be alert: You usually can't just average the rates to get the right answer.
- Counting integers is tricky. You can't just subtract the first number from the last number; you have to add one.

13. (C) Trap: Percent increase/decrease (see p. 176)

14. (C) Trap: Weighted averages (see p. 178)

15. (E) Trap: Ratio:ratio:ratio (see p. 179)

16. (B) Trap: Average rates (see p. 189)

17. (A) Trap: Length:area ratios (see p. 184)

F·A·S·T P·R·E·P

CHAPTER CHECKLIST

Once you've mastered a section, check it off.

MATH GUESSING

❑ ELIMINATE UNREASONABLE ANSWER
CHOICES

❑ ELIMINATE THE OBVIOUS ON HARD
QUESTIONS

❑ EYEBALL LENGTHS, ANGLES, AND AREAS
ON GEOMETRY PROBLEMS

❑ ELIMINATE CHOICE (D) ON SOME QCs

❑ FIND THE RANGE ON GRID-INS—
THEN GUESS

PANICPLAN

If you have less than a month to prep for the SAT, here's the best way to spend your time:

• Guessing is an important strategy for scoring points, so read this chapter carefully. It's a short chapter, and there are no shortcuts to learning how to guess accurately.

CHAPTER 15

MATH GUESSING

O bviously, the best way to find the answer is to actually solve the problem. But if you're stuck or running out of time, guessing can be a good alternative.

The Regular Math and QC sections, like the Verbal sections, are scored to discourage random guessing. For every question you get right you earn a whole point. For every question you get wrong, you lose a fraction of a point. So if you guess at random on a number of questions, the points you gain from correct guesses are canceled out by the points you lose on incorrect guesses, for no overall gain or loss.

But you can make *educated* guesses. This raises the odds of guessing correctly, so the fractional points you lose no longer cancel out all the whole points you gain. You have just raised your score.

To make an educated guess, eliminate answer choices you know to be wrong, and guess from what's left. Of course, the more answer choices you can eliminate, the better chance you have of guessing the correct answer from what's left over.

Here are five strategies for guessing intelligently on all types of math problems.

ELIMINATE UNREASONABLE ANSWER CHOICES

Before you guess, think about the problem, and decide which answers don't make sense. Take as an example the problem on the next page.

GUESSING IS EASY

Quick. Guess the right answer. William H. Harrison's middle name was:
• Hazel
• Hello
• Henry
• Hal
• Herbert

Except for the class clown who said Hazel, most people can safely eliminate two of the five choices. That means you've got a one-in-three chance of guessing Henry.

If you went into the SAT determined not to guess, you would have passed up this great opportunity to score a point.

Remember, if you can eliminate at least one answer, you should guess.

STUCK?

- Stuck on a QC or Regular Math question? Eliminate at least one answer choice and guess.

- Stuck on a Grid-in? You won't lose points for guessing wrong on Grid-ins. So go ahead and guess.

EXAMPLE

The ratio of men to women in a certain room is 13:11. If there are 429 men in the room, how many women are there?

(A) 143
(B) 363
(C) 433
(D) 507
(E) 792

Solution:

- The ratio of men to women is 13:11, so there are more men than women.

- Since there are 429 men, there must be fewer than 429 women.

- So you can eliminate choices (C), (D), and (E).

- The answer must be either (A) or (B), so guess. The correct answer is (B).

ELIMINATE THE OBVIOUS ON HARD QUESTIONS

On the hard questions late in a set, obvious answers are usually wrong. So eliminate them when you guess. That doesn't hold true for early, easy questions, when the obvious answer could be right.

Now apply the rule. In the following difficult problem, which obvious answer should you eliminate?

EXAMPLE

A number x is increased by 30 percent and then the result is decreased by 20 percent. What is the final result of these changes?

(A) x is increased by 10 percent
(B) x is increased by 6 percent
(C) x is increased by 4 percent
(D) x is decreased by 5 percent
(E) x is decreased by 10 percent

NEED MORE HELP?

For more on percent increase/decrease problems, see Top 10 SAT Math Traps, pp. 176–177.

Solution:

If you picked (A) as the obvious choice to eliminate, you'd be right. Most people would combine the decrease of 20 percent with the increase of 30 percent, getting a net increase of 10 percent. That's the easy, obvious answer, but not the correct answer. If you must guess, avoid (A). The correct answer is (C).

EYEBALL LENGTHS, ANGLES, AND AREAS ON GEOMETRY PROBLEMS

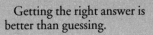

Use diagrams that accompany geometry problems to help you eliminate wrong answer choices. First make sure that the diagram is drawn to scale. Diagrams are always drawn to scale unless there's a note like this: "Note: Figure not drawn to scale." If it's not, don't use this strategy. If it is, estimate quantities or eyeball the diagram. Then eliminate answer choices that are way too large or too small.

KAPLAN RULES

Getting the right answer is better than guessing.

Length

When a geometry question asks for a length, use the given lengths to estimate the unknown length. Measure off the given length by making a nick in your pencil with your thumbnail. Then hold the pencil against the unknown length on the diagram to see how the lengths compare.

In the following problem, which answer choices can you eliminate by eyeballing?

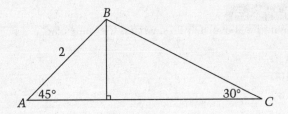

EXAMPLE

In the figure above, what is the length of *BC*?

(A) $\sqrt{2}$
(B) 2
(C) $2\sqrt{2}$
(D) 4
(E) $4\sqrt{2}$

Solution:

- *AB* is 2, so measure off this length on your pencil.
- Compare *BC* with this length.
- *BC* appears almost twice as long as *AB*, so *BC* is about 4.
- Since $\sqrt{2}$ is about 1.4, and *BC* is clearly longer than *AB*, choices (A) and (B) are too small.
- Choice (E) is much greater than 4, so eliminate that.
- Now guess between (C) and (D). The correct answer is (C).

Angles

You can also eyeball angles. To eyeball an angle, compare the angle with a familiar angle, such as a straight angle (180°), a right angle (90°), or half a right angle (45°). The corner of a piece of paper is a right angle, so use that to see if an angle is greater or less than 90°.

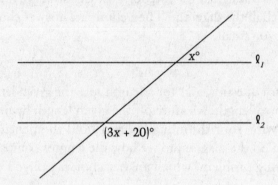

EXAMPLE

In the figure above, if $\ell_1 \parallel \ell_2$, what is the value of x?

(A) 130
(B) 100
(C) 80
(D) 50
(E) 40

Solution:

- You see that x is less than 90 degrees, so eliminate choices (A) and (B).

- Since x appears to be much less than 90 degrees, eliminate choice (C).

- Now pick between (D) and (E). In fact, the correct answer is (E).

Areas

Eyeballing an area is similar to eyeballing a length. You compare an unknown area in a diagram to an area that you do know.

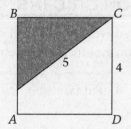

In square *ABCD* above, what is the area of the shaded region?

(A) 10
(B) 9
(C) 8
(D) 6
(E) 4

Solution:

- Since *ABCD* is a square, it has area 4^2, or 16.

- The shaded area is less than one-half the size of the square, so its area must be less than 8.

- Eliminate answer choices (A), (B), and (C). The correct answer is (D).

ELIMINATE CHOICE (D) ON SOME QCs

If both columns of a QC contain only concrete numbers, choice (D)—"the relationship cannot be determined"—can't be right. With no variables in either column, there must be one consistent relationship, even if you can't find it. If you don't know the answer, eliminate (D) as unreasonable and guess.

Column A   Column B

The largest prime   18
factor of 1,224

Solution:

Each column contains only numbers—so eliminate choice (D) and guess. If you were extra clever you may also have seen that since 18 isn't prime, and Column A contains a prime number, the answer cannot be (C) either. The correct answer is (B).

HIGHLIGHTS

- Eliminate answer choices
- Eyeball geometry diagrams
- Find the range

FIND THE RANGE ON GRID-INS—THEN GUESS

On Grid-ins, there are no answer choices to eliminate, but you won't lose points for guessing. So if you are stuck, try to estimate the general range of the answer, and guess.

Here are some examples of hard Grid-in questions.

> **EXAMPLES**
>
> 1. If the three-digit number 11Q is a prime number, what digit is repre-sented by Q?
>
> 2. The sum of five consecutive odd integers is 425. What is the greatest of these integers?
>
> 3. A triangle has one side of length 3 and another of length 7. If the length of the third side is a solution to the equation $x^2 - 2x = 63$, what is the length of the third side?

Solutions:

1. Since Q is a digit, it must be one of the integers 0 through 9. Eliminate all the even digits, since they are divisible by 2. And eliminate 5, since any number ending with 5 is divisible by 5. You can also eliminate 1 and 7, because they are divisible by 3 (the digits add up to a multiple of 3). You are left with 3 and 9 to pick between. The correct answer is 3.

2. Since the integers are consecutive, they are all about the same size. So the number we are looking for is an odd number around 425 ÷ 5, which is 85. The right answer is 89.

3. Even if you can't solve that quadratic, you know that one side of a triangle has to be less than the sum and greater than the difference of the other two sides. So the third side is less than 7 + 3, or 10, and greater than 7 – 3, or 4. Since solutions to SAT quadratics are usually integers, pick an integer from 5 to 9. If you picked 9, you'd be right.

CHAPTER 16

WHAT DO
I DO NOW?

Is it starting to feel like your whole life is a buildup to the SAT? You've known about it for years, worried about it for months, and now spent at least a few hours in solid preparation for it. As the test gets closer, you may find your anxiety is on the rise. You shouldn't worry. After the preparation you've received from this book, you're in good shape for the test.

To calm any pretest jitters you may have, this chapter leads you through a sane itinerary for the last week.

THE WEEK BEFORE THE TEST

Review the FastPrep checklists at the beginning of the chapters. Are there major holes in your preparation? If there are, choose a few of these areas to work on—but don't overload. You can't cram for the SAT.

Take a full-length SAT. If you haven't done so already, take the practice test at the end of this book. Actual SATs released by ETS are available in libraries and bookstores. You could also pick up Kaplan's *SAT In-a-Week*, or get from your guidance counselor a copy of *Taking the SAT I*, a College Board publication with a practice test. All of these are good practice for the real thing.

TWO DAYS BEFORE THE TEST

Do your last studying—a few more practice problems, a few more vocabulary words, and call it quits.

THE NIGHT BEFORE THE TEST

Don't study.
  Get together the following items:
  • A calculator with fresh batteries
  • A watch
  • A few #2 pencils

THINGS NOT TO DO THE NIGHT BEFORE THE TEST

• Try to copy the dictionary onto your fingernails
• Stay up all night watching all the *Friday the 13th* movies
• Eat a large double anchovy, sausage, and pepper pizza with a case of chocolate soda
• Send away for brochures from vocational schools
• Begin prepping for the LSAT
• Start making flashcards
• Tattoo yourself

NEED MORE HELP?

Call 1–800–KAP–TEST if you have any questions about the SAT or want more information about our other books or courses.

- Erasers

- Photo ID card

- Your admission ticket from ETS

- A snack—there are two breaks and you'll probably get hungry

Know exactly where you're going and exactly how you're getting there.

Relax the night before the test. Read a good book, take a bubble bath, watch TV. Get a good night's sleep. Go to bed at a reasonable hour and leave yourself extra time in the morning.

THE MORNING OF THE TEST

Eat breakfast. Make it something substantial, but not anything too heavy or greasy. Don't drink a lot of coffee if you're not used to it; bathroom breaks cut into your time.

Dress in layers so that you can adjust to the temperature of the test room.

Read something. Warm up your brain with a newspaper or a magazine. You shouldn't let the SAT be the first thing you read that day.

Be sure to get there early.

DURING THE TEST

Don't be shaken. If you find your confidence slipping, remind yourself how well you've prepared. You know the structure of the test; you know the instructions; you've studied for every question type.

Even if something goes really wrong, don't panic. If the test booklet is defective—two pages are stuck together or the ink has run—try to stay calm. Raise your hand, tell the proctor you need a new book. If you accidentally misgrid your answer page or put the answers in the wrong section, again don't panic. Raise your hand, tell the proctor. He or she might be able to arrange for you to regrid your test after it's over, when it won't cost you any time.

Don't think about which section is experimental. Remember, you never know for sure which section won't count. Besides, you can't work on any other section during that section's designated time slot.

AFTER THE TEST

Once the test is over, put it out of your mind. If you don't plan to take the test again, give this book away and start thinking about more interesting things.

You might walk out of the SAT thinking that you blew it. You probably didn't. You tend to remember the questions that stumped you, not the many that you knew. If you're really concerned, you can call ETS within 24 hours to find out about canceling your score. But there is usually no good reason to do so. Remember, you can retake the test as many times as you want, and most colleges consider only your highest scores.

If you want more help, or just want to know more about the SAT, college admissions, or Kaplan prep courses for the PSAT, SAT, and ACT, give us a call at 1–800–KAP–TEST. We're here to answer your questions and to help you in any way that we can.

HIGHLIGHTS

- Don't study the night before the SAT.
- Make sure you know where the test center is. Arrive there early.
- Don't let yourself get shaken during or after the test.

F·A·S·T P·R·E·P

CHAPTER CHECKLIST

 Once you've mastered a section, check it off.

LEARNING NEW WORDS
- ☐ THE WORD LIST
- ☐ THE ROOT LIST
- ☐ WORD FAMILIES

WORD AND ROOT LISTS

The Word List and Root List can boost your knowledge of SAT-level words, and that can help you get more questions right. No one can predict exactly which words will show up on your SAT test. But there are certain words that the test makers favor. The more of these you know, the better.

The Word List that follows contains typical SAT words, and the Root List gives you their component parts. Knowing these words can help you because you may run across them on *your* SAT. Also, becoming comfortable with the types of words that pop up will reduce your anxiety about the test.

Knowing roots can help you in two ways. First, instead of learning one word at a time, you can learn a whole group of words that contain a certain root. They'll be related in meaning, so if you remember one, it will be easier for you to remember others. Second, roots can often help you decode an unknown SAT word. If you recognize a familiar root, you could get a good enough idea of the word to answer the question.

GET TO YOUR ROOTS

Most of the words you use every day have their origins in simple roots. Once you know the root, it's much easier to figure out what a strange word means.

For example, the root *mal* means bad. So *malodorous* must mean bad-smelling.

Take a look through this appendix. Many of the roots are easy to learn, and they'll help you on the test.

SHORT ON TIME?

If you have less than a month to go before you take the SAT, your study time would be best spent learning the vocabulary strategies in Chapter 4. If you have more than a month to go and you have at least two hours a week to devote to studying vocabulary, follow the plan of study outlined below. If you do learn a lot of SAT-type words, it can only help you on the test.

MEMORIZING SAT WORDS

In general, the very best way to improve your vocabulary is to read. Choose challenging, college-level material. If you encounter an unknown word, put it on a flashcard or in your vocabulary notebook.

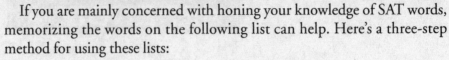

INTIMIDATED?

If you've got two months to prepare for the SAT, you can learn 10 words a day and walk in to the exam knowing an extra 600 words. Not a bad start.

If you are mainly concerned with honing your knowledge of SAT words, memorizing the words on the following list can help. Here's a three-step method for using these lists:

1. Memorize 10 new words and roots a day, using one or more of the techniques below.

2. Reinforce what you've learned. Periodically quiz yourself on all the words you've learned so far.

3. Two weeks before the test, stop learning new words. Spend a week reviewing the word list. Rest up during the last week.

Here are some techniques for memorizing words.

1. Learn words in groups. You can group words by a common root they contain (see the Root list for examples of this), or you can group words together if they are related in meaning. If you memorize words in this way, it may help you to remember them.

2. Use flashcards. Write down new words or word groups and run through them when you have a few minutes to spare. Put one new word or word group on one side of a 3 x 5 card and put a short definition or definitions on the back.

3. Make a vocabulary notebook. List words in one column and their definitions in another. Test yourself. Cover up the meanings, and see which words you can define from memory. Make a sample sentence using each word in context.

NEED MORE HELP?

The lists that follow come from Kaplan's *SAT Verbal Workbook*. For more help with the Verbal section of the SAT, the workbook is a great place to start.

4. Think of hooks that lodge a new word in your mind—create visual images of words.

5. Use rhymes, pictures, songs, and any other devices that help you remember words.

To get the most out of your remaining study time, use the techniques that work for you, and stick with them.

THE KAPLAN WORD LIST

A

- ABANDON (n.)—total lack of inhibition
- ABASE—to humble; disgrace
- ABATEMENT—decrease, reduction
- ABDICATE—to give up a position, right, or power
- ABERRATION—something different from the usual or normal
- ABET—to aid; act as accomplice
- ABEYANCE—temporary suppression or suspension
- ABHOR—to loathe, detest
- ABJECT—miserable, pitiful
- ABJURE—to reject, abandon formally
- ABLUTION—act of cleansing
- ABNEGATE—to deny; renounce
- ABOLITIONIST—one who opposes the practice of slavery
- ABORTIVE—interrupted while incomplete
- ABRIDGE—to condense, shorten
- ABROGATE—to abolish or invalidate by authority
- ABSCOND—to depart secretly
- ABSOLVE—to forgive, free from blame
- ABSTEMIOUS—moderate in appetite
- ABSTRACT (adj.)—theoretical; complex, difficult
- ABSTRUSE—difficult to comprehend
- ACCEDE—to express approval; agree to
- ACCESSIBLE—attainable, available; approachable
- ACCESSORY—attachment, ornament; accomplice, partner
- ACCOLADE—praise, distinction
- ACCOST—to approach and speak to someone
- ACCRETION—growth in size or increase in amount
- ACCRUE—to accumulate, grow by additions
- ACERBIC—bitter, sharp in taste or temper
- ACME—highest point; summit
- ACQUIESCE—to agree; comply quietly
- ACQUITTAL—release from blame
- ACRID—harsh, bitter
- ACRIMONY—bitterness, animosity
- ACUITY—sharpness
- ACUMEN—sharpness of insight
- ACUTE—sharp, pointed
- ADAGE—old saying or proverb
- ADAMANT—uncompromising, unyielding
- ADAPT—to accommodate; adjust

- ADHERE—to cling or follow without deviation
- ADJACENT—next to
- ADJUNCT—something added, attached, or joined
- ADMONISH—to caution or reprimand
- ADROIT—skillful, accomplished, highly competent
- ADULATION—high praise
- ADULTERATE—to corrupt or make impure
- ADUMBRATE—to sketch, outline in a shadowy way
- ADVANTAGEOUS—favorable, useful
- ADVERSARIAL—antagonistic, competitive
- ADVERSE—unfavorable, unlucky; harmful
- AERIAL—having to do with the air
- AERIE—nook or nest built high in the air
- AERODYNAMIC—relating to objects moving through the air
- AESTHETIC—pertaining to beauty or art
- AFFABLE—friendly, easy to approach
- AFFECTED (adj.)—pretentious, phony
- AFFINITY—fondness, liking; similarity
- AFFLUENT—rich, abundant
- AFFRONT (n.)—personal offense, insult
- AGENDA—plan, schedule
- AGGRANDIZE—to make larger or greater in power
- AGGREGATE (n.)—collective mass or sum; total
- AGGRIEVE—to afflict, distress
- AGILE—well coordinated, nimble
- AGITATION—commotion, excitement; uneasiness
- AGNOSTIC—one who doubts that God exists
- AGRARIAN—relating to farming or rural matters
- ALACRITY—cheerful willingness, eagerness; speed
- ALCHEMY—medieval chemical philosophy aimed at trying to change metal into gold
- ALGORITHM—mechanical problem-solving procedure
- ALIAS—assumed name
- ALIENATED—distanced, estranged
- ALIGNED—precisely adjusted; committed to one side
- ALLAY—to lessen, ease, or soothe
- ALLEGORY—symbolic representation
- ALLEVIATE—to relieve, improve partially
- ALLITERATION—repetition of the beginning sounds of words
- ALLOCATION—allowance, portion, share
- ALLURE (v.)—to entice by charm; attract
- ALLUSION—indirect reference

- ❑ ALLUSIVENESS—quality of making many indirect references
- ❑ ALOOF—detached, indifferent
- ❑ ALTERCATION—noisy dispute
- ❑ ALTRUISM—unselfish concern for others' welfare
- ❑ AMALGAM—mixture, combination, alloy
- ❑ AMBIDEXTROUS—able to use both hands equally well
- ❑ AMBIGUOUS—uncertain; subject to multiple interpretations
- ❑ AMBIVALENCE—attitude of uncertainty; conflicting emotions
- ❑ AMELIORATE—to make better, improve
- ❑ AMENABLE—agreeable, cooperative
- ❑ AMEND—to improve or correct flaws in
- ❑ AMENITY—pleasantness; something increasing comfort
- ❑ AMIABLE—friendly, pleasant, likable
- ❑ AMICABLE—friendly, agreeable
- ❑ AMITY—friendship
- ❑ AMORAL—unprincipled, unethical
- ❑ AMOROUS—strongly attracted to love; showing love
- ❑ AMORPHOUS—having no definite form
- ❑ AMORTIZE—to diminish by installment payments
- ❑ AMPHIBIAN—creature equally at home on land or in water
- ❑ AMPHITHEATER—arena theater with rising tiers around a central open space
- ❑ AMPLE—abundant, plentiful
- ❑ AMPLIFY—increase, intensify
- ❑ AMULET—ornament worn as a charm against evil spirits
- ❑ ANACHRONISM—something chronologically inappropriate
- ❑ ANACHRONISTIC—outdated
- ❑ ANALOGOUS—comparable, parallel
- ❑ ANARCHY—absence of government or law; chaos
- ❑ ANATHEMA—ban, curse; something shunned or disliked
- ❑ ANCILLARY—accessory; subordinate; helping
- ❑ ANECDOTE—short, usually funny account of an event
- ❑ ANGULAR—characterized by sharp angles; lean and gaunt
- ❑ ANIMATION—enthusiasm, excitement
- ❑ ANIMOSITY—hatred, hostility
- ❑ ANNUL—to cancel, nullify, declare void, or make legally invalid
- ❑ ANODYNE—something that calms or soothes pain
- ❑ ANOINT—to apply oil to, esp. as a sacred rite
- ❑ ANOMALY—irregularity or deviation from the norm
- ❑ ANONYMITY—condition of having no name or an unknown name
- ❑ ANTAGONIST—foe, opponent, adversary
- ❑ ANTECEDENT (adj.)—coming before in place or time
- ❑ ANTEDILUVIAN—prehistoric, ancient beyond measure
- ❑ ANTEPENULTIMATE—third from last
- ❑ ANTERIOR—preceding, previous, before, prior (to)
- ❑ ANTHOLOGY—collection of literary works
- ❑ ANTHROPOMORPHIC—attributing human qualities to nonhumans
- ❑ ANTIPATHY—dislike, hostility; extreme opposition or aversion
- ❑ ANTIQUATED—outdated, obsolete
- ❑ ANTIQUITY—ancient times; the quality of being old or ancient
- ❑ ANTITHESIS—exact opposite or direct contrast
- ❑ APATHETIC—indifferent, unconcerned
- ❑ APATHY—lack of feeling or emotion
- ❑ APHASIA—inability to speak or use words
- ❑ APHELION—point in a planet's orbit that is farthest from the sun
- ❑ APHORISM—old saying or short, pithy statement
- ❑ APOCRYPHAL—not genuine; fictional
- ❑ APOSTATE—one who renounces a religious faith
- ❑ APOSTROPHE—an address to the reader or someone not present
- ❑ APOTHEOSIS—glorification; glorified ideal
- ❑ APPEASE—to satisfy, placate, calm, pacify
- ❑ APPROBATION—praise; official approval
- ❑ APPROPRIATE (v.)—to take possession of
- ❑ AQUATIC—belonging or living in water
- ❑ ARABLE—suitable for cultivation
- ❑ ARBITRARY—depending solely on individual will; inconsistent
- ❑ ARBITRATOR—mediator, negotiator
- ❑ ARBOREAL—relating to trees; living in trees
- ❑ ARBORETUM—place where trees are displayed and studied
- ❑ ARCANE—secret, obscure, known only to a few
- ❑ ARCHAIC—antiquated, from an earlier time; outdated
- ❑ ARCHIPELAGO—large group of islands
- ❑ ARDENT—passionate, enthusiastic, fervent
- ❑ ARDOR—great emotion or passion
- ❑ ARDUOUS—extremely difficult, laborious
- ❑ ARID—extremely dry or deathly boring
- ❑ ARRAIGN—to call to court to answer an indictment
- ❑ ARROGATE—to demand, claim arrogantly
- ❑ ARSENAL—ammunition storehouse
- ❑ ARTICULATE (adj.)—well spoken, expressing oneself clearly
- ❑ ARTIFACT—historical relic, item made by human craft
- ❑ ARTISAN—craftsperson; expert

❑ ASCEND—to rise or climb

❑ ASCENDANCY—state of rising, ascending; power or control

❑ ASCERTAIN—to determine, discover, make certain of

❑ ASCETIC—self-denying, abstinent, austere

❑ ASCRIBE—to attribute to, assign

❑ ASHEN—resembling ashes; deathly pale

❑ ASKEW—crooked, tilted

❑ ASPERSION—false rumor, damaging report, slander

❑ ASPIRE—to have great hopes; to aim at a goal

❑ ASSAIL—to attack, assault

❑ ASSENT—to express agreement

❑ ASSERT—to affirm, attest

❑ ASSIDUOUS—diligent, persistent, hard-working

❑ ASSIGNATION—appointment for lovers' meeting; assignment

❑ ASSIMILATION—act of blending in, becoming similar

❑ ASSONANCE—resemblance in sound, especially in vowel sounds; partial rhyme

❑ ASSUAGE—to make less severe, ease, relieve

❑ ASTRINGENT—harsh, severe, stern

❑ ASTUTE—having good judgment

❑ ASUNDER (adv.)—into different parts

❑ ASYMMETRICAL—not corresponding in size, shape, position, etcetera

❑ ATONE—to make amends for a wrong

❑ ATROCIOUS—monstrous, shockingly bad, wicked

❑ ATROPHY—to waste away, wither from disuse

❑ ATTAIN—to accomplish, gain

❑ ATTENUATE—to make thin or slender; weaken

❑ ATTEST—to testify, stand as proof of, bear witness

❑ AUDACIOUS—bold, daring, fearless

❑ AUDIBLE—capable of being heard

❑ AUDIT—formal examination of financial records

❑ AUDITORY—having to do with hearing

❑ AUGMENT—to expand, extend

❑ AUGURY—prophecy, prediction of events

❑ AUGUST—dignified, awe-inspiring, venerable

❑ AUSPICIOUS—having favorable prospects, promising

❑ AUSTERE—stern, strict, unadorned

❑ AUTHORITARIAN—extremely strict, bossy

❑ AUTOCRAT—dictator

❑ AUTONOMOUS—separate, independent

❑ AUXILIARY—supplementary, reserve

❑ AVARICE—greed

❑ AVENGE—to retaliate, take revenge for an injury or crime

❑ AVER—to declare to be true, affirm

❑ AVERSION—intense dislike

❑ AVERT—to turn (something) away; prevent, hinder

❑ AVIARY—large enclosure housing birds

❑ AVOW—to state openly or declare

❑ AWRY—crooked, askew, amiss

❑ AXIOM—premise, postulate, self-evident truth

B

❑ BALEFUL—harmful, with evil intentions

❑ BALK—to refuse, shirk; prevent

❑ BALLAD—folk song, narrative poem

❑ BALM—soothing, healing influence

❑ BAN—to forbid, outlaw

❑ BANAL—trite, overly common

❑ BANE—something causing death, destruction, or ruin

❑ BANTER—playful conversation

❑ BASTION—fortification, stronghold

❑ BAY (v.)—to bark, especially in a deep, prolonged way

❑ BECALM—to make calm or still; keep motionless by lack of wind

❑ BECLOUD—to confuse; darken with clouds

❑ BEGUILE—to deceive, mislead; charm

❑ BEHEMOTH—huge creature

❑ BELABOR—to insist repeatedly or harp on

❑ BELATED—late

❑ BELEAGUER—to harass, plague

❑ BELFRY—bell tower, room in which a bell is hung

❑ BELIE—to misrepresent; expose as false

❑ BELITTLE—to represent as unimportant, make light of

❑ BELLICOSE—warlike, aggressive

❑ BELLIGERENT—hostile, tending to fight

❑ BELLOW—to roar, shout

❑ BEMUSE—to confuse, stupefy; plunge deep into thought

❑ BENCHMARK—standard of measure

❑ BENEFACTOR—someone giving aid or money

❑ BENEFICENT—kindly, charitable; doing good deeds; producing good effects

❑ BENIGHTED—unenlightened

❑ BENIGN—kindly, gentle, or harmless

❑ BEQUEATH—to give or leave through a will; to hand down

❑ BERATE—to scold harshly

❑ BESEECH—to beg, plead, implore

❑ BESTIAL—beastly, animal-like

❑ BESTOW—to give as a gift

❑ BETOKEN—to indicate, signify, give evidence of

❑ BEVY—group

❑ BIAS—prejudice, slant

❑ BIBLIOGRAPHY—list of books

❑ BIBLIOPHILE—book lover

❑ BILATERAL—two-sided

❑ BILK—to cheat, defraud

❑ BILLET—board and lodging for troops

❑ BIPED—two-footed animal

❑ BISECT—to cut into two (usually equal) parts

❑ BLANCH—to pale; take the color out of

❑ BLANDISH—to coax with flattery

❑ BLASPHEMOUS—cursing, profane, irreverent

❑ BLATANT—glaring, obvious, showy

❑ BLIGHT (v.)—to afflict, destroy

❑ BLITHE—joyful, cheerful, or without appropriate thought

❑ BLUDGEON—to hit as with a short, heavy club

❑ BOISTEROUS—rowdy, loud, unrestrained

❑ BOMBASTIC—using high-sounding but meaningless language

❑ BONANZA—extremely large amount; something profitable

❑ BONHOMIE—good-natured geniality; atmosphere of good cheer

❑ BOON—blessing, something to be thankful for

❑ BOOR—crude person, one lacking manners or taste

❑ BOTANIST—scientist who studies plants

❑ BOUNTIFUL—plentiful

❑ BOURGEOIS—middle-class

❑ BOVINE—cow-like; relating to cows

❑ BRAZEN—bold, shameless, impudent; of or like brass

❑ BREACH—act of breaking, violation

❑ BRIGAND—bandit, outlaw

❑ BROACH—to mention or suggest for the first time

❑ BRUSQUE—rough and abrupt in manner

❑ BUFFET (v.)—to toss about

❑ BUFFOON—clown or fool

❑ BULWARK—defense wall; anything serving as defense

❑ BURGEON—to sprout or flourish

❑ BURLY—brawny, husky

❑ BURNISH—to polish, make smooth and bright

❑ BURSAR—treasurer

❑ BUSTLE—commotion, energetic activity

❑ BUTT—person or thing that is object of ridicule

❑ BUTTRESS (n.)—to reinforce or support

❑ BYWAY—back road

C

❑ CACOPHONOUS—jarring, unpleasantly noisy

❑ CADENCE—rhythmic flow of poetry; marching beat

❑ CAJOLE—to flatter, coax, persuade

❑ CALAMITOUS—disastrous, catastrophic

❑ CALLOUS—thick-skinned, insensitive

❑ CALLOW—immature, lacking sophistication

❑ CALUMNY—false and malicious accusation, misrepresentation, slander

❑ CANDOR—honesty of expression

❑ CANNY—smart; founded on common sense

❑ CANONIZE—to declare a person a saint; raise to highest honors

❑ CANVASS—to examine thoroughly; conduct a poll

❑ CAPACIOUS—large, roomy; extensive

❑ CAPITULATE—to submit completely, surrender

❑ CAPRICIOUS—impulsive, whimsical, without much thought

❑ CARDIOLOGIST—physician specializing in diseases of the heart

❑ CARICATURE—exaggerated portrait, cartoon

❑ CARNAL—of the flesh

❑ CARNIVOROUS—meat-eating

❑ CARP (v.)—to find fault, complain constantly

❑ CARTOGRAPHY—science or art of making maps

❑ CAST (n.)—copy, replica

❑ CAST (v.)—to fling, to throw

❑ CASTIGATE—to punish, chastise, criticize severely

❑ CATALYST—something causing change without being changed

❑ CATEGORICAL—absolute, without exception

❑ CATHARSIS—purification, cleansing

❑ CATHOLIC—universal; broad and comprehensive

❑ CAUCUS—smaller group within an organization; a meeting of such a group

❑ CAULK—to make watertight

❏ CAUSALITY—cause-and-effect relationship

❏ CAUSTIC—biting, sarcastic; able to burn

❏ CAVALIER—carefree, happy; with lordly disdain

❏ CAVORT—to frolic, frisk

❏ CEDE—to surrender possession of something

❏ CELEBRITY—fame, widespread acclaim

❏ CENSORIOUS—severely critical

❏ CENTRIPETAL—directed or moving toward the center

❏ CERTITUDE—assurance, certainty

❏ CESSATION—temporary or complete halt

❏ CESSION—act of surrendering something

❏ CHAGRIN—shame, embarrassment, humiliation

❏ CHALICE—goblet, cup

❏ CHAMPION (v.)—to defend or support

❏ CHAOTIC—extremely disorderly

❏ CHARLATAN—quack, fake

❏ CHARY—watchful, cautious, extremely shy

❏ CHASTISE—to punish, discipline, scold

❏ CHERUBIC—sweet, innocent, resembling a cherub angel

❏ CHICANERY—trickery, fraud, deception

❏ CHIDE—to scold, express disapproval

❏ CHIMERICAL—fanciful, imaginary, visionary, impossible

❏ CHOLERIC—easily angered, short-tempered

❏ CHOICE (adj.)—specially selected, preferred

❏ CHORTLE—to chuckle

❏ CHROMATIC—relating to color

❏ CHRONICLER—one who keeps records of historical events

❏ CIRCUITOUS—roundabout

❏ CIRCUMFERENCE—boundary or distance around a circle or sphere

❏ CIRCUMLOCUTION—roundabout, lengthy way of saying something

❏ CIRCUMNAVIGATE—to sail completely around

❏ CIRCUMSCRIBE—to encircle; set limits on, confine

❏ CIRCUMSPECT—cautious, wary

❏ CIRCUMVENT—to go around; avoid

❏ CISTERN—tank for rainwater

❏ CITADEL—fortress or stronghold

❏ CIVIL—polite; relating to citizens

❏ CIVILITY—courtesy, politeness

❏ CLAIRVOYANT (adj.)—having ESP, psychic

❏ CLAMOR (v.) to make a noisy outcry

❏ CLAMOR (n.)—noisy outcry

❏ CLANDESTINE—secretive, concealed for a darker purpose

❏ CLARITY—clearness; clear understanding

❏ CLAUSTROPHOBIA—fear of small, confined places

❏ CLEAVE—to split or separate or to stick, cling, adhere

❏ CLEMENCY—merciful leniency

❏ CLOISTER (v.)—to confine, seclude

❏ COAGULATE—to clot or change from a liquid to a solid

❏ COALESCE—to grow together or cause to unite as one

❏ CODDLE—to baby, treat indulgently

❏ COERCE—to compel by force or intimidation

❏ COFFER—strongbox, large chest for money

❏ COGENT—logically forceful, compelling, convincing

❏ COGNATE—related, similar, akin

❏ COGNITION—mental process by which knowledge is acquired

❏ COGNOMEN—family name; any name, especially a nickname

❏ COHABIT—to live together

❏ COHERENT—intelligible, lucid, understandable

❏ COLLATERAL—accompanying

❏ COLLOQUIAL—characteristic of informal speech

❏ COLLOQUY—dialogue or conversation, conference

❏ COLLUSION—collaboration, complicity, conspiracy

❏ COMELINESS—physical grace and beauty

❏ COMMEND—to compliment, praise

❏ COMMENSURATE—proportional

❏ COMMISSION—fee payable to an agent; authorization

❏ COMMODIOUS—roomy, spacious

❏ COMMONPLACE—ordinary, found every day

❏ COMMUNICABLE—transmittable

❏ COMMUTE—to change a penalty to a less severe one

❏ COMPATRIOT—fellow countryman

❏ COMPELLING (adj.)—having a powerful and irresistible effect

❏ COMPENSATE—to repay or reimburse

❏ COMPLACENT—self-satisfied, smug

❏ COMPLEMENT—to complete, perfect

❏ COMPLIANT—submissive and yielding

❏ COMPLICITY—knowing partnership in wrongdoing

❏ COMPOUND (adj.)—complex; composed of several parts

❏ COMPOUND (v.)—to combine, augment

❏ COMPRESS—to reduce, squeeze

❏ COMPULSIVE—obsessive, fanatic

❏ COMPUNCTION—feeling of uneasiness caused by guilt or regret

☐ CONCAVE—curving inward

☐ CONCEDE—to yield, admit

☐ CONCEPTUALIZE—to envision, imagine

☐ CONCERTO—musical composition for orchestra and one or more soloists

☐ CONCILIATORY—overcoming distrust or hostility

☐ CONCORD—agreement

☐ CONCUR—to agree

☐ CONDONE—to pardon or forgive; overlook, justify, or excuse a fault

☐ CONDUIT—tube, pipe, or similar passage

☐ CONFECTION—something sweet to eat

☐ CONFISCATE—to appropriate, seize

☐ CONFLAGRATION—big, destructive fire

☐ CONFLUENCE—meeting place; meeting of two streams

☐ CONFOUND—to baffle, perplex

☐ CONGEAL—to become thick or solid, as a liquid freezing

☐ CONGENIAL—similar in tastes and habits

☐ CONGENITAL—existing since birth

☐ CONGLOMERATE—collected group of varied things

☐ CONGRESS—formal meeting or assembly

☐ CONGRUITY—correspondence, harmony, agreement

☐ CONJECTURE—speculation, prediction

☐ CONJUGAL—pertaining to marriage

☐ CONJURE—to evoke a spirit, cast a spell

☐ CONNIVE—to conspire, scheme

☐ CONSANGUINEOUS—of the same origin; related by blood

☐ CONSCIENTIOUS—governed by conscience; careful and thorough

☐ CONSECRATE—to declare sacred; dedicate to a goal

☐ CONSENSUS—unanimity, agreement of opinion or attitude

☐ CONSIGN—to commit, entrust

☐ CONSOLATION—something providing comfort or solace for a loss or hardship

☐ CONSOLIDATE—to combine, incorporate

☐ CONSONANT (adj.)—consistent with, in agreement with

☐ CONSTITUENT—component, part; citizen, voter

☐ CONSTRAINED—forced, compelled; confined, restrained

☐ CONSTRAINT—something that forces or compels; something that restrains or confines

☐ CONSTRUE—to explain or interpret

☐ CONSUMMATE (adj.)—accomplished, complete, perfect

☐ CONSUMMATE (v.)—to complete, fulfill

☐ CONTEND—to battle, clash; compete

☐ CONTENTIOUS—quarrelsome, disagreeable, belligerent

☐ CONTINENCE—self-control, self-restraint

☐ CONTRAVENE—to contradict, deny, act contrary to

☐ CONTRITE—deeply sorrowful and repentant for a wrong

☐ CONTUSION—bruise

☐ CONUNDRUM—riddle, puzzle or problem with no solution

☐ CONVALESCENCE—gradual recovery after an illness

☐ CONVENE—to meet, come together, assemble

☐ CONVENTIONAL—typical, customary, commonplace

☐ CONVEX—curved outward

☐ CONVIVIAL—sociable; fond of eating, drinking, and people

☐ CONVOKE—to call together, summon

☐ CONVOLUTED—twisted, complicated, involved

☐ COPIOUS—abundant, plentiful

☐ COQUETTE—woman who flirts

☐ CORPOREAL—having to do with the body; tangible, material

☐ CORPULENCE—obesity, fatness, bulkiness

☐ CORRELATION—association, mutual relation of two or more things

☐ CORROBORATE—to confirm, verify

☐ CORRUGATE—to mold in a shape with parallel grooves and ridges

☐ COSMETIC (adj.)—relating to beauty; affecting the surface of something

☐ COSMOGRAPHY—science that deals with the nature of the universe

☐ COSMOPOLITAN—sophisticated, free from local prejudices

☐ COSSET—to pamper, treat with great care

☐ COTERIE—small group of persons with a similar purpose

☐ COUNTENANCE (n.)—facial expression; look of approval or support

☐ COUNTENANCE (v.)—to favor, support

☐ COUNTERMAND—to annul, cancel, make a contrary order

☐ COUNTERVAIL—to counteract, to exert force against

☐ COVEN—group of witches

☐ COVERT—hidden; secret

☐ COVET—to desire strongly something possessed by another

☐ CRASS—crude, unrefined

☐ CRAVEN—cowardly

☐ CREDENCE—acceptance of something as true or real

☐ CREDIBLE—plausible, believable

☐ CREDULOUS—gullible, trusting

☐ CREED—statement of belief or principle

- CRESCENDO—gradual increase in volume of sound
- CRITERION—standard for judging, rule for testing
- CRYPTIC—puzzling
- CUISINE—characteristic style of cooking
- CULMINATION—climax, final stage
- CULPABLE—guilty, responsible for wrong
- CULPRIT—guilty person
- CUMULATIVE—resulting from gradual increase
- CUPIDITY—greed
- CURATOR—caretaker and overseer of an exhibition, esp. in a museum
- CURMUDGEON—cranky person
- CURSORY—hastily done, superficial
- CURT—abrupt, blunt
- CURTAIL—to shorten
- CUTLERY—cutting instruments; tableware
- CYGNET—young swan
- CYNIC—person who distrusts the motives of others

D

- DAINTY—delicate, sweet
- DAUNT—to discourage, intimidate
- DEARTH—lack, scarcity, insufficiency
- DEBASE—to degrade or lower in quality or stature
- DEBAUCH—to corrupt, seduce from virtue or duty; indulge
- DEBILITATE—to weaken, enfeeble
- DEBUNK—to discredit, disprove
- DEBUTANTE—young woman making debut in high society
- DECAPITATE—to behead
- DECATHLON—athletic contest with 10 events
- DECIDUOUS—losing leaves in the fall; short-lived, temporary
- DECLIVITY—downward slope
- DECOROUS—proper, tasteful, socially correct
- DECORUM—proper behavior, etiquette
- DECRY—to belittle, openly condemn
- DEFACE—to mar the appearance of, vandalize
- DEFAMATORY—slanderous, injurious to the reputation
- DEFENDANT—person required to answer a legal action or suit
- DEFERENTIAL—respectful and polite in a submissive way
- DEFILE—to dirty, spoil; to disgrace, dishonor

- DEFINITIVE—clear-cut, explicit or decisive
- DEFLATION—decrease, depreciation
- DEFORM—to disfigure, distort
- DEFT—skillful, dexterous
- DEFUNCT—no longer existing, dead, extinct
- DELECTABLE—appetizing, delicious
- DELEGATE (v.)—to give powers to another
- DELETERIOUS—harmful, destructive, detrimental
- DELINEATION—depiction, representation
- DELTA—tidal deposit at the mouth of a river
- DELUGE (n.)—flood
- DELUGE (v.)—to submerge, overwhelm
- DEMAGOGUE—leader, rabble-rouser, usually using appeals to emotion or prejudice
- DEMARCATION—borderline; act of defining or marking a boundary or distinction
- DEMEAN—to degrade, humiliate, humble
- DEMOGRAPHICS—data relating to study of human population
- DEMOTE—to reduce to a lower grade or rank
- DEMOTION—lowering in rank or grade
- DEMUR—to express doubts or objections
- DEMYSTIFY—to remove mystery from, clarify
- DENIGRATE—to slur or blacken someone's reputation
- DENOUNCE—to accuse, blame
- DENUDE—to make bare, uncover, undress
- DENUNCIATION—public condemnation
- DEPICT—to describe, represent
- DEPLETE—to use up, exhaust
- DEPLORE—to express or feel disapproval of; regret strongly
- DEPLOY—to spread out strategically over an area
- DEPOSE—to remove from a high position, as from a throne
- DEPRAVITY—sinfulness, moral corruption
- DEPRECATE—to belittle, disparage
- DEPRECIATE—to lose value gradually
- DERIDE—to mock, ridicule, make fun of
- DERIVATIVE—copied or adapted; not original
- DERIVE—to originate; take from a certain source
- DEROGATE—to belittle, disparage
- DESECRATE—to abuse something sacred
- DESICCATE—to dry completely, dehydrate
- DESIST—to stop doing something
- DESPONDENT—feeling discouraged and dejected
- DESPOT—tyrannical ruler

- ❏ DESTITUTE—very poor, poverty-stricken
- ❏ DESULTORY—at random, rambling, unmethodical
- ❏ DETER—to discourage; prevent from happening
- ❏ DETERMINATE—having defined limits; conclusive
- ❏ DETRIMENTAL—causing harm or injury
- ❏ DEVIATE—to stray, wander
- ❏ DEVIATION—departure, exception, anomaly
- ❏ DEVOID—totally lacking
- ❏ DEVOUT—deeply religious
- ❏ DEXTEROUS—skilled physically or mentally
- ❏ DIABOLICAL—fiendish; wicked
- ❏ DIALECT—regional style of speaking
- ❏ DIAPHANOUS—allowing light to show through; delicate
- ❏ DIATRIBE—bitter verbal attack
- ❏ DICHOTOMY—division into two parts
- ❏ DICTUM—authoritative statement; popular saying
- ❏ DIDACTIC—excessively instructive
- ❏ DIFFERENTIATE—to distinguish between two items
- ❏ DIFFIDENCE—shyness, lack of confidence
- ❏ DIFFRACT—to cause to separate into parts, esp. light
- ❏ DIFFUSE—widely spread out
- ❏ DIGRESS—to turn aside; to stray from the main point
- ❏ DILAPIDATED—in disrepair, run down, neglected
- ❏ DILATE—to enlarge, swell, extend
- ❏ DILATORY—slow, tending to delay
- ❏ DILUVIAL—relating to a flood
- ❏ DIMINUTIVE—small
- ❏ DIPLOMACY—discretion, tact
- ❏ DIRGE—funeral hymn
- ❏ DISAFFECTED—discontented and disloyal
- ❏ DISARRAY—clutter, disorder
- ❏ DISBAND—to break up
- ❏ DISBAR—to expel from legal profession
- ❏ DISBURSE—to pay out
- ❏ DISCERN—to perceive something obscure
- ❏ DISCLAIM—to deny, disavow
- ❏ DISCLOSE—to confess, divulge
- ❏ DISCONCERTING—bewildering, perplexing, slightly disturbing
- ❏ DISCORDANT—harsh-sounding, badly out of tune
- ❏ DISCREDIT—to dishonor or disgrace
- ❏ DISCREDITED—disbelieved, discounted; disgraced, dishonored
- ❏ DISCREPANCY—difference between

- ❏ DISCRETIONARY—subject to one's own judgment
- ❏ DISCURSIVE—wandering from topic to topic
- ❏ DISDAIN—to regard with scorn and contempt
- ❏ DISDAINFUL—contemptuous, scornful
- ❏ DISENGAGED—disconnected, disassociated
- ❏ DISGORGE—to vomit, discharge violently
- ❏ DISHEVELED—untidy, disarranged, unkempt
- ❏ DISINCLINED—averse, unwilling, lacking desire
- ❏ DISPARAGE—to belittle, speak disrespectfully about
- ❏ DISPARATE—dissimilar, different in kind
- ❏ DISPARITY—contrast, dissimilarity
- ❏ DISPASSIONATE—free from emotion; impartial, unbiased
- ❏ DISPEL—to drive out or scatter
- ❏ DISPENSE—to distribute, administer
- ❏ DISPENSE WITH—to suspend the operation of, do without
- ❏ DISPERSE—to break up, scatter
- ❏ DISPIRIT—to dishearten, make dejected
- ❏ DISREPUTE—disgrace, dishonor
- ❏ DISSEMBLE—to pretend, disguise one's motives
- ❏ DISSEMINATE—to spread far and wide
- ❏ DISSENSION—difference of opinion
- ❏ DISSIPATE—to scatter; to pursue pleasure to excess
- ❏ DISSOCIATE—to separate; remove from an association
- ❏ DISSONANT—harsh and unpleasant sounding
- ❏ DISSUADE—to persuade someone to alter original intentions
- ❏ DISTEND—to swell, inflate, bloat
- ❏ DISTRAUGHT—very worried and distressed
- ❏ DISTRUST (n.)—disbelief and suspicion
- ❏ DITHER—to move or act confusedly or without clear purpose
- ❏ DIURNAL—daily
- ❏ DIVINE (v.)—to foretell or know by inspiration
- ❏ DIVISIVE—creating disunity or conflict
- ❏ DOCILE—tame, willing to be taught
- ❏ DOCTRINAIRE—rigidly devoted to theories
- ❏ DOGMATIC—rigidly fixed in opinion, opinionated
- ❏ DOLEFUL—sad, mournful
- ❏ DOLT—idiot, dimwit, foolish person
- ❏ DOMINEER—to rule over something in a tyrannical way
- ❏ DONOR—benefactor, contributor
- ❏ DORMANT—at rest, inactive, in suspended animation
- ❏ DOTARD—senile old person
- ❏ DOTING—excessively fond, loving to excess

- DOUR—sullen and gloomy; stern and severe
- DOWRY—money or property given by a bride to her husband
- DRAFT (v.)—to plan, outline; to recruit, conscript
- DRIVEL—stupid talk; slobber
- DROLL—amusing in a wry, subtle way
- DROSS—waste produced during metal smelting; garbage
- DULCET—pleasant sounding, soothing to the ear
- DUPE (v.)—to deceive, trick
- DUPE (n.)—fool, pawn
- DUPLICITY—deception, dishonesty, double-dealing
- DURABILITY—strength, sturdiness
- DURATION—period of time that something lasts
- DURESS—threat of force or intimidation; imprisonment
- DYSPEPTIC—suffering from indigestion; gloomy and irritable

E

- EBB—to fade away, recede
- EBULLIENT—exhilarated, full of enthusiasm and high spirits
- ECLECTIC—selecting from various sources
- ECSTATIC—joyful
- EDDY—air or wind current
- EDICT—law, command, official public order
- EDIFICE—building
- EDIFY—to instruct morally and spiritually
- EDITORIALIZE—to express an opinion on an issue
- EFFACE—to erase or make illegible
- EFFERVESCENT—bubbly, lively
- EFFICACIOUS—effective, efficient
- EFFIGY—stuffed doll; likeness of a person
- EFFLUVIA—outpouring of gases or vapors
- EFFRONTERY—impudent boldness; audacity
- EFFULGENT—brilliantly shining
- EFFUSIVE—expressing emotion without restraint
- EGOCENTRIC—acting as if things are centered around oneself
- EGREGIOUS—conspicuously bad
- EGRESS—exit
- ELATION—exhilaration, joy
- ELEGY—mournful poem, usually about the dead

- ELICIT—to draw out, provoke
- ELOQUENCE—fluent and effective speech
- ELUCIDATE—to explain, clarify
- EMACIATED—skinny, scrawny, gaunt, esp. from hunger
- EMANCIPATE—to set free, liberate
- EMBELLISH—to ornament; make attractive with decoration or details; add details to a statement
- EMBEZZLE—to steal money in violation of a trust
- EMBROIL—to involve in; cause to fall into disorder
- EMEND—to correct a text
- EMINENT—celebrated, distinguished; outstanding, towering
- EMOLLIENT—having soothing qualities, especially for skin
- EMOTIVE—appealing to or expressing emotion
- EMPATHY—identification with another's feelings
- EMULATE—to copy, imitate
- ENCIPHER—to translate a message into code
- ENCORE—additional performance, often demanded by audience
- ENCUMBER—to hinder, burden, restrict motion
- ENDEMIC—belonging to a particular area, inherent
- ENDURANCE—ability to withstand hardships
- ENERVATE—to weaken, sap strength from
- ENGENDER—to produce, cause, bring about
- ENIGMATIC—puzzling, inexplicable
- ENJOIN—to urge, order, command; forbid or prohibit, as by judicial order
- ENMITY—hostility, antagonism, ill-will
- ENNUI—boredom, lack of interest and energy
- ENORMITY—state of being gigantic or terrible
- ENSCONCE—to settle comfortably into a place
- ENSHROUD—to cover, enclose with a dark cover
- ENTAIL—to involve as a necessary result, necessitate
- ENTHRALL—to captivate, enchant, enslave
- ENTITY—something with its own existence or form
- ENTOMOLOGIST—scientist who studies insects
- ENTREAT—to plead, beg
- ENUMERATE—to count, list, itemize
- ENUNCIATE—to pronounce clearly
- EPHEMERAL—momentary, transient, fleeting
- EPICURE—person with refined taste in food and wine
- EPIGRAM—short, witty saying or poem
- EPIGRAPH—quotation at the beginning of a literary work
- EPILOGUE—concluding section of a literary work

❑ EPITOME—representative of an entire group; summary

❑ EPOCHAL—very significant or influential; defining an epoch or time period

❑ EQUANIMITY—calmness, composure

❑ EQUESTRIAN—one who rides on horseback

❑ EQUINE—relating to horses

❑ EQUIVOCAL—ambiguous, open to two interpretations

❑ EQUIVOCATE—to use vague or ambiguous language intentionally

❑ ERADICATE—to erase or wipe out

❑ ERRANT—straying, mistaken, roving

❑ ERUDITE—learned, scholarly

❑ ESCHEW—to abstain from, avoid

❑ ESOTERIC—understood only by a learned few

❑ ESPOUSE—to support or advocate; to marry

❑ ESTRANGE—to alienate, keep at a distance

❑ ETHEREAL—not earthly, spiritual, delicate

❑ ETHOS—beliefs or character of a group

❑ ETYMOLOGY—origin and history of a word; study of words

❑ EULOGY—high praise, often in a public speech

❑ EUPHEMISM—use of an inoffensive word or phrase in place of a more distasteful one

❑ EUPHONY—pleasant, harmonious sound

❑ EUPHORIA—feeling of well-being or happiness

❑ EURYTHMICS—art of harmonious bodily movement

❑ EUTHANASIA—mercy killing; intentional, easy, and painless death

❑ EVADE—to avoid, dodge

❑ EVANESCENT—momentary, transitory, short-lived

❑ EVICT—to put out or force out

❑ EVINCE—to show clearly, display, signify

❑ EVOKE—to inspire memories; to produce a reaction

❑ EXACERBATE—to aggravate, intensify the bad qualities of

❑ EXASPERATION—irritation

❑ EXCERPT (n.)—selection from a book or play

❑ EXCOMMUNICATE—to bar from membership in the church

❑ EXCRUCIATING—agonizing, intensely painful

❑ EXCULPATE—to clear of blame or fault, vindicate

❑ EXECRABLE—utterly detestable, abhorrent

❑ EXHILARATION—state of being energetic or filled with happiness

❑ EXHORT—to urge or incite by strong appeals

❑ EXHUME—to remove from a grave; uncover a secret

❑ EXIGENT—urgent; excessively demanding

❑ EXONERATE—to clear of blame, absolve

❑ EXORBITANT—extravagant, greater than reasonable

❑ EXORCISE—to expel evil spirits

❑ EXOTIC—foreign; romantic, excitingly strange

❑ EXPANSIVE—sweeping, comprehensive; tending to expand

❑ EXPATRIATE (n.)—one who lives outside one's native land

❑ EXPATRIATE (v.)—to drive someone from his/her native land

❑ EXPEDIENT (adj.)—convenient, efficient, practical

❑ EXPIATE—to atone for, make amends for

❑ EXPIRE—to come to an end; die; breathe out

❑ EXPLICABLE—capable of being explained

❑ EXPLICIT—clearly defined, specific; forthright in expression

❑ EXPLODE—to debunk, disprove; blow up, burst

❑ EXPONENT—one who champions or advocates

❑ EXPOUND—to elaborate; to expand or increase

❑ EXPUNGE—to erase, eliminate completely

❑ EXPURGATE—to censor

❑ EXTEMPORANEOUS—unrehearsed, on the spur of the moment

❑ EXTENUATE—to lessen the seriousness, strength or effect of

❑ EXTINCTION—end of a living thing or species

❑ EXTOL—to praise

❑ EXTORT—to obtain something by threats

❑ EXTRANEOUS—irrelevant, unrelated, unnecessary

❑ EXTREMITY—outermost or farthest point

❑ EXTRICATE—to free from, disentangle

❑ EXTRINSIC—not inherent or essential, coming from without

❑ EXUBERANT—lively, happy, and full of good spirits

❑ EXUDE—to give off, ooze

❑ EXULT—to rejoice

F

❑ FABRICATE—to make or devise; construct

❑ FABRICATED—constructed, invented; faked, falsified

❑ FACADE—face, front; mask, superficial appearance

❑ FACILE—very easy

❑ FACILITATE—to aid, assist

❑ FACILITY—aptitude, ease in doing something

❑ FALLACIOUS—wrong, unsound, illogical

- ❏ FALLOW—uncultivated, unused
- ❏ FANATICISM—extreme devotion to a cause
- ❏ FARCICAL—absurd, ludicrous
- ❏ FASTIDIOUS—careful with details
- ❏ FATHOM (v.)—to measure the depth of, gauge
- ❏ FATUOUS—stupid; foolishly self-satisfied
- ❏ FAULT—break in a rock formation; mistake or error
- ❏ FAWN (v.)—to flatter excessively, seek the favor of
- ❏ FAZE—to bother, upset, or disconcert
- ❏ FEASIBLE—possible, capable of being done
- ❏ FECKLESS—ineffective, careless, irresponsible
- ❏ FECUND—fertile, fruitful, productive
- ❏ FEDERATION—union of organizations; union of several states, each of which retains local power
- ❏ FEIGN—to pretend, give a false impression; to invent falsely
- ❏ FEISTY—excitable, easily drawn into quarrels
- ❏ FELICITOUS—suitable, appropriate; well-spoken
- ❏ FELL (v.)—to chop, cut down
- ❏ FERVID—passionate, intense, zealous
- ❏ FETID—foul-smelling, putrid
- ❏ FETTER—to bind, chain, confine
- ❏ FIASCO—disaster, utter failure
- ❏ FICTIVE—fictional, imaginary
- ❏ FIDELITY—loyalty
- ❏ FILCH—to steal
- ❏ FILIBUSTER—use of obstructive tactics in a legislative assembly to prevent adoption of a measure
- ❏ FINICKY—fussy, difficult to please
- ❏ FISSION—process of splitting into two parts
- ❏ FITFUL—intermittent, irregular
- ❏ FLACCID—limp, flabby, weak
- ❏ FLAGRANT—outrageous, shameless
- ❏ FLAMBOYANT—flashy, garish; exciting, dazzling
- ❏ FLAMMABLE—combustible, being easily burned
- ❏ FLAUNT—to show off
- ❏ FLEDGLING—young bird just learning to fly; beginner, novice
- ❏ FLORA—plants
- ❏ FLORID—gaudy, extremely ornate; ruddy, flushed
- ❏ FLOUNDER—to falter, waver; to muddle, struggle
- ❏ FLOUT—to treat contemptuously, scorn
- ❏ FLUCTUATE—to alternate, waver
- ❏ FODDER—raw material; feed for animals
- ❏ FOIBLE—minor weakness or character flaw

- ❏ FOIL (v.)—to defeat, frustrate
- ❏ FOLIATE—to grow, sprout leaves
- ❏ FOMENT—to arouse or incite
- ❏ FORBEARANCE—patience, restraint, leniency
- ❏ FORECLOSE—to rule out; to seize debtor's property for lack of payments
- ❏ FORD (v.)—to cross a body of water at a shallow place
- ❏ FOREBODING—dark sense of evil to come
- ❏ FORENSIC—relating to legal proceedings; relating to debates
- ❏ FORESTALL—to prevent, delay; anticipate
- ❏ FORETHOUGHT—anticipation, foresight
- ❏ FORGO—to go without, refrain from
- ❏ FORLORN—dreary, deserted; unhappy; hopeless, despairing
- ❏ FORMULATE—to conceive, devise; to draft, plan; to express, state
- ❏ FORSAKE—to abandon, withdraw from
- ❏ FORSWEAR—to repudiate, renounce, disclaim, reject
- ❏ FORTE—strong point, something a person does well
- ❏ FORTUITOUS—happening by luck, fortunate
- ❏ FOSTER—to nourish, cultivate, promote
- ❏ FOUNDATION—groundwork, support; institution established by donation to aid a certain cause
- ❏ FOUNDER (v.)—to fall helplessly; sink
- ❏ FRACAS—noisy dispute
- ❏ FRACTIOUS—unruly, rebellious
- ❏ FRAGMENTATION—division, separation into parts, disorganization
- ❏ FRANK—honest and straightforward
- ❏ FRAUD—deception, hoax
- ❏ FRAUDULENT—deceitful, dishonest, unethical
- ❏ FRAUGHT—full of, accompanied by
- ❏ FRENETIC—wildly frantic, frenzied, hectic
- ❏ FRENZIED—feverishly fast, hectic, and confused
- ❏ FRIVOLOUS—petty, trivial; flippant, silly
- ❏ FROND—leaf
- ❏ FULSOME—sickeningly excessive; repulsive
- ❏ FUNEREAL—mournful, appropriate to a funeral
- ❏ FURTIVE—secret, stealthy
- ❏ FUSION—process of merging things into one

G

- ❑ GALL (n.)—bitterness; careless nerve
- ❑ GALL (v.)—to exasperate and irritate
- ❑ GAMBOL—to dance or skip around playfully
- ❑ GAMELY—courageously
- ❑ GARGANTUAN—giant, tremendous
- ❑ GARNER—to gather and store
- ❑ GARRULOUS—very talkative
- ❑ GAUNT—thin and bony
- ❑ GAVEL—mallet used for commanding attention
- ❑ GENRE—type, class, category
- ❑ GERMINATE—to begin to grow (as with a seed or idea)
- ❑ GESTATION—growth process from conception to birth
- ❑ GIBE—to make heckling, taunting remarks
- ❑ GIRTH—distance around something
- ❑ GLIB—fluent in an insincere manner; offhand, casual
- ❑ GLOBAL—involving the entire world; relating to a whole
- ❑ GLOWER—to glare, stare angrily and intensely
- ❑ GLUTTONY—eating and drinking to excess
- ❑ GNARL—to make knotted, deform
- ❑ GNOSTIC—having to do with knowledge
- ❑ GOAD—to prod or urge
- ❑ GRADATION—process occurring by regular degrees or stages; variation in color
- ❑ GRANDILOQUENCE—pompous talk, fancy but meaningless language
- ❑ GRANDIOSE—magnificent and imposing; exaggerated and pretentious
- ❑ GRANULAR—having a grainy texture
- ❑ GRASP (v.)—to perceive and understand; to hold securely
- ❑ GRATIS—free, costing nothing
- ❑ GRATUITOUS—free, voluntary; unnecessary and unjustified
- ❑ GRATUITY—something given voluntarily, tip
- ❑ GREGARIOUS—outgoing, sociable
- ❑ GRIEVOUS—causing grief or sorrow; serious and distressing
- ❑ GRIMACE—facial expression showing pain or disgust
- ❑ GRIMY—dirty, filthy
- ❑ GROSS (adj.)—obscene; blatant, flagrant
- ❑ GROSS (n.)—total before deductions
- ❑ GROVEL—to humble oneself in a demeaning way
- ❑ GUILE—trickery, deception
- ❑ GULLIBLE—easily deceived
- ❑ GUSTATORY—relating to sense of taste

H

- ❑ HABITAT—dwelling place
- ❑ HACKNEYED—worn out by overuse
- ❑ HALLOW—to make holy; treat as sacred
- ❑ HAMLET—small village
- ❑ HAPLESS—unfortunate, having bad luck
- ❑ HARBINGER—precursor, sign of something to come
- ❑ HARDY—robust, vigorous
- ❑ HARROWING—extremely distressing, terrifying
- ❑ HASTEN—to hurry, to speed up
- ❑ HAUGHTY—arrogant and condescending
- ❑ HEADSTRONG—reckless; insisting on one's own way
- ❑ HEATHEN—pagan; uncivilized and irreligious
- ❑ HECTIC—hasty, hurried, confused
- ❑ HEDONISM—pursuit of pleasure as a goal
- ❑ HEGEMONY—leadership, domination, usually by a country
- ❑ HEIGHTEN—to raise
- ❑ HEINOUS—shocking, wicked, terrible
- ❑ HEMICYCLE—semicircular form or structure
- ❑ HEMORRHAGE (n.)—heavy bleeding
- ❑ HEMORRHAGE (v.)—to bleed heavily
- ❑ HERETICAL—opposed to an established religious orthodoxy
- ❑ HERMETIC—tightly sealed
- ❑ HETERODOX—unorthodox, not widely accepted
- ❑ HETEROGENEOUS—composed of unlike parts, different, diverse
- ❑ HEW—to cut with an ax
- ❑ HIATUS—break, interruption, vacation
- ❑ HIDEBOUND—excessively rigid; dry and stiff
- ❑ HINDSIGHT—perception of events after they happen
- ❑ HINTERLAND—wilderness
- ❑ HOARY—very old; whitish or gray from age
- ❑ HOLISTIC—emphasizing importance of the whole and interdependence of its parts
- ❑ HOLOCAUST—widespread destruction, usually by fire
- ❑ HOMAGE—public honor and respect
- ❑ HOMOGENEOUS—composed of identical parts
- ❑ HOMONYM—word identical in pronunciation and spelling but different in meaning
- ❑ HONE—to sharpen
- ❑ HONOR—to praise, glorify, pay tribute to
- ❑ HUMANE—merciful, kindly

- ❑ HUSBAND (v.)—to farm; manage carefully and thriftily
- ❑ HUTCH—pen or coop for animals; shack, shanty
- ❑ HYDRATE—to add water to
- ❑ HYGIENIC—clean, sanitary
- ❑ HYMN—religious song, usually of praise or thanks
- ❑ HYPERBOLE—purposeful exaggeration for effect
- ❑ HYPERVENTILATE—to breathe abnormally fast
- ❑ HYPOCHONDRIA—unfounded belief that one is often ill
- ❑ HYPOCRITE—person claiming beliefs or virtues he or she doesn't really possess
- ❑ HYPOTHERMIA—abnormally low body temperature
- ❑ HYPOTHESIS—assumption subject to proof
- ❑ HYPOTHETICAL—theoretical, speculative

I

- ❑ ICONOCLAST—one who attacks traditional beliefs
- ❑ IDEALISM—pursuit of noble goals
- ❑ IDIOSYNCRASY—peculiarity of temperament, eccentricity
- ❑ IGNOBLE—dishonorable, not noble in character
- ❑ IGNOMINIOUS—disgraceful and dishonorable
- ❑ ILK—type or kind
- ❑ ILLICIT—illegal, improper
- ❑ ILLIMITABLE—limitless
- ❑ ILLUSORY—unreal, deceptive
- ❑ ILLUSTRIOUS—famous, renowned
- ❑ IMBUE—to infuse; dye, wet, moisten
- ❑ IMMACULATE—spotless; free from error
- ❑ IMMATERIAL—extraneous, inconsequential, nonessential; not consisting of matter
- ❑ IMMENSE—enormous, huge
- ❑ IMMERSE—to bathe, dip; to engross, preoccupy
- ❑ IMMOBILE—not moveable; still
- ❑ IMMUNE—exempt; protected from harm or disease; unresponsive to
- ❑ IMMUNOLOGICAL—relating to immune system
- ❑ IMMUTABLE—unchangeable, invariable
- ❑ IMPAIR—to damage, injure
- ❑ IMPASSE—blocked path, dilemma with no solution
- ❑ IMPASSIONED—with passion
- ❑ IMPASSIVE—showing no emotion
- ❑ IMPEACH—to charge with misdeeds in public office; accuse
- ❑ IMPECCABLE—flawless, without fault

- ❑ IMPECUNIOUS—poor, having no money
- ❑ IMPEDIMENT—barrier, obstacle; speech disorder
- ❑ IMPERATIVE—essential; mandatory
- ❑ IMPERIOUS—arrogantly self-assured, domineering, overbearing
- ❑ IMPERTINENT—rude
- ❑ IMPERTURBABLE—not capable of being disturbed
- ❑ IMPERVIOUS—impossible to penetrate; incapable of being affected
- ❑ IMPETUOUS—quick to act without thinking
- ❑ IMPIOUS—not devout in religion
- ❑ IMPLACABLE—inflexible, incapable of being pleased
- ❑ IMPLANT (v.)—to set securely or deeply; to instill
- ❑ IMPLAUSIBLE—improbable, inconceivable
- ❑ IMPLICATE—to involve in a crime, incriminate
- ❑ IMPLICIT—implied, not directly expressed
- ❑ IMPORTUNE—to ask repeatedly, beg
- ❑ IMPOSE—to inflict, force upon
- ❑ IMPOSING—dignified, grand
- ❑ IMPOTENT—powerless, ineffective, lacking strength
- ❑ IMPOUND—to seize and confine
- ❑ IMPOVERISH—to make poor or bankrupt
- ❑ IMPRECATION—curse
- ❑ IMPREGNABLE—totally safe from attack, able to resist defeat
- ❑ IMPRESSIONABLE—easily influenced or affected
- ❑ IMPROMPTU—spontaneous, without rehearsal
- ❑ IMPROVIDENT—without planning or foresight, negligent
- ❑ IMPUDENT—arrogant, audacious
- ❑ IMPUGN—to call into question, attack verbally
- ❑ IMPULSE—sudden tendency, inclination
- ❑ IMPULSIVE—spontaneous, unpredictable
- ❑ INADVERTENTLY—unintentionally
- ❑ INANE—foolish, silly, lacking significance
- ❑ INAUGURATE—to begin or start officially; to induct into office
- ❑ INCANDESCENT—shining brightly
- ❑ INCARCERATE—to put in jail; to confine
- ❑ INCARCERATION—imprisonment
- ❑ INCARNADINE—blood-red in color
- ❑ INCARNATE—having bodily form
- ❑ INCENDIARY—combustible, flammable, burning easily
- ❑ INCENSE (v.)—to infuriate, enrage
- ❑ INCEPTION—beginning

❑ INCESSANT—continuous, never ceasing

❑ INCHOATE—imperfectly formed or formulated

❑ INCIPIENT—beginning to exist or appear; in an initial stage

❑ INCISIVE—perceptive, penetrating

❑ INCLINATION—tendency towards

❑ INCLUSIVE—comprehensive, all-encompassing

❑ INCOGNITO—in disguise, concealing one's identity

❑ INCONCEIVABLE—impossible, unthinkable

❑ INCONSEQUENTIAL—unimportant, trivial

❑ INCONTROVERTIBLE—unquestionable, beyond dispute

❑ INCORRIGIBLE—incapable of being corrected

❑ INCREDULOUS—skeptical, doubtful

❑ INCULCATE—to teach, impress in the mind

❑ INCULPATE—to blame, charge with a crime

❑ INCUMBENT—holding a specified office, often political

❑ INCURSION—sudden invasion

❑ INDEFATIGABLE—never tired

❑ INDEFENSIBLE—inexcusable, unforgivable

❑ INDELIBLE—permanent, not erasable

❑ INDICATIVE—showing or pointing out, suggestive of

❑ INDICT—to accuse formally, charge with a crime

❑ INDIGENOUS—native, occurring naturally in an area

❑ INDIGENT—very poor

❑ INDIGNANT—angry, incensed, offended

❑ INDOLENT—habitually lazy, idle

❑ INDOMITABLE—fearless, unconquerable

❑ INDUBITABLE—unquestionable

❑ INDUCE—to persuade; bring about

❑ INDUCT—to place ceremoniously in office

❑ INDULGE—to give in to a craving or desire

❑ INDUSTRY—business or trade; diligence, energy

❑ INEBRIATED—drunk, intoxicated

❑ INEPT—clumsy, awkward

❑ INERT—unable to move, tending to inactivity

❑ INESTIMABLE—too great to be estimated

❑ INEVITABLE—certain, unavoidable

❑ INEXORABLE—inflexible, unyielding

❑ INEXTRICABLE—incapable of being disentangled

❑ INFALLIBLE—incapable of making a mistake

❑ INFAMY—reputation for bad deeds

❑ INFANTILE—childish, immature

❑ INFATUATED—strongly or foolishly attached to, inspired with foolish passion, overly in love

❑ INFER—to conclude, deduce

❑ INFILTRATE—to pass secretly into enemy territory

❑ INFINITESIMAL—extremely tiny

❑ INFIRMITY—disease, ailment

❑ INFRINGE—to encroach, trespass; to transgress, violate

❑ INFURIATE—to anger, provoke, outrage

❑ INFURIATING—provoking anger or outrage

❑ INGENIOUS—original, clever, inventive

❑ INGENUOUS—straightforward, open; naive and unsophisticated

❑ INGRATE—ungrateful person

❑ INGRATIATE—to bring oneself purposely into another's good graces

❑ INGRESS—entrance

❑ INHIBIT—to hold back, prevent, restrain

❑ INIMICAL—hostile, unfriendly

❑ INIQUITY—sin, evil act

❑ INITIATE—to begin, introduce; to enlist, induct

❑ INJECT—to force into; to introduce into conversation

❑ INJUNCTION—command, order

❑ INKLING—hint; vague idea

❑ INNATE—natural, inborn

❑ INNATENESS—state of being natural or inborn

❑ INNOCUOUS—harmless; inoffensive

❑ INNOVATE—to invent, modernize, revolutionize

❑ INNUENDO—indirect and subtle criticism, insinuation

❑ INNUMERABLE—too many to be counted

❑ INOFFENSIVE—harmless, innocent

❑ INOPERABLE—not operable; incurable by surgery

❑ INQUEST—investigation; court or legal proceeding

❑ INSATIABLE—never satisfied

❑ INSCRUTABLE—impossible to understand fully

❑ INSENTIENT—unfeeling, unconscious

❑ INSIDIOUS—sly, treacherous, devious

❑ INSINUATE—to suggest, say indirectly, imply

❑ INSIPID—bland, lacking flavor; lacking excitement

❑ INSOLENT—insulting and arrogant

❑ INSOLUBLE—not able to be solved or explained

❑ INSOLVENT—bankrupt, unable to pay one's debts

❑ INSTIGATE—to incite, urge, agitate

❑ INSUBSTANTIAL—modest, insignificant

❑ INSULAR—isolated, detached

❑ INSUPERABLE—insurmountable, unconquerable

❑ INSURGENT (adj.)—rebellious, insubordinate

- ❏ INSURRECTION—rebellion
- ❏ INTEGRAL—central, indispensable
- ❏ INTEGRITY—decency, honesty; wholeness
- ❏ INTEMPERATE—not moderate
- ❏ INTER—to bury
- ❏ INTERDICT—to forbid, prohibit
- ❏ INTERJECT—to interpose, insert
- ❏ INTERLOCUTOR—someone taking part in a dialogue
- ❏ INTERLOPER—trespasser; meddler in others' affairs
- ❏ INTERMINABLE—endless
- ❏ INTERMITTENT—starting and stopping
- ❏ INTERNECINE—deadly to both sides
- ❏ INTERPOLATE—to insert; change by adding new words or material
- ❏ INTERPOSE—to insert; to intervene
- ❏ INTERREGNUM—interval between reigns
- ❏ INTERROGATE—to question formally
- ❏ INTERSECT—to divide by passing through or across
- ❏ INTERSPERSE—to distribute among, mix with
- ❏ INTIMATION—clue, suggestion
- ❏ INTRACTABLE—not easily managed
- ❏ INTRAMURAL—within an institution, such as a school
- ❏ INTRANSIGENT—uncompromising, refusing to be reconciled
- ❏ INTREPID—fearless
- ❏ INTRINSIC—inherent, internal
- ❏ INTROSPECTIVE—contemplating one's own thoughts and feelings
- ❏ INTROVERT—someone given to self-analysis
- ❏ INTRUSION—trespass, invasion of another's privacy
- ❏ INTUITIVE—instinctive, untaught
- ❏ INUNDATE—to cover with water; overwhelm
- ❏ INURE—to harden; accustom; become used to
- ❏ INVALIDATE—to negate or nullify
- ❏ INVECTIVE—verbal abuse
- ❏ INVESTITURE—ceremony conferring authority
- ❏ INVETERATE—confirmed, long-standing, deeply rooted
- ❏ INVIDIOUS—likely to provoke ill-will, offensive
- ❏ INVINCIBLE—invulnerable, unbeatable
- ❏ INVIOLABLE—safe from violation or assault
- ❏ INVOKE—to call upon, request help
- ❏ IOTA—very tiny amount
- ❏ IRASCIBLE—easily angered
- ❏ IRIDESCENT—showing many colors

- ❏ IRRESOLVABLE—unable to be resolved; not analyzable
- ❏ IRREVERENT—disrespectful
- ❏ IRREVOCABLE—conclusive, irreversible
- ❏ ITINERANT—wandering from place to place, unsettled
- ❏ ITINERARY—route of a traveler's journey

J

- ❏ JADED—tired by excess or overuse; slightly cynical
- ❏ JANGLING—clashing, jarring; harshly unpleasant (in sound)
- ❏ JARGON—nonsensical talk; specialized language
- ❏ JAUNDICE—yellowish discoloration of skin
- ❏ JAUNDICED—affected by jaundice; prejudiced or embittered
- ❏ JETTISON—to cast off, throw cargo overboard
- ❏ JINGOISM—belligerent support of one's country
- ❏ JOCULAR—jovial, playful, humorous
- ❏ JUBILEE—special anniversary
- ❏ JUDICIOUS—sensible, showing good judgment
- ❏ JUGGERNAUT—huge force destroying everything in its path
- ❏ JUNCTURE—point where two things are joined
- ❏ JURISPRUDENCE—philosophy of law
- ❏ JUXTAPOSITION—side-by-side placement

K

- ❏ KEEN (adj.)—having a sharp edge; intellectually sharp, perceptive
- ❏ KERNEL—innermost, essential part; seed grain, often in a shell
- ❏ KEYNOTE—note or tone on which a musical key is founded; main idea of a speech, program, etcetera
- ❏ KINDLE—to set fire to or ignite; excite or inspire
- ❏ KINETIC—relating to motion; characterized by movement
- ❏ KNELL—sound of a funeral bell; omen of death or failure
- ❏ KUDOS—fame, glory, honor

L

- ❏ LABYRINTH—maze
- ❏ LACERATION—cut or wound

- ❑ LACHRYMOSE—tearful
- ❑ LACKADAISICAL—idle, lazy; apathetic, indifferent
- ❑ LACONIC—using few words
- ❑ LAGGARD—dawdler, loafer, lazy person
- ❑ LAMENT (v.)—to deplore, grieve
- ❑ LAMPOON—to attack with satire, mock harshly
- ❑ LANGUID—lacking energy, indifferent, slow
- ❑ LAP (v.)—to drink using the tongue; to wash against
- ❑ LAPIDARY—relating to precious stones
- ❑ LARCENY—theft of property
- ❑ LARDER—place where food is stored
- ❑ LARGESS—generosity; gift
- ❑ LARYNX—organ containing vocal cords
- ❑ LASSITUDE—lethargy, sluggishness
- ❑ LATENT—present but hidden; potential
- ❑ LAUDABLE—deserving of praise
- ❑ LAXITY—carelessness
- ❑ LEERY—suspicious
- ❑ LEGERDEMAIN—trickery
- ❑ LEGIBLE—readable
- ❑ LEGISLATE—to decree, mandate, make laws
- ❑ LENIENT—easygoing, permissive
- ❑ LETHARGY—indifferent inactivity
- ❑ LEVITATE—to rise in the air or cause to rise
- ❑ LEVITY—humor, frivolity, gaiety
- ❑ LEXICON—dictionary, list of words
- ❑ LIBERAL—tolerant, broad-minded; generous, lavish
- ❑ LIBERATION—freedom, emancipation
- ❑ LIBERTARIAN—one who believes in unrestricted freedom
- ❑ LIBERTINE—one without moral restraint
- ❑ LICENTIOUS—immoral; unrestrained by society
- ❑ LIEN—right to possess and sell the property of a debtor
- ❑ LIMPID—clear, transparent
- ❑ LINEAGE—ancestry
- ❑ LINGUISTICS—study of language
- ❑ LINIMENT—medicinal liquid used externally to ease pain
- ❑ LIONIZE—to treat as a celebrity
- ❑ LISSOME—easily flexed, limber, agile
- ❑ LISTLESS—lacking energy and enthusiasm
- ❑ LITERATE—able to read and write; well-read and educated
- ❑ LITHE—moving and bending with ease; graceful
- ❑ LITIGATION—lawsuit
- ❑ LIVID—discolored from a bruise; reddened with anger

- ❑ LOATHE—to abhor, despise, hate
- ❑ LOCOMOTION—movement from place to place
- ❑ LOGO—corporate symbol
- ❑ LOITER—to stand around idly
- ❑ LOQUACIOUS—talkative
- ❑ LOW (v.)—to make a sound like a cow, moo
- ❑ LUCID—clear and easily understood
- ❑ LUDICROUS—laughable, ridiculous
- ❑ LUGUBRIOUS—sorrowful, mournful; dismal
- ❑ LUMBER (v.)—to move slowly and awkwardly
- ❑ LUMINARY—bright object; celebrity; source of inspiration
- ❑ LUMINOUS—bright, brilliant, glowing
- ❑ LUNAR—relating to the moon
- ❑ LURID—harshly shocking, sensational; glowing
- ❑ LURK—to prowl, sneak
- ❑ LUSCIOUS—tasty
- ❑ LUXURIANCE—elegance, lavishness
- ❑ LYRICAL—suitable for poetry and song; expressing feeling

M

- ❑ MACHINATION—plot or scheme
- ❑ MACROBIOTICS—art of prolonging life by special diet of organic nonmeat substances
- ❑ MACROCOSM—system regarded as an entity with subsystems
- ❑ MAELSTROM—whirlpool; turmoil; agitated state of mind
- ❑ MAGNANIMOUS—generous, noble in spirit
- ❑ MAGNATE—powerful or influential person
- ❑ MAGNITUDE—extent, greatness of size
- ❑ MALADROIT—clumsy, tactless
- ❑ MALADY—illness
- ❑ MALAPROPISM—humorous misuse of a word
- ❑ MALCONTENT—discontented person, one who holds a grudge
- ❑ MALEDICTION—curse
- ❑ MALEFACTOR—evil-doer; culprit
- ❑ MALEVOLENT—ill-willed; causing evil or harm to others
- ❑ MALFUNCTION (v.)—to fail to work
- ❑ MALFUNCTION (n.)—breakdown, failure
- ❑ MALICE—animosity, spite, hatred
- ❑ MALINGER—to evade responsibility by pretending to be ill
- ❑ MALNUTRITION—undernourishment

❑ MALODOROUS—foul-smelling

❑ MANDATORY—necessary, required

❑ MANIFEST (adj.)—obvious

❑ MANIFOLD—diverse, varied, comprised of many parts

❑ MANNERED—artificial or stilted in character

❑ MANUAL (adj.)—hand-operated; physical

❑ MAR—to damage, deface; spoil

❑ MARGINAL—barely sufficient

❑ MARITIME—relating to the sea or sailing

❑ MARTIAL—warlike, pertaining to the military

❑ MARTINET—strict disciplinarian, one who rigidly follows rules

❑ MARTYR—person dying for his or her beliefs

❑ MASOCHIST—one who enjoys pain or humiliation

❑ MASQUERADE—disguise; action that conceals the truth

❑ MATERIALISM—preoccupation with material things

❑ MATRICULATE—to enroll as a member of a college or university

❑ MATRILINEAL—tracing ancestry through mother's line rather than father's

❑ MAUDLIN—overly sentimental

❑ MAWKISH—sickeningly sentimental

❑ MEDDLER—person interfering in others' affairs

❑ MEDIEVAL—relating to the Middle Ages (about A.D. 500–1500)

❑ MEGALITH—huge stone used in prehistoric structures

❑ MEGALOMANIA—mental state with delusions of wealth and power

❑ MELANCHOLY—sadness, depression

❑ MELODY—pleasing musical harmony; related musical tunes

❑ MENAGERIE—various animals kept together for exhibition

❑ MENDACIOUS—dishonest

❑ MENDICANT—beggar

❑ MENTOR—experienced teacher and wise adviser

❑ MERCENARY (n.)—soldier for hire in foreign countries

❑ MERCENARY (adj.)—motivated only by greed

❑ MERCURIAL—quick, shrewd, and unpredictable

❑ MERETRICIOUS—gaudy, falsely attractive

❑ MERIDIAN—circle passing through the two poles of the earth

❑ MERITORIOUS—deserving reward or praise

❑ METAMORPHOSIS—change, transformation

❑ METAPHOR—figure of speech comparing two different things

❑ METICULOUS—extremely careful, fastidious, painstaking

❑ METRONOME—time-keeping device used in music

❑ METTLE—courageousness; endurance

❑ MICROBE—microorganism

❑ MICROCOSM—tiny system used as analogy for larger system

❑ MIGRATORY—wandering from place to place with the seasons

❑ MILITATE—to operate against, work against

❑ MINIMAL—smallest in amount, least possible

❑ MINUSCULE—very small

❑ MIRTH—frivolity, gaiety, laughter

❑ MISANTHROPE—person who hates human beings

❑ MISAPPREHEND—to misunderstand, fail to know

❑ MISCONSTRUE—to misunderstand, fail to discover

❑ MISERLINESS—extreme stinginess

❑ MISGIVING—apprehension, doubt, sense of foreboding

❑ MISHAP—accident; misfortune

❑ MISNOMER—an incorrect name or designation

❑ MISSIVE—note or letter

❑ MITIGATE—to soften, or make milder

❑ MNEMONIC—relating to memory; designed to assist memory

❑ MOBILITY—ease of movement

❑ MOCK—to deride, ridicule

❑ MODERATE (adj.)—reasonable, not extreme

❑ MODERATE (v.)—to make less excessive, restrain; regulate

❑ MOLLIFY—to calm or make less severe

❑ MOLLUSK—sea animal with soft body

❑ MOLT (v.)—to shed hair, skin, or an outer layer periodically

❑ MONASTIC—extremely plain or secluded, as in a monastery

❑ MONOCHROMATIC—having one color

❑ MONOGAMY—custom of marriage to one person at a time

❑ MONOLITH—large block of stone

❑ MONOLOGUE—dramatic speech performed by one actor

❑ MONTAGE—composite picture

❑ MOOT—debatable; purely academic, deprived of practical significance

❑ MORBID—gruesome; relating to disease; abnormally gloomy

❑ MORES—customs or manners

❑ MORIBUND—dying, decaying

❑ MOROSE—gloomy, sullen, or surly

❑ MORSEL—small bit of food

❑ MOTE—small particle, speck

❑ MOTLEY—many-colored; composed of diverse parts

❑ MOTTLE—to mark with spots

❑ MULTIFACETED—having many parts, many-sided

❑ MULTIFARIOUS—diverse

❑ MUNDANE—worldly; commonplace

❑ MUNIFICENT—generous

❑ MUNITIONS—ammunition

❑ MUTABILITY—changeability

❑ MYOPIC—nearsighted

❑ MYRIAD—immense number, multitude

N

❑ NADIR—lowest point

❑ NARRATIVE—account, story

❑ NASCENT—starting to develop, coming into existence

❑ NATAL—relating to birth

❑ NEBULOUS—vague, cloudy

❑ NECROMANCY—black magic

❑ NEFARIOUS—vicious, evil

❑ NEGLIGENT—careless, inattentive

❑ NEGLIGIBLE—not worth considering

❑ NEOLOGISM—new word or expression

❑ NEONATE—newborn child

❑ NEOPHYTE—novice, beginner

❑ NETHER—located under or below

❑ NETTLE (v.)—to irritate

❑ NEUTRALITY—disinterest, impartiality

❑ NEUTRALIZE—to balance, offset

❑ NICETY—elegant or delicate feature; minute distinction

❑ NICHE—recess in a wall; best position for something

❑ NIGGARDLY—stingy

❑ NIHILISM—belief that existence and all traditional values are meaningless

❑ NOCTURNAL—pertaining to night; active at night

❑ NOISOME—stinking, putrid

❑ NOMADIC—moving from place to place

❑ NOMENCLATURE—terms used in a particular science or discipline

❑ NOMINAL—existing in name only; negligible

❑ NONSEQUITUR—conclusion not following from apparent evidence

❑ NONDESCRIPT—lacking interesting or distinctive qualities; dull

❑ NOTORIETY—unfavorable fame

❑ NOVICE—apprentice, beginner

❑ NOVITIATE—state of being a beginner or novice

❑ NOXIOUS—harmful, unwholesome

❑ NUANCE—shade of meaning

❑ NULLIFY—to make legally invalid; to counteract the effect of

❑ NUMISMATICS—coin collecting

❑ NUPTIAL—relating to marriage

❑ NUTRITIVE—relating to nutrition or health

O

❑ OBDURATE—stubborn

❑ OBFUSCATE—to confuse, obscure

❑ OBLIQUE—indirect, evasive; misleading, devious

❑ OBLITERATE—demolish, wipe out

❑ OBLIVIOUS—unaware, inattentive

❑ OBSCURE (adj.)—dim, unclear; not well known

❑ OBSCURITY—a state of being obscure

❑ OBSEQUIOUS—overly submissive, brownnosing

❑ OBSEQUIES—funeral ceremony

❑ OBSESSIVE—preoccupying, all-consuming

❑ OBSOLETE—no longer in use

❑ OBSTINATE—stubborn

❑ OBSTREPEROUS—troublesome, boisterous, unruly

❑ OBTRUSIVE—pushy, too conspicuous

❑ OBTUSE—insensitive, stupid, dull

❑ OBVIATE—to make unnecessary; to anticipate and prevent

❑ OCCLUDE—to shut, block

❑ ODIOUS—hateful, contemptible

❑ OFFICIOUS—too helpful, meddlesome

❑ OFFSHOOT—branch

❑ OMINOUS—menacing, threatening, indicating misfortune

❑ OMNIPOTENT—having unlimited power

❑ OMNISCIENT—having infinite knowledge

❑ OMNIVOROUS—eating everything; absorbing everything

❑ ONEROUS—burdensome

❑ ONTOLOGY—theory about the nature of existence

❑ OPALESCENT—iridescent, displaying colors

❑ OPAQUE—impervious to light; difficult to understand

❑ OPERATIVE (adj.)—functioning, working

❑ OPINE—to express an opinion

❑ OPPORTUNE—appropriate, fitting

❑ OPPORTUNIST—one who takes advantage of circumstances

❑ OPPROBRIOUS—disgraceful, contemptuous

❑ OPULENCE—wealth

❑ ORACLE—person who foresees the future and gives advice

❑ ORATION—lecture, formal speech

❑ ORATOR—lecturer, speaker

❑ ORB—spherical body; eye

❑ ORCHESTRATE—to arrange music for performance; to coordinate, organize

❑ ORDAIN—to make someone a priest or minister; to order

❑ ORNITHOLOGIST—scientist who studies birds

❑ OSCILLATE—to move back and forth

❑ OSSIFY—to turn to bone; to become rigid

❑ OSTENSIBLE—apparent

❑ OSTENTATIOUS—showy

❑ OSTRACISM—exclusion, temporary banishment

❑ OUSTER—expulsion, ejection

❑ OVERSTATE—to embellish, exaggerate

❑ OVERTURE—musical introduction; proposal, offer

❑ OVERWROUGHT—agitated, overdone

P

❑ PACIFIC—calm, peaceful

❑ PACIFIST—one opposed to war

❑ PACIFY—to restore calm, bring peace

❑ PALATIAL—like a palace, magnificent

❑ PALAVER—idle talk

❑ PALEONTOLOGY—study of past geological eras through fossil remains

❑ PALETTE—board for mixing paints; range of colors

❑ PALISADE—fence made up of stakes

❑ PALL (n.)—covering that darkens or obscures; coffin

❑ PALL (v.)—to lose strength or interest

❑ PALLIATE—to make less serious, ease

❑ PALLID—lacking color or liveliness

❑ PALPABLE—obvious, real, tangible

❑ PALPITATION—trembling, shaking

❑ PALTRY—pitifully small or worthless

❑ PANACEA—cure-all

❑ PANACHE—flamboyance, verve

❑ PANDEMIC—spread over a whole area or country

❑ PANEGYRIC—elaborate praise; formal hymn of praise

❑ PANOPLY—impressive array

❑ PANORAMA—broad view; comprehensive picture

❑ PARADIGM—ideal example, model

❑ PARADOX—contradiction, incongruity; dilemma, puzzle

❑ PARADOXICAL—self-contradictory but true

❑ PARAGON—model of excellence or perfection

❑ PARAMOUNT—supreme, dominant, primary

❑ PARAPHRASE—to reword, usually in simpler terms

❑ PARASITE—person or animal that lives at another's expense

❑ PARCH—to dry or shrivel

❑ PARE—to trim

❑ PARIAH—outcast

❑ PARITY—equality

❑ PARLEY—discussion, usually between enemies

❑ PAROCHIAL—of limited scope or outlook, provincial

❑ PARODY—humorous imitation

❑ PAROLE—conditional release of a prisoner

❑ PARRY—to ward off or deflect

❑ PARSIMONY—stinginess

❑ PARTISAN (n.)—strong supporter

❑ PARTISAN (adj.)—biased in favor of

❑ PASTICHE—piece of literature or music imitating other works

❑ PATENT (adj.)—obvious, unconcealed

❑ PATENT (n.)—official document giving exclusive right to sell an invention

❑ PATERNITY—fatherhood; descent from father's ancestors

❑ PATHOGENIC—causing disease

❑ PATHOS—pity, compassion

❑ PATRICIAN—aristocrat

❑ PATRICIDE—murder of one's father

❑ PATRIMONY—inheritance or heritage derived from one's father

❑ PATRONIZE—to condescend to, disparage; to buy from

❑ PAUCITY—scarcity, lack

❑ PAUPER—very poor person

❑ PAVILION—tent or light building used for shelter or exhibitions

❑ PECCADILLO—minor sin or offense

❑ PECULATION—theft of money or goods

❑ PEDAGOGUE—teacher

- ❑ PEDANT—uninspired, boring academic
- ❑ PEDESTRIAN (adj.)—commonplace
- ❑ PEDIATRICIAN—doctor specializing in children and their ailments
- ❑ PEDIMENT—triangular gable on a roof or facade
- ❑ PEER (n.)—contemporary, equal, match
- ❑ PEERLESS—unequaled
- ❑ PEJORATIVE—having bad connotations; disparaging
- ❑ PELLUCID—transparent; translucent; easily understood
- ❑ PENANCE—voluntary suffering to repent for a wrong
- ❑ PENCHANT—inclination
- ❑ PENDING (adj.)—not yet decided, awaiting decision
- ❑ PENITENT—expressing sorrow for sins or offenses, repentant
- ❑ PENSIVE—thoughtful
- ❑ PENULTIMATE—next to last
- ❑ PENUMBRA—partial shadow
- ❑ PENURY—extreme poverty
- ❑ PERAMBULATOR—baby carriage
- ❑ PERCIPIENT—discerning, able to perceive
- ❑ PERDITION—complete and utter loss; damnation
- ❑ PEREGRINATE—to wander from place to place
- ❑ PERENNIAL—present throughout the years; persistent
- ❑ PERFIDIOUS—faithless, disloyal, untrustworthy
- ❑ PERFUNCTORY—done in a routine way; indifferent
- ❑ PERIHELION—point in orbit nearest to the sun
- ❑ PERIPATETIC—moving from place to place
- ❑ PERJURE—to tell a lie under oath
- ❑ PERMEABLE—penetrable
- ❑ PERNICIOUS—very harmful
- ❑ PERPETUAL—endless, lasting
- ❑ PERSONIFICATION—act of attributing human qualities to objects or abstract qualities
- ❑ PERSPICACIOUS—shrewd, astute, keen-witted
- ❑ PERT—lively and bold
- ❑ PERTINACIOUS—persistent, stubborn
- ❑ PERTINENT—applicable, appropriate
- ❑ PERTURBATION—disturbance
- ❑ PERUSAL—close examination
- ❑ PERVERT (v.)—to cause to change in immoral way; to misuse
- ❑ PESTILENCE—epidemic, plague
- ❑ PETULANCE—rudeness, peevishness
- ❑ PHALANX—massed group of soldiers, people, or things

- ❑ PHILANDERER—pursuer of casual love affairs
- ❑ PHILANTHROPY—love of humanity; generosity to worthy causes
- ❑ PHILISTINE—narrow-minded person, someone lacking appreciation for art or culture
- ❑ PHILOLOGY—study of words
- ❑ PHLEGMATIC—calm in temperament; sluggish
- ❑ PHOBIA—exaggerated, illogical fear
- ❑ PHOENIX—mythical, immortal bird that lives for 500 years, burns itself to death, and rises from its ashes
- ❑ PHONETICS—study of speech sounds
- ❑ PHONIC—relating to sound
- ❑ PIETY—devoutness
- ❑ PILFER—to steal
- ❑ PILLAGE—to loot, especially during a war
- ❑ PINNACLE—peak, highest point of development
- ❑ PIOUS—dedicated, devout, extremely religious
- ❑ PIQUE (n.)—fleeting feeling of hurt pride
- ❑ PITHY—profound, substantial; concise, succinct, to the point
- ❑ PITTANCE—meager amount or wage
- ❑ PLACATE—to soothe or pacify
- ❑ PLACID—calm
- ❑ PLAGIARIST—one who steals words or ideas
- ❑ PLAINTIFF—injured person in a lawsuit
- ❑ PLAIT—to braid
- ❑ PLATITUDE—stale, overused expression
- ❑ PLEBEIAN—crude, vulgar, low-class
- ❑ PLENITUDE—abundance, plenty
- ❑ PLETHORA—excess, overabundance
- ❑ PLIANT—pliable, yielding
- ❑ PLUCK (v.)—to pull strings on musical instrument
- ❑ PLUCKY—courageous, spunky
- ❑ PLUMMET—to fall, plunge
- ❑ PLURALISTIC—including a variety of groups
- ❑ PLY (v.)—to use diligently; to engage; to join together
- ❑ PNEUMATIC—relating to air; worked by compressed air
- ❑ POACH—to steal game or fish; cook in boiling liquid
- ❑ PODIUM—platform or lectern for orchestra conductors or speakers
- ❑ POIGNANT—emotionally moving
- ❑ POLAR—relating to a geographic pole; exhibiting contrast
- ❑ POLARIZE—to tend towards opposite extremes
- ❑ POLEMIC—controversy, argument; verbal attack

- POLITIC—discreet, tactful
- POLYGLOT—speaker of many languages
- PONDEROUS—weighty, heavy, large
- PONTIFICATE—to speak in a pretentious manner
- PORE (v.)—to study closely or meditatively
- POROUS—full of holes, permeable to liquids
- PORTENT—omen
- PORTLY—stout, dignified
- POSIT—to put in position; to suggest an idea
- POSTERIOR—bottom, rear
- POSTERITY—future generations; all of a person's descendants
- POTABLE—drinkable
- POTENTATE—monarch or ruler with great power
- PRAGMATIC—practical; moved by facts rather than abstract ideals
- PRATTLE (n.)—meaningless, foolish talk
- PRECARIOUS—uncertain
- PRECEPT—principle; law
- PRECIPICE—edge, steep overhang
- PRECIPITATE (adj.)—sudden and unexpected
- PRECIPITATE (v.)—to throw down from a height; to cause to happen
- PRECIPITOUS—hasty, quickly, with too little caution
- PRÉCIS—concise summary of facts
- PRECISION—state of being precise
- PRECLUDE—to rule out
- PRECOCIOUS—unusually advanced at an early age
- PRECURSOR—forerunner, predecessor
- PREDATOR—one that preys on others, destroyer, plunderer
- PREDICAMENT—difficult situation
- PREDICATE (v.)—to found or base on
- PREDICTIVE—relating to prediction, indicative of the future
- PREDILECTION—preference, liking
- PREDISPOSITION—tendency, inclination
- PREEMINENT—celebrated, distinguished
- PREFACE (n.)—introduction to a book; introductory remarks to a speech
- PREMEDITATE—to consider, plan beforehand
- PREMONITION—forewarning; presentiment
- PREPONDERANCE—majority in number; dominance
- PREPOSSESSING—attractive, engaging, appealing
- PREPOSTEROUS—absurd, illogical

- PRESAGE—to foretell, indicate in advance
- PRESCIENT—having foresight
- PRESCRIBE—to set down a rule; to recommend a treatment
- PRESENTIMENT—premonition, sense of foreboding
- PRESTIDIGITATION—sleight of hand
- PRESUMPTUOUS—rude, improperly bold
- PRETEXT—excuse, pretended reason
- PREVALENT—widespread
- PREVARICATE—to lie, evade the truth
- PRIMEVAL—ancient, primitive
- PRIMORDIAL—original, existing from the beginning
- PRISTINE—untouched, uncorrupted
- PRIVATION—lack of usual necessities or comforts
- PROBITY—honesty, high-mindedness
- PROCLIVITY—tendency, inclination
- PROCRASTINATOR—one who continually and unjustifiably postpones
- PROCURE—to obtain
- PRODIGAL (adj.)—wasteful, extravagant, lavish
- PRODIGIOUS—vast, enormous, extraordinary
- PROFANE—impure; contrary to religion; sacrilegious
- PROFICIENT—expert, skilled in a certain subject
- PROFLIGATE—corrupt, degenerate
- PROFUSE—lavish, extravagant
- PROGENITOR—originator, forefather, ancestor in a direct line
- PROGENY—offspring, children
- PROGNOSIS—prediction of disease outcome; any prediction
- PROGRESSIVE—favoring progress or change; moving forward, going step-by-step
- PROLIFERATION—propagation, reproduction; enlargement, expansion
- PROLIFIC—productive, fertile
- PROLOGUE—introductory section of a literary work or play
- PROMONTORY—piece of land or rock higher than its surroundings
- PROMULGATE—to make known publicly
- PROPENSITY—inclination, tendency
- PROPINQUITY—nearness
- PROPITIATE—to win over, appease
- PROPITIOUS—favorable, advantageous
- PROPONENT—advocate, defender, supporter
- PROSAIC—relating to prose; dull, commonplace

❑ PROSCRIBE—to condemn; to forbid, outlaw

❑ PROSE—ordinary language used in everyday speech

❑ PROSECUTOR—person who initiates a legal action or suit

❑ PROSELYTIZE—to convert to a particular belief or religion

❑ PROSTRATE—lying face downward, lying flat on ground

❑ PROTAGONIST—main character in a play or story, hero

❑ PROTEAN—readily assuming different forms or characters

❑ PROTESTATION—declaration

❑ PROTOCOL—ceremony and manners observed by diplomats

❑ PROTRACT—to prolong, draw out, extend

❑ PROTRUSION—something that sticks out

❑ PROVINCIAL—rustic, unsophisticated, limited in scope

❑ PROVOCATION—cause, incitement to act or respond

❑ PROWESS—bravery, skill

❑ PROXIMITY—nearness

❑ PROXY—power to act as a substitute for another

❑ PRUDE—one who is excessively proper or modest

❑ PRUDENT—careful, cautious

❑ PRURIENT—lustful, exhibiting lewd desires

❑ PRY—to intrude into; force open

❑ PSEUDONYM—pen name; fictitious or borrowed name

❑ PSYCHIC (adj.)—perceptive of nonmaterial, spiritual forces

❑ PUERILE—childish, immature, silly

❑ PUDGY—chubby, overweight

❑ PUGILISM—boxing

❑ PUGNACIOUS—quarrelsome, eager and ready to fight

❑ PULCHRITUDE—beauty

❑ PULVERIZE—to pound, crush, or grind into powder; destroy

❑ PUMMEL—to pound, beat

❑ PUNCTILIOUS—careful in observing rules of behavior or ceremony

❑ PUNGENT—strong or sharp in smell or taste

❑ PUNITIVE—having to do with punishment

❑ PURGATION—catharsis, purification

❑ PURGE—to cleanse or free from impurities

❑ PURITANICAL—adhering to a rigid moral code

❑ PURPORT—to profess, suppose, claim

Q

❑ QUACK—faker; one who falsely claims to have medical skill

❑ QUADRILATERAL—four-sided polygon

❑ QUADRUPED—animal having four feet

❑ QUAGMIRE—marsh; difficult situation

❑ QUALIFY—to provide with needed skills; modify, limit

❑ QUANDARY—dilemma, difficulty

❑ QUARANTINE—isolation period, originally 40 days, to prevent spread of disease

❑ QUATERNARY—consisting of or relating to four units or members

❑ QUELL—to crush or subdue

❑ QUERULOUS—inclined to complain, irritable

❑ QUERY (n.)—question

❑ QUIBBLE—to argue about insignificant and irrelevant details

❑ QUICKEN (v.)—to hasten, arouse, excite

❑ QUIESCENCE—inactivity, stillness

❑ QUINTESSENCE—most typical example; concentrated essence

❑ QUIVER—to shake slightly, tremble, vibrate

❑ QUIXOTIC—overly idealistic, impractical

❑ QUOTIDIAN—occurring daily; commonplace

R

❑ RACONTEUR—witty, skillful storyteller

❑ RADICAL—fundamental; drastic

❑ RAIL (v.)—to scold with bitter or abusive language

❑ RALLY (v.)—to assemble; recover, recuperate

❑ RAMBLE—to roam, wander; to babble, digress

❑ RAMIFICATION—an implication, outgrowth, or consequence

❑ RAMSHACKLE—likely to collapse

❑ RANCID—spoiled, rotten

❑ RANCOR—bitter hatred

❑ RANT—to harangue, rave, forcefully scold

❑ RAPPORT—relationship of trust and respect

❑ RAPT—deeply absorbed

❑ RAREFY—to make thinner, purer, or more refined

❑ RASH (adj.)—careless, hasty, reckless

❑ RATIFY—to approve formally, confirm

- ❑ RATIOCINATION—methodical, logical reasoning
- ❑ RATION (n.)—portion, share
- ❑ RATION (v.)—to supply; to restrict consumption of
- ❑ RATIONAL—logical, reasonable
- ❑ RAUCOUS—harsh-sounding; boisterous
- ❑ RAVAGE—to destroy, devastate
- ❑ RAVENOUS—extremely hungry
- ❑ RAVINE—deep, narrow gorge
- ❑ RAZE—to tear down, demolish
- ❑ REACTIONARY—marked by extreme conservatism, esp. in politics
- ❑ REBUFF (n.)—blunt rejection
- ❑ REBUKE—to reprimand, scold
- ❑ REBUT—to refute by evidence or argument
- ❑ RECALCITRANT—resisting authority or control
- ❑ RECANT—to retract a statement, opinion, etc.
- ❑ RECAPITULATE—to review by a brief summary
- ❑ RECEPTIVE—open to others' ideas; congenial
- ❑ RECLUSIVE—shut off from the world
- ❑ RECONDITE—relating to obscure learning; known to only a few
- ❑ RECOUNT—to describe facts or events
- ❑ RECRUIT (v.)—to draft, enlist; to seek to enroll
- ❑ RECTIFY—to correct
- ❑ RECTITUDE—moral uprightness
- ❑ RECURRENCE—repetition
- ❑ REDRESS—relief from wrong or injury
- ❑ REDUNDANCY—unnecessary repetition
- ❑ REFECTORY—room where meals are served
- ❑ REFLECTION—image, likeness; opinion, thought, impression
- ❑ REFORM—to change, correct
- ❑ REFRACT—to deflect sound or light
- ❑ REFUGE—escape, shelter
- ❑ REFURBISH—to renovate
- ❑ REFUTE—to contradict, discredit
- ❑ REGIMEN—government rule; systematic plan
- ❑ REGRESS—to move backward; revert to an earlier form or state
- ❑ REHABILITATE—to restore to good health or condition; re-establish a person's good reputation
- ❑ REITERATE—to say or do again, repeat
- ❑ REJOINDER—response
- ❑ REJUVENATE—to make young again; renew

- ❑ RELEGATE—to assign to a class, especially an inferior one
- ❑ RELINQUISH—to renounce or surrender something
- ❑ RELISH (v.)—to enjoy greatly
- ❑ REMEDIABLE—capable of being corrected
- ❑ REMEDY (v.)—to cure, correct
- ❑ REMINISCENCE—remembrance of past events
- ❑ REMISSION—lessening, relaxation
- ❑ REMIT—to send (usually money) as payment
- ❑ REMOTE—distant, isolated
- ❑ REMUNERATION—pay or reward for work, trouble, etc.
- ❑ RENASCENT—reborn, coming into being again
- ❑ RENEGADE—traitor, person abandoning a cause
- ❑ RENEGE—to go back on one's word
- ❑ RENOUNCE—to give up or reject a right, title, person, etc.
- ❑ RENOWN—fame, widespread acclaim
- ❑ REPAST—meal or mealtime
- ❑ REPEAL—to revoke or formally withdraw (often a law)
- ❑ REPEL—to rebuff, repulse; disgust, offend
- ❑ REPENT—to regret a past action
- ❑ REPENTANT—apologetic, guilty, remorseful
- ❑ REPLETE—abundantly supplied
- ❑ REPLICATE—to duplicate, repeat
- ❑ REPOSE—relaxation, leisure
- ❑ REPRESS—to restrain or hold in
- ❑ REPRESSION—act of restraining or holding in
- ❑ REPREHENSIBLE—blameworthy, disreputable
- ❑ REPRISE—repetition, esp. of a piece of music
- ❑ REPROACH—to find fault with; blame
- ❑ REPROBATE—morally unprincipled person
- ❑ REPROVE—to criticize or correct
- ❑ REPUDIATE—to reject as having no authority
- ❑ REPULSE—repel, fend off; sicken, disgust
- ❑ REQUIEM—hymns or religious service for the dead
- ❑ REQUITE—to return or repay
- ❑ RESCIND—to repeal, cancel
- ❑ RESIDUE—remainder, leftover, remnant
- ❑ RESILIENT—able to recover quickly after illness or bad luck; able to bounce back to shape
- ❑ RESOLUTE—determined; with a clear purpose
- ❑ RESOLVE (n.)—determination, firmness of purpose
- ❑ RESOLVE (v.)—to conclude, determine
- ❑ RESONATE—to echo
- ❑ RESPIRE—to breathe

❏ RESPITE—interval of relief

❏ RESPLENDENT—splendid, brilliant

❏ RESTITUTION—act of compensating for loss or damage

❏ RESTIVE—impatient, uneasy, restless

❏ RESTORATIVE—having the power to renew or revitalize

❏ RESTRAINED—controlled, repressed, restricted

❏ RESUSCITATE—to revive, bring back to life

❏ RETAIN—to hold, keep possession of

❏ RETARD (v.)—to slow, hold back

❏ RETICENT—not speaking freely; reserved

❏ RETINUE—group of attendants with an important person

❏ RETIRING—shy, modest, reserved

❏ RETORT (n.)—cutting response

❏ RETRACT—to draw in or take back

❏ RETRENCH—to regroup, reorganize

❏ RETRIEVE—to bring, fetch; reclaim

❏ RETROACTIVE—applying to an earlier time

❏ RETROGRADE—having a backward motion or direction

❏ RETROSPECTIVE—review of the past

❏ REVELRY—boisterous festivity

❏ REVERE—to worship, regard with awe

❏ REVERT—to backslide, regress

❏ REVILE—to criticize with harsh language, verbally abuse

❏ REVITALIZE—to renew; give new energy to

❏ REVOKE—to annul, cancel, call back

❏ REVULSION—strong feeling of repugnance or dislike

❏ RHAPSODY—emotional literary or musical work

❏ RHETORIC—persuasive use of language

❏ RHYTHM—regular pattern or variation of sounds and stresses

❏ RIBALD—humorous in a vulgar way

❏ RIDDLE (v.)—to make many holes in; permeate

❏ RIFE—widespread, prevalent; abundant

❏ RISQUÉ —bordering on being inappropriate or indecent

❏ ROBUST—strong and healthy; hardy

❏ ROCOCO—very highly ornamented

❏ ROOT (v.)—to dig with a snout (like a pig)

❏ ROSTRUM—stage for public speaking

❏ ROTUND—round in shape; fat

❏ RUE—to regret

❏ RUMINATE—to contemplate, reflect upon

❏ RUSTIC—rural

S

❏ SACCHARINE—excessively sweet or sentimental

❏ SACROSANCT—extremely sacred; beyond criticism

❏ SAGACIOUS—shrewd

❏ SALIENT—prominent or conspicuous

❏ SALLOW—sickly yellow in color

❏ SALUBRIOUS—healthful

❏ SALUTATION—greeting

❏ SANCTION (n.)—permission, support; law; penalty

❏ SANCTUARY—haven, retreat

❏ SANGUINE—ruddy; cheerfully optimistic

❏ SARDONIC—cynical, scornfully mocking

❏ SATIATE—to satisfy

❏ SAUNTER—to amble; walk in a leisurely manner

❏ SAVANT—learned person

❏ SAVORY—agreeable in taste or smell

❏ SCABBARD—sheath for sword or dagger

❏ SCALE (v.)—to climb to the top of

❏ SCATHING—harshly critical; painfully hot

❏ SCENARIO—plot outline; possible situation

❏ SCINTILLA—trace amount

❏ SCINTILLATE—to sparkle, flash

❏ SCOFF—to deride, ridicule

❏ SCORE (n.)—notation for a musical composition

❏ SCORE (v.)—to make a notch or scratch

❏ SCRIVENER—professional copyist

❏ SCRUPULOUS—restrained; careful and precise

❏ SCRUTINY—careful observation

❏ SCURRILOUS—vulgar, low, indecent

❏ SECANT—straight line intersecting a curve at two points

❏ SECEDE—to withdraw formally from an organization

❏ SECLUDED—isolated and remote

❏ SECTARIAN—narrow-minded; relating to a group or sect

❏ SECULAR—not specifically pertaining to religion

❏ SEDENTARY—inactive, stationary; sluggish

❏ SEDITION—behavior promoting rebellion

❏ SEISMOLOGY—science of earthquakes

❏ SEMINAL—relating to the beginning or seeds of something

❏ SENESCENT—aging, growing old

❏ SENSUAL—satisfying or gratifying the senses; suggesting sexuality

❏ SENTENTIOUS   having a moralizing tone

- ❑ SENTIENT—aware, conscious, able to perceive
- ❑ SEQUEL—anything that follows
- ❑ SEQUESTER—to remove or set apart; put into seclusion
- ❑ SERAPHIC—angelic, pure, sublime
- ❑ SERENDIPITY—habit of making fortunate discoveries by chance
- ❑ SERENITY—calm, peacefulness
- ❑ SERPENTINE—serpent-like; twisting, winding
- ❑ SERRATED—saw-toothed, notched
- ❑ SERVILE—submissive, obedient
- ❑ SHARD—piece of broken glass or pottery
- ❑ SHEEPISH—timid, meek, or bashful
- ❑ SHIRK—to avoid a task due to laziness or fear
- ❑ SIGNIFY—denote, indicate; symbolize
- ❑ SIMIAN—apelike; relating to apes
- ❑ SIMPER—to smirk, smile foolishly
- ❑ SINECURE—well-paying job or office that requires little or no work
- ❑ SINGE—to burn slightly, scorch
- ❑ SINUOUS—winding; intricate, complex
- ❑ SKEPTICAL—doubtful, questioning
- ❑ SKULK—to move in a stealthy or cautious manner; sneak
- ❑ SLIGHT—to treat as unimportant; insult
- ❑ SLIPSHOD—careless, hasty
- ❑ SLOTH—sluggishness, laziness
- ❑ SLOUGH—to discard or shed
- ❑ SLOVENLY—untidy, messy
- ❑ SLUGGARD—lazy, inactive person
- ❑ SMELT (v.)—to melt metal in order to refine it
- ❑ SNIPPET—tiny part, tidbit
- ❑ SOBRIETY—seriousness
- ❑ SOBRIQUET—nickname
- ❑ SODDEN—thoroughly soaked; saturated
- ❑ SOJOURN—visit, stay
- ❑ SOLACE—comfort in distress; consolation
- ❑ SOLARIUM—room or glassed-in area exposed to the sun
- ❑ SOLECISM—grammatical mistake
- ❑ SOLICITOUS—concerned, attentive; eager
- ❑ SOLIDARITY—unity based on common aims or interests
- ❑ SOLILOQUY—literary or dramatic speech by one character, not addressed to others
- ❑ SOLIPSISM—belief that oneself is the only reality
- ❑ SOLSTICE—shortest and longest day of the year
- ❑ SOLUBLE—capable of being solved or dissolved
- ❑ SOMBER—dark and gloomy; melancholy, dismal
- ❑ SOMNAMBULIST—sleepwalker
- ❑ SOMNOLENT—drowsy, sleepy; inducing sleep
- ❑ SONIC—relating to sound
- ❑ SONOROUS—producing a full, rich sound
- ❑ SOPHIST—person good at arguing deviously
- ❑ SOPHISTRY—deceptive reasoning or argumentation
- ❑ SOPHOMORIC—immature and overconfident
- ❑ SOPORIFIC—sleepy or tending to cause sleep
- ❑ SORDID—filthy; contemptible and corrupt
- ❑ SOVEREIGN—having supreme power
- ❑ SPARTAN—austere, severe, grave; simple, bare
- ❑ SPAWN—to generate, produce
- ❑ SPECULATION—contemplation; act of taking business risks for financial gain
- ❑ SPECULATIVE—involving assumption; uncertain; theoretical
- ❑ SPONTANEOUS—on the spur of the moment, impulsive
- ❑ SPORADIC—infrequent, irregular
- ❑ SPORTIVE—frolicsome, playful
- ❑ SPRIGHTLY—lively, animated, energetic
- ❑ SPUR (v.)—to prod
- ❑ SPURIOUS—lacking authenticity; counterfeit, false
- ❑ SPURN—to reject or refuse contemptuously; scorn
- ❑ SQUALID—filthy; morally repulsive
- ❑ SQUANDER—to waste
- ❑ STACCATO—marked by abrupt, clear-cut sounds
- ❑ STAGNANT—immobile, stale
- ❑ STAID—self-restrained to the point of dullness
- ❑ STALK (v.)—to hunt, pursue
- ❑ STAND (n.)—group of trees
- ❑ STARK—bare, empty, vacant
- ❑ STASIS—motionless state; standstill
- ❑ STIFLE—to smother or suffocate; suppress
- ❑ STIGMA—mark of disgrace or inferiority
- ❑ STILTED—stiff, unnatural
- ❑ STINT (n.)—period of time spent doing something
- ❑ STINT (v.)—to be sparing or frugal
- ❑ STIPEND—allowance; fixed amount of money paid regularly
- ❑ STOCKADE—enclosed area forming defensive wall
- ❑ STOIC—indifferent to or unaffected by emotions
- ❑ STOLID—having or showing little emotion
- ❑ STRATAGEM—trick designed to deceive an enemy
- ❑ STRATIFY—to arrange into layers

❑ STRICTURE—something that restrains; negative criticism

❑ STRIDENT—loud, harsh, unpleasantly noisy

❑ STRINGENT—imposing severe, rigorous standards

❑ STULTIFY—to impair or reduce to uselessness

❑ STUNTED—having arrested growth or development

❑ STUPEFY—to dull the senses of; stun, astonish

❑ STYLIZE—to fashion, formalize

❑ STYMIE—to block or thwart

❑ SUAVE—smoothly gracious or polite; blandly ingratiating

❑ SUBDUED—suppressed, stifled

❑ SUBJECTION—dependence, obedience, submission

❑ SUBJUGATE—to conquer, subdue; enslave

❑ SUBLIME—awe-inspiring; of high spiritual or moral value

❑ SUBLIMINAL—subconscious; imperceptible

❑ SUBMISSIVE—tending to be meek and submit

❑ SUBPOENA—notice ordering someone to appear in court

❑ SUBSEQUENT—following in time or order

❑ SUBTERFUGE—trick or tactic used to avoid something

❑ SUBTERRANEAN—hidden, secret; underground

❑ SUBTLE—hard to detect or describe; perceptive

❑ SUBVERT—to undermine or corrupt

❑ SUCCINCT—terse, brief, concise

❑ SUCCULENT—juicy; full of vitality or freshness

❑ SUFFERABLE—bearable

❑ SUFFRAGIST—one who advocates extended voting rights

❑ SULLEN—brooding, gloomy

❑ SULLY—to soil, stain, tarnish, taint

❑ SUMPTUOUS—lavish, splendid

❑ SUPERANNUATED—too old, obsolete, outdated

❑ SUPERCILIOUS—arrogant, haughty, overbearing, condescending

❑ SUPERFICIAL—hasty; shallow and phony

❑ SUPERFLUOUS—extra, more than necessary

❑ SUPERSEDE—to take the place of; replace

❑ SUPERVISE—to direct or oversee the work of others

❑ SUPPLANT—replace, substitute

❑ SUPPLE—flexible, pliant

❑ SUPPLICANT—one who asks humbly and earnestly

❑ SURFEIT—excessive amount

❑ SURLY—rude and bad-tempered

❑ SURMISE—to make an educated guess

❑ SURMOUNT—to conquer, overcome

❑ SURPASS—to do better than, be superior to

❑ SURPLUS—excess

❑ SURREPTITIOUS—characterized by secrecy

❑ SURVEY (v.)—to examine in a comprehensive way

❑ SUSCEPTIBLE—vulnerable, unprotected

❑ SUSPEND—to defer, interrupt; dangle, hang

❑ SUSTAIN—support, uphold; endure, undergo

❑ SWARTHY—having a dark complexion

❑ SYBARITE—person devoted to pleasure and luxury

❑ SYCOPHANT—self-serving flatterer, yes-man

❑ SYLLABUS—outline of a course

❑ SYMBIOSIS—cooperation, mutual helpfulness

❑ SYMPOSIUM—meeting with short presentations on related topics

❑ SYNCOPATION—temporary irregularity in musical rhythm

❑ SYNOPSIS—plot summary

❑ SYNTHESIS—blend, combination

❑ SYNTHETIC—artificial, imitation

T

❑ TABLEAU—vivid description, striking incident or scene

❑ TACIT—silently understood or implied

❑ TACITURN—uncommunicative, not inclined to speak much

❑ TACTILE—relating to the sense of touch

❑ TAINT—to spoil or infect; to stain honor

❑ TAINTED—stained, tarnished; corrupted, poisoned

❑ TALON—claw of an animal, esp. a bird of prey

❑ TANG—sharp flavor or odor

❑ TANGENTIAL—digressing, diverting

❑ TANGIBLE—able to be sensed, perceptible, measurable

❑ TANTAMOUNT—equivalent in value or significance; amounting to

❑ TARNISHED—corroded, discolored; discredited, disgraced

❑ TAWDRY—gaudy, cheap, showy

❑ TAXONOMY—science of classification

❑ TECHNOCRAT—strong believer in technology; technical expert

❑ TEMPERANCE—restraint, self-control, moderation

❑ TEMPERED—moderated, restrained

❑ TEMPESTUOUS—stormy, raging, furious

❑ TENABLE—defensible, reasonable

❑ TENACIOUS—stubborn, holding firm

- ❑ TENET—belief, doctrine
- ❑ TENSILE—capable of withstanding physical stress
- ❑ TENUOUS—weak, insubstantial
- ❑ TEPID—lukewarm; showing little enthusiasm
- ❑ TERMINAL (adj.)—concluding, final; fatal
- ❑ TERMINAL (n.)—depot, station
- ❑ TERRESTRIAL—earthly; down-to-earth, commonplace
- ❑ TERSE—concise, brief, free of extra words
- ❑ TESTAMENT—statement of belief; will
- ❑ TESTIMONIAL—statement testifying to a truth; something given in tribute to a person's achievement
- ❑ TETHER—to bind, tie
- ❑ THEOCRACY—government by priests representing a god
- ❑ THEOLOGY—study of God and religion
- ❑ THEORETICAL—abstract
- ❑ THERAPEUTIC—medicinal
- ❑ THESAURUS—book of synonyms and antonyms
- ❑ THESIS—theory or hypothesis; dissertation or long, written composition
- ❑ THWART—to block or prevent from happening; frustrate
- ❑ TIDINGS—news
- ❑ TIMOROUS—timid, shy, full of apprehension
- ❑ TINGE (v.)—to color slightly
- ❑ TINGE (n.)—slight amount
- ❑ TIRADE—long, violent speech; verbal assault
- ❑ TITAN—person of colossal stature or achievement
- ❑ TOADY—flatterer, hanger-on, yes-man
- ❑ TOLERANCE—capacity to respect different values; capacity to endure or resist something
- ❑ TOME—book, usually large and academic
- ❑ TONAL—relating to pitch or sound
- ❑ TOPOGRAPHY—art of making maps or charts
- ❑ TORPID—lethargic; unable to move; dormant
- ❑ TORRID—burning hot; passionate
- ❑ TORSION—act of twisting and turning
- ❑ TORTUOUS—having many twists and turns; highly complex
- ❑ TOTTERING—barely standing
- ❑ TOXIN—poison
- ❑ TRACTABLE—obedient, yielding
- ❑ TRANSCEND—to rise above, go beyond
- ❑ TRANSCENDENT—rising above, going beyond
- ❑ TRANSCRIPTION—copy, reproduction; record
- ❑ TRANSGRESS—to trespass, violate a law
- ❑ TRANSIENT (adj.)—temporary, short-lived, fleeting

- ❑ TRANSITORY—short-lived, existing only briefly
- ❑ TRANSLUCENT—partially transparent
- ❑ TRANSMUTE—to change in appearance or shape
- ❑ TRANSPIRE—to happen, occur; become known
- ❑ TRAVESTY—parody, exaggerated imitation, caricature
- ❑ TREMULOUS—trembling, quivering; fearful, timid
- ❑ TRENCHANT—acute, sharp, incisive; forceful, effective
- ❑ TREPIDATION—fear and anxiety
- ❑ TRIFLING—of slight worth, trivial, insignificant
- ❑ TRITE—shallow, superficial
- ❑ TROUNCE—to beat severely, defeat
- ❑ TROUPE—group of actors
- ❑ TRUNCATE—to cut off, shorten by cutting
- ❑ TRYING—difficult to deal with
- ❑ TRYST—agreement between lovers to meet; rendezvous
- ❑ TUMULT—state of confusion; agitation
- ❑ TUNDRA—treeless plain found in arctic or subarctic regions
- ❑ TURBULENCE—commotion, disorder
- ❑ TURGID—swollen, bloated
- ❑ TURPITUDE—inherent vileness, foulness, depravity
- ❑ TYRO—beginner, novice

U

- ❑ UBIQUITOUS—being everywhere simultaneously
- ❑ UMBRAGE—offense, resentment
- ❑ UNADULTERATED—absolutely pure
- ❑ UNANIMITY—state of total agreement or unity
- ❑ UNAPPEALING—unattractive, unpleasant
- ❑ UNAVAILING—hopeless, useless
- ❑ UNCONSCIONABLE—unscrupulous; shockingly unfair or unjust
- ❑ UNCTUOUS—greasy, oily; smug and falsely earnest
- ❑ UNDERMINE—to sabotage, thwart
- ❑ UNDOCUMENTED—not certified, unsubstantiated
- ❑ UNDULATING—moving in waves
- ❑ UNEQUIVOCAL—absolute, certain
- ❑ UNFROCK—to strip of priestly duties
- ❑ UNHERALDED—unannounced, unexpected, not publicized
- ❑ UNIDIMENSIONAL—having one size or dimension, flat
- ❑ UNIFORM (adj.)—consistent and unchanging; identical
- ❑ UNIMPEACHABLE—beyond question

❑ UNINITIATED—not familiar with an area of study

❑ UNKEMPT—uncombed, messy in appearance

❑ UNOBTRUSIVE—modest, unassuming

❑ UNSCRUPULOUS—dishonest

❑ UNSOLICITED—unrequested

❑ UNWARRANTED—groundless, unjustified

❑ UNWITTING—unconscious; unintentional

❑ UNYIELDING—firm, resolute

❑ UPBRAID—to scold sharply

❑ UPROARIOUS—loud and forceful

❑ URBANE—courteous, refined, suave

❑ USURP—to seize by force

❑ USURY—practice of lending money at exorbitant rates

❑ UTILITARIAN—efficient, functional, useful

❑ UTOPIA—perfect place

V

❑ VACILLATE—to waver, show indecision

❑ VACUOUS—empty, void; lacking intelligence, purposeless

❑ VAGRANT—poor person with no home

❑ VALIDATE—to authorize, certify, confirm

❑ VANQUISH—to conquer, defeat

❑ VAPID—tasteless, dull

❑ VARIABLE—changeable, inconstant

❑ VARIEGATED—varied; marked with different colors

❑ VAUNTED—boasted about, bragged about

❑ VEHEMENTLY—strongly, urgently

❑ VENDETTA—prolonged feud marked by bitter hostility

❑ VENERABLE—respected because of age

❑ VENERATION—adoration, honor, respect

❑ VENT (v.)—to express, say out loud

❑ VERACIOUS—truthful, accurate

❑ VERACITY—accuracy, truth

❑ VERBATIM—word for word

❑ VERBOSE—wordy

❑ VERDANT—green with vegetation; inexperienced

❑ VERDURE—fresh, rich vegetation

❑ VERIFIED—proven true

❑ VERISIMILITUDE—quality of appearing true or real

❑ VERITY—truthfulness; belief viewed as true and enduring

❑ VERMIN—small creatures offensive to humans

❑ VERNACULAR—everyday language used by ordinary people; specialized language of a profession

❑ VERNAL—related to spring

❑ VERSATILE—adaptable, all-purpose

❑ VESTIGE—trace, remnant

❑ VETO (v.)—to reject formally

❑ VEX—to irritate, annoy; confuse, puzzle

❑ VIABLE—workable, able to succeed or grow

❑ VIADUCT—series of elevated arches used to cross a valley

❑ VICARIOUS—substitute, surrogate; enjoyed through imagined participation in another's experience

❑ VICISSITUDE—change or variation; ups and downs

❑ VIE—to compete, contend

❑ VIGILANT—attentive, watchful

❑ VIGNETTE—decorative design; short literary composition

❑ VILIFY—to slander, defame

❑ VIM—energy, enthusiasm

❑ VINDICATE—to clear of blame; support a claim

❑ VINDICATION—clearance from blame or suspicion

❑ VINDICTIVE—spiteful, vengeful, unforgiving

❑ VIRILE—manly, having qualities of an adult male

❑ VIRTUOSO—someone with masterly skill; expert musician

❑ VIRULENT—extremely poisonous; malignant; hateful

❑ VISCOUS—thick, syrupy, and sticky

❑ VITRIOLIC—burning, caustic; sharp, bitter

❑ VITUPERATE—to abuse verbally

❑ VIVACIOUS—lively, spirited

❑ VIVID—bright and intense in color; strongly perceived

❑ VOCIFEROUS—loud, vocal, and noisy

❑ VOID (adj.)—not legally enforceable; empty

❑ VOID (n.)—emptiness, vacuum

❑ VOID (v.)—to cancel, invalidate

❑ VOLITION—free choice, free will; act of choosing

❑ VOLLEY (n.)—flight of missiles, round of gunshots

❑ VOLUBLE—speaking much and easily, talkative; glib

❑ VOLUMINOUS—large, having great volume

❑ VORACIOUS—having a great appetite

❑ VULNERABLE—defenseless, unprotected; innocent, naive

W

- ❑ WAIVE—to refrain from enforcing a rule; to give up a legal right
- ❑ WALLOW—to indulge oneself excessively, luxuriate
- ❑ WAN—sickly pale
- ❑ WANTON—undisciplined, unrestrained, reckless
- ❑ WARRANTY—guarantee of a product's soundness
- ❑ WARY—careful, cautious
- ❑ WAYWARD—erratic, unrestrained, reckless
- ❑ WEATHER (v.)—to endure, undergo
- ❑ WHET—to sharpen, stimulate
- ❑ WHIMSY—playful or fanciful idea
- ❑ WILY—clever, deceptive
- ❑ WINDFALL—sudden, unexpected good fortune
- ❑ WINSOME—charming, happily engaging
- ❑ WITHDRAWN—unsociable, aloof; shy, timid
- ❑ WIZENED—withered, shriveled, wrinkled
- ❑ WRIT—written document, usually in law
- ❑ WRY—amusing, ironic

X

- ❑ XENOPHOBIA—fear or hatred of foreigners or strangers

Y

- ❑ YOKE (v.)—to join together

Z

- ❑ ZEALOT—someone passionately devoted to a cause
- ❑ ZENITH—highest point, summit
- ❑ ZEPHYR—gentle breeze
- ❑ ZOOLOGIST—scientist who studies animals

THE KAPLAN ROOT LIST

❑ A, AN—not, without
amoral, atrophy, asymmetrical, anarchy, anesthetic, anonymity, anomaly

❑ AB, A—from, away, apart
abnormal, abdicate, aberration, abhor, abject, abjure, ablution, abnegate, abortive, abrogate, abscond, absolve, abstemious, abstruse, annul, avert, aversion

❑ AC, ACR—sharp, sour
acid, acerbic, exacerbate, acute, acuity, acumen, acrid, acrimony

❑ AD, A—to, toward
adhere, adjacent, adjunct, admonish, adroit, adumbrate, advent, abeyance, abet, accede, accretion, acquiesce, affluent, aggrandize, aggregate, alleviate, alliteration, allude, allure, ascribe, aspersion, aspire, assail, assonance, attest

❑ ALI, ALTR—another
alias, alienate, inalienable, altruism

❑ AM, AMI—love
amorous, amicable, amiable, amity

❑ AMBI, AMPHI—both
ambiguous, ambivalent, ambidextrous, amphibious

❑ AMBL, AMBUL—walk
amble, ambulatory, perambulator, somnambulist

❑ ANIM—mind, spirit, breath
animal, animosity, unanimous, magnanimous

❑ ANN, ENN—year
annual, annuity, superannuated, biennial, perennial

❑ ANTE, ANT—before
antecedent, antediluvian, antebellum, antepenultimate, anterior, antiquity, antiquated, anticipate

❑ ANTHROP—human
anthropology, anthropomorphic, misanthrope, philanthropy

❑ ANTI, ANT—against, opposite
antidote, antipathy, antithesis, antacid, antagonist, antonym

❑ AUD—hear
audio, audience, audition, auditory, audible

❑ AUTO—self
autobiography, autocrat, autonomous

❑ BELLI, BELL—war
belligerent, bellicose, antebellum, rebellion

❑ BENE, BEN—good
benevolent, benefactor, beneficent, benign

❑ BI—two
bicycle, bisect, bilateral, bilingual, biped

❏ BIBLIO—book
Bible, bibliography, bibliophile

❏ BIO—life
biography, biology, amphibious, symbiotic, macrobiotics

❏ BURS—money, purse
reimburse, disburse, bursar

❏ CAD, CAS, CID—happen, fall
accident, cadence, cascade, deciduous

❏ CAP, CIP—head
captain, decapitate, capitulate, precipitous, precipitate, recapitulate

❏ CARN—flesh
carnal, carnage, carnival, carnivorous, incarnate

❏ CAP, CAPT, CEPT, CIP—take, hold, seize
capable, capacious, captivate, deception, intercept, precept, inception, anticipate, emancipation, incipient, percipient

❏ CED, CESS—yield, go
cease, cessation, incessant, cede, precede, accede, recede, antecedent, intercede, secede, cession

❏ CHROM—color
chrome, chromatic, monochrome

❏ CHRON—time
chronology, chronic, anachronism

❏ CIDE—murder
suicide, homicide, regicide, patricide

❏ CIRCUM—around
circumference, circumlocution, circumnavigate, circumscribe, circumspect, circumvent

❏ CLIN, CLIV—slope
incline, declivity, proclivity

❏ CLUD, CLUS, CLAUS, CLOIS—shut, close
conclude, reclusive, claustrophobia, cloister, preclude, occlude

❏ CO, COM, CON—with, together
coeducation, coagulate, coalesce, coerce, cogent, cognate, collateral, colloquial, colloquy, commensurate, commodious, compassion, compatriot, complacent, compliant, complicity, compunction, concerto, conciliatory, concord, concur, condone, conflagration, congeal, congenial, congenital, conglomerate, conjugal, conjure, conscientious, consecrate, consensus, consonant, constrained, contentious, contrite, contusion, convalescence, convene, convivial, convoke, convoluted, congress

❏ COGN, GNO—know
recognize, cognition, cognizance, incognito, diagnosis, agnostic, prognosis, gnostic, ignorant

❏ CONTRA—against
controversy, incontrovertible, contravene

❏ CORP—body
corpse, corporeal, corpulence

❏ COSMO, COSM—world
cosmopolitan, cosmos, microcosm, macrocosm

❏ CRAC, CRAT—rule, power
democracy, bureaucracy, theocracy, autocrat, aristocrat, technocrat

❏ CRED—trust, believe
incredible, credulous, credence

❏ CRESC, CRET—grow
crescent, crescendo, accretion

❏ CULP—blame, fault
culprit, culpable, inculpate, exculpate

❏ CURR, CURS—run
current, concur, cursory, precursor, incursion

❏ DE—down, out, apart
depart, debase, debilitate, declivity, decry, deface, defamatory, defunct, delegate, demarcation, demean, demur, deplete, deplore, depravity, deprecate, deride, derivative, desist, detest, devoid

❏ DEC—ten, tenth
decade, decimal, decathlon, decimate

❏ DEMO, DEM—people
democrat, demographics, demagogue, epidemic, pandemic, endemic

❏ DI, DIURN—day
diary, quotidian, diurnal

❏ DIA—across
diagonal, diatribe, diaphanous

❏ DIC, DICT—speak
abdicate, diction, interdict, predict, indict, verdict

❏ DIS, DIF, DI—not, apart, away
disaffected, disband, disbar, disburse, discern, discordant, discredit, discursive, disheveled, disparage, disparate, dispassionate, dispirit, dissemble, disseminate, dissension, dissipate, dissonant, dissuade, distend, differentiate, diffidence, diffuse, digress, divert

❏ DOC, DOCT—teach
docile, doctrine, doctrinaire

❏ DOL—pain
condolence, doleful, dolorous, indolent

❏ DUC, DUCT—lead
seduce, induce, conduct, viaduct, induct

❏ EGO—self
ego, egoist, egocentric

❏ EN, EM—in, into
enter, entice, encumber, endemic, ensconce, enthrall, entreat, embellish, embezzle, embroil, empathy

❏ ERR—wander
erratic, aberration, errant

❑ EU—well, good
eulogy, euphemism, euphony, euphoria, eurythmics, euthanasia

❑ EX, E—out, out of
exit, exacerbate, excerpt, excommunicate, exculpate, execrable, exhume, exonerate, exorbitant, exorcise, expatriate, expedient, expiate, expunge, expurgate, extenuate, extort, extremity, extricate, extrinsic, exult, evoke, evict, evince, elicit, egress, egregious

❑ FAC, FIC, FECT, FY, FEA—make, do
factory, facility, benefactor, malefactor, fiction, fictive, beneficent, affect, confection, refectory, magnify, unify, rectify, vilify, feasible

❑ FAL, FALS—deceive
infallible, fallacious, false

❑ FERV—boil
fervent, fervid, effervescent

❑ FID—faith, trust
confident, diffidence, perfidious, fidelity

❑ FLU, FLUX—flow
fluent, affluent, confluence, effluvia, superfluous, flux

❑ FORE—before
forecast, foreboding, forestall

❑ FRAG, FRAC—break
fragment, fracture, diffract, fractious, refract

❑ FUS—pour
profuse, infusion, effusive, diffuse

❑ GEN—birth, class, kin
generation, congenital, homogeneous, heterogeneous, ingenious, engender, progenitor, progeny

❑ GRAD, GRESS—step
graduate, gradual, retrograde, centigrade, degrade, gradation, gradient, progress, congress, digress, transgress, ingress, egress

❑ GRAPH, GRAM—writing
biography, bibliography, epigraph, grammar, epigram

❑ GRAT—pleasing
grateful, gratitude, gratis, ingrate, congratulate, gratuitous, gratuity

❑ GRAV, GRIEV—heavy
grave, gravity, aggravate, grieve, aggrieve, grievous

❑ GREG—crowd, flock
segregate, gregarious, egregious, congregate, aggregate

❑ HABIT, HIBIT—have, hold
habit, cohabit, habitat, inhibit

❑ HAP—by chance
happen, haphazard, hapless, mishap

❑ HELIO, HELI—sun
heliocentric, heliotrope, aphelion, perihelion, helium

❏ HETERO—other
heterosexual, heterogeneous, heterodox

❏ HOL—whole
holocaust, catholic, holistic

❏ HOMO—same
homosexual, homogenize, homogeneous, homonym

❏ HOMO—man
homo sapiens, homicide, bonhomie

❏ HYDR—water
hydrant, hydrate, dehydration

❏ HYPER—too much, excess
hyperactive, hyperbole, hyperventilate

❏ HYPO—too little, under
hypodermic, hypothermia, hypochondria, hypothesis, hypothetical

❏ IN, IG, IL, IM, IR—not
incorrigible, indefatigable, indelible, indubitable, inept, inert, inexorable, insatiable, insentient, insolvent, insomnia, interminable, intractable, incessant, inextricable, infallible, infamy, innumerable, inoperable, insipid, intemperate, intrepid, inviolable, ignorant, ignominious, ignoble, illicit, illimitable, immaculate, immutable, impasse, impeccable, impecunious, impertinent, implacable, impotent, impregnable, improvident, impassioned, impervious, irregular

❏ IN, IL, IM, IR—in, on, into
invade, inaugurate, incandescent, incarcerate, incense, indenture, induct, ingratiate, introvert, incarnate, inception, incisive, infer, infusion, ingress, innate, inquest, inscribe, insinuate, inter, illustrate, imbue, immerse, implicate, irrigate, irritate

❏ INTER—between, among
intercede, intercept, interdiction, interject, interlocutor, interloper, intermediary, intermittent, interpolate, interpose, interregnum, interrogate, intersect, intervene

❏ INTRA, INTR—within
intrastate, intravenous, intramural, intrinsic

❏ IT, ITER—between, among
transit, itinerant, transitory, reiterate

❏ JECT, JET—throw
eject, interject, abject, trajectory, jettison

❏ JOUR—day
journal, adjourn, sojourn

❏ JUD—judge
judge, judicious, prejudice, adjudicate

❏ JUNCT, JUG—join
junction, adjunct, injunction, conjugal, subjugate

❏ JUR—swear, law
jury, abjure, adjure, conjure, perjure, jurisprudence

❏ LAT—side
lateral, collateral, unilateral, bilateral, quadrilateral

❑ LAV, LAU, LU—wash
   lavatory, laundry, ablution, antediluvian

❑ LEG, LEC, LEX—read, speak
   legible, lecture, lexicon

❑ LEV—light
   elevate, levitate, levity, alleviate

❑ LIBER—free
   liberty, liberal, libertarian, libertine

❑ LIG, LECT—choose, gather
   eligible, elect, select

❑ LIG, LI, LY—bind
   ligament, oblige, religion, liable, liaison, lien, ally

❑ LING, LANG—tongue
   lingo, language, linguistics, bilingual

❑ LITER—letter
   literate, alliteration, literal

❑ LITH—stone
   monolith, lithograph, megalith

❑ LOQU, LOC, LOG—speech, thought
   eloquent, loquacious, colloquial, colloquy, soliloquy, circumlocution, interlocutor, monologue, dialogue, eulogy, philology, neologism

❑ LUC, LUM—light
   lucid, elucidate, pellucid, translucent, illuminate

❑ LUD, LUS—play
   ludicrous, allude, delusion, allusion, illusory

❑ MACRO—great
   macrocosm, macrobiotics

❑ MAG, MAJ, MAS, MAX—great
   magnify, magnanimous, magnate, magnitude, majesty, master, maximum

❑ MAL—bad
   malady, maladroit, malevolent, malodorous

❑ MAN—hand
   manual, manuscript, emancipate, manifest

❑ MAR—sea
   submarine, marine, maritime

❑ MATER, MATR—mother
   maternal, matron, matrilineal

❑ MEDI—middle
   intermediary, medieval, mediate

❑ MEGA—great
megaphone, megalomania, megaton, megalith

❑ MEM, MEN—remember
memory, memento, memorabilia, reminisce

❑ METER, METR, MENS—measure
meter, thermometer, perimeter, metronome, commensurate

❑ MICRO—small
microscope, microorganism, microcosm, microbe

❑ MIS—wrong, bad, hate
misunderstand, misanthrope, misapprehension, misconstrue, misnomer, mishap

❑ MIT, MISS—send
transmit, emit, missive

❑ MOLL—soft
mollify, emollient, mollusk

❑ MON, MONIT—warn
admonish, monitor, premonition

❑ MONO—one
monologue, monotonous, monogamy, monolith, monochrome

❑ MOR—custom, manner
moral, mores, morose

❑ MOR, MORT—dead
morbid, moribund, mortal, amortize

❑ MORPH—shape
amorphous, anthropomorphic, metamorphosis, morphology

❑ MOV, MOT, MOB, MOM—move
remove, motion, mobile, momentum, momentous

❑ MUT—change
mutate, mutability, immutable, commute

❑ NAT, NASC—born
native, nativity, natal, neonate, innate, cognate, nascent, renascent, renaissance

❑ NAU, NAV—ship, sailor
nautical, nauseous, navy, circumnavigate

❑ NEG—not, deny
negative, abnegate, renege

❑ NEO—new
neoclassical, neophyte, neologism, neonate

❑ NIHIL—none, nothing
annihilation, nihilism

❑ NOM, NYM—name
nominate, nomenclature, nominal, cognomen, misnomer, ignominious, antonym, homonym, pseudonym, synonym, anonymity

❑ NOX, NIC, NEC, NOC—harm
obnoxious, noxious, pernicious, internecine, innocuous

❑ NOV—new
novelty, innovation, novitiate

❑ NUMER—number
numeral, numerous, innumerable, enumerate

❑ OB—against
obstruct, obdurate, obfuscate, obnoxious, obsequious, obstinate, obstreperous, obtrusive

❑ OMNI—all
omnipresent, omnipotent, omniscient, omnivorous

❑ ONER—burden
onerous, onus, exonerate

❑ OPER—work
operate, cooperate, inoperable

❑ PAC—peace
pacify, pacifist, pacific

❑ PALP—feel
palpable, palpitation

❑ PAN—all
panorama, panacea, panegyric, pandemic, panoply

❑ PATER, PATR—father
paternal, paternity, patriot, compatriot, expatriate, patrimony, patricide, patrician

❑ PATH, PASS—feel, suffer
sympathy, antipathy, empathy, apathy, pathos, impassioned

❑ PEC—money
pecuniary, impecunious, peculation

❑ PED, POD—foot
pedestrian, pediment, expedient, biped, quadruped, tripod

❑ PEL, PULS—drive
compel, compelling, expel, propel, compulsion

❑ PEN—almost
peninsula, penultimate, penumbra

❑ PEND, PENS—hang
pendant, pendulous, compendium, suspense, propensity

❑ PER—through, by, for, throughout
perambulator, percipient, perfunctory, permeable, perspicacious, pertinacious, perturbation, perusal, perennial, peregrinate

❑ PER—against, destruction
perfidious, pernicious, perjure

❑ PERI—around
perimeter, periphery, perihelion, peripatetic

❑ PET—seek, go toward
petition, impetus, impetuous, petulant, centripetal

❑ PHIL—love
philosopher, philanderer, philanthropy, bibliophile, philology

❑ PHOB—fear
phobia, claustrophobia, xenophobia

❑ PHON—sound
phonograph, megaphone, euphony, phonetics, phonics

❑ PLAC—calm, please
placate, implacable, placid, complacent

❑ PON, POS—put, place
postpone, proponent, exponent, preposition, posit, interpose, juxtaposition, depose

❑ PORT—carry
portable, deportment, rapport

❑ POT—drink
potion, potable

❑ POT—power
potential, potent, impotent, potentate, omnipotence

❑ PRE—before
precede, precipitate, preclude, precocious, precursor, predilection, predisposition, preponderance, prepossessing, presage, prescient, prejudice, predict, premonition, preposition

❑ PRIM, PRI—first
prime, primary, primal, primeval, primordial, pristine

❑ PRO—ahead, forth
proceed, proclivity, procrastinator, profane, profuse, progenitor, progeny, prognosis, prologue, promontory, propel, proponent, propose, proscribe, protestation, provoke

❑ PROTO—first
prototype, protagonist, protocol

❑ PROX, PROP—near
approximate, propinquity, proximity

❑ PSEUDO—false
pseudoscientific, pseudonym

❑ PYR—fire
pyre, pyrotechnics, pyromania

❑ QUAD, QUAR, QUAT—four
quadrilateral, quadrant, quadruped, quarter, quarantine, quaternary

❑ QUES, QUER, QUIS, QUIR—question
quest, inquest, query, querulous, inquisitive, inquiry

❑ QUIE—quiet
disquiet, acquiesce, quiescent, requiem

❑ QUINT, QUIN—five
quintuplets, quintessence

❑ RADI, RAMI—branch
radius, radiate, radiant, eradicate, ramification

❑ RECT, REG—straight, rule
rectangle, rectitude, rectify, regular

❑ REG—king, rule
regal, regent, interregnum

❑ RETRO—backward
retrospective, retroactive, retrograde

❑ RID, RIS—laugh
ridiculous, deride, derision

❑ ROG—ask
interrogate, derogatory, abrogate, arrogate, arrogant

❑ RUD—rough, crude
rude, erudite, rudimentary

❑ RUPT—break
disrupt, interrupt, rupture

❑ SACR, SANCT—holy
sacred, sacrilege, consecrate, sanctify, sanction, sacrosanct

❑ SCRIB, SCRIPT, SCRIV—write
scribe, ascribe, circumscribe, inscribe, proscribe, script, manuscript, scrivener

❑ SE—apart, away
separate, segregate, secede, sedition

❑ SEC, SECT, SEG—cut
sector, dissect, bisect, intersect, segment, secant

❑ SED, SID—sit
sedate, sedentary, supersede, reside, residence, assiduous, insidious

❑ SEM—seed, sow
seminar, seminal, disseminate

❑ SEN—old
senior, senile, senescent

❑ SENT, SENS—feel, think
sentiment, nonsense, assent, sentient, consensus, sensual

❑ SEQU, SECU—follow
sequence, sequel, subsequent, obsequious, obsequy, nonsequitur, consecutive

❑ SIM, SEM—similar, same
similar, verisimilitude, semblance, dissemble

❑ SIGN—mark, sign
signal, designation, assignation

❑ SIN—curve
sine curve, sinuous, insinuate

❑ SOL—sun
solar, parasol, solarium, solstice

❑ SOL—alone
solo, solitude, soliloquy, solipsism

❑ SOMN—sleep
insomnia, somnolent, somnambulist

❑ SON—sound
sonic, consonance, dissonance, assonance, sonorous, resonate

❑ SOPH—wisdom
philosopher, sophistry, sophisticated, sophomoric

❑ SPEC, SPIC—see, look
spectator, circumspect, retrospective, perspective, perspicacious, perspicuous

❑ SPER—hope
prosper, prosperous, despair, desperate

❑ SPERS, SPAR—scatter
disperse, sparse, aspersion, disparate

❑ SPIR—breathe
respire, inspire, spiritual, aspire, transpire

❑ STRICT, STRING—bind
strict, stricture, constrict, stringent, astringent

❑ STRUCT, STRU—build
structure, obstruct, construe

❑ SUB—under
subconscious, subjugate, subliminal, subpoena, subsequent, subterranean, subvert

❑ SUMM—highest
summit, summary, consummate

❑ SUPER, SUR—above
supervise, supercilious, supersede, superannuated, superfluous, insurmountable, surfeit

❑ SURGE, SURRECT—rise
surge, resurgent, insurgent, insurrection

❑ SYN, SYM—together
synthesis, sympathy, synonym, syncopation, synopsis, symposium, symbiosis

❑ TACIT, TIC—silent
tacit, taciturn, reticent

❑ TACT, TAG, TANG—touch
tact, tactile, contagious, tangent, tangential, tangible

251

❑ TEN, TIN, TAIN—hold, twist
detention, tenable, tenacious, pertinacious, retinue, retain

❑ TEND, TENS, TENT—stretch
intend, distend, tension, tensile, ostensible, contentious

❑ TERM—end
terminal, terminus, terminate, interminable

❑ TERR—earth, land
terrain, terrestrial, extraterrestrial, subterranean

❑ TEST—witness
testify, attest, testimonial, testament, detest, protestation

❑ THE—god
atheist, theology, apotheosis, theocracy

❑ THERM—heat
thermometer, thermal, thermonuclear, hypothermia

❑ TIM—fear, frightened
timid, intimidate, timorous

❑ TOP—place
topic, topography, utopia

❑ TORT—twist
distort, extort, tortuous

❑ TORP—stiff, numb
torpedo, torpid, torpor

❑ TOX—poison
toxic, toxin, intoxication

❑ TRACT—draw
tractor, intractable, protract

❑ TRANS—across, over, through, beyond
transport, transgress, transient, transitory, translucent, transmutation

❑ TREM, TREP—shake
tremble, tremor, tremulous, trepidation, intrepid

❑ TURB—shake
disturb, turbulent, perturbation

❑ UMBR—shadow
umbrella, umbrage, adumbrate, penumbra

❑ UNI, UN—one
unify, unilateral, unanimous

❑ URB—city
urban, suburban, urbane

❑ VAC—empty
vacant, evacuate, vacuous

❏ VAL, VAIL—value, strength
valid, valor, ambivalent, convalescence, avail, prevail, countervail

❏ VEN, VENT—come
convene, contravene, intervene, venue, convention, circumvent, advent, adventitious

❏ VER—true
verify, verity, verisimilitude, veracious, aver, verdict

❏ VERB—word
verbal, verbose, verbiage, verbatim

❏ VERT, VERS—turn
avert, convert, pervert, revert, incontrovertible, divert, subvert, versatile, aversion

❏ VICT, VINC—conquer
victory, conviction, evict, evince, invincible

❏ VID, VIS—see
evident, vision, visage, supervise

❏ VIL—base, mean
vile, vilify, revile

❏ VIV, VIT—life
vivid, vital, convivial, vivacious

❏ VOC, VOK, VOW—call, voice
vocal, equivocate, vociferous, convoke, evoke, invoke, avow

❏ VOL—wish
voluntary, malevolent, benevolent, volition

❏ VOLV, VOLUT—turn, roll
revolve, evolve, convoluted

❏ VOR—eat
devour, carnivore, omnivorous, voracious

WORD FAMILIES

Note: These are samples of the kinds of word groups you can create to memorize words more efficiently.

❑ **Talkative**

garrulous
glib
loquacious
raconteur
verbose
voluble

❑ **Secret/Hidden**

abscond
alias
arcane
clandestine
covert
cryptic
enigma
furtive
incognito
inconspicuous
lurk
obscure
skulk
subterranean
surreptitious

❑ **Not Talkative**

concise
curt
laconic
pithy
reticent
succinct
taciturn

❑ **Praise**

accolade
adulation
commend
eulogize

exalt
extol
laud
lionize
plaudit
revere

❑ **Criticize/Scold**

admonish
berate
castigate
censure
chastise
defame
denigrate
disdain
disparage
excoriate
malign
obloquy
rail
rebuke
reproach
reprimand
reprove
revile
upbraid
vilify

❑ **Stubborn**

intractable
mulish
obdurate
obstinate
pertinacious
recalcitrant
refractory
tenacious

❑ Lazy/Lacking Energy

indolent
lackadaisical
laggard
languid
lassitude
lethargic
listless
loiter
phlegmatic
sluggard
somnolent
torpid

❑ Cowardly

craven
diffident
pusillanimous
timid
timorous

❑ Inexperienced

callow
fledgling
infantile
ingenuous
neophyte
novice
tyro

❑ Obedient

amenable
assent
compliant
deferential
docile
pliant
submissive
tractable

❑ Haughty/Pretentious

affected
aloof
bombastic
grandiloquent
grandiose
magniloquent
mannered
ostentatious
pontificate
supercilious

❑ Friendly

affable
amiable
amicable
bonhomie
convivial
gregarious

❑ Lucky

auspicious
fortuitous
opportune
serendipity
windfall

❑ Soothe

allay
alleviate
anodyne
assuage
liniment
mitigate
mollify
pacify
palliate
placate

❏ Hostility/Hatred
abhor
anathema
animosity
antagonism
antipathy
aversion
contentious
deplore
odious
rancor

❏ Stupid
buffoon
dolt
dupe
fatuous
imbecile
inane
insipid
obtuse
simpleton
vacuous
vapid

❏ Subservient
fawn
grovel
obsequious
servile
subjection
sycophant
toady

❏ Argumentative
adversarial
bellicose
belligerent
fractious
irascible
obstreperous
pugnacious
quibble

❏ Cautious
chary
circumspect
discretion
leery
prudent
wary

❏ Impermanent
ephemeral
evanescent
fleeting
transient
transitory

❏ Ability/Intelligence
acumen
adept
adroit
agile
astute
cogent
deft
dexterous
erudite
literate
lithe
lucidity
sagacious
trenchant

❏ Kind/Generous
altruistic
beneficent
benevolent
bestow
largess
liberal
magnanimous
munificent
philanthropic

APPENDIX B

SAT MATH IN A NUTSHELL

The math on the SAT covers a lot of ground—from arithmetic to algebra to geometry.

Don't let yourself be intimidated. We've highlighted the 100 most important concepts that you'll need for SAT Math and listed them in this chapter.

You've probably been taught most of these in school already, so this list is a great way to refresh your memory.

A MATH STUDY PLAN

Use this list to remind yourself of the key areas you'll need to know. Do four concepts a day, and you'll be ready within a month. If a concept continually causes you trouble, circle it and refer back to it as you try to do the questions.

> **NEED MORE HELP?**
>
> The math reference list comes from Kaplan's *SAT Math Workbook*. For more help with the Math section of the SAT, the workbook is a great place to start.

NUMBER PROPERTIES

1. Integer/Noninteger

Integers are **whole numbers**; they include negative whole numbers and zero.

2. Rational/Irrational Numbers

A rational number is a number that can be expressed as a **ratio of two integers. Irrational numbers** are real numbers—they have locations on the number line; they just **can't be expressed precisely as fractions or decimals.** For the purposes of the SAT, the most important **irrational numbers** are $\sqrt{2}$, $\sqrt{3}$, and π.

3. Adding/Subtracting Signed Numbers

To **add a positive and a negative**, first ignore the signs and find the positive difference between the number parts. Then attach the sign of the original number with the larger number part. For example, to add 23 and –34, first we ignore the minus sign and find the positive difference between 23 and 34—that's 11. Then we attach the sign of the number with the larger number part—in this case it's the minus sign from the –34. So, 23 + (–34) = –11.

Make **subtraction** situations simpler by turning them into addition. For example, think of –17 – (–21) as –17 + (+21).

To **add or subtract a string of positives and negatives**, first turn everything into addition. Then combine the positives and negatives so that the string is reduced to the sum of a single positive number and a single negative number.

4. Multiplying/Dividing Signed Numbers

To multiply and/or divide positives and negatives, treat the number parts as usual and **attach a minus sign if there were originally an odd number of negatives.** For example, to multiply –2, –3, and –5, first multiply the number parts: 2 x 3 x 5 = 30. Then go back and note that there were three—an odd number—negatives, so the product is negative: (–2) x (–3) x (–5) = –30.

5. PEMDAS

When performing multiple operations, remember **PEMDAS**, which means **Parentheses** first, then **Exponents**, then **Multiplication and Division** (left to right), and lastly, **Addition and Subtraction** (left to right). In the expression $9 - 2 \times (5 - 3)^2 + 6 \div 3$, begin with the parentheses: $(5 - 3) = 2$. Then do the exponent: $2^2 = 4$. Now the expression is: $9 - 2 \times 4 + 6 \div 3$. Next do the multiplication and division to get: $9 - 8 + 2$, which equals 3. If you have difficulty remembering PEMDAS, use this sentence to recall it: Please Excuse My Dear Aunt Sally.

6. Counting Consecutive Integers

To count consecutive integers, **subtract the smallest from the largest and add 1.** To count the integers from 13 through 31, subtract: 31 – 13 = 18. Then add 1: 18 + 1 = 19.

DIVISIBILITY

7. Factor/Multiple

The factors of integer n are the positive integers that divide into n with no remainder. The multiples of n are the integers that n divides into with no remainder. For example, 6 is a factor of 12, and 24 is a multiple of 12. 12 is both a factor and a multiple of itself, since $12 \times 1 = 12$ and $12 \div 1 = 12$.

8. Prime Factorization

To find the prime factorization of an integer, just keep breaking it up into factors until **all the factors are prime.** To find the prime factorization of 36, for example, you could begin by breaking it into 4×9: $36 = 4 \times 9 = 2 \times 2 \times 3 \times 3$.

9. Relative Primes

Relative primes are integers that have no common factor other than 1. To determine whether two integers are relative primes, break them both down to their prime factorizations. For example: $35 = 5 \times 7$, and $54 = 2 \times 3 \times 3 \times 3$. They have **no prime factors in common,** so 35 and 54 are relative primes.

10. Common Multiple

A common multiple is a number that is a multiple of two or more integers. You can always get a common multiple of two integers by **multiplying** them, but, unless the two numbers are relative primes, the product will not be the *least* common multiple. For example, to find a common multiple for 12 and 15, you could just multiply: $12 \times 15 = 180$.

11. Least Common Multiple (LCM)

To find the least common multiple, check out the **multiples of the larger integer** until you find one that's also **a multiple of the smaller.** To find the LCM of 12 and 15, begin by taking the multiples of 15: 15 is not divisible by 12; 30 is not; nor is 45. But the next multiple of 15, 60, *is* divisible by 12, so it's the LCM.

12. Greatest Common Factor (GCF)

To find the greatest common factor, break down both integers into their prime factorizations and multiply **all the prime factors they have in common.** $36 = 2 \times 2 \times 3 \times 3$, and $48 = 2 \times 2 \times 2 \times 2 \times 3$. What they have in common is two 2s and one 3, so the GCF is $2 \times 2 \times 3 = 12$.

13. Even/Odd

To predict whether a sum, difference, or product will be even or odd, just **take simple numbers such as 1 and 2 and see what happens.** There are rules—"odd times even is even," for example—but there's no need to memorize them. What happens with one set of numbers generally happens with all similar sets.

14. Multiples of 2 and 4

An integer is divisible by 2 (even) if the **last digit is even.** An integer is divisible by 4 if the **last two digits form a multiple of 4.** The last digit of 562 is 2, which is even, so 562 is a multiple of 2. The last two digits form 62, which is *not* divisible by 4, so 562 is not a multiple of 4. The integer 512, however is divisible by four because the last two digits form 12, which is a multiple of 4.

15. Multiples of 3 and 9

An integer is divisible by 3 if the **sum of its digits is divisible by 3.** An integer is divisible by 9 if the **sum of its digits is divisible by 9.** The sum of the digits in 957 is 21, which is divisible by 3 but not by 9, so 957 is divisible by 3 but not by 9.

16. Multiples of 5 and 10

An integer is divisible by 5 if the **last digit is 5 or 0.** An integer is divisible by 10 if the **last digit is 0.** The last digit of 665 is 5, so 665 is a multiple of 5 but *not* a multiple of 10.

17. Remainders

The remainder is the **whole number left over after division.** 487 is 2 more than 485, which is a multiple of 5, so when 487 is divided by 5, the remainder will be 2.

FRACTIONS AND DECIMALS

18. Reducing Fractions

To reduce a fraction to lowest terms, **factor out and cancel** all factors the numerator and denominator have in common.

$$\frac{28}{36} = \frac{4 \times 7}{4 \times 9} = \frac{7}{9}$$

19. Adding/Subtracting Fractions

To add or subtract fractions, first find a **common denominator,** then add or subtract the numerators.

$$\frac{2}{15} + \frac{3}{10} = \frac{4}{30} + \frac{9}{30} = \frac{4+9}{30} = \frac{13}{30}$$

20. Multiplying Fractions

To multiply fractions, **multiply the numerators and multiply the denominators.**

$$\frac{5}{7} \times \frac{3}{4} = \frac{5 \times 3}{7 \times 4} = \frac{15}{28}$$

21. Dividing Fractions

To divide fractions, **invert the second one and multiply.**

$$\frac{1}{2} \div \frac{3}{5} = \frac{1}{2} \times \frac{5}{3} = \frac{1 \times 5}{2 \times 3} = \frac{5}{6}$$

22. Converting a Mixed Number to an Improper Fraction

To convert a mixed number to an improper fraction, **multiply the whole number part by the denominator, then add the numerator.** The result is the new numerator (over the same denominator). To convert $7\frac{1}{3}$, first multiply 7 by 3, then add 1, to get the new numerator of 22. Put that over the same denominator, 3, to get $\frac{22}{3}$.

23. Converting an Improper Fraction to a Mixed Number

To convert an improper fraction to a mixed number, divide the denominator into the numerator to get a **whole number quotient with a remainder.** The quotient becomes the whole number part of the mixed number, and the remainder becomes the new numerator—with the same denominator. For example, to convert $\frac{108}{5}$, first divide 5 into 108, which yields 21 with a remainder of 3. Therefore, $\frac{108}{5} = 21\frac{3}{5}$.

24. Reciprocal

To find the reciprocal of a fraction, switch the numerator

and the denominator. The reciprocal of $\frac{3}{7}$ is $\frac{7}{3}$. The reci-

procal of 5 is $\frac{1}{5}$. The product of reciprocals is 1.

25. Comparing Fractions

One way to compare fractions is to re-express them with a

common denominator. $\frac{3}{4} = \frac{21}{28}$ and $\frac{5}{7} = \frac{20}{28}$. $\frac{21}{28}$ is

greater than $\frac{20}{28}$, so $\frac{3}{4}$ is greater than $\frac{5}{7}$. Another way to

compare fractions is to convert them both to decimals. $\frac{3}{4}$

converts to .75, and $\frac{5}{7}$ converts to approximately .714.

26. Converting Fractions to Decimals

To convert a fraction to a decimal, **divide the bottom into

the top.** To convert $\frac{5}{8}$, divide 8 into 5, yielding .625.

27. Converting Decimals to Fractions

To convert a decimal to a fraction, set the decimal over 1
and **multiply the numerator and denominator by ten raised
to the number of digits to the right of the decimal point.**
For instance, to convert .625 to a fraction, you would multi-

ply $\frac{.625}{1}$ by $\frac{10^3}{10^3}$, or $\frac{1000}{1000}$. Then simplify:

$$\frac{625}{1000} = \frac{5 \times 125}{8 \times 125} = \frac{5}{8}.$$

28. Repeating Decimal

To find a particular digit in a repeating decimal, note the

number of digits in the cluster that repeats. If there are 2

digits in that cluster, then every second digit is the same. If

there are three digits in that cluster, then every third digit is

the same. And so on. For example, the decimal equivalent of

$\frac{1}{27}$ is .037037037..., which is best written $.\overline{037}$. There are

three digits in the repeating cluster, so every third digit is the

same: 7. To find the 50th digit, look for the multiple of

three just less than 50—that's 48. The 48th digit is 7, and with

the 49th digit the pattern repeats with 0. The 50th digit is 3.

29. Identifying the Parts and the Whole

The key to solving most fractions and percents story problems is to identify the part and the whole. Usually you'll find
the **part** associated with the verb "**is/are**" and the **whole** associated with the word "**of.**" In the sentence, "Half of the boys
are blonds," the whole is the boys ("of the boys"), and the
part is the blonds ("are blonds").

PERCENTS

30. Percent Formula

Whether you need to find the part, the whole, or the percent, use the same formula:

Part = Percent × Whole

Example:	What is 12% of 25?
Setup:	Part = .12 × 25

Example:	15 is 3% of what number?
Setup:	15 = .03 × Whole

Example:	45 is what percent of 9?
Setup:	45 = Percent × 9

31. Percent Increase and Decrease

To increase a number by a percent, **add the percent to 100
percent,** convert to a decimal, and multiply. To increase 40
by 25 percent, add 25 percent to 100 percent, convert 125
percent to 1.25, and multiply by 40. 1.25 × 40 = 50.

32. Finding the Original Whole

To find the **original whole before a percent increase or
decrease,** set up an equation. Think of the result of a 15 percent increase over x as $1.15x$.

Example:	After a 5 percent increase, the population was 59,346. What was the population before the increase?
Setup:	$1.05x = 59{,}346$

33. Combined Percent Increase and Decrease

To determine the combined effect of multiple percent increases and/or decreases, **start with 100 and see what happens.**

Example:	A price went up 10 percent one year, and the new price went up 20 percent the next year. What was the combined percent increase?
Setup:	First year: 100 + (10 percent of 100) = 110. Second year: 110 + (20 percent of 110) = 132. That's a combined 32 percent increase.

RATIOS, PROPORTIONS, AND RATES

34. Setting up a Ratio

To find a ratio, put the number associated with the word **"of"** on top and the quantity associated with the word **"to"** on the bottom and reduce. The ratio of 20 oranges to 12 apples is $\frac{20}{12}$, which reduces to $\frac{5}{3}$.

35. Part-to-Part Ratios and Part-to-Whole Ratios

If the parts add up to the whole, a part-to-part ratio can be turned into two part-to-whole ratios by putting **each number in the original ratio over the sum of the numbers.** If the ratio of males to females is 1 to 2, then the males-to-people ratio is $\frac{1}{1+2} = \frac{1}{3}$ and the females-to-people ratio is $\frac{2}{1+2} = \frac{2}{3}$. In other words, $\frac{2}{3}$ of all the people are female.

36. Solving a Proportion

To solve a proportion, **cross-multiply:**

$$\frac{x}{5} = \frac{3}{4}$$
$$4x = 3 \times 5$$
$$x = \frac{15}{4} = 3.75$$

37. Rate

To solve a rates problem, **use the units** to keep things straight.

Example: If snow is falling at the rate of one foot every four hours, how many inches of snow will fall in seven hours?

Setup:

$$\frac{1 \text{ foot}}{4 \text{ hours}} = \frac{x \text{ inches}}{7 \text{ hours}}$$

$$\frac{12 \text{ inches}}{4 \text{ hours}} = \frac{x \text{ inches}}{7 \text{ hours}}$$

$$4x = 12 \times 7$$
$$x = 21$$

38. Average Rate

Average rate is *not* simply the average of the rates.

$$\text{Average } A \text{ per } B = \frac{\text{Total } A}{\text{Total } B}$$

$$\text{Average Speed} = \frac{\text{Total distance}}{\text{Total time}}$$

To find the average speed for 120 miles at 40 mph and 120 miles at 60 mph, **don't just average the two speeds.** First figure out the total distance and the total time. The total distance is 120 + 120 = 240 miles. The times are two hours for the first leg and three hours for the second leg, or five hours total. The average speed, then, is $\frac{240}{5} = 48$ miles per hour.

AVERAGES

39. Average Formula

To find the average of a set of numbers, **add them up and divide by the number of numbers.**

$$\text{Average} = \frac{\text{Sum of the terms}}{\text{Number of terms}}$$

To find the average of the five numbers 12, 15, 23, 40, and 40, first add them: 12 + 15 + 23 + 40 + 40 = 130. Then divide the sum by 5: 130 ÷ 5 = 26.

40. Average of Evenly Spaced Numbers

To find the average of evenly spaced numbers, just **average the smallest and the largest.** The average of all the integers from 13 through 77 is the same as the average of 13 and 77:

$$\frac{13+77}{2} = \frac{90}{2} = 45$$

41. Using the Average to Find the Sum

Sum = (Average) × (Number of terms)

If the average of 10 numbers is 50, then they add up to 10 × 50, or 500.

42. Finding the Missing Number

To find a missing number when you're given the average, **use the sum.** If the average of four numbers is 7, then the sum of those four numbers is 4 × 7, or 28. Suppose that three of the numbers are 3, 5, and 8. These three numbers add up to 16 of that 28, which leaves 12 for the fourth number.

43. Median

The median of a set of numbers is the value that falls in the middle of the set. If you have five test scores, and they are 88, 86, 57, 94, and 73, you must first list the scores in increasing or decreasing order: 57, 73, 86, 88, 94.

The median is the middle number, or 86. If there is an even number of values in a set (six test scores, for instance), simply take the average of the two middle numbers.

44. Mode

The mode of a set of numbers is the value that appears most often. If your test scores were 88, 57, 68, 85, 99, 93, 93, 84, and 81, the mode of the scores would be 93 because it appears more often than any other score. If there is a tie for the most common value in a set, the set has more than one mode.

POSSIBILITIES AND PROBABILITY

45. Counting the Possibilities

The fundamental counting principle: If there are *m* **ways** one event can happen and *n* **ways** a second event can happen, then there are *m* × *n* **ways** for the two events to happen. For example, with five shirts and seven pairs of pants to choose from, you can put together 5 × 7 = 35 different outfits.

46. Probability

$$\text{Probability} = \frac{\text{Favorable outcomes}}{\text{Total possible outcomes}}$$

For example, if you have 12 shirts in a drawer and nine of them are white, the probability of picking a white shirt at random is $\frac{9}{12} = \frac{3}{4}$. This probability can also be expressed as .75 or 75 percent.

POWERS AND ROOTS

47. Multiplying and Dividing Powers

To multiply powers with the same base, **add the exponents and keep the same base:**

$$x^3 \times x^4 = x^{3+4} = x^7$$

To divide powers with the same base, **subtract the exponents and keep the same base:**

$$y^{13} \div y^8 = y^{13-8} = y^5$$

48. Raising Powers to Powers

To raise a power to a power, **multiply the exponents:**

$$(x^3)^4 = x^{3 \times 4} = x^{12}$$

49. Simplifying Square Roots

To simplify a square root, **factor out the perfect squares** under the radical, unsquare them and put the result in front.

$$\sqrt{12} = \sqrt{4 \times 3} = \sqrt{4} \times \sqrt{3} = 2\sqrt{3}$$

50. Adding and Subtracting Roots

You can add or subtract radical expressions **when the part under the radicals is the same:**

$$2\sqrt{3} + 3\sqrt{3} = 5\sqrt{3}$$

Don't try to add or subtract when the radical parts are different. There's not much you can do with an expression like:

$$3\sqrt{5} + 3\sqrt{7}$$

51. Multiplying and Dividing Roots

The product of square roots is equal to the **square root of the product:**

$$\sqrt{3} \times \sqrt{5} = \sqrt{3 \times 5} = \sqrt{15}$$

The quotient of square roots is equal to the **square root of the quotient:**

$$\frac{\sqrt{6}}{\sqrt{3}} = \sqrt{\frac{6}{3}} = \sqrt{2}$$

ALGEBRAIC EXPRESSIONS

52. Evaluating an Expression

To evaluate an algebraic expression, **plug in** the given values for the unknowns and calculate according to PEMDAS. To find the value of $x^2 + 5x - 6$ when $x = -2$, plug in -2 for x: $(-2)^2 + 5(-2) - 6 = 4 - 10 - 6 = -12$.

53. Adding and Subtracting Monomials

To combine like terms, **keep the variable part unchanged while adding or subtracting the coefficients:**

$$2a + 3a = (2 + 3)a = 5a$$

54. Adding and Subtracting Polynomials

To add or subtract polynomials, **combine like terms.**

$$(3x^2 + 5x - 7) - (x^2 + 12) =$$
$$(3x^2 - x^2) + 5x + (-7 - 12) =$$
$$2x^2 + 5x - 19$$

55. Multiplying Monomials

To multiply monomials, **multiply the coefficients and the variables separately:**

$$2a \cdot 3a = (2 \cdot 3)(a \cdot a) = 6a^2$$

56. Multiplying Binomials—FOIL

To multiply binomials, use **FOIL**. To multiply $(x + 3)$ by $(x + 4)$, first multiply the <u>F</u>irst terms: $x \cdot x = x^2$. Next the <u>O</u>uter terms: $x \cdot 4 = 4x$. Then the <u>I</u>nner terms: $3 \cdot x = 3x$. And finally the <u>L</u>ast terms: $3 \cdot 4 = 12$. Then add and combine like terms:

$$x^2 + 4x + 3x + 12 = x^2 + 7x + 12$$

57. Multiplying Other Polynomials

FOIL works only when you want to multiply two binomials. If you want to multiply polynomials with more than two terms, make sure you **multiply each term in the first polynomial by each term in the second.**

$$(x^2 + 3x + 4)(x + 5) =$$
$$x^2(x + 5) + 3x(x + 5) + 4(x + 5) =$$
$$x^3 + 5x^2 + 3x^2 + 15x + 4x + 20 =$$
$$x^3 + 8x^2 + 19x + 20$$

After multiplying two polynomials together, the number of terms in your expression before simplifying should equal the number of terms in one polynomial multiplied by the number of terms in the second. In the example above, you should have $3 \times 2 = 6$ terms in the product before you simplify like terms.

FACTORING ALGEBRAIC EXPRESSIONS

58. Factoring out a Common Divisor

A factor common to all terms of a polynomial can be **factored out.** Each of the three terms in the polynomial $3x^3 + 12x^2 - 6x$ contains a factor of $3x$. Pulling out the common factor yields $3x(x^2 + 4x - 2)$.

59. Factoring the Difference of Squares

One of the test maker's favorite factorables is the **difference of squares.**

$$a^2 - b^2 = (a - b)(a + b)$$

$x^2 - 9$, for example, factors to $(x - 3)(x + 3)$.

60. Factoring the Square of a Binomial

Learn to recognize polynomials that are squares of binomials:

$$a^2 + 2ab + b^2 = (a+b)^2$$
$$a^2 - 2ab + b^2 = (a-b)^2$$

For example, $4x^2 + 12x + 9$ factors to $(2x + 3)^2$, and $n^2 - 10n + 25$ factors to $(n - 5)^2$.

61. Factoring Other Polynomials—FOIL in Reverse

To factor a quadratic expression, **think about what binomials you could use FOIL on to get that quadratic expression.** To factor $x^2 - 5x + 6$, think about what First terms will produce x^2 , what Last terms will produce $+6$, and what Outer and Inner terms will produce $-5x$. Some common sense—and a little trial and error—lead you to $(x - 2)(x - 3)$.

62. Simplifying an Algebraic Fraction

Simplifying an algebraic fraction is a lot like simplifying a numerical fraction. The general idea is to **find factors common to the numerator and denominator and cancel them.** Thus, simplifying an algebraic fraction begins with factoring.

For example, to simplify $\dfrac{x^2 - x - 12}{x^2 - 9}$, first factor the numer-

ator and denominator:

$$\frac{x^2 - x - 12}{x^2 - 9} = \frac{(x-4)(x+3)}{(x-3)(x+3)}$$

Canceling $x + 3$ from the numerator and denominator

leaves you with $\dfrac{x-4}{x-3}$.

SOLVING EQUATIONS

63. Solving a Linear Equation

To solve an equation, do whatever is necessary to both sides to **isolate the variable.** To solve the equation $5x - 12 = -2x + 9$, first get all the xs on one side by adding $2x$ to both sides: $7x - 12 = 9$. Then add 12 to both sides: $7x = 21$. Then divide both sides by 7: $x = 3$.

64. Solving "in Terms Of"

To solve an equation for one variable **in terms of** another means to **isolate the one variable on one side of the equation,** leaving an expression containing the other variable on the other side of the equation. To solve the equation $3x - 10y = -5x + 6y$ for x in terms of y, isolate x:

$$3x - 10y = -5x + 6y$$
$$3x + 5x = 6y + 10y$$
$$8x = 16y$$
$$x = 2y$$

65. Translating from English into Algebra

To translate from English into algebra, look for the key words and systematically turn phrases into algebraic expressions and sentences into equations. Be careful about order, especially when subtraction is called for.

Example: The charge for a phone call is r cents for the first three minutes and s cents for each minute thereafter. What is the cost, in cents, of a phone call lasting exactly t minutes? $(t > 3)$

Setup: The charge begins with r, and then something more is added, depending on the length of the call. The amount added is s times the number of minutes past three minutes. If the total number of minutes is t, then the number of minutes past three is $t - 3$. So the charge is $r + s(t - 3)$.

66. Solving a Quadratic Equation

To solve a quadratic equation, put it in the "$ax^2 + bx + c = 0$" form, **factor** the left side (if you can), and set each factor equal to 0 separately to get the two solutions. To solve $x^2 + 12 = 7x$, first rewrite it as $x^2 - 7x + 12 = 0$. Then factor the left side:

$$(x-3)(x-4) = 0$$
$$x - 3 = 0 \text{ or } x - 4 = 0$$
$$x = 3 \text{ or } 4$$

67. Solving a System of Equations

You can solve for two variables only if you have two distinct equations. Two forms of the same equation will not be adequate. **Combine the equations** in such a way that **one of the variables cancels out.** To solve the two equations $4x + 3y = 8$ and $x + y = 3$, multiply both sides of the second equation by -3 to get: $-3x - 3y = -9$. Now add the two equations; the $3y$ and the $-3y$ cancel out, leaving: $x = -1$. Plug that back into either one of the original equations and you'll find that $y = 4$.

68. Solving an Inequality

To solve an inequality, do whatever is necessary to both sides to **isolate the variable.** Just remember that when you **multiply or divide both sides by a negative number,** you must **reverse the sign.** To solve $-5x + 7 < -3$, subtract 7 from both sides to get: $-5x < -10$. Now divide both sides by -5, remembering to reverse the sign: $x > 2$.

COORDINATE GEOMETRY

69. Finding the Distance Between Two Points

To find the distance between points, **use the Pythagorean theorem or special right triangles.** The difference between the xs is one leg and the difference between the ys is the other.

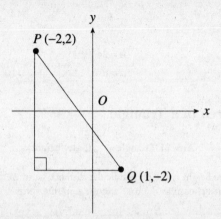

In the figure above, PQ is the hypotenuse of a 3-4-5 triangle, so $PQ = 5$.

You can also use the **distance formula**:

$$d = \sqrt{(x_1 - x_2)^2 + (y_1 - y_2)^2}$$

To find the distance between $R(3,6)$ and $S(5,-2)$:

$$d = \sqrt{(3 - 5)^2 + [6 - (-2)]^2}$$
$$= \sqrt{(-2)^2 + (8)^2}$$
$$= \sqrt{68} = 2\sqrt{17}$$

70. Using Two Points to Find the Slope

$$\text{Slope} = \frac{\textbf{Change in } y}{\textbf{Change in } x} = \frac{\textbf{Rise}}{\textbf{Run}}$$

The slope of the line that contains the points $A(2,3)$ and $B(0,-1)$ is:

$$\frac{y_A - y_B}{x_A - x_B} = \frac{3 - (-1)}{2 - 0} = \frac{4}{2} = 2$$

71. Using an Equation to Find the Slope

To find the slope of a line from an equation, put the equation into the **slope-intercept** form:

$$y = mx + b$$

The **slope is** m. To find the slope of the equation $3x + 2y = 4$, rearrange it:

$$3x + 2y = 4$$
$$2y = -3x + 4$$
$$y = -\frac{3}{2}x + 2$$

The slope is $-\dfrac{3}{2}$.

72. Using an Equation to Find an Intercept

To find the y-intercept, you can either put the equation into $y = mx + b$ (**slope-intercept**) form—in which case b is the y-intercept—or you can just **plug $x = 0$** into the equation and **solve for y**. To find the x-intercept, **plug $y = 0$** into the equation and **solve for x**.

LINES AND ANGLES

73. Intersecting Lines

When two lines intersect, **adjacent angles are supplementary and vertical angles are equal**.

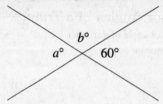

In the figure above, the angles marked $a°$ and $b°$ are adjacent and supplementary, so $a + b = 180$. Furthermore, the angles marked $a°$ and $60°$ are vertical and equal, so $a = 60$.

74. Parallel Lines and Transversals

A transversal across parallel lines forms **four equal acute angles and four equal obtuse angles**.

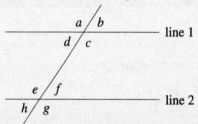

In the figure above, line 1 is parallel to line 2. Angles a, c, e, and g are obtuse, so they are all equal. Angles b, d, f, and h are acute, so they are all equal.

Furthermore, **any of the acute angles is supplementary to any of the obtuse angles**. Angles a and h are supplementary, as are b and e, c and f, and so on.

267

TRIANGLES—GENERAL

75. Interior Angles of a Triangle

The three angles of any triangle **add up to 180°.**

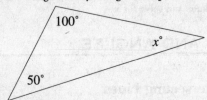

In the figure above, $x + 50 + 100 = 180$, so $x = 30$.

76. Exterior Angles of a Triangle

An exterior angle of a triangle is equal to the **sum of the remote interior angles.**

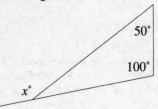

In the figure above, the exterior angle labeled $x°$ is equal to the sum of the remote angles: $x = 50 + 100 = 150$.

The three exterior angles of a triangle add up to 360°.

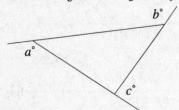

In the figure above, $a + b + c = 360$.

77. Similar Triangles

Similar triangles have the same shape; **corresponding angles are equal and corresponding sides are proportional.**

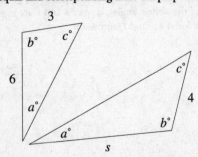

The triangles above are similar because they have the same angles. The 3 corresponds to the 4 and the 6 corresponds to the s.

$$\frac{3}{4} = \frac{6}{s}$$
$$3s = 24$$
$$s = 8$$

78. Area of a Triangle

$$\text{Area of Triangle} = \frac{1}{2}\,(\text{base})(\text{height})$$

The height is the perpendicular distance between the side that's chosen as the base and the opposite vertex.

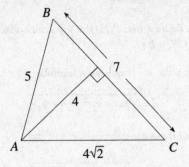

In the triangle above, 4 is the height when the 7 is chosen as the base.

$$\text{Area} \ = \frac{1}{2}bh = \frac{1}{2}(7)(4) = 14$$

79. Triangle Inequality Theorem

The length of one side of a triangle must be **greater than the difference and less than the sum** of the lengths of the other two sides. For example, if it is given that the length of one side is 3 and the length of another side is 7, then you know that the length of the third side must be greater than $7 - 3 = 4$ and less than $7 + 3 = 10$.

80. Isosceles Triangles

An isosceles triangle is a triangle that has **two equal sides.** Not only are two sides equal, but the angles opposite the equal sides, called base angles, are also equal.

81. Equilateral Triangles

Equilateral triangles are triangles in which **all three sides are equal.** Since all the sides are equal, all the angles are also equal. All three angles in an equilateral triangle measure 60 degrees, regardless of the lengths of sides.

RIGHT TRIANGLES

82. Pythagorean Theorem

For all right triangles:

$$(\text{leg}_1)^2 + (\text{leg}_2)^2 = (\text{hypotenuse})^2$$

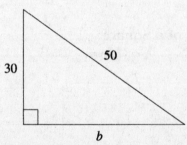

If one leg is 2 and the other leg is 3, then:

$$2^2 + 3^2 = c^2$$
$$c^2 = 4 + 9$$
$$c = \sqrt{13}$$

83. The 3–4–5 Triangle

If a right triangle's leg-to-leg ratio is 3:4, or if the leg-to-hypotenuse ratio is 3:5 or 4:5, it's a 3–4–5 triangle and you don't need to use the Pythagorean theorem to find the third side. Just figure out what multiple of 3–4–5 it is.

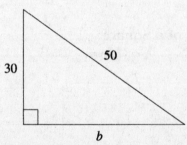

In the right triangle shown, one leg is 30 and the hypotenuse is 50. This is 10 times 3–4–5. The other leg is 40.

84. The 5–12–13 Triangle

If a right triangle's leg-to-leg ratio is 5:12, or if the leg-to-hypotenuse ratio is 5:13 or 12:13, then it's a 5–12–13 triangle and you don't need to use the Pythagorean theorem to find the third side. Just figure out what multiple of 5–12–13 it is.

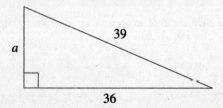

Here one leg is 36 and the hypotenuse is 39. This is 3 times 5–12–13. The other leg is 15.

85. The 30–60–90 Triangle

The sides of a 30–60–90 triangle are in a ratio of

$x : x\sqrt{3} : 2x$ You don't need to use the Pythagorean theorem.

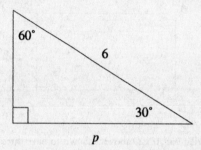

If the hypotenuse is 6, then the shorter leg is half that, or 3; and then the longer leg is equal to the short leg times $\sqrt{3}$, or $3\sqrt{3}$.

86. The 45–45–90 Triangle

The sides of a 45–45–90 triangle are in a ratio of

$x : x : x\sqrt{2}$.

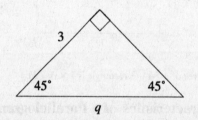

If one leg is 3, then the other leg is also 3, and the hypotenuse is equal to a leg times $\sqrt{2}$, or $3\sqrt{2}$.

OTHER POLYGONS

87. Characteristics of a Rectangle

A rectangle is a **four-sided figure with four right angles.**
Opposite sides are equal. Diagonals are equal.

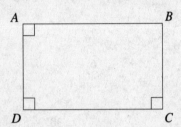

Quadrilateral *ABCD* above is shown to have three right angles. The fourth angle therefore also measures 90°, and *ABCD* is a rectangle. The perimeter of a rectangle is equal to the sum of the lengths of the four sides, which is equivalent to 2(Length + Width).

88. Area of a Rectangle

Area of Rectangle = length × width

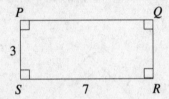

The area of a 7-by-3 rectangle is 7 × 3 = 21.

89. Characteristics of a Parallelogram

A parallelogram has **two pairs of parallel sides.** Opposite sides are equal. Opposite angles are equal. Consecutive angles add up to 180°.

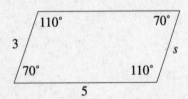

In the figure above, *s* is the length of the side opposite the 3, so *s* = 3.

90. Area of a Parallelogram

Area of Parallelogram = base × height

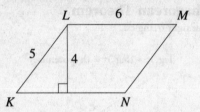

In parallelogram *KLMN* above, 4 is the height when *LM* or *KN* is used as the base. Base × height = 6 × 4 = 24.

91. Characteristics of a Square

A square is a **rectangle with four equal sides.**

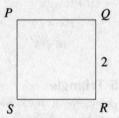

If *PQRS* is a square, all sides are the same length as *QR.* The perimeter of a square is equal to four times the length of one side.

92. Area of a Square

Area of Square = (side)^2

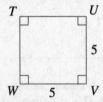

The square above, with sides of length 5, has an area of 5^2 = 25.

93. Interior Angles of a Polygon

The sum of the measures of the interior angles of a polygon = $(n - 2) \times 180$, where *n* is the number of sides.

Sum of the Angles = $(n - 2) \times 180$

The eight angles of an octagon, for example, add up to $(8 - 2) \times 180 = 1,080$.

CIRCLES

94. Circumference of a Circle

Circumference = $2\pi r$

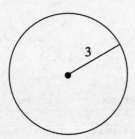

In the circle above, the radius is 3, and so the circumference is $2\pi(3) = 6\pi$.

95. Length of an Arc

An arc is a piece of the circumference. If n is the degree measure of the arc's central angle, then the formula is:

$$\text{Length of an Arc} = \left(\frac{n}{360}\right)(2\pi r)$$

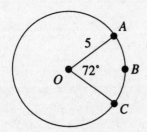

In the figure above, the radius is 5 and the measure of the central angle is 72°. The arc length is $\frac{72}{360}$ or $\frac{1}{5}$ of the circumference:

$$\left(\frac{72}{360}\right)(2\pi)(5)=\left(\frac{1}{5}\right)(10\pi)=2\pi$$

96. Area of a Circle

Area of a Circle = πr^2

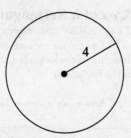

The area of the circle is $\pi(4)^2 = 16\pi$.

97. Area of a Sector

A sector is a piece of the area of a circle. If n is the degree measure of the sector's central angle, then the formula is:

$$\text{Area of a Sector} = \left(\frac{n}{360}\right)(\pi r^2)$$

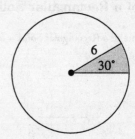

In the figure above, the radius is 6 and the measure of the sector's central angle is 30°. The sector has $\frac{30}{360}$ or $\frac{1}{12}$ of the area of the circle:

$$\left(\frac{30}{360}\right)(\pi)(6^2)=\left(\frac{1}{12}\right)(36\pi)=3\pi$$

SOLIDS

98. Surface Area of a Rectangular Solid

The surface of a rectangular solid consists of three pairs of identical faces. To find the surface area, find the area of each face and add them up. If the length is l, the width is w, and the height is h, the formula is:

Surface Area = $2lw + 2wh + 2lh$

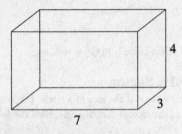

The surface area of the box above is: $2 \cdot 7 \cdot 3 + 2 \cdot 3 \cdot 4 + 2 \cdot 7 \cdot 4 = 42 + 24 + 56 = 122$

99. Volume of a Rectangular Solid

Volume of a Rectangular Solid = lwh

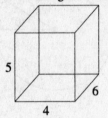

The volume of a 4-by-5-by-6 box is

$$4 \times 5 \times 6 = 120$$

A cube is a rectangular solid with length, width, and height all equal. If e is the length of an edge of a cube, the volume formula is:

Volume of a Cube = e^3

The volume of this cube is $2^3 = 8$.

100. Volume of a Cylinder

Volume of a Cylinder = $\pi r^2 h$

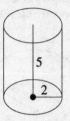

In the cylinder above, $r = 2$, $h = 5$, so:

$$\text{Volume} = \pi(2^2)(5) = 20\pi$$

APPENDIX C

COLLEGE ADMISSIONS

APPENDIX C

COLLEGE ADMISSIONS

1. THE ROAD TO COLLEGE

2. SHOW AND REPLY

3. ESSAYS THAT WORK

4. RECOMMENDATIONS

5. INTERVIEWS AND CAMPUS VISITS

6. MAKING YOUR FINAL DECISION

1

THE ROAD TO COLLEGE

Many high school students think that applying for admission to colleges—particularly the most competitive ones—is much like taking a chance at the lottery. They believe that decisions are made arbitrarily. A student once asked us whether admissions officers used the "stair-step approach" to make their admissions decisions. That is, do they take a stack of applications and throw them down the stairs, admitting students whose applications land on the first step, wait-listing the ones that land on the second step, and rejecting the rest?

Now that you'll be taking the SAT, this helpful section will show you how your test results will fit in with the entire admissions process. Take heart that there is a form of logic to the process. Each college and university has an admissions system, and each works fairly well. Admissions officers really want to make the best fit between applicants and their institution. To do that, they sift through all the material that you and other applicants provide, make evaluations, and decide. Their job is to take the information from you and give it a fair review.

Your job is to decide how you're going to present yourself to the readers of your application file. That's the part of the process you control. Maximizing every part of the application process to cast yourself in a positive light will give you the best chance to stand apart from the competition. To accomplish this goal, you must have a strategy. You must be aware of your strengths and prepare your applications in a way that focuses attention on your strongest qualities. That's what this section will help you do. You'll learn the ins and outs of when to apply, how to apply, how to sell yourself, and how to make your final decision.

IN THE SAME BOAT

You're not alone. Thousands of people are applying to colleges along with you. Many share your fears and concerns about the admissions process.

GETTING STARTED

The admissions process can be long and involved. But there are things you can do to avoid the last-minute crunch. Ideally, you should begin thinking about college as early as your junior year. The first thing you

PENCIL ME IN

Get yourself a calendar, preferably one of those 18-month numbers with a page for every day so you can jot down all the requirements for the college admissions process, starting as early as spring of your junior year. Don't make the mistake of writing down your notations only on the day of the deadline. Give yourself at least two weeks notice before each deadline to get things done.

ADVANTAGES OF EARLY DECISION

• You don't have to wait around so long to find out if you're in.

• You don't spend time and money filing a lot of applications.

• You have more time to plan how to pay for college.

should do is go to your guidance office in September of your junior year and do the following:

• Ask for the PSAT Registration Booklet.
• Talk with your guidance counselor about planning for college.
• Start thinking about the qualities you want in your ideal college.

Once you've taken these initial steps, you'll want to start planning your application schedule. The application process requires that you compile loads of information about yourself, fill out a lot of forms, and meet rigid deadlines. You'll have to get organized to make sure you know all the important dates and to avoid missing any deadlines.

Timing is everything in the college admissions process. You face deadlines for taking standardized tests, deadlines for submitting your admissions applications, deadlines for financial aid applications, and deadlines for returning all of the other bits and pieces to the admissions office. Colleges also have deadlines—for sending decision letters and notices for financial aid and scholarships. Keep in mind that each step in the process takes time and that there's often a lot of waiting between steps. And remember the most important piece of advice: Never, ever, miss a deadline.

EARLY DECISION

Early decision plans are designed for students who have evaluated their college choices at an early date, have determined which school is their first choice, and want to settle their college decision relatively early in their senior year of high school. The rule for early decision is simple: Use it only if you're certain of the college that you want to attend. If you decide to apply for early decision, you're entering a binding agreement with the college. If you're admitted, you'll attend and pay your non-refundable commitment deposit up front. Therefore, if you're not absolutely certain that you want to attend a particular college, you may be able to opt for early admission (you find out early, but it's nonbinding) or stick with the regular timeline.

Some colleges will say that you have a better chance of admission if you apply using early decision, but it really depends upon the applicant pool and how selective the college is overall. Don't count on early decision to increase your chances of admission greatly, but if you're sure that this college is the one, it won't hurt your chances if you let them know that you care enough to make this early commitment.

A couple of caveats: If you think your senior grades or SAT/ACT scores from your senior year will help your case, early decision or early admission probably isn't for you. If financial aid is a major consideration, you'll only be able to get an estimate of your likely financial aid package—rather than a firm offer—if you apply for early decision. Keep these factors in mind when you make the decision.

THE APPLICATION SCHEDULE

Many students wonder when to begin the college admissions process in earnest. You should begin as early as fall of your junior year. It's the most important year academically because it's the last complete year that the colleges will have to evaluate. Junior year is also the time to start preparing for the SAT I and II and/or the ACT. If you're already a senior, don't despair. Although you can't change your junior grades, you still have enough time to make sure your application stands out from the crowd.

Applications for admission generally don't appear until the summer between your junior and senior year. If you checked the box on the PSAT registration materials to enter in the Student Search Service, colleges all over the country will send you their promotional materials in an effort to recruit you. Keep in mind that this type of popularity is fleeting and that you must separate the information you need about a college from the hype in its catalog.

DISADVANTAGES OF EARLY DECISION

- If accepted, you're obliged to attend.
- You may discover a more suitable college later.
- The earliness of the deadline may force you to submit a less-polished application, unless you begin planning your application extra early

---

June 30, 1996

College of Michoice
100 Old Main
Michoice, MI 00000

To Whom It May Concern:

I will graduate from Central High School in June 1997, and I am interested in possibly attending your institution. Please send me all pertinent information about your institution so that I can apply for admission, financial aid, and scholarships.

I am particularly interested in your departments of underwater weaving and extraterrestrial real estate management. I would also appreciate information on your hackey-sack team and your student-operated radio station.

Thank you for your assistance.

Sincerely,

Angela Chase
101 Plaza del Flannel
Catalano, CA 90210

Sample Expression-of-Interest Letter

THE THREE FLAVORS OF ADMISSION

Early decision: You find out early, and you must attend.

Early admission: You find out early, but you can choose whether to attend.

Regular admission: You find out later, and you can choose whether to attend.

DON'T FREAK

Organize your college stategies—send for your free copy of our KaPlanner calendar. Just fill out and mail in the business reply card in this book.

TO AVOID CATASTROPHE

- Plan ahead.
- Spread out your work.
- Give yourself plenty of time to complete each facet of the application.
- Don't wait until the last minute.

Once you know which colleges or universities you want to consider, make sure you're on their mailing lists. You can do this by returning the cards you receive from Student Search mailings, filling out the response cards at college fairs, or by writing a letter to the colleges you're considering. Use the sample expression-of-interest letter on the previous page as a guide.

AVOID THE CRUNCH

One of the greatest pitfalls encountered by students in the application process is procrastination—putting off the applications until the last minute. You can avoid this trap by setting up a calendar with all of the deadlines for each college you intend to apply to. Your 18-month calendar will help you with this, but you should put all the dates on a single piece of paper, so you see exactly how big the job is.

Your calendar should highlight dates for getting the recommendations that you will need from counselors and teachers. Remember: The most popular teachers will be swamped with requests. A high school biology teacher once told us that he was asked to write more than 50 recommendations one year. Don't be number 50! (We'll look more closely at recommendations in the fourth section of this appendix.)

Your calendar should also include the big events for you in high school, such as deadlines for activities in which you are involved, final exams, and family trips to visit colleges. You'll have to work your college application schedule around these dates, but don't use your activities as an excuse to miss those application deadlines.

That should answer most of your questions about when to apply. The main things to remember are: Get organized and don't procrastinate. Use our Applications Flowchart Worksheet on the next page to help you organize your application schedule and keep track of all the deadlines (make as many photocopies of the worksheet as you need).

APPLICATIONS FLOWCHART WORKSHEET

OFFICIAL DEADLINES

College	1	2	3
Preliminary application deadline			
Application deadline			
College financial aid application deadline			
National financial aid application forms deadline			
Candidate notification date			
Candidate reply date			
Personal Timetable			
Application completed and mailed			
Application acknowledgment received			
High school record form and counselor recommendation form delivered to guidance counselor			
Forms mailed			
First recommendation form delivered to _____ (name)			
Form mailed			
Second recommendation form delivered to _____ (name)			
Form mailed			
Midyear school report form delivered to guidance counselor			
Form mailed			
SAT I/SAT II/ACT scores requested to be sent to college			
Institutional financial aid form completed and mailed			

██████████████████████████████████

2

HOW TO APPLY

O nce you start receiving applications, you'll quickly notice one thing: Almost none of them are exactly alike. Some may require no essays or recommendations; others might require two or more of each. Some have very detailed forms requiring extensive background information; others are satisfied with just your name and address and very little else.

Despite these differences, most applications follow a general pattern with variations on the same kinds of questions. So read this chapter with the understanding that, although not all of it is relevant to all parts of every application, these guidelines will be valuable for just about any college application you'll encounter.

DEVELOPING YOUR APPLICATION STRATEGY

The first part of your application strategy should be to aim high. But before you can determine what is an appropriate range of college competitiveness for you, you need to have a firm grasp of how the colleges will review your application. College admissions committees will consider your academic record as the primary factor in determining your admissibility. They will scrutinize the following parts of your academic record.

Courses. The more demanding your academic program, the higher your evaluation will be in this area.

Grades. The admissions committee will consider how well you've done in the context of the norms for your school. If you attend a very competitive high school and you're doing well, that will be more impressive than an equally strong showing at a less demanding school.

Standardized Test Scores. SAT, ACT, and other standardized test scores are a nationally normed measure designed to predict your first-year performance in college. College admissions committees give them a lot of weight—but, despite what you may have heard, not as much as your courses and grades.

WHAT THEY WANT

Colleges want you to show them why they should accept you. Taken together, the elements of your application should accomplish this task.

Counselor/Teacher Recommendations. Competitive colleges, particularly the smaller ones, put a good deal of weight on teacher recommendations. That's why you should choose your recommendation writers carefully.

As for other admissions criteria, private college admissions committees are much more interested in extracurriculars and personal qualities than are public universities. Private colleges will review the contributions you've made to your school and community. They'll also consider your writing skills, which will be reflected in your essays, and what other people think of you as a person, as evidenced by the recommendations you receive from teachers and counselors. Personal interviews with admissions staff or alumni will also contribute to their impression of you as a person.

Nonacademic factors are important, particularly for the private institutions, but they do not make up for a less-than-outstanding academic record. In a competitive admissions environment, you'll need all of these factors working for you in order to be successful.

HOW COMPETITIVE ARE YOU?

You can use the scale on the following page to give yourself a rating—much like an admissions committee will do when it reviews your credentials. You'll need to be honest with yourself in evaluating where your high school career would be ranked.

This rating system does not take into account a wide swing in one category or another. In general, if you're strong in GPA (grade point average) and courses, you can consider yourself a bit stronger than your point total indicates. The most competitive colleges, however, require successful candidates to be superior in all aspects of their applications.

CHOOSING YOUR COLLEGES

You may be wondering how many colleges to include on your applications list. There's no magic number. The length of your list depends upon your range of interests and the kind of institution you want. If size, geographic location, and academic program are not limiting factors, your list may include institutions from all over the country and would be longer than the list of someone who wants to stay close to home and attend a state institution.

But no matter how many schools you apply to, you want to ensure that you'll be receiving a good number of those big, fat envelopes full of information for admitted students. These envelopes always contain a letter that has the word "congratulations" written somewhere in the text. Those are the letters you want. Not those skinny No. 10 envelopes that usually contain the word "unfortunately" somewhere in the text. The Three-Tier approach to choosing your colleges will guarantee that at least some of your envelopes will be of the large variety.

COMPETITIVENESS SCALE

GPA of 3.75–4.00   = 5 points
GPA of 3.50–3.74   = 4 points
GPA of 3.00–3.49   = 3 points
GPA of 2.75–2.99   = 2 points
GPA of 2.50–2.74   = 1 point

Note: The Grade Point Averages (GPAs) are considered unweighted even though most colleges will give you extra credit for Advanced Placement or International Baccalaureate grades.

SAT I of 1300–1600 (ACT Comp. 30–36)   = 5 points
SAT I of 1200–1290 (ACT Comp. 27–29)   = 4 points
SAT I of 1100–1190 (ACT Comp. 24–26)   = 3 points
SAT I of 1000–1090 (ACT Comp. 22–23)   = 2 points
SAT I of   900–990 (ACT Comp. 19–21)   = 1 point

If you have a record of outstanding extracurricular achievement—such as all-state orchestra, student body leadership, other local, regional, or national recognition for citizenship, leadership, or academic achievement—*and* you feel your recommendations will be outstanding, give yourself another *3 points.*

Or: If your extracurriculars are solid, but not at the highest leadership or recognition level, and you feel your recommendations will be very positive, give yourself another *2 points.*

Or: If your extracurriculars are limited to participation—but little leadership—in a relatively narrow range of activities and your recommendations will be good, give yourself another *1 point.*

If you are part of an underrepresented ethnic minority group (African American, Latino, Native American, etc.), give yourself another *2 points.*

If your mother or father attended the college you're considering, give yourself another *1 point.*

The maximum number of points you could get is 16 (although very few people will actually get the full 16 points). Add your point total and see where you are on the following scale:

11 to 16 Points = You have a shot at the most competitive colleges in the country. There is no guarantee that you'll be admitted, but it does mean that an application to this level of institution is warranted.

7 to 10 Points = While you would have only a long-shot at the most competitive colleges, you would be a good candidate at the second-tier (less competitive, but well respected) colleges in America.

6 Points or Below = You will be competitive at colleges that are less selective but still are looking for good students.

The Three-Tier approach allows you to make sense out of the selection process as it relates to your academic and extracurricular record. Use our Application List for schools to which you plan to send an application.

Tier One: This group of colleges will include your long shots. Aiming high is okay. In fact, it's desirable. If you don't receive at least one rejection letter, it probably means you didn't aim high enough. (You probably should apply to two to four institutions in this category.)

Tier Two: These institutions provide all the things that you are looking for in a college but are less selective than the Tier One places. They'll give you a better chance for admission but are still selective. (You should probably apply to two to four institutions in this category.)

Tier Three: These colleges also meet your requirements, but they are virtually certain to offer you admission based on what you know about your academic record and their admitted student profile. Some students make the mistake of paying too little attention to this group of colleges. Choose them carefully and do as good a job completing the applications as you do with your Tier-One colleges, because you may actually have to attend one of these colleges if your Tier-One and Tier-Two choices don't work out. (You should apply to at least two institutions in this category.)

If you are applying to a public university system—such as the University of California or the University of North Carolina—remember that campuses within those systems have different levels of selectivity for both in-state and out-of-state applicants. Moreover, some universities may have a variety of campuses fitting into all three tiers of selectivity. Don't limit your applications to only the most selective campus if you think your chances for admission there are small. Place the various campuses in the appropriate tiers to maximize your chances for admission.

THE APPLICATION EVALUATION PROCESS

At this point, you're probably asking yourself: How do colleges determine which students to admit? College admissions procedures vary according to the type of institution. Public universities tend to use a formula-based approach. Your GPA and SAT I, SAT II, and ACT scores are combined to give you a selection score or academic number, and this number will be used to determine your admissibility.

The formula system has come under attack, however, because it uses test scores inappropriately and makes hard distinctions on factors that are difficult to compare. The GPA component, for example, varies in meaning according to the difficulty of the courses taken by the student and the relative competitiveness of the school. In other words, a student at a very

TRAFFIC JAM

Here are a dozen schools that receive more than 15,000 applications each year:
Boston U.
U. of California–Berkeley
U. of California–Los Angeles
U. of California–San Diego
Cornell U.
Indiana U.
U. of Michigan
Ohio State U.
Penn State U.
Purdue U.
Rutgers–New Brunswick
U. of Virginia

BASIC APPLICATION STRATEGY

• Apply to at least two "safety" schools.

• Apply to a few "wishful-thinking" schools.

• Apply to several schools between these extremes.

APPLICATION LIST

Break down your list of schools into the three tiers as discussed in this chapter. The number of schools on the list depends on your individual circumstances.

Tier One: "Wishful-Thinking" Schools

1.
2.
3.
4.

Tier Two: "In-Between" Schools

1.
2.
3.
4.

Tier Three: "Safety" Schools

1.
2.
3.
4.

GO FOR IT!

Apply to several schools that seem just beyond your reach. You might be pleasantly surprised!

demanding high school who chooses the most challenging courses and earns a 3.5 GPA will be at a distinct disadvantage when compared to a student at a less demanding high school who takes only the minimum level of courses and earns a higher GPA. The system does give some extra consideration to students who elect honors and AP-type courses by adding points through a 5.0 scale (A = 5, B = 4, and so forth) or by adding a "plus" for a strong program of study. These formulaic systems give relatively little weight to extracurricular and personal factors. Ethnicity and personal hardships do figure into an adjustment to the academic scale at many schools, but they do little to offset the very strong emphasis on the objective criteria.

Again, private colleges and universities tend to give much greater weight to extracurricular and personal factors in the evaluation process. When applying to these colleges, it's more important for you to concentrate on the subjective portions of your application such as your essays and the recommendation writers you choose.

Deciding on the Numbers

Every year admissions deans or directors are given an enrollment target by their presidents or chancellors. College administrators determine these numbers by looking at the budget and tuition revenue and projecting how many tuition dollars the institution will need in order to function. Enrollment targets are less critical for public universities because they receive enrollment-based revenue streams from state government, but the principle is still the same. In either case, the admissions office is charged with generating enough applications to allow them to choose the class they want, with the kind of academic credentials that will keep the faculty happy, and with enough diversity and talent to satisfy all the other interests represented in the campus community. Not an easy job!

Once the applications are in, the dean or director must decide how many of these applicants to admit. To do this, he or she must predict what hundreds of 18-year-olds will do about their college careers. The deans use sophisticated statistical information about the applicant pool that's based on gender, geographic location, academic ability, financial need, desired majors, and other factors. These statistics give them a clue about what will happen if they admit various numbers of students.

This process is, at best, imprecise, so admissions officers hedge their bets by "overbooking." If the college's goal is a freshman class of 500 students, the admissions dean may decide to admit 1,000 students, which means she is betting on a "yield" of 50 percent. You may think that a 50 percent rate of acceptance of admission offers is low. In fact, it's quite high. Harvard University, for example, has a yield of about 70 percent. Looked at another way, 30 percent of the students admitted to Harvard end up going somewhere else. The highest yields in the land are at the military service academies, which makes sense when you consider all the obstacles that an applicant to West Point, Annapolis, or the Air Force Academy must negotiate in order to gain admission.

Admissions officers further protect themselves by assigning a number of applicants to the waiting list. The waiting list doesn't protect applicants. It gives the college some insurance in case they have miscalculated the yield (in other words, if fewer admittees accept their offers of admission than they had anticipated).

NUMBER CRUNCH

Some colleges will decide which students to admit merely by using a formula that combines each applicant's SAT/ACT score and GPA. More weight will be given to your GPA than your standardized test scores.

YIELDS

Check out the yields at these colleges:

U.S. Naval Academy	81%
Princeton	57%
Birmingham-Southern	49%
Indiana	44%
Michigan	39%
Pomona	35%
UCLA	34%
SUNY–Binghamton	29%
Washington U.	25%
Bucknell	22%

The evaluation process itself involves a review of your credentials and the assignment of some rating. This is done in a variety of ways, such as by the numerical formula described above. Private colleges are more likely to assign an evaluation to both academic and nonacademic factors. Once these ratings, or readings, have been done, the usual practice is for the top 20 percent of the pool to be admitted outright. The bottom 20 percent of the pool will be set aside for those dreaded skinny-envelope letters.

This leaves the remaining 60 percent of the applicant pool. This group is sometimes referred to as the muddy, or murky, middle. The freshmen class is rounded out with this group of applicants. The admissions committee will spend most of its time discussing these applicants, poring over their letters of recommendation, essays, counselor comments, and the other factors that they will throw into the acceptance mix.

You should know that you'll be considered, in most cases, with other applicants from your high school. The committee does this to make sure that there's some consistency of decisions within the applicant group from the same school. They may decide to deny the valedictorian and admit someone just barely in the top half of the class, provided that person can reverse-jam a basketball. But the committee certainly wants your high school to know that they are making that kind of decision, and may contact your school to let the counselor know what's happening.

Many college admissions offices will contact their "feeder" high schools before the decisions go out to alert the counselors if there's an apparent inconsistency in the decisions or if it has been a particularly difficult year for the high school. Also, the counselor may be able to help the admissions officer sort out some of the more difficult decisions and also soften the blow for the students who are going to be getting bad news.

The Committee

College admissions committees are usually made up of members of the admissions staff, faculty, students, alumni, and occasionally guests, such as high school counselors. Some colleges hire "readers" who just do the first readings of applications. These people may be members of the campus community, such as faculty spouses or retirees from the faculty or staff. Ordinarily, readers aren't members of the actual committee. In some cases, the professional admissions officers are not voting members of the committee or they have a combined vote. The dean or director of admissions usually chairs the committee, but not always. There may also be a faculty chair, particularly at small colleges where admissions decisions are seen as much more important to the faculty.

The professional admissions officers are often young, and many are recent graduates of the institution they represent. They tend to be "people persons" and enjoy meeting the public and talking about their institution. Some large offices have regional directors who are responsible for a particular part of the country. They will be the first reader on the

THE WAITING GAME

Colleges put some applicants on a waiting list just in case they've underestimated the number of admitted students who actually decide to enroll. They use wait-listed students to fill up any empty slots in the incoming class.

applications from their region and often will make a presentation on the applicants to the full committee. They'll also make recommendations on the decisions and answer any questions the other committee members may have about the applicants from their region.

There are also "regional reps" who live in the region they represent but return to the campus during file-reading time, for decision making, and for training in the fall. You may find the regional reps visiting your school if you live on the opposite coast from the college or university you're considering. It's well worth your time to meet these reps; they may be the people ultimately making the case for your admission before the full committee.

Many colleges include other members of the community on the admissions committee. Faculty representatives, student representatives, and an alumni representative will often have seats on a committee. Some offices invite local high school guidance counselors to participate in the evaluation phase of the process. Because there's such diversity on any admissions committee, there's no way to tailor your application to appeal to one segment or another. However, you can be sure that all members of the committee—no matter how different from each other—will be literate, sophisticated, humane, and intensely interested in everything about you that might reflect on your potential as a member of their community.

Admissions Scheduling
College admissions officers are on a schedule that has definite seasons. In the fall they're on the road visiting high schools, attending college fairs, and appearing at college nights—sometimes in drafty gyms and crowded lunch rooms—as the guests of the school guidance counselors. In the winter they're busy reading applications. The file-reading season is the most intense time of the year because the admissions office is facing deadlines just as the applicants were when filling out their application forms.

There's no disadvantage to sending your application right at the deadline, but there are pluses if you get your application in early:

- If any component of your application is missing, you'll have time to get it in before it's too late.
- Admissions officers become weary as the file-reading season wears on; the files that are complete and ready to be read early in the process may be reviewed more carefully when the staff is not at the edge of exhaustion.
- Some institutions, including Harvard and Radcliffe, like all applicants to have an interview with a staff member or a local alumnus. The earlier your application is received, the sooner the college can contact you about an interview.
- If you get your applications completed and sent well in advance of the deadline, you avoid the stress of squeezing everything into the last minute.

COMMITTEE COMPOSITION

The typical admissions committee has several different types of members, including admissions office staff, faculty members, current students, and alumni.

APPLICATION TYPES

The conventional college application comes in a packet that includes the application, detailed instructions, and, in some cases, a separate institutional financial aid application. This conventional application will describe the notification options the college offers, such as early decision, early action, rolling admissions, and regular decision. The deadline dates will be clearly stated along with the testing requirements and the last test date that can be used for consideration in that admissions cycle (usually the last test for fall admission is in January for the SAT I and II or February for the ACT).

Don't forget to read the instructions and other material in the application completely before you begin to fill out the forms. It's amazing how many students forget the simplest elements of the process, such as enclosing the check for the processing fee or signing the application. These oversights will, at best, slow down the processing of your application, and they may even stop it altogether until the problem has been resolved.

You'll find the last word on the requirements for admission right there in the instructions for this year's application. Don't rely on what the college required last year or what one of the big, fat reference books in your school's library or counselor's office says. Fee amounts, deadlines, test requirements, and essay questions are only some of the items on college admission applications that are subject to change every year.

Preliminary, or Part I, Applications

Several selective private and public colleges and universities use a two-part application process. The Part I form usually consists of questions of a demographic type—name, address, high school, and so forth. This information is used to open your application file and is requested earlier than the Part II forms. Part II forms usually consist of sections on activities, secondary school report form, counselor and teacher recommendation forms, and the essay questions. Be mindful of the deadlines on this type of application because the Part I forms often must be received before the Part II forms will be processed. Most institutions using this type of form require that the application processing fee be submitted with Part I. This fee is usually nonrefundable, even if you decide not to complete Part II.

The Common Application

The Common Application has been in existence for many years. It offers one standard form that's used by a great many private colleges and universities. The applicant completes the form as thoughtfully and carefully as possible and then makes photocopies, which can be sent to as many of the participating colleges as the applicant wishes. Copies may also be made of the School Report form and the Teacher Evaluation pages to cover the requirements of the individual colleges. Almost all the colleges

EARLY BIRDS

The advantages of submitting your application early include:

- You have time to correct any problems or omissions.
- Admissions officers will be fresher and less harried when they read your application.
- You have time to set up an interview, if required.
- You won't have to rush to meet any deadlines.

ALWAYS READ THE INSTRUCTIONS

Before you start filling out an application, make sure you know exactly what the application asks you to submit. Double-check that each element is enclosed in the envelope before you mail it.

subscribing to the Common Application require the School Report, but not all require Teacher Evaluations.

Some of the colleges that use the Common Application, particularly the more selective ones, will require additional information or writing samples. Some will send you a supplement with instructions on submitting other material. Each college has separate instructions about processing fees, deadlines, and other requirements. The Common Application also allows you to use a computer disk to complete the application, but the colleges vary in which computer software format they require: DOS for PC, Windows, or Macintosh. You may be asked to submit only a printout of the application, a disk only, or a printout and disk.

The Common Application saves a great deal of time for the applicant and for the college. Some colleges use it exclusively; others have their own applications but will accept the Common Application. Members of the Common Application organization "encourage its use and all give equal consideration to the Common Application and the college's own form." Remember that this form should be completed very carefully. Some applicants have added colleges as "backups" with the Common Application and dashed off their essays without too much thought. That does not serve the student well and only adds to the processing burden of the colleges. Make the effort to thoughtfully fill out the Common Application. It will save you time and give you some excellent college choices.

Computer-Supported Applications

The latest wrinkle in the world of college admissions applications is the use of the computer-generated application on a disk. The Common Application allows the use of computer disks to create an application. But some colleges and universities now have additional computer-assisted options for their applicants. Some of the more popular of these alternatives include:

- **College Link.** College Link sends applicants a disk that they can use to apply to as many as 12 of the colleges that subscribe to College Link. More than 800 colleges subscribe to the College Link program. For more information, call (800) 394–0505.

- **Discover.** The Discover Information and Guidance System is now being offered in a Computer Disk Interactive (CDI) format. Students using this system are able to interact with the system using a mouse or infrared remote controller to assess their interests, abilities, experiences, and values and receive results immediately for use in investigating educational and occupational options. For more information contact Discover at (319) 337–1000.

- **College Connector.** ACT is now offering a new computer-based college planning and application service. (Although it's administered by ACT, the service is available to SAT takers also.) The system includes a college-search component to identify the colleges that meet their requirements; an inquiry service to allow students to request information from participating colleges and to send those colleges information about themselves and their interests; an application service that students can use to complete their admission applications and apply electronically to participating colleges; and a financial-need estimator for students and families to receive college cost information and preliminary estimates of their eligibility for federal financial aid programs. For more information contact College Connector at (800) 525–3729.

- **MacApply.** This system allows students to fill in a replica of each college's application form on a Macintosh. Many colleges and universities are in the MacApply library, and those listed in it have agreed to evaluate applications submitted using Macintosh software on an equal basis with conventional applications. For more information, call (800) 932–7759.

- **Xap Co.** The Xap Company is working with a number of colleges and universities to provide software for students to fill out and send their applications using computer disks. The University of Southern California and the Claremont Colleges are using Xap for their applicants. You can find instructions on how to request the disks in the application instructions of the colleges that subscribe to Xap.

If you decide to take advantage of computer technology, remember that it's new and that some bugs need to be worked out. The best thing you can do is work on these applications early just in case there are problems that you can't solve from your computer. The programs themselves are relatively simple and user-friendly. They're menu driven, so all you have to do is follow the instructions built into the program.

APPLICATION BASICS

One of the greatest fears applicants have about the admissions process is that the information they convey to the committee doesn't accurately reflect their true selves. Or that somehow the information provided will be misinterpreted by the readers, and the applicants' wonderful qualities won't be recognized. How do you avoid either of those possibilities? Here are some suggestions:

Be yourself. Application readers usually aren't looking for a specific type of student. Sure, if you're applying to Harvey Mudd or MIT, there will be a pretty strong emphasis on your ability in science and mathematics. But even in specialized places like those, they're still looking for balance—both among individual applicants and in the class as a whole. That means there's room for the unidirectionally brilliant—the students who are focused on a particular part of the academic spectrum. But there's also room for the "Renaissance man or woman." (Don't describe yourself that way. That is one of the clichés recommendation writers often use. But you should avoid it in your essays. It's almost as bad as: "She marches to the beat of a different drummer.")

Some application readers put great store in leadership ability among applicants. Other readers like seeing students who combine athletic and artistic qualities. All combinations of positive qualities will be valued. But you need to present yourself as who you are and what you have done. And you need to do so in a way that strongly emphasizes what contributions you will make to the campus.

Be positive. All aspects of your application should indicate that you're moving in a positive direction toward the realization of your academic goals. Even if you have endured great difficulties in your life, it's important to indicate how you've learned from those experiences and, as a result, are stronger and better able to face what lies ahead.

Use anecdotes. An anecdote is a brief account of an interesting or humorous incident. There's no better way to convey to a reader who you are than through the use of anecdotes. Begin right now to think about things that have happened in your life that will help your reader know you better and understand what you have to offer to their campus. These incidents don't have to be big life-or-death kinds of things. They can be relatively mundane, but they should be meaningful to you and should illustrate some trait you possess or significant learning experience that you've had. Here are several types of anecdotes that will get you thinking and that will keep application evaluators reading:

- *Your intellectual development.* Do you remember the first book you ever read? What was it and how did reading it make you feel? When was the first time you actually thought about thinking? Was it when you were watching television (unlikely), watching a movie, reading a book, talking with friends, or simply lying in bed pondering the day's events?

- *Significant people in your life.* Obviously there are your parents, but what about brothers or sisters, other relatives who have had a real impact on who you are, coaches, employers, someone who gave you a chance to show what you can do?

- *Influential teachers.* Almost every college-bound student we know has had at least one memorable teacher. What made that person unique? Was it personality, knowledge, caring, or all of these? What did they do in the classroom to grab your attention? Did they dress in costumes, dance, sing, make cookies, have you teach the class?

SEARCH FOR TOMORROW

Kaplan's five-disk CD-ROM college search program, *On Campus*, is the ideal way to find the college that's right for you. Call 1–800–KAP–ITEM for more info.

COLLEGE APPLICATION CHECKLIST

The following list of things to do with every application should be used with all the applications you submit. Not every application will require all these steps, but they're all worth considering for each one:

❑ Proofread your applications to make sure you have completed all required items or put an "NA" (not applicable) in the appropriate places. **Make photocopies of your finished applications.**

❑ Sign and date each application and sign recommendation forms if a waiver of your right to review the recommendation is requested.

❑ Submit printouts or carefully typed applications only. Use black ink and definitely don't use pencil for anything.

❑ Make sure you enclose a check, money order, or fee waiver request for the processing fee. Make sure it's for the proper amount and made out to the correct party, such as "The Regents of the University of California."

❑ Make a photocopy of your check and keep it in your admissions file.

❑ Submit your School Report and Teacher Recommendation forms to your counselor. Make a note of the date for each of these forms you give to your counselor.

❑ Keep track of the Teacher Recommendation forms given to your recommendation writers. Keep careful records of whom you ask to write recommendations for you and the date you made the request. Don't forget to give your recommendation writers a stamped, addressed envelope to send in the recommendation, or else a note telling them that you'll pick up the completed, signed, and sealed recommendation to be included in your application packet.

❑ Give a transcript (or School Report transcript) request to your counselor or registrar with a notation of the date it was requested.

❑ Ask for a Midyear School Report or transcript request covering your grades through the first trimester or semester of your senior year.

❑ Request SAT I/II or ACT score reports, if the official report is required. Some colleges will take scores from the transcript. Others require an official report from the Educational Testing Service (ETS) or ACT. Score Request Forms are available in your counselor's office.

❑ Enclose your essays. Carefully proofread for content, grammar, punctuation, spelling, etc. If you have printed out or typed your applications on separate pages, make sure your name and Social Security number are on each page. **Make photocopies of your essays.**

❑ Attach photographs, if requested. Photos are used to identify you as a person rather than just a set of numbers. Be sure your name and Social Security number are carefully printed on the back of each photo. No shots from kindergarten, please.

❑ Mail your applications using a U.S. Postal Service Certificate of Mailing. Get one of these from your post office for each of your applications. The cost is low, and the peace of mind is well worth it.

- *Special hardships that you have overcome.* Has your family gone through a difficult time, such as separation, divorce, financial troubles, many moves, illness, death, natural disasters, dislocations? If so, how have these things affected you and your development?

- *Community service.* Have you been involved in volunteer activities in your community, such as church or temple programs, hospitals, nursing homes, tutoring programs, working with disadvantaged/low income students? What have these kinds of activities meant to you?

- *Travel or living abroad.* Have you had any significant travel experiences or have you lived in another country? Have any of these experiences taught you something important about yourself or how you live?

- *Leadership.* Have you been in a position of leadership in which your participation made a difference? For example, have you revitalized a club that had ceased to function? One student was elected activities director of a nearly defunct science club and brought it back to life by programming such events as a school science fair, trips to a local amusement park for their science day, and visits by scientists and students from the local university.

- *Business/job experiences.* Have you had a job or formed a business that gave you insight into the world of work or how businesses are organized? Another student learned an important lesson in life by serving for two summers as a busboy at a popular restaurant. He developed immense respect for the busboys who were supporting their families through their work and putting themselves through college.

COMPLETING THE APPLICATION

Keeping the three basics in mind—be yourself, be positive, and use anecdotes—it's time to get down to filling out the application.

Read the instructions again. The most important advice about completing your applications is to read the instructions carefully before you begin. Do this early to be sure you know the deadlines and all application requirements, such as standardized tests, essays, and letters of recommendation. Be sure you do everything that the application asks you to do.

There are no trick questions. College application questions tend to fall into categories, but none of them is a "trick" category. College admissions officers want the most accurate information about you that they can get. They aren't interested in making this process any more difficult than necessary. But admissions offices vary in the amount of information

SELL YOURSELF

Try to create an image of yourself that will stick in the minds of admissions officers. Remember to:

- Present facts concisely
- Double-check to make sure facts don't conflict
- Exclude any useless, unnecessary facts

THE REAL YOU

Don't try to make yourself sound like someone you're not. Your application will sound forced, and admissions officers can detect most attempts at deception.

they need. You'll find that some applications consist of little more than questions about your name, address, and where you attended high school. Others, from the more competitive colleges, may ask for two creative essays, plus short essays on your activities, as well as teacher recommendations.

Tooting your own horn. Many applicants feel uncomfortable engaging too much in self-aggrandizement. In other words, they don't like bragging about themselves. As with most things in life, there's a continuum of self-described achievement. No one likes the person who's obnoxiously self-centered and self-promoting. On the other hand, college applications want you to divulge your strengths. If you don't provide the information on your accomplishments, the admissions committee won't have it. View the application process as your opportunity to showcase what you've accomplished. You should do so with pride. Here are two simple rules to keep in mind:

- *Limit your recitation of accomplishments to your high school years only*. The exception is if what you're doing in high school goes back to beginnings in earlier years. Then a mention of how you began your interest in swimming, the violin, or journalism might be helpful.

- *Pay particular attention to those activities that have been most meaningful to you*. Even if you weren't the class leader but were just involved in planning, say, a fund-raiser to help the homeless in your community, discuss what it meant to you. The committee will want to know about your activity and why it was important.

Typical application questions. The following questions may not all appear on every application that you complete, but they're likely to appear on some applications:

Personal information. These questions ask for objective information—names, addresses, and the like. Make sure you use the same name throughout. That means don't use your nickname unless they ask for it with a "name you preferred to be called" question.

Enrollment information. These questions ask when you hope to start your college career—fall semester 1997, for example—and whether you're going to use any special admission options, such as early decision or early admission.

Major or anticipated academic concentration. Many students spend hours agonizing over this question. Some feel that the wrong choice here will jeopardize their chances for admission. If you're applying to a professional program—such as engineering, architecture, nursing, or business—your choice will make a difference in your admissibility. You'll be competing against students who consider themselves competitive for

DON'T BE JUST ANOTHER FACE IN THE CROWD

In your application, focus on what you think makes you stand out, what makes you better prepared for college than other applicants. Accentuate your strong points.

STORY TIME

Using anecdotes in your essays is a good way to show the admissions committee who you really are.

programs with high demand and relatively few spaces available. That means the requirements are going to be more stringent, the competition keener. If, on the other hand, you're looking for a good liberal arts and sciences program and you aren't sure about your major, that's okay. In some ways it's even preferred for you to indicate "undecided" as your major. Undecided, in fact, is one of the most popular major choices. Some large public universities will have a very competitive situation for such high-demand majors as computer science or psychology. Read the information in the application to determine if there are such popular majors. If there are, the best advice is to avoid these majors because citing a preference for one of them could affect your admission chances. Going undeclared or undecided does not prevent you from choosing any major once you're enrolled, unless it is specifically stated that you can't apply for admission to a particular major unless you indicate it on your application.

Don't worry too much about premed or prelaw majors. On most college campuses you can major in any area and still consider yourself to be premed or prelaw. Premedical students, however, must take a prescribed sequence of courses, including general and organic chemistry, biology with laboratory, physics, mathematics, and English. The medical college bulletins or your health sciences adviser can give you precise information on the requirements, including the tests you must take, such as the MCAT (Medical College Admissions Test), for medical school admission.

Prelaw students should choose a major they really enjoy because admission to law school is almost exclusively based on college GPA and LSAT (Law School Admissions Test) scores. Your major matters relatively little, as long as you emerge from your course of study with good communication and logic skills.

Transfer students, on the other hand, must be much more careful about indicating a major on their application. If you're planning to transfer as an "upper division" or junior-level student, that means you must have completed the lower-division prerequisites for your proposed major. Some majors have many more prerequisites than others. Upper-division transfers aren't usually allowed to apply as "undeclared" because they should have completed prerequisite requirements for a major during their first two years. These regulations vary quite a bit from institution to institution. Check with your transfer-student adviser at your college or at the college you're considering for transfer.

Residency information. These questions help the college determine whether you're a resident of the state (for publicly supported institutions) and of the United States. (for all institutions).

Language proficiency. Some applications ask this question in order to determine your English ability. They may also ask whether English is

UNDECIDED?

Many college-bound students don't know what their majors will be. If you're one of them, don't worry about indicating "undecided" as your major. In most instances, you really don't need to declare a specific major on your application.

your native language and whether you've taken the TOEFL (Test of English as a Foreign Language).

Statistical information. These questions, which are usually optional, ask about the applicant's ethnicity. These questions won't have a negative effect on your chances for admissions but they'll help if you're from an underrepresented ethnic group.

Income information. This information should not affect your admissions status because most colleges operate under what's referred to as the "need-blind" policy. This means that your financial aid status will have no effect on the committee's evaluation of your application.

Parents' levels of education. Some colleges will give preference to students who are in the first generation of persons from their family to attend college.

Parents' occupations. If your family is of modest means and paying for your college education will be a challenge, this information may give your application special consideration.

Institution outreach questions. These questions ask how you found out about the college. They help the school fine-tune its recruitment activities.

Scholastic information. You'll be asked to provide information about all your previous schooling through high school. They will ask if you've attended any other high schools or colleges, the dates of attendance, and any schooling you might have had outside the United States. Don't leave anything out. If it comes to light later that you failed to mention some part of your academic career, you might have a problem. If you're in doubt about this, ask your counselor.

Test information. The colleges want to know what standardized tests you've taken, as well as the scores and dates of the tests you plan to take. Most require an official score report.

Academic record. Many colleges ask you to submit official transcripts. But some colleges ask you to self-report your courses and grades and compute an academic GPA. This self-reporting of grades and courses can be tricky, so read the instructions carefully and follow the rules to the letter. If your report contradicts your official transcript, your admissions status could be in jeopardy. Don't complete these sections from memory. *Always work from your transcript to avoid potentially embarrassing or disastrous errors.*

Transfer academic record. Transfer applicants may be asked to report all colleges they have attended and provide information about college courses and grades. Again, be sure to mention all institutions you've attended and all courses you've attempted. This information will be verified by official transcripts later. Here again, always use your transcript to complete this section. Don't work from memory.

REPORT CARD

If an application asks you to report your own grades, get your official transcript from your guidance counselor. Reporting a wrong grade could be embarrassing, and it might even hurt your chances of admission.

Scholarships and financial aid. A Common Application question asks whether you plan to apply for merit-based scholarships or need-based financial aid. You should always apply for the merit-based awards unless you're clearly not competitive for them. Applying for need-based financial aid should *not* affect your chances for admission. There's a continuing controversy in higher education, however, over the precise meaning of the term "need-blind" admissions. As the term implies, if the college to which you're applying states that it is need-blind, it means that it's not influenced in its admission decisions by the applicant's financial aid status. Many colleges, however, don't meet the full need of the students who apply and who have demonstrated financial need. Because of this, they tend to offer the best financial aid packages to the best students. All in all, this is sometimes referred to as "preferential packaging." In some cases, colleges simply run out of grant (gift) money and decide not to offer admission to marginal high-need students. This is a hazy area where ethics, institutional viability, truth in advertising, and recruitment pressures all collide. The best advice is that if you think you will qualify for need-based aid, you should plan to apply for it and not worry about the consequences. This means that you have to be careful about where you apply and be prepared to ask questions about the financial aid policy and the number of applying students who receive financial aid.

Activities. These questions often state that you should list only activities engaged in during the high school years. They are often broken down into in-school and out-of-school categories. In-school includes high school or (for transfers) college activities in which you have participated. You'll be asked to rank these activities in order of importance and specify in which years you engaged in these activities and how much time per week was involved. Don't worry about absolute precision here. An estimate of the average time spent will suffice. You may also be asked about positions you held in these organizations or honors you might have won. The questions may also ask if you intend to continue these activities in college. If you're unsure of the answer to that question, answer "yes." Your answer is non-binding and a "yes" will show that you're enthusiastic about contributing to your college community.

Honors and awards. Some applications will ask you to list separately any honors or awards you've received. They will want the name of the

WHOA!

Occasionally students get a bit overly enthusiastic about reporting their activities. Or, they may take the instructions too literally. As the applicant did a few years ago when, under the heading "Activity," she wrote "Horseback riding" and under "Positions Held" she wrote, "On top!"

award, a brief description, and the date you received it. Keep this list limited to the important awards in your life but don't neglect to mention things that may seem unimportant, such as promotions at your job and recognition for hours of volunteer service. These kinds of awards and recognition give the committee a glimpse into the kind of person you are.

Your signature. You must sign the application in order for it to be processed. Your signature simply informs the college or university that you know that the information you have provided in the application is true. If it's later determined that you have misrepresented any information, your admission or enrollment may be rescinded.

YOUR PERSONAL DATA SHEET

A good way to organize your thinking for college is to compile a Personal Data Sheet (PDS), on which you can list all of your extracurricular activities, relevant dates of participation, and any honors or positions of leadership you won. You can divide the list into in-school, out-of-school, employment, and honors and awards. You can give this same form to your recommendation writers to remind them of your accomplishments. The PDS can also contain your name, address, phone number, GPA, and senior year courses. You might think of it as your high school résumé.

ACTIVITIES OVERLOAD

Don't make the mistake of listing every possible activity you can think of. As with most things in life, quality is more important than quantity. And an admissions officer's eyes may well glaze over if you include a super-long list of activities.

PERSONAL DATA SHEET

NAME
Social Security Number
Address
Phone Number

High School
Academic GPA

Test Scores (Include your best SAT I/II and/or ACT scores and any Advanced Placement scores that you've received.)

Senior Year Courses

Activities and Awards (Include jobs, academic and nonacademic honors, and awards by year.)
SENIOR YEAR

JUNIOR YEAR

SOPHOMORE YEAR

FRESHMAN YEAR

ESSAYS THAT WORK

The part of the application process that you have the greatest control over—and that causes the greatest difficulty—is, without a doubt, the essay. Applicants are vexed by such concerns as: What makes a good essay? How important is this essay, anyway? Is anyone really going to read it? These are important questions, so let's take a close look at each of them.

THE IMPORTANCE OF ESSAYS

Private colleges and universities tend to place more importance on essays than do public universities. There are some exceptions to this general rule, and you don't want to assume that no one will read your essay if you're writing it for a public institution. But because private institutions put more weight on the personal factors, the essay takes on greater importance for them. At such schools, a brilliant essay won't make up for serious academic shortcomings, but it will make a great deal of difference in a highly competitive admissions situation where all other factors are more or less equal. Remember: You want everything in your application working for you. The essays are a big part of what you control in this process and can leave a lasting positive impression on your readers.

There's a myth that at many large public universities the admissions staff simply checks to see if the required essay is there, but no one actually reads them. If your application is very strong or very weak academically, your essay may receive only a cursory glance. However, if you fall in the murky middle group of applicants at either a public or a private institution, then the essay becomes much more important. It may make the difference between admission and rejection. It's much safer to assume that your essay will be read and that it will count in the final determination of your admissibility. This will keep you focused on writing the best essay possible.

THE FOUR Cs OF ESSAY WRITING

If you want to write a distinctive essay, you should be:

- **Creative.** Try to be creative, but be careful not to offend your reader. Avoid clichés and bromides. College admissions officers

THE WRITE STUFF

Application essays should be viewed as an opportunity for you to show admissions officers what you're really made of.

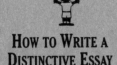

HOW TO WRITE A DISTINCTIVE ESSAY

- Create a quick image of who you are and why you want to go to college.
- Sell your image briefly and accurately.
- Include real-life examples to support your points.
- Make sure your enthusiasm shines through.

ESSAY NO-NOS

- Don't dwell on your weak points.
- Don't employ dull chronological histories.
- Don't disregard length limitations.
- Don't lie in your essay—or in any part of your application.

hate them. Students who write in an engaging, interesting manner will be miles ahead of those who plod through a predictable writing exercise. Enliven your writing by using anecdotes, bits of dialogue, and humor. And don't forget to structure your essays effectively. The first and last paragraphs should be the most important ones in any essay that you write. Grab your reader's attention in the first paragraph with something that excites curiosity, and use the closing paragraph to tie your essay together and leave the reader with the desired impression.

- **Concise.** The Harvard and Radcliffe bulletin encourages applicants to write concisely, saying, "The best essays are not necessarily long essays." Take this advice to heart. Use only as many words as you need to say what you want to say. College admissions officers are very busy during the reading season. Long, tedious essays tend to make them impatient.

- **Casual.** Your college essays aren't formal writing exercises. The tone should be casual but not chatty. A personal statement loses some of its vibrancy when the writing is too stiff and formal. Use language that's appropriate to the subject. And remember to avoid sesquipedalianism (the unnecessary use of big words).

- **Careful.** Be sure your essays are grammatically correct, properly spelled, and appropriately punctuated. Don't rely exclusively on your word processor's spell-checking program. Remember that the computer doesn't know whether you've used the wrong word in those instances where the word is another correctly spelled word, such as "piers" for "peers." Your essays should be typed or printed out, if possible. As a last resort, you can handwrite your essay; colleges understand that some people don't have access to a computer or a typewriter. Make sure it's legible and use black ink, even if green ink is your favorite.

YOUR BASIC ESSAY

A good way to begin your serious essay writing is to compose a basic essay, which should probably discuss the following topic: "Describe a personal experience that will tell the committee more about the person you are." Your response should be based on a personal anecdote—something that has happened to you.

Here are the elements of the basic essay:

- **Strong opening.** Make your first paragraph a grabber. Don't start with a recitation of facts about yourself unless they're facts that aren't found elsewhere in the application. For example, instead of saying, "I have a job as assistant manager at McDonald's." You could say, "What do you do when the number two french-fry vat

ESSAY WRITING WORKSHEET

Use this Essay Writing Worksheet to plan, organize, and draft your essays.

Name of college: _____

Essay topic or question: _____

First thoughts about the topic: _____
_____

Possible responses or approaches: _____
_____
_____

Working title: _____

Outline of introduction: _____
_____
_____
_____
_____
_____

Middle paragraph: _____
_____
_____
_____
_____
_____

Conclusion: _____
_____
_____
_____
_____
_____

COMPUTER GLITCH

If you're using a word processor to write your essays and you've stated that "The University of Awesome Parties is definitely my first choice," be sure to change the school name if you recycle the same essay when you apply to the College of Serious Studying.

THE BASICS

Your basic essay—and all of your essays—should have a title, a strong opening, and a strong closing.

is down, the drive-through window microphone is not working, and there is a potential confrontation between rival gangs in the parking lot? Answer: Call me, the assistant manager."

- **Strong closing.** Your basic essay—and all your essays—should leave readers with a clear sense of what you were trying to say. The last paragraph should tie the essay together and make it memorable. It should relate back to the opening paragraph, answering the questions of what happened and what the experience meant to you. In our example the writer might conclude, "We were able to bring another french-fry maker on line. We found that the drive-through cord was unplugged. A call to 911, resulting in a police cruise-by, calmed things down in the parking lot. It was a typical day for me at McDonald's, but I loved it because it let me be a creative and caring leader for my staff and my customers at the same time. I plan to bring those same skills to college and develop them even further."

- **Title.** Always title your major essays so that your readers will be prepared for what they encounter. A title also allows you to set the tone for the essay from the beginning. Using our example again, you might call it, "My Experience as Assistant Manager at McDonald's," or "French Fries and Gang Fights: A Typical Day at McDonald's." Which of these titles do you think might attract more interest from a potential reader? The latter gives the reader a taste of what you'll be saying in your essay and does so in a way that's at once arresting and ingenious.

THE SHORT-ANSWER ESSAY

Short-answer essay questions are usually specific to your extracurricular activities or academic interests. The committee wants to know something pretty specific, such as, "We are curious about your current academic interests and goals. Please discuss the subjects or areas that most interest you." You may be instructed to use the space available or attach extra pages if necessary. Writing these essays is definitely an opportunity to put into practice the adage "less is more." Answer the questions succinctly and directly. Don't hesitate to make your responses personal, but keep them brief. It isn't necessary to give titles to short-answer essays.

ESSAY TIPS

Here are some tips that will help make sure essays work:

- **Feedback.** It's okay—in fact, advisable—for you to ask your teacher, counselor, parents, or anyone else, to discuss essay topics or read a rough draft of your essay and give you their impressions. As long as the thinking and writing is your own, seeking advice from others won't violate the spirit of the process.

- **Rough drafts.** Always write rough drafts of your essays, even the short-answer variety, and let them "cool off" for a day or two. Then go back and reread them to make sure that they say exactly what you want them to say.

- **Identify your essays.** If you're given a choice of options, be sure to indicate on your essays which question you're addressing. You may do this by writing or typing the question before you begin your essay, unless it takes up needed space. If this turns out to be the case, just list the number or letter that corresponds to the question or topic you're addressing.

- **Proofread.** "I always wanted to be a collage student and now I almost are one." This is an extreme example, but it gets across the point: Check and double-check your essays for grammatical and spelling errors before mailing them in. Proofread your essays by reading them backwards one word at a time. This will help you pick up any misspelled words. Then read the essays front to back for content. Check out our Proofreading Hit List on the next page for commonly misspelled words.

- **Timing.** Some colleges, like Harvard, tell you that you can send in your essays after you submit your application, to avoid missing the application deadline. This gives you some flexibility, but it's dangerous because it allows for more procrastination. Resolve that you'll have your essays ready with everything else that goes into your application packet when it is to be mailed.

GOOD ESSAYS DON'T JUST HAPPEN

Don't just dash off your essays. Write rough drafts. Reread them. Rethink them, if necessary. And revise them as needed.

NAIL IT

If an application asks you a specific question, answer the question clearly and concisely and don't stray from the topic at hand.

**SMALL ERRORS—
BIG MISTAKE**

Once you've finished your essays, get other people to read them. Type your final drafts and proofread them carefully. Make sure it's perfect—that means no typos!

PROOFREADING HIT LIST

Spellcheck and carefully proofread your application to catch misspellings and typos. Here are the most commonly misspelled words on applications:

Incorrect	Correct
alot	a lot
athelete	athlete
calculas	calculus
calender	calendar
candy stripper	candy striper
cirriculum	curriculum
colledge	college
compleat	complete
conncellor	counselor (or counsellor)
docter	doctor
eleminate	eliminate
excelerate	accelerate
lecrosse	lacrosse
medecine	medicine
metriculate	matriculate
oppertunity	opportunity
perspective	prospective (as in "prospective student")
persued	pursued
piers	peers
psycology	psychology
sensative	sensitive
seperate	separate
sponser	sponsor
studnet (most frequent typo)	student

4

RECOMMENDATIONS

Not every college application asks you to submit recommendations. Public universities are less likely to ask you for recommendations than private schools are. The exceptions are usually when public universities require recommendations for students seeking admission to a special program, such as an honors program, or for consideration in a scholarship competition. Private colleges and universities—again in keeping with their stronger emphasis on the personal factors—are much more likely to require one, two, or, in some unusual cases, three recommendations.

Colleges will typically ask for two types of recommendations: The school report/college counselor recommendation and the teacher evaluation. Everybody has teachers, so the teacher evaluation should be no problem. Not everybody, however, has a college counselor at his or her high school. If your school doesn't have a counselor, you'll still need to have the school report completed by a school official. There's probably an assistant principal, registrar, or other person who takes care of this responsibility. This person will also have to see that an official transcript is either attached to the school report form or sent separately to the college or university admissions office. If you have no idea who that person will be in your school, ask one of your teachers.

CHOOSING YOUR RECOMMENDERS

There's an old saying in college admissions counseling: "When choosing your recommenders, make sure the people you choose like you." Sounds obvious, you may say, but after reading thousands of recommendations, we occasionally wonder how many students keep that admonition in mind. What's the best way to gauge how your teachers will respond to the questions on a teacher recommendation form? Simple. Ask yourself how your teachers would respond to this question (which appears on the Occidental College teacher recommendation form): "What are the first words that come to mind to describe this applicant?"

More recent teachers tend to write the best recommendations, and some colleges even require that your recommenders be teachers who have taught you recently. One college application, for example, stipulates that

THE CASE OF THE APPLICANT WITH GOOD TASTE

Many years ago an admissions office received a rather large package containing a dining hall–type plastic tray with a plate, silverware, and plastic glass carefully glued on. In the middle of the plate was a typed note that said, "I want to go to Pomona College so badly that I can taste it!" The admissions office thought this was clever, and since the student was strong in every way, this added a bit of whimsy to his attractiveness.

The applicant chose not to attend Pomona, however, which made the admissions office wonder if he had sent replicas of the Pomona tray to admissions offices all over the country.

A+ RECOMMENDER

The best recommendation writers will be those who:

• Like you

• Know you well enough to provide a credible opinion

• Write well

recommendation writers must be "academic teachers who have taught you within the last two years."

You may or may not know your counselor very well. You usually don't have any choice who that person will be. The best thing to do for your counselor recommendation is to make sure your counselor gets to know you before the recommendation has to be written.

Taciturn math and science faculty are typically more succinct and direct in their recommendations than are more loquacious English and social studies teachers. Science and math teachers tend to write shorter and less sophisticated recommendations. That's not necessarily bad for you, the applicant, but it's a tendency worth keeping in mind. The ideal approach in choosing recommendation writers is to provide the application reader a balance between math/science and English/social studies recommenders.

PREPPING YOUR RECOMMENDERS

It's a good idea to identify in advance the teachers you think would make good recommendation writers. The qualities you should consider are:

- **Knowledge of you and your academic work.** If your teacher can speak to your qualities (assuming you possess them) of intellectual curiosity, perseverance, discipline, and so forth, it will serve you well.

- **Anecdotal observations.** Are there specific things you did in association with your teacher—such as helping with projects, conducting research, working as a lab assistant, and overcoming obstacles—that will sound really good in a recommendation? Admissions committees enjoy reading accounts of what students have actually done in class rather than just a collection of platitudes about a student's sterling character.

- **Knowledge of you in nonacademic capacities.** Teachers who have worked with you in clubs or other extracurricular activities are even better bets. They'll be able to talk not only about your academic prowess but also mention your qualities as a leader, team player, and organizer.

- **Evidence of good writing skill.** You probably already know who among your potential recommenders will write the best, most lucid, and most easily understood letters. You also probably know the teachers who will write one or two sentences with a scratchy ballpoint pen and let it go at that. Seek out the former and avoid the latter. In some cases you won't have a choice and can't avoid the teacher who hates writing recommendations. Some will warn you that they don't like writing recommendations. Take the warning seriously. Most teachers, however, recognize the importance of good recommendations and will do their best.

SCHMOOZE ALARM

It pays to get to know your high school guidance counselors because they'll write the official school report or counselor recommendation that colleges require.

MAKE IT EASY

What you should do to help your recommenders:

- Tell them early on about the deadline dates.
- Give them materials to help them write recommendations.
- Provide all the forms that they'll need; stamped, addressed envelopes; and your Personal Data Sheet.

You should allow your recommendation writers at least a month before the deadline for the submission of your admissions application. Make a note on your calendar with the names of your recommendation writers, the date you requested the recommendations, and the colleges for which you asked them to write recommendations. A gentle reminder a couple of weeks later is a good idea. Use our Letters of Recommendation Organizer on p. 313 to keep track of all your recommendations.

Students are often confused about what materials or guidance they should give to their recommendation writers. Here's a list of the basics:

- **Exact recommendation requirements.** If you're asking a person to write a recommendation and the college doesn't supply you with a recommendation form, give them a typed page that lists the colleges you would like them to contact and tell them what you need—a letter about your association with them or a testimonial to your particular abilities, for example.

- **Stamped, addressed envelope.** If you're asking your recommendation writers to send your recommendations directly to the college, you should provide the envelope and postage. This also makes it easier for your recommenders to get the recommendations done and in the mail on time. If you're going to send the letters yourself, tell your recommenders what time you'll pick up the recommendations.

- **Your Personal Data Sheet.** Your recommenders may know you very well, but don't count on them to remember all of your achievements. Your Personal Data Sheet will remind them of the things you have done in high school, making it easier for them to write a well-informed recommendation for you. The PDS will also answer the questions about you that may appear on the recommendation forms.

OTHER SUPPORTING MATERIALS

Some colleges actually seek supporting material for admission to such programs as fine and performing arts. They will want to see examples of your work—slides, videotapes, and audio tapes. In that case, follow these suggestions:

- **Never send anything that you want returned.** Admissions offices often don't have the time to return supporting materials. Even if they do have time, they'll return material only if you send a postage-paid return package for the material.

- **Never send originals of works of art.** Instead, send high-quality slides, mounted on clear plastic carrying sheets that are clearly marked with identifying information and dates to help the committee know what they're considering.

BALANCING ACT

Try to find recommenders from different parts of your life. Recommendations from people who know different things about you will draw a more complete picture of you.

WAS HIS NAME MR. DUMM?

If you choose your recommendation writers carefully, you'll avoid receiving a recommendation similar to the one in which the teacher wrote, "Joe is an igma." (The admissions committee thought perhaps the teacher meant Joe was a member of a high school fraternity.) Not only did this teacher not write well, he also didn't seem to know the applicant very well.

WAIVE IT GOOD-BYE

As a general rule, it's advisable to waive your right to read letters of recommendation. Admissions officers place greater trust in recommendations written in confidence.

• **Submit videotapes and audio tapes that are of the highest quality possible.** Many audition-type tapes of good performances are ruined by scratchiness and generally poor sound quality. The same is true of videotapes of performances or auditions. Try to arrange for someone knowledgeable to tape you. Bouncy, poorly lit, and inaudible videotapes don't help your cause.

• **Make sure other materials are clearly marked.** Computer programs you have written, poetry, and screenplays should have your name, social security number, and identifying information attached.

Some schools may not be satisfied with tapes and may actually ask to see you perform. Be prepared: Do your research on who will be evaluating your performance and what they will be observing. Remember that the audition might include an assessment not only of your talent but also of how you would fit into the group for which you're being evaluated. So be prepared for questions about your training, your leadership, and your desire to go on in a career. Have an artistic resume with you to present to your evaluators, even if you've already sent one to them.

LETTERS OF RECOMMENDATION ORGANIZER

✉ Name _____ Title _____

Business address _____

_____

Date recommendation requested _____

Date recommendation sent _____

Date thank-you note sent _____ Date notified of final outcome _____

✉ Name _____ Title _____

Business address _____

_____

Date recommendation requested _____

Date recommendation sent _____

Date thank-you note sent _____ Date notified of final outcome _____

✉ Name _____ Title _____

Business address _____

_____

Date recommendation requested _____

Date recommendation sent _____

Date thank-you note sent _____ Date notified of final outcome _____

✉ Name _____ Title _____

Business address _____

_____

Date recommendation requested _____

Date recommendation sent _____

Date thank-you note sent _____ Date notified of final outcome _____

After you've completed this sheet, make copies of it and place one in the file folder of each school that you're applying to.

5

INTERVIEWS AND CAMPUS VISITS

Interviews, like the essays, are your chance to present your case directly to the admissions committee. The difference is that in an interview you're making contact with someone connected to the admissions office who may become your advocate when your application is reviewed. That's why you want to make the best possible impression you can.

Not every college requires, or even offers, an interview. If you're applying to a college that has a mandatory interview, make sure you schedule one. If you're applying to a college that offers an optional interview, you need to decide whether you want to take them up on their offer. It really depends on you. If the thought of a personal interview terrifies you—and you'd rather have your teeth drilled without painkillers than answer questions about yourself—you should probably skip the interview and let your application speak for itself. If your interpersonal skills are polished, however, you may want to consider arranging an interview, especially if your application could use a little extra boost.

A LITTLE EXTRA PUSH

In a very competitive admissions situation, you want everything working in your favor, including your interview.

PERSONAL INTERVIEWS

Some students are convinced that they can compensate for deficiencies in other parts of their application if they're able to "wow" someone in an interview. This isn't true, unfortunately, because the interviews are relatively less important than other parts of the application process. Most colleges feel they cannot put too much weight on interviews for two reasons: Not all candidates will have the benefit of an interview, and interviews are merely shallow impressions of a person based on a 20- or 30-minute conversation. Other factors are regarded as much more reliable than interviews in determining a candidate's admissibility.

Private institutions want to make a good impression on you, just as you're trying to make a good impression on them. In other words, the interview is part of their recruitment program. They want you to feel good about your encounter with their campus.

ALUMNI INTERVIEWS

Many of the colleges that require or offer interviews have alumni representatives interview students, especially those who live far away from the college.

Public universities are usually less interested in this recruitment aspect of the admissions process and instead focus more on the evaluation of objective data, such as courses, grades, and scores. Admissions interviews are never required for the public universities. For most private colleges and universities, interviews are not required. Some of the more selective institutions, however, require either an interview on campus or with an alumni volunteer who lives near you.

ON-CAMPUS INTERVIEWS

Let's take a look at the things that you should expect to encounter at an on-campus interview.

Who will interview you? Interviewers are most often members of the admissions office's professional staff. You'll most likely be interviewed by an associate or assistant dean (or director), an admissions counselor, an admissions intern (usually a student who's been specially selected and trained for this purpose), or a member of the faculty or other staff person who conducts interviews for the admissions office. Don't be concerned if you're not interviewed by the dean (or director) of admissions. In many offices, they conduct relatively few interviews and are often too busy to do a good job anyway.

Most interviewers will write some comments about their meeting with you. Those comments will go in your application file and will be reviewed by the committee when your application is evaluated. Bring along a copy of your Personal Data Sheet to leave with the interviewers; it will help them remember who you are.

Arriving at the interview. Private colleges take a great deal of pride in offering a warm welcome to the prospective student and her or his family. Admissions offices are usually cozy and well appointed, and interviews are conducted in private offices where there will be no interruptions.

When you arrive at the admissions office, you'll usually check in with a receptionist, who may give you a form to complete with your name, address, and some questions about your academic record and extracurricular activities. Some admissions office waiting areas now have computers you can use to check the status of your application or to access a CD-ROM tour of the campus and the school's various departments and programs.

The admissions officer conducting the interview will come to the waiting area and introduce herself or himself to you and your parents, if they're with you, and escort you back to the office where the interview will take place. Most admissions officers prefer not to sit behind a desk and stare at the interviewee across an expanse of oak. They would rather have a closer setting with you across a small table or some other more relaxed seating arrangement.

TALK THE TALK

You never know when the public university's decision might come down to a review of your file, so you want positive, rather than negative, comments from an interviewer in it.

ON YOUR OWN

The interviewer will want to speak to you alone. Your parents, or whoever is with you, should remain in the waiting area or explore the campus on their own until your interview is over.

The interview itself. Most college admissions interviewers want you to do well in your interview. They will "structure" the interviews by giving you some idea of the kinds of questions they'll be asking—about your academic interests and extracurricular activities, for example—and give you a chance to ask them any questions you may have about their campus.

Interviews usually unfold into three segments: icebreaking, middle section, and closing. Let's take a look at each one:

Icebreaking. The first few minutes of the interview are usually devoted to such pleasantries as the weather, your trip to the campus, or comments about the campus tour. This time will give you an opportunity to calm down and hear the sound of your voice in this new environment. The key is to be natural.

Middle section. Here the interviewer gets to the serious questions of the interview. He or she expects you to do the bulk of the talking. Most interviewers consider the interview a success if the interviewee has talked about 70 percent of the time.

Closing. The interviewer will bring the interview to a close by asking whether you have any questions. It's a good idea to have one or two questions prepared, even if you know the answers, in order to appear engaged and interested. The interviewer may also tell you a little bit about what will happen during the rest of the admissions process. The content of this section of the interview is determined by the time of year and the corresponding phase of the admission cycle of the admissions staff.

Typical interview questions. Below are some of the most-often asked college admission interview questions. It's a good idea to have thought through answers in advance.

- Why are you interested in Nirvana State College?
- What is your best academic subject and your worst?
- Do you have a major in mind? If you answer "yes," the next question will be, "Why did you choose that major?"
- How did you hear about Nirvana State?
- What do you like to do when you aren't studying?
- How would your friends describe you?
- What books/movies have you read/seen lately?

And here are some tougher questions of a more specific nature:

- Do you think your high school education has been relevant to today's competitive world?

NERVOUS?

Some nervousness is natural in an interview situation. Try to calm down during the icebreaking phase of the interview so you can think clearly when the interviewer starts asking the serious questions.

INTERVIEW TIPS

- Practice with friends or family members beforehand.
- Dress appropriately.
- Arrive early.
- Be prepared to discuss the facts in your personal statement.
- Maintain eye contact.
- Don't fidget.
- Try not to speak too quickly.
- Use the interview to flesh out your application and to impress the interviewer.

- Who has been the most influential person in your life and in what way?

- Describe an issue in your community that needs immediate attention. What would you recommend to improve the situation?

- What is your definition of leadership? How would you describe your leadership style?

- If you were given a million dollars and told to spend it on a pressing societal problem, which would you choose and how would you spend the money?

- If you could interview anyone living or dead, who would you choose and what would you ask them first?

- What do you consider to be your greatest strength? Your greatest weakness?

When answering these and any other questions, be as direct as you can but don't answer in monosyllables. And don't answer any question with just a "yup" or "nope." Be prepared for followup questions if you profess real interest in, or knowledge of, a particular topic. It's unimpressive if you mention that you're a great fan of Steven Spielberg films but don't know that he directed *Schindler's List* or *Duel* (Spielberg's first film to receive critical acclaim). You're the interviewee and should do most of the talking, but don't go overboard bragging about yourself. Be matter-of-fact about your accomplishments; the interviewer will recognize the level of your achievements.

What to do after any interview. Be sure to ask your interviewer for her or his business card. When you return home write a thank-you letter. (See the suggested format on the next page.)

CAMPUS VISITS

A campus visit is the best way to see what a college is really like. Here are some common questions (and answers) about visiting college campuses.

When should you visit? Campus visits are best made on a weekday during the regular academic year. College campuses undergo remarkable changes at about 3:00 P.M. on Fridays and don't return to normal until about the same time on Sunday afternoon. Weekend visits and visits during the summer are better than not visiting at all, but keep in mind that college life is different during the academic year.

How do you arrange a campus visit? Contact the Office of Admissions and let them know when you want to visit. Give them at least two weeks' notice. Avoid the last week of the term because that's when students will be taking exams and finishing term papers. College students tend to be somewhat surly during these times and may not make the best impression on a prospective student. The ideal plan is to visit one campus per day. If you

THANK-YOU LETTER FORMAT

Date

Interviewer's Name and Title

College Address

Salutation:

Opening Paragraph: Thank your interviewer for her/his courtesy and interest and mention the date of your interview.

Middle Paragraph(s): Reconfirm your interest in the college, perhaps mentioning something that you learned about the campus during your visit.

If there is information you wish to add to your file, such as newly won honors or just-arrived grades or scores, you can include those here.

Closing Paragraph: Mention that you look forward to learning more about the college and attending in the fall. Suggest that you would be happy to provide any additional information if it is needed.

Sincerely,

(Signature)

Typed Name

Address

Phone Number

must cover a number of colleges in a short time, give yourself no more than two campuses per day. Because of the travel time between campuses, that's pushing pretty hard, though. When you make the call to arrange your visits, make a note of the phone number and name of the person with whom you speak. If you allow enough time, many admissions offices will send you travel, lodging, and parking information.

Where should you stay? The best place to stay is in one of the residence halls (dorms). Many campuses have overnight-stay programs for prospective students. These programs may be called the Student Ambassadors, the Host Program, or something similar, but the idea is usually the same—to match you with a student who will be your host in a residence hall. Some campuses will also include meal coupons for prospective students. Make sure you find out if the food is edible and the dorm life tolerable. The admissions office will also encourage you to attend classes with your host and to tour the campus. Use our Campus Visit Reminders worksheet to help you plan your visit and the Campus Visit Notes sheet to record your visit (see pp. 320–321).

OVERNIGHT SENSATION

If a college you're visiting allows prospective students to spend a night in a residence hall, take them up on their offer.

CAMPUS VISIT REMINDERS

Things to do:

☐ Call campus and make appointment: Telephone _____

Bring the following:

☐ Letter from campus confirming date, time, and location of your interview

☐ List of questions for your interview

☐ Copies of unofficial transcript

☐ Copy of Personal Data Sheet for each interview

☐ SAT I/SAT II and ACT scores

☐ Samples of your work (if appropriate)

☐ Campus map

☐ Parking permit (if necessary)

☐ Airplane tickets (if necessary)

☐ Letter confirming overnight residence hall visit

☐ Confirmed reservations at local hotel (if you're not staying on campus)

☐ Interview clothes (clean)

☐ Copy of this book (or photocopy of this section)

☐ Money or traveler's checks

☐ Camera

CAMPUS VISIT NOTES

Name of college ———————————— Telephone ———————————————

Travel instructions ——————————————————————————————————

Lodging ———————————————— Telephone ———————————————

Interview/date/time/location ——————————————————————————

Name of interviewer ———————————————————————————————

Impression gained from interview ——————————————————————

——

Time of tour ——————————— Tour guide's name —————————————

Impression gained from tour ————————————————————————————

——

——

Places I would like to see again ——————————————————————————

——

Names of faculty, staff, or students met ———————————————————

——

Classes or other activities attended ————————————————————————

——

Overnight visit date and time ————————————————————————————

Name of student host ——————————————————————————————

General impression from visit ————————————————————————————

——

——

6

MAKING YOUR FINAL DECISION

Having filled out your application, written your essays, received your recommendations, gone through interviews, and made campus visits, your next step is to sit back and wait for those fat envelopes we've been talking about. If you followed our advice and maximized every part of your application, you can take a deep breath and rest assured that you presented yourself in the best light. But then you have to start focusing again once letters of acceptance begin to arrive in your mailbox.

NOW WHAT?

Once you've collected all those fat envelopes, it's time for you to make the decision as to which college to attend. You may be surprised to learn that the process has now taken a 180-degree turn since you filed your application: You're now in the position of making the colleges wait as they made you wait while they were reviewing your application.

The colleges that have offered you admission, however, aren't going to wait passively until you decide. They're going to help you choose them. Colleges will inundate you with invitations to teas, receptions, campus "admissions days," and other events designed with one purpose in mind—to convince you to accept their offer of admission.

It's particularly important for you to separate the important information you need from the hype of the recruitment "yield" programs (so called because the colleges want to increase the acceptance rate, or yield, of the students to whom they have offered admission).

This is also a time when you may receive direct phone calls from currently enrolled students, faculty, and local alumni. All these contacts can provide you with valuable information. To take best advantage of this bounty of interest in your decision, you need to know what else can help you make the best choice.

The strategies that worked for you during the first part of the process can be helpful again now. Refer to the list of factors you were considering when you decided where you would apply for admission. See how well the colleges that have offered you admission meet those requirements.

IT FEELS GOOD TO BE WANTED

Once you've received a letter of acceptance from a college, it's likely that they'll call or write to convince you to enroll.

Carefully evaluate the financial aid packages offered by each school and factor all the student aid offered with your actual costs into your final decision. Affordability will be a major factor for the families of many college-bound students. Resist the temptation to make a hasty decision until all of your options are known to you.

A good way to make the final decision is to visit (or revisit) the campuses that are still in the running. As mentioned above, you may be invited to attend special on-campus events held in honor of newly admitted students. Keep in mind that these events are carefully orchestrated to make the most positive impression possible on you and your parents.

But if you look beneath the hype, these events can give you valuable insight into exactly what the campus culture and opportunities are like. By staying overnight in a residence hall, talking with students and faculty, reading the bulletin boards, and eating the food in the dining halls you'll be able to tell if this is the place for you.

WAITING OUT THE WAITING LIST

In addition to overbooking their acceptances, colleges further protect themselves by placing a number of applicants on a waiting list. These students will be re-evaluated if the admissions office determines they need to admit more students to fill the class.

If you find yourself on a college's waiting list, your best bet is to assume that you won't be admitted and protect yourself by accepting an offer of admission from one of your other choices. There's never a guarantee that you'll be admitted from a waiting list. The best you can do is let the admissions office know right away that you're still interested. A letter from you affirming your interest and adding any additional honors or other pertinent information that's not already in the file is a good idea.

If you're admitted from a waiting list and decide to accept the offer, be sure and let the interim college know that you'll be going somewhere else. That will give them time to take someone from their own waiting list to fill the slot you've vacated.

COMPARING THE COLLEGES

Make copies of the College Comparison Worksheet on the next page. As you accumulate information and impressions about the colleges that you've applied to, fill in a worksheet for each school. These worksheets will help you compare the colleges and help you make a decision that you'll be happy with.

WHAT'S NEXT

By getting a complete picture of the college admissions process, you'll have more meaningful context for your SAT preparation and testing experience.

COLLEGE COMPARISON WORKSHEET

Name of college _____

Admissions

Special items to be submitted with application _____

Percent of applicants accepted _____

Tests required _____

Average test scores of applicants _____

Average high school GPA or class rank of applicants _____

Special admissions plans (rolling, early decision, advance placement) _____

Admissions selectivity rating (most selective, highly selective, selective, not selective) _____

Academic Life

Academic or career orientation _____

Majors of interest _____

Special programs (study abroad, internships, unusual degree programs) _____

Individual or dual majors _____

Grading systems _____

Academic calendar _____

Student-faculty ratio/average class size _____

Faculty advising programs _____

Percent of faculty holding Ph.D.s_____

Graduate schools or programs relevant to your interest _____

Student Body

Total enrollment _____

Undergraduate enrollment _____

Geographic area most students come from _____

Male-female ratio _____

Ethnic/religious enrollment _____

Percent of commuters vs. campus residents _____

Percent of students who graduate _____

Percent who go on to graduate study _____

Campus Life

Distance from your home _____

Nearest major city _____

College setting _____

Facilities of interest to you _____

Athletics _____

Extracurricular groups _____

On-/off-campus housing _____

Board plans available _____

Regulations worth noting _____

Costs/Financial Aid

Application fee _____

Enrollment deposit _____

Tuition _____

Room and board _____

Traveling costs _____

Off-campus living, dorms, etc. _____

Forms required for aid _____

Typical aid package _____

Sample on-campus jobs _____

Work-study programs available _____

College's estimated total budget _____

Percent of students receiving aid _____

SAT
PRACTICE TEST

HOW TO TAKE THIS
PRACTICE TEST

Before taking this practice test, find a quiet room where you can work uninterrupted for two and a half hours. Make sure you have a comfortable desk, your calculator, and several #2 pencils.

Use the answer sheet on the previous page to record your answers. (You can cut it out, or photocopy it.)

Once you start this practice test, don't stop until you've finished. Remember—you can review any questions within a section, but you may not go back or forward a section.

You'll find the answers and a score converter following the test.

Good luck.

KAPLAN
PRACTICE TEST

Remove (or photocopy) this answer sheet and use it to complete the practice test.
(See answer key on p. 353 to correct your test when finished.)

Start with number 1 for each new section. If a section has fewer questions than answer spaces, leave the extra spaces blank.

SECTION 1

1 Ⓐ Ⓑ Ⓒ Ⓓ Ⓔ	11 Ⓐ Ⓑ Ⓒ Ⓓ Ⓔ	21 Ⓐ Ⓑ Ⓒ Ⓓ Ⓔ	31 Ⓐ Ⓑ Ⓒ Ⓓ Ⓔ
2 Ⓐ Ⓑ Ⓒ Ⓓ Ⓔ	12 Ⓐ Ⓑ Ⓒ Ⓓ Ⓔ	22 Ⓐ Ⓑ Ⓒ Ⓓ Ⓔ	32 Ⓐ Ⓑ Ⓒ Ⓓ Ⓔ
3 Ⓐ Ⓑ Ⓒ Ⓓ Ⓔ	13 Ⓐ Ⓑ Ⓒ Ⓓ Ⓔ	23 Ⓐ Ⓑ Ⓒ Ⓓ Ⓔ	33 Ⓐ Ⓑ Ⓒ Ⓓ Ⓔ
4 Ⓐ Ⓑ Ⓒ Ⓓ Ⓔ	14 Ⓐ Ⓑ Ⓒ Ⓓ Ⓔ	24 Ⓐ Ⓑ Ⓒ Ⓓ Ⓔ	34 Ⓐ Ⓑ Ⓒ Ⓓ Ⓔ
5 Ⓐ Ⓑ Ⓒ Ⓓ Ⓔ	15 Ⓐ Ⓑ Ⓒ Ⓓ Ⓔ	25 Ⓐ Ⓑ Ⓒ Ⓓ Ⓔ	35 Ⓐ Ⓑ Ⓒ Ⓓ Ⓔ
6 Ⓐ Ⓑ Ⓒ Ⓓ Ⓔ	16 Ⓐ Ⓑ Ⓒ Ⓓ Ⓔ	26 Ⓐ Ⓑ Ⓒ Ⓓ Ⓔ	36 Ⓐ Ⓑ Ⓒ Ⓓ Ⓔ
7 Ⓐ Ⓑ Ⓒ Ⓓ Ⓔ	17 Ⓐ Ⓑ Ⓒ Ⓓ Ⓔ	27 Ⓐ Ⓑ Ⓒ Ⓓ Ⓔ	37 Ⓐ Ⓑ Ⓒ Ⓓ Ⓔ
8 Ⓐ Ⓑ Ⓒ Ⓓ Ⓔ	18 Ⓐ Ⓑ Ⓒ Ⓓ Ⓔ	28 Ⓐ Ⓑ Ⓒ Ⓓ Ⓔ	38 Ⓐ Ⓑ Ⓒ Ⓓ Ⓔ
9 Ⓐ Ⓑ Ⓒ Ⓓ Ⓔ	19 Ⓐ Ⓑ Ⓒ Ⓓ Ⓔ	29 Ⓐ Ⓑ Ⓒ Ⓓ Ⓔ	39 Ⓐ Ⓑ Ⓒ Ⓓ Ⓔ
10 Ⓐ Ⓑ Ⓒ Ⓓ Ⓔ	20 Ⓐ Ⓑ Ⓒ Ⓓ Ⓔ	30 Ⓐ Ⓑ Ⓒ Ⓓ Ⓔ	40 Ⓐ Ⓑ Ⓒ Ⓓ Ⓔ

right in section 1

wrong in section 1

SECTION 2

1 Ⓐ Ⓑ Ⓒ Ⓓ Ⓔ	11 Ⓐ Ⓑ Ⓒ Ⓓ Ⓔ	21 Ⓐ Ⓑ Ⓒ Ⓓ Ⓔ	31 Ⓐ Ⓑ Ⓒ Ⓓ Ⓔ
2 Ⓐ Ⓑ Ⓒ Ⓓ Ⓔ	12 Ⓐ Ⓑ Ⓒ Ⓓ Ⓔ	22 Ⓐ Ⓑ Ⓒ Ⓓ Ⓔ	32 Ⓐ Ⓑ Ⓒ Ⓓ Ⓔ
3 Ⓐ Ⓑ Ⓒ Ⓓ Ⓔ	13 Ⓐ Ⓑ Ⓒ Ⓓ Ⓔ	23 Ⓐ Ⓑ Ⓒ Ⓓ Ⓔ	33 Ⓐ Ⓑ Ⓒ Ⓓ Ⓔ
4 Ⓐ Ⓑ Ⓒ Ⓓ Ⓔ	14 Ⓐ Ⓑ Ⓒ Ⓓ Ⓔ	24 Ⓐ Ⓑ Ⓒ Ⓓ Ⓔ	34 Ⓐ Ⓑ Ⓒ Ⓓ Ⓔ
5 Ⓐ Ⓑ Ⓒ Ⓓ Ⓔ	15 Ⓐ Ⓑ Ⓒ Ⓓ Ⓔ	25 Ⓐ Ⓑ Ⓒ Ⓓ Ⓔ	35 Ⓐ Ⓑ Ⓒ Ⓓ Ⓔ
6 Ⓐ Ⓑ Ⓒ Ⓓ Ⓔ	16 Ⓐ Ⓑ Ⓒ Ⓓ Ⓔ	26 Ⓐ Ⓑ Ⓒ Ⓓ Ⓔ	36 Ⓐ Ⓑ Ⓒ Ⓓ Ⓔ
7 Ⓐ Ⓑ Ⓒ Ⓓ Ⓔ	17 Ⓐ Ⓑ Ⓒ Ⓓ Ⓔ	27 Ⓐ Ⓑ Ⓒ Ⓓ Ⓔ	37 Ⓐ Ⓑ Ⓒ Ⓓ Ⓔ
8 Ⓐ Ⓑ Ⓒ Ⓓ Ⓔ	18 Ⓐ Ⓑ Ⓒ Ⓓ Ⓔ	28 Ⓐ Ⓑ Ⓒ Ⓓ Ⓔ	38 Ⓐ Ⓑ Ⓒ Ⓓ Ⓔ
9 Ⓐ Ⓑ Ⓒ Ⓓ Ⓔ	19 Ⓐ Ⓑ Ⓒ Ⓓ Ⓔ	29 Ⓐ Ⓑ Ⓒ Ⓓ Ⓔ	39 Ⓐ Ⓑ Ⓒ Ⓓ Ⓔ
10 Ⓐ Ⓑ Ⓒ Ⓓ Ⓔ	20 Ⓐ Ⓑ Ⓒ Ⓓ Ⓔ	30 Ⓐ Ⓑ Ⓒ Ⓓ Ⓔ	40 Ⓐ Ⓑ Ⓒ Ⓓ Ⓔ

right in section 2

wrong in section 2

SECTION 3

1 Ⓐ Ⓑ Ⓒ Ⓓ Ⓔ	11 Ⓐ Ⓑ Ⓒ Ⓓ Ⓔ	21 Ⓐ Ⓑ Ⓒ Ⓓ Ⓔ	31 Ⓐ Ⓑ Ⓒ Ⓓ Ⓔ
2 Ⓐ Ⓑ Ⓒ Ⓓ Ⓔ	12 Ⓐ Ⓑ Ⓒ Ⓓ Ⓔ	22 Ⓐ Ⓑ Ⓒ Ⓓ Ⓔ	32 Ⓐ Ⓑ Ⓒ Ⓓ Ⓔ
3 Ⓐ Ⓑ Ⓒ Ⓓ Ⓔ	13 Ⓐ Ⓑ Ⓒ Ⓓ Ⓔ	23 Ⓐ Ⓑ Ⓒ Ⓓ Ⓔ	33 Ⓐ Ⓑ Ⓒ Ⓓ Ⓔ
4 Ⓐ Ⓑ Ⓒ Ⓓ Ⓔ	14 Ⓐ Ⓑ Ⓒ Ⓓ Ⓔ	24 Ⓐ Ⓑ Ⓒ Ⓓ Ⓔ	34 Ⓐ Ⓑ Ⓒ Ⓓ Ⓔ
5 Ⓐ Ⓑ Ⓒ Ⓓ Ⓔ	15 Ⓐ Ⓑ Ⓒ Ⓓ Ⓔ	25 Ⓐ Ⓑ Ⓒ Ⓓ Ⓔ	35 Ⓐ Ⓑ Ⓒ Ⓓ Ⓔ
6 Ⓐ Ⓑ Ⓒ Ⓓ Ⓔ	16 Ⓐ Ⓑ Ⓒ Ⓓ Ⓔ	26 Ⓐ Ⓑ Ⓒ Ⓓ Ⓔ	36 Ⓐ Ⓑ Ⓒ Ⓓ Ⓔ
7 Ⓐ Ⓑ Ⓒ Ⓓ Ⓔ	17 Ⓐ Ⓑ Ⓒ Ⓓ Ⓔ	27 Ⓐ Ⓑ Ⓒ Ⓓ Ⓔ	37 Ⓐ Ⓑ Ⓒ Ⓓ Ⓔ
8 Ⓐ Ⓑ Ⓒ Ⓓ Ⓔ	18 Ⓐ Ⓑ Ⓒ Ⓓ Ⓔ	28 Ⓐ Ⓑ Ⓒ Ⓓ Ⓔ	38 Ⓐ Ⓑ Ⓒ Ⓓ Ⓔ
9 Ⓐ Ⓑ Ⓒ Ⓓ Ⓔ	19 Ⓐ Ⓑ Ⓒ Ⓓ Ⓔ	29 Ⓐ Ⓑ Ⓒ Ⓓ Ⓔ	39 Ⓐ Ⓑ Ⓒ Ⓓ Ⓔ
10 Ⓐ Ⓑ Ⓒ Ⓓ Ⓔ	20 Ⓐ Ⓑ Ⓒ Ⓓ Ⓔ	30 Ⓐ Ⓑ Ⓒ Ⓓ Ⓔ	40 Ⓐ Ⓑ Ⓒ Ⓓ Ⓔ

right in section 3

wrong in section 3

Remove this answer sheet and use it to complete the practice test.

Start with number 1 for each new section. If a section has fewer questions than answer spaces, leave the extra spaces blank.

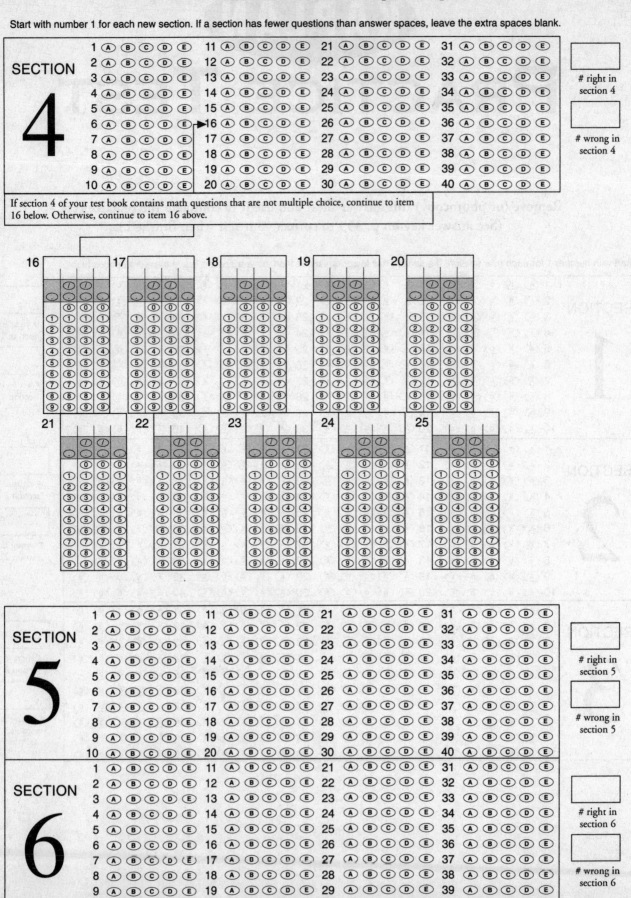

SECTION 1

Time—30 Minutes   For each of the following questions, choose the best answer and darken the
30 Questions   corresponding oval on the answer sheet.

Select the lettered word or set of words that best completes the sentence.

Example:

Today's small, portable computers contrast markedly with the earliest electronic computers, which were ----.

(A) effective
(B) invented
(C) useful
(D) destructive
(E) enormous

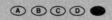

1   More insurers are limiting the sale of property insurance in coastal areas and other regions ---- natural disasters.

    (A) safe from
    (B) according to
    (C) despite
    (D) which include
    (E) prone to

2   Roman legions ---- the mountain ---- of Masada for three years before they were able to seize it.

    (A) dissembled . . bastion
    (B) assailed . . symbol
    (C) besieged . . citadel
    (D) surmounted . . dwelling
    (E) honed . . stronghold

3   Unlike his calmer, more easygoing colleagues, the senator was ----, ready to quarrel at the slightest provocation.

    (A) whimsical
    (B) irascible
    (C) gregarious
    (D) ineffectual
    (E) benign

4   Although historians have long thought of Genghis Khan as a ---- potentate, new research has shown he was ---- by many of his subjects.

    (A) tyrannical . . abhorred
    (B) despotic . . revered
    (C) redundant . . venerated
    (D) jocular . . esteemed
    (E) peremptory . . invoked

5   Jill was ---- by her employees because she often ---- them for not working hard enough.

    (A) deified . . goaded
    (B) loathed . . berated
    (C) disregarded . . eulogized
    (D) cherished . . derided
    (E) execrated . . lauded

6   Reconstructing the skeletons of extinct species like dinosaurs is ---- process that requires much patience and effort by paleontologists.

    (A) a nascent
    (B) an aberrant
    (C) a disheveled
    (D) a worthless
    (E) an exacting

7   Nearly ---- by disease and the destruction of their habitat, koalas are now found only in isolated parts of eucalyptus forests.

    (A) dispersed
    (B) compiled
    (C) decimated
    (D) infuriated
    (E) averted

8   Deep ideological ---- and internal power struggles ---- the government.

    (A) disputes . . facilitated
    (B) similarities . . protracted
    (C) distortions . . accelerated
    (D) agreements . . stymied
    (E) divisions . . paralyzed

9   Medical experts have viewed high doses of vitamins as a popular remedy whose value is, as yet, ----.

    (A) medicinal
    (B) prescribed
    (C) recommended
    (D) unproven
    (E) beneficial

GO ON TO THE NEXT PAGE →

SECTION 1

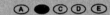
10   TROUT : FISH ::

(A) grain : sand
(B) human : mammal
(C) river : stream
(D) chicken : egg
(E) frog : toad

11   INHALE : LUNGS ::

(A) swallow : stomach
(B) attack : heart
(C) ache : head
(D) pump : blood
(E) travel : foot

12   BRAGGART : BOAST

(A) laggard : tarry
(B) hypocrite : speak
(C) extrovert : brood
(D) mendicant : compromise
(E) boor : gratify

13   ALLEVIATE : PAIN ::

(A) soothe : antidote
(B) depreciate : value
(C) contract : job
(D) deviate : standard
(E) officiate : safety

14   INFURIATE : ANNOY ::

(A) admire : respect
(B) indulge : lure
(C) terrify : frighten
(D) satiate : deprive
(E) vex : startle

15   MISERLY : MAGNANIMITY ::

(A) greedy : mirth
(B) transient : stupefaction
(C) admirable : fastidiousness
(D) innocent : culpability
(E) offensive : avarice

GO ON TO THE NEXT PAGE →

SECTION 1

Answer the questions below based on the information in the accompanying passages.

Questions 16–23 are based on the following passage.

In this excerpt, a Nobel Prize-winning scientist discusses ways of thinking about extremely long periods of time.

There is one fact about the origin of life which is reasonably certain. Whenever and wherever it happened, it started a very long time ago, so long
(5) ago that it is extremely difficult to form any realistic idea of such vast stretches of time. The shortness of human life necessarily limits the span of direct personal recollection.

Human culture has given us the illusion that our memories go further back than that. Before
(10) writing was invented, the experience of earlier generations, embodied in stories, myths, and moral precepts to guide behavior, was passed down verbally or, to a lesser extent, in pictures, carvings, and statues. Writing has made more precise and
(15) more extensive the transmission of such information and, in recent times, photography has sharpened our images of the immediate past. Even so, we have difficulty in contemplating steadily the march of history, from the beginnings of
(20) civilization to the present day, in such a way that we can truly experience the slow passage of time. Our minds are not built to deal comfortably with periods as long as hundreds or thousands of years.

Yet when we come to consider the origin of life,
(25) the time scales we must deal with make the whole span of human history seem but the blink of an eyelid. There is no simple way to adjust one's thinking to such vast stretches of time. The immensity of time passed is beyond our ready
(30) comprehension. One can only construct an impression of it from indirect and incomplete descriptions, just as a blind man laboriously builds up, by touch and sound, a picture of his immediate surroundings.

(35) The customary way to provide a convenient framework for one's thoughts is to compare the age of the universe with the length of a single earthly day. Perhaps a better comparison, along the same lines, would be to equate the age of our earth with
(40) a single week. On such a scale the age of the universe, since the Big Bang, would be about two or three weeks. The oldest macroscopic fossils (those from the start of the Cambrian Period*) would have been alive just one day ago. Modern man would
(45) have appeared in the last 10 seconds and agriculture in the last one or two. Odysseus** would have lived only half a second before the present time.

Even this comparison hardly makes the longer
(50) time scale comprehensible to us. Another alternative is to draw a linear map of time, with the different events marked on it. The problem here is to make the line long enough to show our own experience on a reasonable scale, and yet short
(55) enough for convenient reproduction and examination. But perhaps the most vivid method is to compare time to the lines of print themselves. Let us make a 200-page book equal in length to the time from the start of the Cambrian to the present;
(60) that is, about 600 million years. Then each full page will represent roughly three million years, each line about ninety thousand years and each letter or small space about fifteen hundred years. The origin of the earth would be about seven books ago and
(65) the origin of the universe (which has been dated only approximately) ten or so books before that. Almost the whole of recorded human history would be covered by the last two or three letters of the book.

(70) If you now turn back the pages of the book, slowly reading *one letter at a time*—remember, each letter is fifteen hundred years—then this may convey to you something of the immense stretches of time we shall have to consider. On this scale the span of your own
(75) life would be less than the width of a comma.

*Cambrian: the earliest period in the Paleozoic era, beginning about 600 million years ago.
**Odysseus: the most famous Greek hero of antiquity; he is the hero of Homer's *The Odyssey*, which describes the aftermath of the Trojan War (ca. 1200 B.C.).

16 The word *span* in line 6 most nearly means

(A) rate of increase
(B) value
(C) bridge
(D) extent
(E) accuracy

17 The phrase *to a lesser extent* in line 13, indicates that, before the invention of writing, the wisdom of earlier generations was

(A) rejected by recent generations when portrayed in pictures, carvings, or statues
(B) passed down orally, or not at all
(C) transmitted more effectively by spoken word than by other means
(D) based on illusory memories that turned fact into fiction
(E) more strongly grounded in science than in the arts

GO ON TO THE NEXT PAGE →

331

SECTION 1

18 The author most likely describes the impact of writing (lines 14–17) in order to

(A) illustrate the limitations of the human memory
(B) provide an example of how cultures transmit information
(C) indicate how primitive preliterate cultures were
(D) refute an opinion about the origin of human civilization
(E) explain the difference between historical facts and myth

19 The word *ready* in line 29 most nearly means

(A) set
(B) agreeable
(C) immediate
(D) apt
(E) willing

20 The analogy of the "blind man" (line 32) is presented primarily to show that

(A) humans are unable to comprehend long periods of time
(B) myths and legends fail to give an accurate picture of the past
(C) human history is only a fraction of the time since life began
(D) humans refuse to learn the lessons of the past
(E) long periods of time can only be understood indirectly

21 In lines 40–44, the author mentions the Big Bang and the Cambrian Period in order to demonstrate which point?

(A) The age of the earth is best understood using the time scale of a week.
(B) Agriculture was a relatively late development in human history.
(C) No fossil record exists before the Cambrian Period.
(D) Convenient time scales do not adequately represent the age of the earth.
(E) The customary framework for thinking about the age of the universe should be discarded permanently.

22 According to lines 52–56, one difficulty of using a linear representation of time is that

(A) linear representations of time do not meet accepted scientific standards of accuracy
(B) prehistoric eras overlap each other, making linear representation deceptive
(C) the more accurate the scale, the more difficult the map is to copy and study
(D) there are too many events to represent on a single line
(E) our knowledge of pre-Cambrian time is insufficient to construct an accurate linear map

23 The author of this passage discusses several kinds of time scales primarily in order to illustrate the

(A) difficulty of assigning precise dates to past events
(B) variety of choices faced by scientists investigating the origin of life
(C) evolution of efforts to comprehend the passage of history
(D) immensity of time since life began on earth
(E) development of the technology of communication

GO ON TO THE NEXT PAGE →

SECTION 1

Questions 24–30 are based on the following passage.

The following excerpt is from a speech delivered in 1873 by Susan B. Anthony, a leader in the women's rights movement of the 19th century.

Friends and fellow-citizens: I stand before you tonight under indictment for the alleged crime of having voted at the last Presidential election, without having a lawful right to vote. It shall be my
(5) work this evening to prove to you that in thus voting, I not only committed no crime, but, instead, simply exercised my citizen's rights, guaranteed to me and all United States citizens by the National Constitution, beyond the power of
(10) any State to deny.

The preamble of the Federal Constitution says:
"We, the people of the United States, in order to form a more perfect union, establish justice, insure domestic tranquillity, provide for the common
(15) defense, promote the general welfare, and secure the blessings of liberty to ourselves and our posterity, do ordain and establish this Constitution for the United States of America."

It was we, the people; not we, the white male
(20) citizens; nor yet we, the male citizens; but we, the whole people, who formed the Union. And we formed it, not to give the blessings of liberty, but to secure them; not to the half of ourselves and the half of our posterity, but to the whole people—
(25) women as well as men. And it is a downright mockery to talk to women of their enjoyment of the blessings of liberty while they are denied the use of the only means of securing them provided by this democratic-republican government—the
(30) ballot.

For any State to make sex a qualification that must ever result in the disfranchisement* of one entire half of the people is a violation of the supreme law of the land. By it the blessings of
(35) liberty are forever withheld from women and their female posterity. To them this government had no just powers derived from the consent of the governed. To them this government is not a democracy. It is not a republic. It is an odious
(40) aristocracy; a hateful oligarchy of sex; this oligarchy of sex, which makes father, brothers, husband, sons, the oligarchs over the mother and sisters, the wife and daughters of every household —which ordains all men sovereigns, all women
(45) subjects, carries dissension, discord and rebellion into every home of the nation.

Webster, Worcester and Bouvier all define a citizen to be a person in the United States, entitled to vote and hold office.
(50) The one question left to be settled now is: Are women persons? And I hardly believe any of our opponents will have the hardihood to say they are not. Being persons, then, women are citizens; and no State has a right to make any law, or to enforce
(55) any old law, that shall abridge their privileges or immunities. Hence, every discrimination against women in the constitutions and laws of the several States is today null and void, precisely as is every one against Negroes.

*disfranchisement: to deprive of the right to vote.

24 In the first paragraph, Anthony states that her action in voting was

(A) illegal, but morally justified
(B) the result of her keen interest in national politics
(C) legal, if the Constitution is interpreted correctly
(D) an illustration of the need for a women's rights movement
(E) illegal, but worthy of leniency

25 Which best captures the meaning of the word *promote* in line 15?

(A) further
(B) organize
(C) publicize
(D) commend
(E) motivate

26 By saying "we, the people . . . the whole people, who formed the Union" (lines 19–21), Anthony means that

(A) the founders of the nation conspired to deprive women of their rights
(B) some male citizens are still being denied basic rights
(C) the role of women in the founding of the nation is generally ignored
(D) society is endangered when women are deprived of basic rights
(E) all people deserve to enjoy the rights guaranteed by the Constitution

GO ON TO THE NEXT PAGE →

SECTION 1

27 By "the half of our posterity" (lines 23–24), Anthony means

   (A) the political legacy passed down from her era
   (B) future generations of male United States citizens
   (C) those who wish to enjoy the blessings of liberty
   (D) current and future opponents of the women's rights movement
   (E) future members of the democratic-republican government

28 In the fifth paragraph, lines 31–46, Anthony's argument rests mainly on the strategy of convincing her audience that

   (A) any state which denies women the vote undermines its status as a democracy
   (B) women deprived of the vote will eventually raise a rebellion
   (C) the nation will remain an aristocracy if the status of women does not change
   (D) women's rights issues should be debated in every home
   (E) even an aristocracy cannot survive without the consent of the governed

29 The word *hardihood* in line 52 could best be replaced by

   (A) endurance
   (B) vitality
   (C) nerve
   (D) opportunity
   (E) stupidity

30 When Anthony warns that "no State . . . shall abridge their privileges" (lines 54–55), she means that

   (A) women should be allowed to live a life of privilege
   (B) women on trial cannot be forced to give up their immunity
   (C) every state should repeal its outdated laws
   (D) governments may not deprive citizens of their rights
   (E) the rights granted to women must be decided by the people, not the state

IF YOU FINISH BEFORE TIME IS CALLED, YOU MAY CHECK YOUR WORK ON THIS SECTION ONLY. DO NOT TURN TO ANY OTHER SECTION IN THE TEST **STOP**

334

SECTION 2

Time—30 Minutes 25 Questions	Solve each of the following problems, decide which is the best answer choice, and darken the corresponding oval on the answer sheet. Use available space in the test booklet for scratchwork.*

Notes:

(1) Calculator use is permitted.

(2) All numbers used are real numbers.

(3) Figures are provided for some problems. All figures are drawn to scale and lie in a plane UNLESS otherwise indicated.

Reference Information

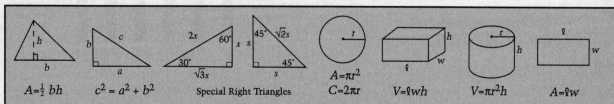

$A = \frac{1}{2} bh$ $c^2 = a^2 + b^2$ Special Right Triangles $A = \pi r^2$
$C = 2\pi r$ $V = \ell wh$ $V = \pi r^2 h$ $A = \ell w$

The sum of the degree measures of the angles of a triangle is 180.
The number of degrees of arc in a circle is 360.
A straight angle has a degree measure of 180.

---

1 Which of the following must be equal to 30 percent of x?

(A) $30x$

(B) $3x$

(C) $\frac{3x}{10}$

(D) $\frac{3x}{100}$

(E) $\frac{3x}{1000}$

2 $(2 \times 10^4) + (5 \times 10^3) + (6 \times 10^2) + (4 \times 10^1) =$

(A)   2,564
(B) 20,564
(C) 25,064
(D) 25,604
(E) 25,640

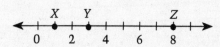

3 On the number line shown above, the length of YZ is how much greater than the length of XY?

(A) 3
(B) 4
(C) 5
(D) 6
(E) 7

4 If $2^{x+1} = 16$, what is the value of x?

(A) 2
(B) 3
(C) 4
(D) 5
(E) 6

---

* The directions on the actual SAT will vary slightly.

GO ON TO THE NEXT PAGE →

SECTION 2

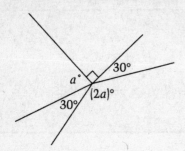

Note: Figure not drawn to scale.

5 In the figure above, what is the value of a?

(A) 50
(B) 55
(C) 60
(D) 65
(E) 70

6 A machine labels 150 bottles in 20 minutes. At this rate, how many minutes does it take to label 60 bottles?

(A) 2
(B) 4
(C) 6
(D) 8
(E) 10

7 If $x - 1$ is a multiple of 3, which of the following must be the next greater multiple of 3?

(A) x
(B) $x + 2$
(C) $x + 3$
(D) $3x$
(E) $3x - 3$

8 When x is divided by 5, the remainder is 4. When x is divided by 9, the remainder is 0. Which of the following is a possible value for x?

(A) 24
(B) 45
(C) 59
(D) 109
(E) 144

9 In triangle ABC, $AB = 6$, $BC = 12$, and $AC = x$. Which of the following cannot be a value of x?

(A) 6
(B) 7

(C) 8
(D) 9
(E) 10

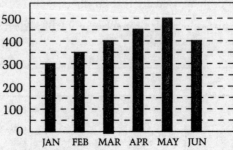

10 The average of 20, 70, and x is 40. If the average of 20, 70, x, and y is 50, then $y =$

(A) 100
(B) 80
(C) 70
(D) 60
(E) 30

NUMBER OF BOOKS BORROWED
FROM MIDVILLE LIBRARY

11 According to the graph above, the number of books borrowed during the month of January was what fraction of the total number of books borrowed during the first six months of the year?

(A) $\frac{1}{8}$

(B) $\frac{1}{7}$

(C) $\frac{1}{6}$

(D) $\frac{3}{16}$

(E) $\frac{5}{12}$

12 If 40 percent of r is equal to s, then which of the following is equal to 10 percent of r?

(A) $4s$

(B) $2s$

(C) $\frac{s}{2}$

(D) $\frac{s}{4}$

(E) $\frac{s}{8}$

GO ON TO THE NEXT PAGE →

SECTION 2

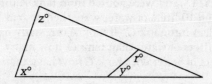

13 In the figure above, which of the following must be true?

(A) $x + r = z + y$
(B) $x + r = z - y$
(C) $x - y = z + r$
(D) $x - r = y - z$
(E) $x + y = z + r$

14 If a *prifact number* is a nonprime integer such that each factor of the integer other than 1 and the integer itself is a prime number, which of the following is a *prifact number*?

(A) 12
(B) 18
(C) 21
(D) 24
(E) 28

15 If $3x + y = 14$, and x and y are positive integers, each of the following could be the value of $x + y$ EXCEPT

(A) 12
(B) 10
(C) 8
(D) 6
(E) 4

16 A certain deck of cards contains r cards. After the cards are distributed evenly among s people, 8 cards are left over. In terms of r and s, how many cards did each person receive?

(A) $\dfrac{s}{8 - r}$

(B) $\dfrac{r - s}{8}$

(C) $\dfrac{r - 8}{s}$

(D) $s - 8r$

(E) $rs - 8$

17 If d is an integer, which of the following CANNOT be an integer?

(A) $\dfrac{d}{2}$

(B) $\dfrac{\sqrt{d}}{2}$

(C) $2d$

(D) $d\sqrt{2}$

(E) $d + 2$

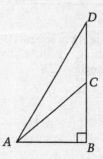

18 In the figure above, the area of triangle ABC is 6. If $BC = CD$, what is the area of triangle ACD?

(A) 6
(B) 8
(C) 9
(D) 10
(E) 12

19 The ratio of x to y to z is 3 to 6 to 8. If $y = 24$, what is the value of $x + z$?

(A) 11
(B) 33
(C) 44
(D) 66
(E) 88

20 What is the minimum number of rectangular tiles, each 12 centimeters by 18 centimeters, needed to completely cover five flat rectangular surfaces, each 60 centimeters by 180 centimeters?

(A) 50
(B) 100
(C) 150
(D) 200
(E) 250

GO ON TO THE NEXT PAGE →

SECTION 2

21 If $x + y = 11$, $y + z = 14$, and $x + z = 13$, what is the value of $x + y + z$?

(A) 16
(B) 17
(C) 18
(D) 19
(E) 20

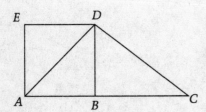

22 In the figure above, side AB of square $ABDE$ is extended to point C. If $BC = 8$ and $CD = 10$, what is the perimeter of triangle ACD?

(A) $18 + 6\sqrt{2}$
(B) $24 + 6\sqrt{2}$
(C) $26 + 6\sqrt{2}$
(D) 30
(E) 36

23 If $r < 0$ and $(4r - 4)^2 = 36$, what is the value of r?

(A) -2

(B) -1

(C) $-\dfrac{1}{2}$

(D) $-\dfrac{1}{4}$

(E) $-\dfrac{1}{8}$

24 Five liters of water were poured from tank A into tank B, and 10 liters of water were then poured from tank A into tank C. If tank A originally had 10 more liters of water than tank C, how many more liters of water does tank C now have than tank A?

(A) 0
(B) 5
(C) 10
(D) 15
(E) 20

25 If a cube has a surface area of $36n^2$ square feet, what is its volume in cubic feet, in terms of n?

(A) $n^3\sqrt{6}$

(B) $6n^3\sqrt{6}$

(C) $36n^3$

(D) $36n^3\sqrt{6}$

(E) $216n^3$

IF YOU FINISH BEFORE TIME IS CALLED, YOU MAY CHECK YOUR WORK ON THIS SECTION ONLY. DO NOT TURN TO ANY OTHER SECTION IN THE TEST. STOP

SECTION 3

Select the lettered word or set of words that best completes the sentence.

Example:

Today's small, portable computers contrast markedly with the earliest electronic computers, which were ----.

(A) effective
(B) invented
(C) useful
(D) destructive
(E) enormous

1   The rain is so rare and the land is so ---- that few of the men who work there see much ---- in farming.

(A) plentiful . . hope
(B) barren . . difficulty
(C) productive . . profit
(D) infertile . . future
(E) dry . . danger

2   The principal declared that the students were not simply ignoring the rules, but openly ---- them.

(A) accepting
(B) redressing
(C) reviewing
(D) flouting
(E) discussing

3   Some critics believe that the ---- of modern art came with dadaism, while others insist that the movement was a ----.

(A) zenith . . sham
(B) pinnacle . . triumph
(C) decline . . disaster
(D) acceptance . . success
(E) originality . . fiasco

4   She would never have believed that her article was so ---- were it not for the ---- of correspondence which followed its publication.

(A) interesting . . dearth
(B) inflammatory . . lack
(C) controversial . . spate
(D) commonplace . . influx
(E) insignificant . . volume

5   The writings of the philosopher Descartes are ----; many readers have difficulty following his complex, intricately woven arguments.

(A) generic
(B) trenchant
(C) reflective
(D) elongated
(E) abstruse

6   The prisoner was ---- even though he presented evidence clearly proving that he was nowhere near the scene of the crime.

(A) abandoned
(B) indicted
(C) exculpated
(D) exhumed
(E) rescinded

7   Many biologists are critical of the film's ---- premise that dinosaurs might one day return.

(A) scientific
(B) tacit
(C) speculative
(D) unwitting
(E) ambiguous

8   Mozart composed music with exceptional ----; he left no rough drafts because he was able to write out his compositions in ---- form.

(A) audacity . . original
(B) facility . . finished
(C) incompetence . . ideal
(D) prestige . . orchestral
(E) independence . . concise

9   Known for their devotion, dogs were often used as symbols of ---- in Medieval and Renaissance painting.

(A) resistance
(B) benevolence
(C) generosity
(D) fidelity
(E) antagonism

10 It is ---- that a people so capable of treachery and brutality should also exhibit such a tremendous capacity for heroism.

(A) unfortunate
(B) explicable
(C) paradoxical
(D) distressing
(E) appalling

GO ON TO THE NEXT PAGE →

339

SECTION 3

Choose the lettered pair of words that is related in the
same way as the pair in capital letters.

Example:

FLAKE : SNOW ::

(A) storm : hail
(B) drop : rain
(C) field : wheat
(D) stack : hay
(E) cloud : fog

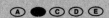

11 CHARLATAN : SCRUPULOUS ::

(A) confidant : virtuous
(B) laborer : stalwart
(C) officer : mutinous
(D) dullard : irritable
(E) tyrant : just

12 GREED : ACQUIRE ::

(A) fear : disguise
(B) inertia : persuade
(C) gluttony : eat
(D) conformity : agree
(E) ignorance : speak

13 PARRY : BLOW ::

(A) counter : argument
(B) sidestep : offense
(C) defer : ruling
(D) stumble : pitfall
(E) shine : light

14 MALIGN : SLURS ::

(A) satisfy : treaties
(B) persecute : complaints
(C) torment : whispers
(D) court : debates
(E) flatter : compliments

15 LENTIL : LEGUME ::

(A) rice : cereal
(B) nutrition : food
(C) horseshoe : pony
(D) husk : corn
(E) baker : cake

16 INDULGE : APPETITE ::

(A) filter : impurity
(B) infuriate : anger
(C) coddle : emotion
(D) humor : whim
(E) liberate : freedom

17 MELLIFLUOUS : SOUND ::

(A) musical : entertainment
(B) fragrant : smell
(C) pale : color
(D) raucous : discussion
(E) auspicious : occasion

18 GUFFAW : LAUGH ::

(A) sniffle : sneeze
(B) whoop : cough
(C) yell : talk
(D) snore : sleep
(E) chuckle : sigh

19 CELESTIAL : HEAVENS ::

(A) planetary : orbit
(B) scientific : experiment
(C) nautical : ships
(D) solar : heat
(E) viscous : matter

20 ENERVATE : VITALITY ::

(A) consolidate : power
(B) energize : action
(C) daunt : courage
(D) estimate : worth
(E) admit : guilt

21 OLIGARCHY : FEW ::

(A) government : majority
(B) authority : consent
(C) constitution : country
(D) monarchy : one
(E) discrimination : minority

22 UNTRUTHFUL : MENDACIOUSNESS ::

(A) circumspect : caution
(B) timid : behavior
(C) agile : physique
(D) sensitive : patient
(E) trusting : honesty

23 INEXCUSABLE : JUSTIFY ::

(A) isolated : abandon
(B) unassailable : attack
(C) affable : like
(D) famous : admire
(E) splendid : revere

GO ON TO THE NEXT PAGE →

SECTION 3

Answer the questions below based on the information in the accompanying passages.

Questions 24–35 are based on the following passage.

In the following passage, a nineteenth-century American writer recalls his boyhood in a small town along the Mississippi River.

My father was a justice of the peace, and I supposed he possessed the power of life and death over all men and could hang anybody that offended
Line him. This was distinction enough for me as a
(5) general thing; but the desire to be a steamboatman kept intruding, nevertheless. I first wanted to be a cabin boy, so that I could come out with a white apron on and shake a tablecloth over the side, where all my old comrades could see me. Later I
(10) thought I would rather be the deck hand who stood on the end of the stage plank with a coil of rope in his hand, because he was particularly conspicuous.

But these were only daydreams—too heavenly to be contemplated as real possibilities. By and by
(15) one of the boys went away. He was not heard of for a long time. At last he turned up as an apprentice engineer or "striker" on a steamboat. This thing shook the bottom out of all my Sunday-school teachings. That boy had been notoriously worldly
(20) and I had been just the reverse—yet he was exalted to this eminence, and I was left in obscurity and misery. There was nothing generous about this fellow in his greatness. He would always manage to have a rusty bolt to scrub while his boat was
(25) docked at our town, and he would sit on the inside guard and scrub it, where we could all see him and envy him and loathe him.

He used all sorts of steamboat technicalities in his talk, as if he were so used to them that he forgot
(30) common people could not understand them. He would speak of the "labboard" side of a horse in an easy, natural way that would make you wish he was dead. And he was always talking about "St. Looy" like an old citizen. Two or three of the boys
(35) had long been persons of consideration among us because they had been to St. Louis once and had a vague general knowledge of its wonders, but the day of their glory was over now. They lapsed into a humble silence, and learned to disappear when the
(40) ruthless "cub" engineer approached. This fellow had money, too, and hair oil, and he wore a showy brass watch chain, a leather belt, and used no suspenders. No girl could withstand his charms. He "cut out" every boy in the village. When his boat blew up at
(45) last, it diffused a tranquil contentment among us such as we had not known for months. But when he came home the next week, alive, renowned, and appeared in church all battered up and bandaged, a shining hero, stared at and wondered over by

(50) everybody, it seemed to us that the partiality of Providence for an undeserving reptile had reached a point where it was open to criticism.

This creature's career could produce but one result, and it speedily followed. Boy after boy
(55) managed to get on the river. Four sons of the chief merchant, and two sons of the county judge became pilots, the grandest position of all. But some of us could not get on the river—at least our parents would not let us.

(60) So by and by I ran away. I said I would never come home again till I was a pilot and could return in glory. But somehow I could not manage it. I went meekly aboard a few of the boats that lay packed together like sardines at the long St. Louis
(65) wharf, and very humbly inquired for the pilots, but got only a cold shoulder and short words from mates and clerks. I had to make the best of this sort of treatment for the time being, but I had comforting daydreams of a future when I should be a great and
(70) honored pilot, with plenty of money, and could kill some of these mates and clerks and pay for them.

---

24 The author makes the statement that "I supposed he . . . offended him" (lines 1–4) primarily to suggest the

(A) power held by a justice of the peace in a frontier town
(B) naive view that he held of his father's importance
(C) respect in which the townspeople held his father
(D) possibility of miscarriages of justice on the American frontier
(E) harsh environment in which he was brought up

25 As used in line 4, the word *distinction* most nearly means

(A) difference
(B) variation
(C) prestige
(D) desperation
(E) clarity

26 The author decides that he would rather become a deck hand than a cabin boy (lines 6–12) because

(A) the job offers higher wages
(B) he believes that the work is easier
(C) he wants to avoid seeing his older friends
(D) deck hands often go on to become pilots
(E) the job is more visible to passersby

GO ON TO THE NEXT PAGE →

SECTION 3

27. The author most likely mentions his "Sunday-school teachings" in lines 18–19 in order to emphasize

    (A) the influence of his early education in later life
    (B) his sense of injustice at the engineer's success
    (C) his disillusionment with longstanding religious beliefs
    (D) his determination to become an engineer at all costs
    (E) the unscrupulous nature of the engineer's character

28. The author most likely concludes that the engineer is not "generous" (line 22) because he

    (A) has no respect for religious beliefs
    (B) refuses to share his wages with friends
    (C) flaunts his new position in public
    (D) takes a pride in material possessions
    (E) ignores the disappointment of other people's ambitions

29. The author most probably mentions the use of "steamboat technicalities" (lines 28–30) in order to emphasize the engineer's

    (A) expertise after a few months on the job
    (B) fascination for trivial information
    (C) ignorance on most other subjects
    (D) desire to appear sophisticated
    (E) inability to communicate effectively

30. The word *consideration* in line 35 most nearly means

    (A) generosity
    (B) deliberation
    (C) contemplation
    (D) unselfishness
    (E) reputation

31. According to the passage, the "glory" of having visited St. Louis (lines 36–38) was over because

    (A) the boys' knowledge of St. Louis was much less detailed than the engineer's
    (B) St. Louis had changed so much that the boys' stories were no longer accurate
    (C) the boys realized that traveling to St. Louis was not a mark of sophistication
    (D) the engineer's account revealed that the boys' stories were lies
    (E) travel to St. Louis had become too commonplace to be envied

32. The author describes the engineer's appearance (lines 41–42) primarily in order to

    (A) suggest one reason why many people found the engineer impressive
    (B) convey the way steamboatmen typically dressed
    (C) emphasize the inadequacy of his own wardrobe
    (D) contrast the engineer's behavior with his appearance
    (E) indicate his admiration for fashionable clothes

33. In lines 50–52, the author's response to the engineer's survival is one of

    (A) thankfulness for what he believes is God's providence
    (B) astonishment at the engineer's miraculous escape
    (C) reflection on the occupational hazards of a steamboating career
    (D) outrage at his rival's undeserved good fortune
    (E) sympathy for the extent of the engineer's wounds

34. The major purpose of the passage is to

    (A) sketch the peaceful life of a frontier town
    (B) relate the events that led to a boy's first success in life
    (C) portray the unsophisticated ambitions of a boy
    (D) describe the characteristics of a small-town boaster
    (E) give a humorous portrayal of a boy's conflicts with his parents

35. At the end of the passage, the author reflects on

    (A) his new ambition to become either a mate or a clerk
    (B) the wisdom of seeking a job in which advancement is easier
    (C) the prospect of abandoning a hopeless search for fame
    (D) the impossibility of returning home and asking his parents' pardon
    (E) his determination to keep striving for success in a glorious career

IF YOU FINISH BEFORE TIME IS CALLED, YOU MAY CHECK YOUR WORK ON THIS SECTION ONLY. DO NOT TURN TO ANY OTHER SECTION IN THE TEST. STOP

SECTION 4

Reference Information

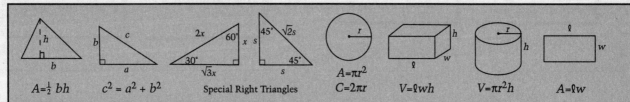

$A=\frac{1}{2}bh$ $c^2 = a^2 + b^2$ Special Right Triangles $A=\pi r^2$ $C=2\pi r$ $V=\ell wh$ $V=\pi r^2 h$ $A=\ell w$

The sum of the degree measures of the angles of a triangle is 180.
The number of degrees of arc in a circle is 360.
A straight angle has a degree measure of 180.

DIRECTIONS FOR QUANTITATIVE COMPARISON QUESTIONS

Compare the boxed quantity in Column A with the boxed quantity in Column B. Select answer choice

   A   if Column A is greater;
   B   if Column B is greater;
   C   if the columns are equal; or
   D   if more information is needed to determine the relationship.

An E response will be treated as an omission.

Notes:

1.   Some questions include information about one or both quantities. That information is centered and unboxed.
2.   A symbol that appears in both Column A and Column B stands for the same thing in both columns.
3.   All numbers used are real numbers.

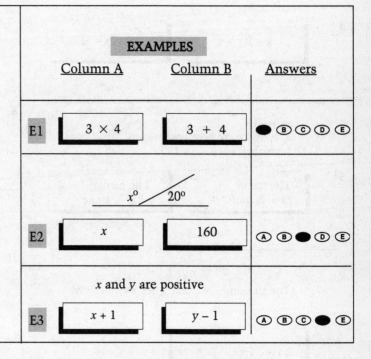

SECTION 4

Column A	Column B

1 $\frac{3}{8} + \frac{2}{5}$ 1

2

The cost of six pens at two for 22 cents	The cost of five pens at 22 cents each

---

$$2a + b = 17$$
$$b - 3 = 2$$

3 a b

---

4 $x - 2(y + z)$ $x - 2y - 2z$

---

a, b, and c are positive integers
such that $a + b + c = 150$.

5

The mean of a, b, and c	The median of a, b, and c

For all numbers x and y, let $x \ast y = (x + y)^3$.

6 $4 \ast 5$ $0 \ast 9$

Column A	Column B

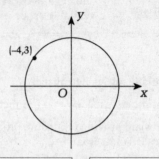

7

The circumference of circle O	30

Jimmy owns a plant he waters every other day.

8

The number of times Jimmy waters the plant during a certain week	The number of times Jimmy waters the plant during the following week

---

A certain line in the rectangular
coordinate plane contains the points
$(1,1)$, $(3,r)$, $(s,9)$, and $(6,11)$.

9 r s

$$r^2 + 4 = 21$$

10 r 4

GO ON TO THE NEXT PAGE →

SECTION 4

| Column A | Column B | | Column A | Column B |

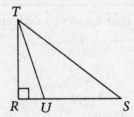

In right triangle *RST*,
$RT = US = 6$ and $RU < 2$.

11

| The perimeter of RST | 24 |

At a science fair, five students are semifinalists for first- and second-place prizes.

12

| The total number of ways to select the two science fair prize winners | 10 |

$$x > 0$$
$$0 < x^2 < 1$$

13

| $1 - x^2$ | $1 - x$ |

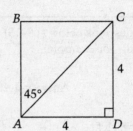

<u>Note</u>: Figure not drawn to scale.

14

| The length of *AB* | 4 |

t is a positive integer.

15

| The number of distinct prime factors of $2t$ | The number of distinct prime factors of $8t$ |

GO ON TO THE NEXT PAGE →

SECTION 4

DIRECTIONS FOR STUDENT-PRODUCED RESPONSE QUESTIONS

For each of the questions below (16–25), solve the problem and indicate your answer by darkening the ovals in the special grid. For example:

Answer: 1.25 or $\frac{5}{4}$ or 5/4

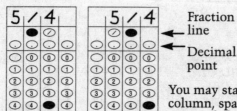

Write answer in boxes.

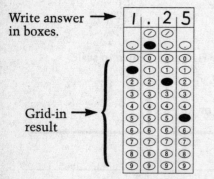

Grid-in result

Fraction line

Decimal point

Either position is correct.

You may start your answers in any column, space permitting. Columns not needed should be left blank.

- It is recommended, though not required, that you write your answer in the boxes at the top of the columns. However, you will receive credit only for darkening the ovals correctly.

- Grid only one answer to a question, even though some problems have more than one correct answer.

- Darken no more than one oval in a column.

- No answers are negative.

- Mixed numbers cannot be gridded. For example: the number $1\frac{1}{4}$ must be gridded as 1.25 or 5/4.

  (If $\boxed{1\,1/4}$ is gridded, it will be interpreted as $\frac{11}{4}$, not $1\frac{1}{4}$.)

- Decimal Accuracy: Decimal answers must be entered as accurately as possible. For example, if you obtain an answer such as 0.1666..., you should record the result as .166 or .167. **Less accurate values such as .16 or .17 are not acceptable.**

Acceptable ways to grid $\frac{1}{6}$ = .1666...

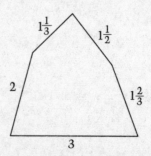

---

16 If $A = 2.54$ and $20B = A$, what is the value of B?

17 What is the perimeter of the figure shown above?

GO ON TO THE NEXT PAGE →

SECTION 4

18 If $\frac{h}{3}$ and $\frac{h}{4}$ are integers, and if $75 < h < 100$, what is one possible value of h?

19 A retailer buys 16 shirts at $4.50 each, and she sells all 16 shirts for $6.75 each. If the retailer purchases more of these shirts at $4.50 each, what is the greatest number of these shirts that she can buy with the profit she made on the 16 shirts?

20 Lines ℓ and m intersect at a point to form four angles. If one of the angles formed is 15 times as large as an adjacent angle, what is the measure, in degrees, of the smaller angle?

21 If $x = -4$ when $x^2 + 2xr + r^2 = 0$, what is the value of r?

22 Let $n\text{✻} = n^2 - n$ for all positive numbers n.

What is the value of $\frac{1}{4}\text{✻} - \frac{1}{2}\text{✻}$?

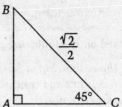

23 What is the area of $\triangle ABC$ shown above?

24 If x is a factor of 8,100 and if x is an odd integer, what is the greatest possible value of x?

25 In a certain class, $\frac{1}{2}$ of the male students and $\frac{2}{3}$ of the female students speak French. If there are $\frac{3}{4}$ as many girls as boys in the class, what fraction of the entire class speaks French?

SECTION 5

Questions 1–12 are based on the following passages.

The controversy over the authorship of Shakespeare's plays began in the 18th century and continues to this day. Here, the author of Passage 1 embraces the proposal that Francis Bacon actually wrote the plays, while the author of Passage 2 defends the traditional attribution to Shakespeare himself.

Passage 1

Anyone with more than a superficial knowledge of Shakespeare's plays must necessarily entertain some doubt concerning their true authorship. Can
(5) scholars honestly accept the idea that such masterworks were written by a shadowy actor with limited formal education and a social position that can most charitably be called "humble"? Obviously, the author of the plays must have traveled widely,
(10) yet there is no record that Shakespeare ever left his native England. Even more obviously, the real author had to have intimate knowledge of life within royal courts and palaces, yet Shakespeare was a commoner, with little firsthand experience of the aristocracy. No, common sense tells us that the
(15) plays must have been written by someone with substantial expertise in the law, the sciences, classics, foreign languages, and the fine arts—someone, in other words, like Shakespeare's eminent contemporary, Sir Francis Bacon.
(20) The first person to suggest that Bacon was the actual author of the plays was Reverend James Wilmot. Writing in 1785, Wilmot argued that someone of Shakespeare's educational background could hardly have produced works of such erudition
(25) and insight. But a figure like Bacon, a scientist and polymath* of legendary stature, would certainly have known about, for instance, the circulation of the blood as alluded to in *Coriolanus*. And as an aristocrat, Bacon would have possessed the
(30) familiarity with court life required to produce a *Love's Labour's Lost*.

Delia Bacon (no relation to Sir Francis) was next to make the case for Francis Bacon's authorship. In 1856, in collaboration with Nathaniel Hawthorne,
(35) she insisted that it was ridiculous to look for the creator of Hamlet among "that dirty, doggish group of players, who come into the scene [of the play Hamlet] summoned like a pack of hounds to his service." Ultimately, she concluded that the plays
(40) were actually composed by a committee consisting of Bacon, Edmund Spenser, Walter Raleigh, and several others.

Still, some might wonder why Bacon, if indeed the plays were wholly or partly his work, would not

(45) put his own name on them. But consider the political climate of England in Elizabethan times. Given that it would have been politically and personally damaging for a man of Bacon's position to associate himself with such controversial plays,
(50) it is quite understandable that Bacon would hire a lowly actor to take the credit—and the consequences.

But perhaps the most convincing evidence of all comes from the postscript of a 1624 letter sent to
(55) Bacon by Sir Tobie Matthew. "The most prodigious wit that I ever knew...is your lordship's name," Matthew wrote, "though he be known by another." That name, of course, was William Shakespeare.

*polymath—a person of wide and varied learning

Passage 2

(60) Over the years, there have been an astonishing number of persons put forth as the "true author" of Shakespeare's plays. Some critics have even gone so far as to claim that only a "committee" could have possessed the abundance of talent and energy
(65) necessary to produce Shakespeare's thirty-seven plays. Among the individual figures most seriously promoted as "the real Shakespeare" is Sir Francis Bacon. Apparently, the fact that Bacon wrote most of his own work in academic Latin does nothing to
(70) deter those who would crown him the premier stylist in the English language.

Although the entire controversy reeks of scholarly gamesplaying, the issue underlying it is worth considering: how could an uneducated actor
(75) create such exquisite works? But the answer to that is easy. Shakespeare's dramatic gifts had little to do with encyclopedic knowledge, complex ideas, or a fluency with great systems of thought. Rather, Shakespeare's genius was one of common sense and
(80) perceptive intuition—a genius that grows not out of book-learning, but out of a deep understanding of human nature and a keen grasp of basic emotions, passions, and jealousies.

One of the most common arguments advanced
(85) by skeptics is that the degree of familiarity with the law exhibited in a *Hamlet* or a *Merchant of Venice* can only have been achieved by a lawyer or other man of affairs. The grasp of law evidenced in these plays, however, is not a detailed knowledge of
(90) formal law, but a more general understanding of so-called "country law." Shakespeare was a landowner—an extraordinary achievement in itself for an ill-paid Elizabethan actor—and so would have been

GO ON TO THE NEXT PAGE →

(95) it is quite understandable that Bacon would hire a lowly actor to take the credit — and the consequences.

(100) But perhaps the most convincing evidence of all comes from the postscript of a 1624 letter sent to Bacon by Sir Tobie Matthew. "The most prodigious wit that I ever knew...is your lordship's name," Matthew wrote, "though he be known by another." That name, of course, was William Shakespeare.

(105) *polymath — a person of wide and varied learning

Passage 2

Over the years, there have been an astonishing number of persons put forth as the "true author" of Shakespeare's plays. Some critics have even gone so far as to claim that only a "committee" could have possessed the abundance of talent and energy necessary to produce Shakespeare's thirty-seven plays. Among the individual figures most seriously promoted as "the real Shakespeare" is Sir Francis Bacon. Apparently, the fact that Bacon wrote most of his own work in academic Latin does nothing to deter those who would crown him the premier stylist in the English language.

Although the entire controversy reeks of scholarly gamesplaying, the issue underlying it is worth considering: how could an uneducated actor create such exquisite works? But the answer to that is easy. Shakespeare's dramatic gifts had little to do with encyclopedic knowledge, complex ideas, or a fluency with great systems of thought. Rather, Shakespeare's genius was one of common sense and perceptive intuition — a genius that grows not out of book-learning, but out of a deep understanding of human nature and a keen grasp of basic emotions, passions, and jealousies.

One of the most common arguments advanced by skeptics is that the degree of familiarity with the law exhibited in a *Hamlet* or a *Merchant of Venice* can only have been achieved by a lawyer or other man of affairs. The grasp of law evidenced in these plays, however, is not a detailed knowledge of formal law, but a more general understanding of so-called "country law". Shakespeare was a landowner — an extraordinary achievement in itself for an ill-paid Elizabethan actor — and so would have been knowledgeable about legal matters related to the buying, selling, and renting of real estate. Evidence of such a common understanding of land regulations can be found, for instance, in the gravedigging scene of *Hamlet*.

So no elaborate theories of intrigue and secret identity are necessary to explain the accomplishment of William Shakespeare. Scholars who have made a career of ferreting out "alternative bards" may be reluctant to admit it, but literary genius can flower in any socioeconomic bracket. Shakespeare, in short, was Shakespeare—an observation that one would have thought was obvious to everyone.

1 In line 2, *entertain* most nearly means

(A) amuse
(B) harbor
(C) occupy
(D) cherish
(E) engage

2 In Passage 1, the author draws attention to Shakespeare's social standing as a "commoner" (line 13) in order to cast doubt on the Elizabethan actor's

(A) aptitude for writing poetically
(B) knowledge of foreign places and habits
(C) ability to support himself by playwriting
(D) familiarity with life among persons of high rank
(E) understanding of the problems of government

3 *Coriolanus* and *Love's Labour's Lost* are mentioned in lines 28–31 as examples of works that

(A) only Francis Bacon could have written
(B) exhibit a deep understanding of human nature
(C) resemble works written by Francis Bacon under his own name
(D) portray a broad spectrum of Elizabethan society
(E) reveal expertise more likely held by Bacon than Shakespeare

4 In Passage 1, the quotation from Delia Bacon (lines 36–39) conveys a sense of

(A) disdain for the disreputable vulgarity of Elizabethan actors
(B) resentment at the way Shakespeare's characters were portrayed
(C) regret that conditions for Elizabethan actors were not better
(D) doubt that Shakespeare could actually have created such unsavory characters
(E) disappointment at the incompetence of Elizabethan actors

5 The author of Passage 1 maintains that Bacon did not put his own name on the plays attributed to Shakespeare because he

(A) regarded writing as an unsuitable occupation for an aristocrat
(B) wished to protect himself from the effects of controversy
(C) preferred being known as a scientist and

GO ON TO THE NEXT PAGE →

politician rather than as a writer

(D) did not want to associate himself with lowly actors

(E) sought to avoid the attention that fame brings

6   In the first paragraph of Passage 2, the author calls into question Bacon's likely ability to

(A) write in a language with which he was unfamiliar

(B) make the transition between scientific writing and playwriting

(C) produce the poetic language evident in the plays

(D) cooperate with other members of a committee

(E) single-handedly create thirty-seven plays

7   The word *premier* in line 69 most nearly means

(A) earliest

(B) influential

(C) inaugural

(D) greatest

(E) original

8   In line 76, the word *encyclopedic* most nearly means

(A) technical

(B) comprehensive

(C) abridged

(D) disciplined

(E) specialized

9   The author of Passage 2 cites Shakespeare's status as a landowner in order to

(A) prove that Shakespeare was a success as a playwright

(B) refute the claim that Shakespeare had little knowledge of aristocratic life

(C) prove that Shakespeare didn't depend solely on acting for his living

(D) dispute the notion that Shakespeare was a commoner

(E) account for Shakespeare's apparent knowledge of the law

10   In lines 100–103, the author maintains that literary genius

(A) is not dependent on a writer's external circumstances

(B) must be based on an inborn comprehension of human nature

(C) is enhanced by the suffering that poverty brings

(D) frequently goes unrecognized among those of modest means and position

(E) can be stifled by too much book-learning and academic training

11   The author of Passage 2 would probably respond to the speculation in the fourth paragraph of Passage 1 by pointing out that

(A) Shakespeare's plays would not have seemed particularly controversial to Elizabethan audiences

(B) The extent and range of Bacon's learning has been generally exaggerated

(C) such scenarios are farfetched and unnecessary if one correctly understands Shakespeare's genius

(D) Bacon would not have had the knowledge of the lower classes required to produce the plays

(E) the claim implies that Shakespeare was disreputable when in fact he was a respectable landowner

12   The author of Passage 1 would probably respond to the skepticism expressed in lines 67–70 by making which of the following statements?

(A) The similarities between English and Latin make it plausible that one person could write well in both languages.

(B) Plays written in Latin would not have been likely to attract a wide audience in Elizabethan England.

(C) The premier stylist in the English language is more likely to have been an eminent scholar than an uneducated actor.

(D) Writing the plays in Latin would have shielded Bacon from much of the political damage he wanted to avoid.

(E) The style of the plays is notable mostly for the clarity of thought behind the lines rather than their musicality or beauty.

IF YOU FINISH BEFORE TIME IS CALLED, YOU MAY CHECK YOUR WORK ON THIS SECTION ONLY. DO NOT TURN TO ANY OTHER SECTION IN THE TEST. **STOP**

SECTION 6

| Time—15 Minutes
10 Questions | Solve each of the following problems, decide which is the best answer choice, and darken the corresponding oval on the answer sheet. Use available space in the test booklet for scratchwork.* |

Notes:

(1) Calculator use is permitted.

(2) All numbers used are real numbers.

(3) Figures are provided for some problems. All figures are drawn to scale and lie in a plane UNLESS otherwise indicated.

Reference Information

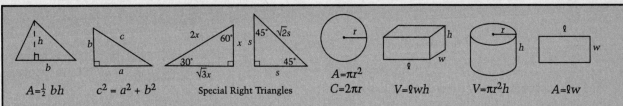

$A=\frac{1}{2}bh$ $c^2 = a^2 + b^2$ Special Right Triangles $A=\pi r^2$ $C=2\pi r$ $V=\ell wh$ $V=\pi r^2 h$ $A=\ell w$

The sum of the degree measures of the angles of a triangle is 180.
The number of degrees of arc in a circle is 360.
A straight angle has a degree measure of 180.

---

1 If $p = -2$ and $q = 3$, then $p^3 q^2 + p^2 q =$

(A) −84
(B) −60
(C) 36
(D) 60
(E) 84

A   B   C D E

Note: Figure not drawn to scale.

2 In the figure above, B is the midpoint of AC and D is the midpoint of CE. If $AB = 5$ and $BD = 8$, what is the length of DE?

(A) 8
(B) 6
(C) 5
(D) 4
(E) 3

N	P
2	7
4	13
6	19
8	25

3 Which of the following equations describes the relationship of each pair of numbers (N,P) in the table above?

(A) $P = N + 5$
(B) $P = 2N + 3$
(C) $P = 2N + 5$
(D) $P = 3N + 1$
(E) $P = 3N - 1$

---

* The directions on the actual SAT will vary slightly.

GO ON TO THE NEXT PAGE →

SECTION 6

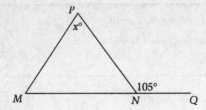

Note: Figure not drawn to scale.

4   In the figure above, *MQ* is a straight line. If *PM* = *PN*, what is the value of *x*?

(A) 30
(B) 45
(C) 60
(D) 75
(E) 90

5   Marty has exactly five blue pens, six black pens, and four red pens in his knapsack. If he pulls out one pen at random from his knapsack, what is the probability that the pen is either red or black?

(A) $\frac{11}{15}$

(B) $\frac{2}{3}$

(C) $\frac{1}{2}$

(D) $\frac{1}{3}$

(E) $\frac{1}{5}$

6   Two hot dogs and a soda cost $3.25. If three hot dogs and a soda cost $4.50, what is the cost of two sodas?

(A) $0.75
(B) $1.25
(C) $1.50
(D) $2.50
(E) $3.00

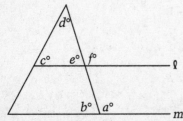

7   In the figure above, if $\ell \parallel m$, which of the following must be equal to *a*?

(A) $b + c$
(B) $b + e$
(C) $c + d$
(D) $d + e$
(E) $d + f$

8   A certain phone call cost 75 cents for the first three minutes plus 15 cents for each additional minute. If the call lasted *x* minutes and *x* is an integer greater than 3, which of the following expresses the cost of the call, in dollars?

(A) $0.75(3) + 0.15x$
(B) $0.75(3) + 0.15(x + 3)$
(C) $0.75 + 0.15(3 - x)$
(D) $0.75 + 0.15(x - 3)$
(E) $0.75 + 0.15x$

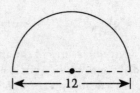

9   The figure above shows a piece of wire in the shape of a semicircle. If the piece of wire is bent to form a circle without any of the wire overlapping, what is the area of the circle?

(A) 6π
(B) 9π
(C) 12π
(D) 18π
(E) 36π

10   If $a^2 - a = 72$, and *b* and *n* are integers such that $b^n = a$, which of the following cannot be a value for *b*?

(A) -8
(B) -2
(C) 2
(D) 3
(E) 9

PRACTICE TEST ANSWER KEY

SECTION 1

1.....E
2.....C
3.....B
4.....B
5.....B
6.....E
7.....C
8.....E
9.....D
10.....B
11.....A
12.....A
13.....B
14.....C
15.....D
16.....D
17.....C
18.....B
19.....C
20.....E
21.....A
22.....C
23.....D
24.....C
25.....A
26.....E
27.....B
28.....A
29.....C
30.....D

SECTION 2

1.....C
2.....E
3.....A
4.....B
5.....E
6.....D
7.....B
8.....E
9.....A
10.....B
11.....A
12.....D
13.....D
14.....C
15.....E
16.....C
17.....D
18.....A
19.....C
20.....E
21.....D
22.....B
23.....C
24.....D
25.....B

SECTION 3

1.....D
2.....D
3.....A
4.....C
5.....E
6.....B
7.....C
8.....B
9.....D
10.....C
11.....E
12.....C
13.....A
14.....E
15.....A
16.....D
17.....B
18.....C
19.....C
20.....C
21.....D
22.....A
23.....B
24.....B
25.....C
26.....E
27.....B
28.....C
29.....D
30.....E
31.....A
32.....A
33.....D
34.....C
35.....E

SECTION 4

1.....B
2.....B
3.....A
4.....C
5.....D
6.....C
7.....A
8.....D
9.....C
10.....D
11.....B
12.....A
13.....A
14.....D
15.....C
16.....127
17.....9.5 or 19/2
18.....84 or 96
19.....8
20.....45/4, 11.2, or
　　　　11.3
21.....4
22.....1/16, .062, or
　　　　.063
23.....1/8 or .125
24.....2025
25.....4/7 or .571

SECTION 5

1.....B
2.....D
3.....E
4.....A
5.....B
6.....C
7.....D
8.....B
9.....E
10.....A
11.....C
12.....C

SECTION 6

1.....B
2.....E
3.....D
4.....A
5.....B
6.....C
7.....C
8.....D
9.....B
10.....C

COMPUTE YOUR RAW SCORE

First, check your answers against the answer key on p. 353 and count up the number right and the number wrong for each section (there are boxes on your answer sheet to record these numbers). Remember not to count omissions as wrong.

Then figure out your raw scores using the table below. The Verbal raw score is equal to the total right in the three Verbal sections minus one-fourth of the number wrong in those sections. The Math raw score is equal to the total right in the three Math sections minus one-fourth of the number wrong in the two Regular Math sections and minus one-third the number wrong in the QCs. (Remember: There is no deduction for wrong answers in the Grid-ins.) Round each raw score to the nearest whole number.

Finally, use the tables on p. 355 to convert each raw score to a range of scaled scores.

	NUMBER RIGHT		NUMBER WRONG		RAW SCORE
SECTION 1:	☐	−[.25 x	☐]	=	☐
SECTION 3:	☐	−[.25 x	☐]	=	☐
SECTION 5:	☐	−[.25 x	☐]	=	☐
VERBAL RAW SCORE:					☐ (ROUNDED)
SECTION 4A: (Questions 1 to 15)	☐	−[.33 x	☐]	=	☐
SECTION 4B: (Questions 16 to 25)	☐		(No wrong-answer penalty)	=	☐
SECTION 2:	☐	−[.25 x	☐]	=	☐
SECTION 6:	☐	−[.25 x	☐]	=	☐
MATH RAW SCORE:					☐ (ROUNDED)

VERBAL

Raw	Scaled	Raw	Scaled	Raw	Scaled
−3 or		22	450	48	620
less	200	23	460	49	630
−2	230	24	470	50	640
−1	270	25	470	51	640
0	290	26	480	52	650
1	300	27	490	53	660
2	310	28	490	54	670
3	320	29	500	55	670
4	330	30	510	56	670
5	330	31	510	57	680
6	340	32	520	58	690
7	350	33	530	59	690
8	360	34	530	60	700
9	370	35	540	61	710
10	370	36	550	62	720
11	380	37	550	63	730
12	390	38	560	64	730
13	390	39	570	65	740
14	400	40	570	66	750
15	410	41	580	67	760
16	410	42	590	68	770
17	420	43	590	69	780
18	430	44	600	70	790
19	430	45	600	71 or	
20	440	46	610	more	800
21	450	47	610		

MATH

Raw	Scaled	Raw	Scaled	Raw	Scaled
−1 or		19	440	40	600
less	200	20	450	41	610
0	220	21	460	42	620
1	240	22	470	43	630
2	260	23	480	44	640
3	280	24	480	45	650
4	300	25	490	46	650
5	310	26	500	47	660
6	330	27	510	48	670
7	340	28	520	49	680
8	350	29	520	50	690
9	360	30	530	51	700
10	370	31	530	52	720
11	380	32	540	53	730
12	390	33	550	54	740
13	400	34	560	55	760
14	410	35	560	56	770
15	420	36	570	57	780
16	430	37	580	58	790
17	430	38	590	59	800
18	440	39	600	60	800

Don't take these scores too literally. Practice test conditions cannot precisely mirror real test conditions. Your actual SAT scores will almost certainly vary from your practice test scores.

Your score on the practice test gives you a rough idea of your range on the actual exam. Use the list on the following page to help you set a goal for the real SAT. It is a partial list of schools from around the country, together with the median scores of their incoming freshmen, based on available published data.

If you don't like your score, it's not too late to do something about it. Work your way way through this book again, and turn to Kaplan's *SAT Verbal Workbook* and *SAT Math Workbook* for even more help.

What follows is just a partial list of schools from around the country (ask your guidance counselor for more alternatives) with the average SAT scores of their incoming freshmen. If the schools you're interested in have average SAT scores higher than your score on the practice test, it's not too late to do something about it. Try Kaplan's *SAT Verbal Workbook* and *SAT Math Workbook,* or call 1–800–KAP–TEST for information on one of Kaplan's courses.

AVERAGE SAT OVER 1300

Amherst College, MA

Bowdoin College, ME

Brown U., RI

California Institute of Technology, CA

Carnegie Mellon U., PA

Case Western Reserve U., OH

Claremont McKenna College, CA

Columbia U. School of Engineering and Applied Science, NY

Cooper Union for the Advancement of Science and Art, NY

Dartmouth College, NH

Duke U., NC*

Harvard U./Harvard and Radcliffe Colleges, MA

Harvey Mudd College, CA

Johns Hopkins U., MD

Massachusetts Institute of Technology, MA

Pomona College, CA

Princeton U., NJ

Reed College, OR*

Rice U., TX

Stanford U., CA

Swarthmore College, PA

U. of Richmond, VA*

Washington and Lee U., VA

Washington U., MO

Wesleyan U., CT

Williams College, MA

Yale U., CT

AVERAGE SAT 1201–1300

Bates College, ME

Birmingham-Southern College, AL*

Boston College, MA

Bryn Mawr College, PA

College of William and Mary, VA*

Columbia U./Columbia College, NY

Connecticut College, CT* .

Cornell U., NY

Davidson College, NC

Emory U., GA

Franklin and Marshall College, PA

Georgetown U., DC

Grinnell College, IA

Hampshire College, MA

Illinois Wesleyan U., IL*

Lehigh U., PA

Lewis and Clark College, OR*

Middlebury College, VT

Northwestern U., IL

Oberlin College, OH

Rensselaer Polytechnic Institute, NY

Rutgers U./Rutgers College, NJ*

Southwestern U., TX*

Trinity College, CT*

Tufts U., MA

Tulane U., LA

United States Naval Academy, MD

U. of California/Berkeley, CA

U. of Chicago, IL

U. of Notre Dame, IN

U. of Pennsylvania, PA

Vassar College, NY*

Wake Forest U., NC

Wellesley College, MA

AVERAGE SAT 1051–1200

American U., DC

Austin College, TX*

Bennington College, VT

Boston U., MA

Clark U., MA

Clemson U., SC

DePauw U., IN

Drew U., NJ

Fairfield U., CT

Fordham U./College/ Lincoln Center, NY

George Washington U., DC

Hendrix College, AR.

Louisiana College, LA*

Loyola College, MD

Lyon College, AR

Mills College, CA

Mount Holyoke College, MA

North Carolina State U., NC

Ohio U., OH*

Pacific Lutheran U., WA*

Penn State U./U. Park, PA

Rhode Island School of Design, RI

Rhodes College, TN

Rutgers U./Camden College of Arts and Sciences, NJ*

Sacred Heart U., CT*

Samford U., AL

Sarah Lawrence College, NY

Seattle U., WA*

Skidmore College, NY

Smith College, MA

State U. of New York College/Buffalo, NY

Stonehill College, MA*

Sweet Briar College, VA

Syracuse U., NY

*This school's score is "recentered." When the SAT was first introduced, the average SAT score was 500 for Math and 500 for Verbal, on a scale of 200 to 800. But over the years, the average score slipped. In the 1993–94 school year, for example, students scoring at the fiftieth percentile level received a 423 on Verbal and a 479 on Math. Over the 1994–95 school year, the College Board adjusted the scale on both tests so that average-scoring students were once more getting a 500, making it easier for students to understand their scores. NOTE: Although most students' scores have been higher on the new scale, this hasn't given students taking the recentered test any advantage in the admissions process. All students taking the recentered test are compared on the same scale, and colleges have adjusted their admissions standards accordingly.

U. of Arizona, AZ*

U. of California/
Los Angeles, CA

U. of Cincinnati, OH*

U. of Dallas, TX

U. of Florida, FL

U. of Maryland/Baltimore
County, MD

U. of Massachusetts/
Amherst, MA

U. of Michigan/
Ann Arbor, MI.

U. of North Carolina/
Chapel Hill, NC

U. of Portland, OR*

U. of Southern Calif., CA

U. of Washington, WA

U. of Wisconsin/
Madison, WI

Valparaiso U., IN

Vanderbilt U., TN

Villanova U., PA

AVERAGE SAT 900–1050

Adelphi U., NY

Alaska Pacific U., AK

Arizona State U./Main
Campus, AZ

Ball State U., IN*

Boise State U., ID

Bowling Green State U., OH

California State U./
Northridge, CA

City U. of New York/
City College, NY

Colorado State U., CO

Drexel U., PA

Emerson College, MA

Fairleigh Dickinson U., NJ

George Mason U., VA*

Georgia State U., GA

Greenville College, IL

Hawaii Pacific U., HI

Hofstra U., NY*

Huntingdon College, AL*

Indiana U./Bloomington, IN*

Iowa State U., IA

Loyola U. of Chicago, IL

Marietta College, OH*

Marymount U., VA

McMurry U., TX

Northeastern U., MA

Ohio State U., OH

Oregon State U., OR

Pace U., NY

Prescott College, AZ

Purdue U./Calumet, IN

Queens College, NC

Rider U., NJ*

Rochester Institute of
Technology, NY

Saint Cloud State U., MN

Sam Houston State U., TX

San Diego State U., CA*

Seton Hall, NJ

Southern Methodist U., TX

Spring Hill College, AL

State U. of New York/
Purchase College, NY

Temple U., PA

Texas Southern U., TX

U. of Alabama/
Huntsville, AL

U. of Charleston, WV

U. of Colorado/Boulder, CO

U. of Connecticut, CT

U. of Delaware, DE

U. of Hartford, CT

U. of Illinois/
Urbana-Champaign, IL

U. of Maine, ME

U. of Massachusetts/
Boston, MA

U. of Nebraska/
Lincoln, NE*

U. of Nevada/Reno, NV

U. of New Orleans, LA

U. of Rhode Island, RI

U. of Utah, UT

U. of Vermont, VT

Washington State U., WA.

AVERAGE SAT UNDER 900

Alabama State U., AL

Arkansas State U., AR

Augusta College, GA*

Barton College, NC

Bowie State U., MD

California State U./
Long Beach, CA

Chadron State College, NE

Cleveland State U., OH

Cumberland College, KY

East Texas State U., TX

Fayetteville State U., NC*

Georgia College, GA

Howard U., DC

Indiana U./Northwest, IN

Iona College, NY

Jacksonville State U., AL

Johnson and Wales U., RI

Kent State U., OH*

Lincoln U., PA

Midwestern State U., TX

Norfolk State U., VA

Northern Illinois U., IL

Pembroke State U., NC

Roger Williams U., RI

Saint Thomas U., FL

Salem State College, MA

San Francisco State U., CA

School of Visual Arts, NY*

Slippery Rock U., PA

South Carolina
State U., SC*

Springfield College, MA

Talladega College, AL

Texas Wesleyan U., TX

Union College, KY

U. of Akron, OH

U. of Bridgeport, CT

U. of Illinois/Chicago, IL

U. of Maine/Augusta, ME

U. of Mississippi, MS

U. of Pittsburgh/
Greensburg, PA

U. of Texas/El Paso, TX

Virginia State U., VA

Western New
Mexico U., NM

Xavier U. of Louisiana, LA

Want more information about our services, products, or the nearest Kaplan educational center?

HERE

↓

Call our nationwide toll-free numbers:

1–800–KAP–TEST
(for information on our live courses)

1–800–KAP–ITEM
(for information on our products)

1–888–KAP–LOAN*
(for information on student loans)

Connect with us in cyberspace:
On **AOL**, keyword **"Kaplan"**
On the Internet's World Wide Web, open **"http://www.kaplan.com"**
On The **MSN**™** online service, Go Word **"KAPLAN"**
Via E-mail, **"info@kaplan.com"**

Write to:
Kaplan Educational Centers
810 Seventh Avenue
New York, NY 10019